The Political and Economic Challenges of Energy in the Middle East and North Africa

The Middle East and North Africa (MENA) are in disarray, and shifts in the field of energy have the potential to drastically affect the course of political and economic developments in the region. Declining oil prices, skyrocketing domestic demand, the rise of unconventional oil and natural gas production in North America, as well as shifting patterns of global energy trade all put severe pressures on both producing and importing countries in the MENA region. Policymakers are facing fundamental challenges in light of the duality of grand transformations in (geo-)politics and energy. Changes in the field of energy require substantial political and economic reforms, affecting the very fabric of sociopolitical arrangements. At the same time, the MENA region's geopolitical volatility makes any such reforms extremely risky.

Including contributions by academics and analysts from both inside and outside the MENA region, this volume explores the changes in global and regional energy, the impact of changing international energy dynamics on politics and economies in the MENA region, and the challenges that will result.

Essential reading for researchers, postgraduates, and professionals in Middle-Eastern and North African politics, global energy governance and regionalism.

David Ramin Jalilvand works with the Middle East and North Africa department of the Friedrich-Ebert-Foundation in Berlin. He holds a PhD in political science from the Free University of Berlin, examining the role of the energy sector in the political economy of Iran. David earned an MSc in Global Politics from the London School of Economics and Political Science and a BA in Government Studies from Erfurt University. During his undergraduate studies, he spent one year at the Moscow State Institute for International Relations. He specializes in energy and international politics, especially in the Middle East.

Kirsten Westphal is Senior Associate at the German Institute for Politics and Security in Berlin (SWP). In the Global Issues Division, she works on international energy relations and energy security issues. Her expertise are in Global Energy Issues and Security of Supply (Oil and Gas), Renewables, International Energy-Governance; Non-conventional Oil and Gas; EU Foreign Energy Relations with the US, Russia, Caspian Region, MENA and Emerging Powers Brazil, China, India and South Africa.

Global Governance

Series Editor: John J. Kirton
University of Toronto, Canada

Global governance is growing rapidly to meet the compounding challenges of a globalized twenty-first-century world. Many issues once dealt with largely at the local, national or regional level are now going global, in the economic, social and political security domains. In response, new and renewed intergovernmental institutions are arising and adapting, multilevel governance is expanding, and sub-national actors are playing a greater role, and create complex combinations and private partnerships to this end.

This series focuses on the new dynamics of global governance in the twenty-first century by:

- Addressing the changes in the structure, operation and impact of individual intergovernmental institutions, above all their innovative responses to the growing global challenges they confront.
- Exploring how they affect, are affected by and relate to non-state actors of global relevance and reach.
- Examining the processes of cooperation, competition and convergence among international institutions and the many global governance gaps where global challenges such as terrorism, transnational crime and energy do not confront powerful international institutions devoted to their control.
- Dealing with how global institutions govern the links among key issues such as climate change and health.

In all cases, it focuses on the central questions of how global governance institutions and processes generate the effective, legitimate, accountable results required to govern today's interconnected, complex, uncertain and crisis-ridden world.

See the webpage for a full list of titles: www.routledge.com/Global-Governance/book-series/ASHSER1420.

The Political and Economic Challenges of Energy in the Middle East and North Africa

Edited by
David Ramin Jalilvand
and Kirsten Westphal

Routledge
Taylor & Francis Group
LONDON AND NEW YORK

First published 2018
by Routledge
2 Park Square, Milton Park, Abingdon, Oxon OX14 4RN

and by Routledge
605 Third Avenue, New York, NY 10017

First issued in paperback 2021

Routledge is an imprint of the Taylor & Francis Group, an informa business

Publisher's Note
The publisher has gone to great lengths to ensure the quality of this reprint but points out that some imperfections in the original copies may be apparent.

British Library Cataloguing in Publication Data
A catalogue record for this book is available from the British Library

Library of Congress Cataloging in Publication Data
Names: Jalilvand, David Ramin, editor. | Westphal, Kirsten, editor.
Title: The political and economic challenges of energy in the Middle East and North Africa / edited by David Ramin Jalilvand and Kirsten Westphal.
Description: Milton Park, Abingdon, Oxon ; New York, NY : Routledge, 2018. | Series: Global governance | Includes bibliographical references and index.
Identifiers: LCCN 2017031176| ISBN 9781138706224 (hardback) | ISBN 9781315201917 (e-book)
Subjects: LCSH: Petroleum industry and trade–Middle East. | Petroleum industry and trade–Political aspects–Middle East. | Petroleum industry and trade–Africa, North. | Petroleum industry and trade–Political aspects–Africa, North.
Classification: LCC HD9576.N36 P63 2018 | DDC 338.2/728–dc23
LC record available at https://lccn.loc.gov/2017031176

ISBN 13: 978-1-03-209607-0 (pbk)
ISBN 13: 978-1-138-70622-4 (hbk)

Typeset in Times New Roman
by Wearset Ltd, Boldon, Tyne and Wear

Contents

Figures

Tables

Contributors

Ayoub Abu-Dayyeh is a civil engineer and Doctor of Philosophy, and head of a chartered consultancy office for energy studies and green buildings design in Amman, Jordan. He has authored several books on energy efficiency, green buildings design, renewable energy, the downfall of nuclear power after Fukushima, etc. He is an ex-president of the Energy Conservation Society and a winner of many prizes: the Jordan State Prize for Engineering 1992, the Green Apple Award golden prize for the built environment 2010 and the Environmental Advocate award by Arab Cities Organization 2015. Currently, he is Vice-president of the Center of Strategic Energy Studies based in Amman.

Anne-Sophie Corbeau is head of gas analysis in BP group's economics team after three years at KAPSARC. She has over 15 years' experience in the energy industry, notably on global gas markets. She recently co-edited the KAPSARC/OIES book, *LNG markets in transition: The great reconfiguration* (2016). Previously, she worked for the International Energy Agency and IHS CERA. At the IEA, she was responsible for managing the research on global gas markets. She was the main author of the *Medium Term Gas Market Report* and (co-)authored several publications on China, India, trading hubs and LNG markets. She also worked in the fuel cell and hydrogen area.

Laura El-Katiri is a freelance consultant based in Abu Dhabi. She has written widely on the politics and economics of oil and development, energy pricing and subsidy reform, and sustainable development with a focus on the Middle East and North Africa region. She has published for the German Marshall Fund of the United States, the United Nations Development Programme (UNDP), the United Nations Economic and Social Commission for Western Asia (UN ESCWA), and the International Renewable Energy Agency (IRENA). She formerly worked as a Research Fellow at the Oxford Institute for Energy Studies, and taught Middle East economic and financial development at the School of Oriental African Studies (SOAS), University of London.

Charles Ellinas has over 35 years' experience in the oil and gas sector in senior management positions. Currently, he is CEO of e-CNHC (E-C Cyprus

Natural Hydrocarbons Company Ltd), providing management and advisory services in the oil and gas and energy sectors in Cyprus and the region. The aim of the company is to contribute to the successful development of these sectors for the future of Cyprus. Prior to this, as CEO of KRETYK he was responsible for implementing the Cyprus government's strategy for the development of its hydrocarbons sector. Up until 2012 he was a Director of Mott MacDonald's for 25 years and Managing Director of Mott MacDonald's oil, gas and petrochemicals business worldwide.

Gonzalo Escribano holds a PhD in Economics from the Universidad Complutense. He is Director of the Energy Programme at the Elcano Royal Institute and Professor of Economics at the Spanish Open University (UNED). His most recent publications include *Energy Security for the EU in the 21st Century* (Routledge, 2012), and articles in journals such as *Energy Policy, Renewable and Sustainable Energy Reviews, European Journal of Political Economy, Geopolitics, Global Policy, Turkish Studies, Global Governance, Mediterranean Politics* and *Environmental Science and Policy*. Most of his publications may be accessed at his Google scholar profile and he may be followed at @g_escribano.

Thomas Fink is a Research Fellow at the Wuppertal Institute in Research Group I, "Future Energy and Mobility Structures". For several years he has been doing research on the MENA region, socioeconomic impacts of renewable energies, market development and green investments. Furthermore, he has worked on several international projects assessing the local manufacturing potential of renewable energy technologies in Tunisia, Morocco and Egypt. He studied economics at the Schumpeter School of Business and Economics at the University of Wuppertal. As part of his PhD, he has developed a framework for companies to assess strategic investments under high dynamic and uncertain business environments (system transformations).

Manfred Fischedick has been a member of the Wuppertal Institute's management as its authorized representative since 2010 and was appointed Vice-president of the Wuppertal Institute in 2006. Up until 2010 he was Director of the Research Group 1, "Future Energy and Mobility Structures" (including more than 50 scientists from different disciplines as well as PhD students). In November 2008 he was appointed Professor at the Schumpeter School of Business and Economics at the University of Wuppertal. He is adviser to the EU and the German government as well as to the Bundesland North Rhine-Westphalia and companies in various sectors. He was coordinating lead author of the IPCC Fifth Assessment Report.

Luay Al-Khatteeb is founding Director of the Iraq Energy Institute, non-resident Fellow at the Center on Global Energy Policy (Columbia University), and was previously a Foreign Policy Fellow at Brookings Institution. His past experience spans over 20 years in business development and public policies with executive capacities at various multinational companies. He focuses on

Middle East political economy and global energy dynamics. His writing has appeared in *Foreign Affairs*, *New York Times*, *Huffington Post*, *Al-Monitor*, *Petroleum-Economist*, *CNN*, *About Oil*, *The National* and *MEES*, among others. He earned his PhD in Middle East Politics from the University of Exeter.

Giacomo Luciani leads the Master in International Energy at the Paris School of International Affairs, Sciences Po, and is Adjunct Professor at the Graduate Institute of International and Development Studies in Geneva. His work has focused on the political economy of the Middle East and North Africa. With Hazem Beblawi, he edited a book on *The Rentier State* (1987), which is frequently cited as one of the origins of the concept. In his subsequent work he has focused on the linkage between evolving sources of government revenue and democratization, on the emergence of a GCC bourgeoisie, and on the economic causes of the Arab Spring. His latest edited book, "Combining Economic and Political Development" (2017), discusses economic policies to support democratic transitions and address popular expectations.

Ayla Gürel Moran is Senior Research Consultant at the PRIO Cyprus Centre (PCC) in Nicosia, Cyprus. She has been engaged in research on energy, particularly on issues related to hydrocarbons exploration and exploitation offshore Cyprus, since 2011. She has written several publications on this topic. She has also been involved in organizing a series of PCC conferences on energy, aimed at contributing to an informed debate at the domestic and regional levels, as well as facilitating a constructive inter-communal dialogue in Cyprus on related questions. Before joining PRIO in 2002 she was an academic engineer based at the Eastern Mediterranean University in Famagusta, Cyprus.

Mohammed Qader is a geoscientist with a PhD in environmental geochemistry from Johannes Gutenberg University in Mainz. He worked at the IASS on soil, environmental and renewable energy issues from November 2012 to December 2016. He is passionate about solar energy and the water–energy nexus.

Elai Rettig is an advanced-stage PhD candidate and a lecturer at the School of Political Science in the University of Haifa. He is also a Research Fellow at the Institute for National Security Studies (INSS) in Tel-Aviv and a Fellow at the Haifa Research Center for Maritime Policy and Strategy. His research focuses on energy security and policy in Israel and in the Middle East. He has received grants from Israel's Ministry of Energy, Israel's Ministry of Science, and from the Chaikin Chair in Geostrategy.

Sybille Roehrkasten leads the Energy Transition Project at the IASS. In her research, she focuses on international policy and governance to foster global energy transition. Before joining the IASS, she engaged in foreign policy consultancy on energy and climate issues at the German Institute for

International and Security Affairs (SWP) in Berlin. She holds Master's degrees in International Economics and Political Science from the University of Tübingen, as well as a PhD from the Free University of Berlin.

Stephan Roll holds a diploma in Business Economics from Freie Universität Berlin and a PhD in Economics from the Friedrich-Alexander-Universität Erlangen-Nürnberg. Since 2009 he has been a researcher at Stiftung Wissenschaft und Politik (SWP) and, since 2017, deputy head of SWP's Middle East and Africa Division. He has lived and studied in Yemen, Syria and Egypt, and lectured at the Friedrich-Alexander-Universität Erlangen-Nürnberg. His research focuses on the interdependencies of economic and political developments in the Arab world, mainly in Egypt.

Ellen Scholl is Associate Director of The Atlantic Council's Global Energy Center. She has experience handling energy policy for the Texas Senate and U.S. Congress, and worked on energy issues as a Robert Bosch Fellow at the German Institute for International and Security Affairs (SWP) and the Federation of German Industries (BDI). She has also worked at the Robert S. Strauss Center for International Security and Law, and was in the initial cohort of the U.S. State Department's Foreign Service Internship Program. She has a Master's Degree in Global Policy Studies from the LBJ School of Public Affairs.

Sebastian Sons is Associate Fellow at the German Council on Foreign Relations (DGAP). Previously, he was involved in the DGAP's research project on "Engagement of the Arab Gulf States Saudi Arabia, Qatar, and the United Arab Emirates in Egypt and Tunisia." He also headed the research unit at the German Orient-Institute in Berlin. Currently, he is writing his PhD dissertation on labor migration from Pakistan to Saudi Arabia at the Humboldt University Berlin. His book "Built on Sand – Saudi Arabia: A Problematic Ally" (in German) was published in 2016. He studied Near and Middle Eastern Studies, Modern History and Political Science.

Guido Steinberg specializes in Middle East and Gulf Affairs and Terrorism at the German Institute for International and Security Affairs (Stiftung Wissenschaft und Politik, SWP) in Berlin. An Islamicist by training, he has worked as a research coordinator at the Free University Berlin (2001) and as an advisor on international terrorism in the German Federal Chancellery (2002–2005). He has published widely on the Middle East, Saudi Arabian and Iraqi History and Politics, the Wahhabiya, Islamism and Terrorism, and, most recently, *German Jihad. The Internationalisation of Jihadist Terrorism* (New York: Columbia University Press 2013).

Harry Tzimitras is Director of the Peace Research Institute Oslo – PRIO Cyprus Centre. In this capacity, he coordinates research and dialogue activities on the search for a political settlement to the island's division. He is also Senior Fellow of the Atlantic Council in Washington, DC. He is Associate

Professor of International Law and International Relations, specializing in the law of the sea, energy geopolitics, foreign policy and the Eastern Mediterranean. Previously, he has been with Istanbul Bilgi University, Koç University, the University of Cambridge and the Institute of International Relations, Athens.

Georgeta Vidican-Auktor is a (substitute) professor at the Institute of Economics, Friedrich Alexander University Erlangen-Nürnberg and Associate Researcher at the German Development Institute in Bonn. She earned her PhD in 2008 from the Massachusetts Institute of Technology, United States, in international development and regional planning. She is working on issues related to industrial policy, energy policy, and science and technology policy, especially as they relate to the process of transition to a low-carbon economy in developing countries and emerging economies. She has published in peer-reviewed journals and worked with development policy organizations to advise both development cooperation agencies and national governments.

Isabelle Werenfels is Head of the Middle East and Africa Research Division at Stiftung Wissenschaft und Politik (SWP) in Berlin. She holds a PhD in Political Science from Humboldt Universität zu Berlin, and a MSc in Development Studies from SOAS. Since joining SWP in 2001 she has broadly published on political transformation and authoritarian resilience in the Maghreb (e.g., *Managing Instability in Algeria*, Routledge 2007), on Political Islam and on Sufi orders, as well as on German and European policies towards the EU's Southern Neighborhood. She is a member of several boards, including, since 2007, the Graduate Institute for International and Development Studies in Geneva.

Acknowledgments

The authors of this book came together in a joint project by the Friedrich-Ebert-Stiftung (FES) and the German Institute for International and Security Affairs (SWP).

Puzzled by the fundamental transformations which the Middle East and North Africa have begun to experience in the realms of both (geo-)politics and energy, this project set out to explore the political and economic challenges emanating from these developments. The contributions to this book have been discussed and further developed in Berlin during an authors' conference in June 2016 as well as during a series of four workshops, featuring experts from academia, industry, and policy.

As editors, we are – of course – extremely grateful to all authors, who patiently went with us through numerous rounds of revisions. Moreover, the valuable feedback and insights from the experts who have participated in the workshops is greatly appreciated. Important advice was further provided by our colleagues from the FES's Middle East and North Africa Department as well as the SWP's Global Issues and Middle East and Africa Research Divisions. Ellen Scholl deserves special credit for supporting the editorial process. Maria Pastukhova and Sergio Rakotozafy provided valuable assistance. We are further indebted to Routledge's editorial team, especially Claire Maloney and Robert Sorsby, for walking us through the publication process.

The project was financed by the German Federal Ministry for Economic Cooperation and Development.

Berlin, autumn 2017
The editors

Introduction

David Ramin Jalilvand and Kirsten Westphal

The Middle East and North Africa (MENA) are in disarray, and shifts in the field of energy have the potential to drastically affect the course of political and economic developments in the region. Trends in regional politics and international energy are coinciding, with the potential for each to impact the other. First, the political and economic order in the region is deteriorating, made evident by political upheaval and violent conflict. Meanwhile, global energy is witnessing fundamental changes, as new technologies are expanding supply and demand growth has proved weaker than expected, sinking oil prices and reshaping producer–consumer relations.

Occurring in tandem, these developments may fundamentally alter the political and economic landscape of the wider MENA region. While energy is at the heart of any national economy, this is more pronounced in the MENA region than perhaps anywhere else in the world, as energy is central to political power, economic development, and foreign relations in most countries. This edited volume examines the confluence of these two trends, analyzing the impact of changing international energy dynamics upon politics and economies in the MENA region.

A region in flux

Not long ago, in 2010, the state of affairs in the swathe of land constituting the MENA region, stretching from the Atlantic Ocean to the borderlands of Central Asia, appeared anything but unusual – at least on the surface. The political order, by and large established by former colonial powers France and Great Britain in the aftermath of the First World War, seemed relatively intact. In most cases, political rule was authoritarian,[1] which seemed to ensure a fair degree of stability throughout the region (if at a cost), home to vast reserves of oil and natural gas as well as crucial chokepoints of global trade, including Bab al-Mandab, the Strait of Hormuz, and the Suez Canal.

At the time, oil prices were recovering at full speed from the 2007/2008 global financial crisis. In 2010 alone, Brent spot prices grew by some 16 percent: to $93 per barrel by the end of the year. Shortly after, they rose to above $110 in April 2011.

However, in late 2010, the political situation began to change drastically as the region's assumed stability proved increasingly fragile. Demonstrations were held throughout the MENA region's Arab countries, with citizens' demands ranging from reform to regime change. In Tunisia and later in Egypt, demonstrations turned into protests that led to the resignation of long-term autocrats. In other parts of the region, government crackdown as well as outside interference sparked violence and repression.

In the intervening years, conflicts have erupted in all corners of the MENA region, from the Arabian Peninsula (Yemen) to the Levant (Iraq, Syria), and North Africa (Libya). These conflicts involve complex blends of local, regional, and international actors, each following different agendas. In these cases, the very question of statehood is at stake as central governments' authority and legitimacy is eroding.

Instability, turmoil, and conflict have contributed to the erosion of political order in the MENA region.[2] In many countries across the region, fundamental political and economic challenges remain unaddressed. Even countries that have thus far avoided the outbreak of violence are affected, as they have largely failed to successfully ameliorate the issues giving rise to the uprisings in the first place, putting stability at risk. At the general level, this includes the lack of political participation and the absence of inclusive economic growth, shortcomings that have given rise to economic and social inequalities as well as to ethnic and sectarian tensions.[3] Demography adds further pressure: due to a youth bulge, each year millions of young women and men are entering job markets that fail to provide sufficient employment. As a result, a growing number of (young) people feel excluded and left behind with little hope that things will change for the better.[4]

In this context, *energy* is of great importance in several ways. First, in producing and importing countries, *energy is part and parcel of the social contract* (perhaps with the exception of Israel and Turkey). In important ways, various regimes legitimize their rule on the basis of energy. Second, in many MENA countries, the economic (growth) model is based on revenues resulting from the extraction and export of hydrocarbons. Third, energy has and continues to substantially *define foreign relations within and beyond the MENA region.* A particularly salient example, and an important relationship, is the region's relations with the United States. The United States has long sought to promote policies and governments ensuring the free flow of oil from the region. Its interests in the region extend back several decades, even pre-dating Carter's emphasis in 1980 on the importance of the "vital oil-producing area of the Persian Gulf".[5] As a result, several leaders and regimes in the MENA region have been able to sustain their rule in part thanks to Washington's political, financial, and military support. The United States has also had a strong and increasing military presence in the region since the end of the Cold War, a presence that sharply accelerated following the 2003 invasion of Iraq.

Against the backdrop of these geopolitical factors, changes in international energy are affecting the MENA region. When attempting to assess the political and economic challenges of energy for the region, it is of crucial importance to consider this delicate mélange.

Changes in international energy

About three years after the 2010/2011 uprisings in the Arab world, fundamental changes in the international energy landscape became increasingly apparent. The most prominent of these changes is symbolized by the dramatic decline in the oil price following a period of high and stable prices. Brent crude prices plummeted from $114 per barrel in June 2014 to as low as $26 in January 2016, later recovering to $50 to $55 at the end of that year.

The changing oil price dynamic is a symptom of a variety of underlying developments. On the supply side, technological advancements have allowed for the production of "unconventional"[6] oil and natural gas, particularly in North America. In response to rising unconventional production, many conventional producers, most notably Saudi Arabia, have initially expanded output in the hopes of being able to beat the new competition on price.[7] At the same time, the surge in demand that had driven up oil prices in the 2000s slowed down more than expected. In particular, slower economic growth in China and East Asia has had a moderating effect on global consumption.[8]

As a result, international oil production expanded at a faster rate than consumption. Investments in exploration and production made during the high price environment of the 2000s paid dividends in the ample availability of supplies by the middle of the decade. Overall, between 2013 and 2015, total world oil production increased by 2.1 mbpd faster than consumption.[9] In short, the oil price decline was underwritten by the ample availability of global supplies. Oil markets turned into buyers' markets as producers competed for customers and market share. A joint initiative by OPEC and several non-OPEC members to reduce supplies in November 2016, meanwhile extended until March 2018, has proven unable to alter market fundamentals. Expanding production and increasing supply was not solely an oil market phenomenon. Thanks to the shale revolution in the United States, gas markets followed the same path as gas production and thus supply rapidly expanded.

In parallel, an evolution has happened in renewable energy technologies as the costs for solar photovoltaics and onshore wind have come down significantly in recent years. The deployment of these technologies means that additional energy supply is increasingly provided by renewable energy sources. The proliferation of renewables is indicative of the fact that changes in energy extend far beyond oil markets, and indeed over the long term a fundamental global energy system transformation is required if the Paris Agreement on Climate Change is implemented. The Agreement's target to limit global warming below 2° centigrade will highly affect energy systems, which are responsible for two-thirds of global greenhouse emissions.

Taken together, these developments have contributed to the prevailing notions of an "era of plenty" and "low for longer" energy prices stretching over many energy sources and sectors.[10]

The MENA region and changing international energy

In the MENA region, recent (oil) supply-side developments have been mixed. Attempting to drive competition from unconventional production out of the market, Saudi Arabia, the top MENA (and OPEC) oil producer, expanded its output following its November 2014 decision to depart from its traditional policy of upholding price in favor of pursuing market share. The kingdom was joined by the UAE, a fellow GCC state, while Iraq substantially increased production following years of conflict. Iran's output grew gradually as the country struggled to recover from sanctions. However, other producers, namely Algeria, Kuwait, and Qatar, maintained more or less constant production levels while war-torn Libya continued to produce below traditional levels (Table I.1).

While supply-side developments varied, the demand-side picture is more uniform: domestic consumption is skyrocketing across the entire MENA region. Between 2005 and 2015, primary energy demand in the Middle East increased by some 56 percent. In North Africa, the two most populous countries, namely Algeria and Egypt, saw primary energy demand increase by 67 percent and 39 percent, respectively (see Table I.2).

Increased domestic energy consumption in the MENA region has been triggered by consumer subsidies, which have led to massive overconsumption. As a result, energy efficiency levels in the MENA region are among the lowest worldwide. Average MENA energy efficiency, measured as energy consumption per unit of GDP, is over 40 percent worse than the world average. While several

Table I.1 MENA oil production by country (mbpd)

	2005	*2006*	*2007*	*2008*	*2009*	*2010*	*2011*	*2012*	*2013*	*2014*	*2015*
Algeria	2.0	2.0	2.0	2.0	1.8	1.7	1.6	1.5	1.5	1.6	1.6
Iran	4.2	4.3	4.3	4.4	4.2	4.4	4.5	3.8	3.6	3.7	3.9
Iraq	1.8	2.0	2.1	2.4	2.5	2.5	2.8	3.1	3.1	3.3	4.0
Kuwait	2.7	2.7	2.7	2.8	2.5	2.6	2.9	3.2	3.1	3.1	3.1
Libya	1.7	1.8	1.8	1.8	1.7	1.7	0.5	1.5	1.0	0.5	0.4
Qatar	1.2	1.2	1.3	1.4	1.4	1.6	1.8	1.9	1.9	1.9	1.9
Saudi Arabia	10.9	10.7	10.3	10.7	9.7	10.1	11.1	11.6	11.4	11.5	12.0
UAE	2.9	3.1	3.0	3.0	2.7	2.9	3.3	3.4	3.6	3.7	3.9

Source: BP (2016).

Table I.2 Middle East, Algeria, and Egypt primary energy consumption (mtoe)

	2005	*2006*	*2007*	*2008*	*2009*	*2010*	*2011*	*2012*	*2013*	*2014*	*2015*
Middle East	568	592	625	669	694	742	755	784	822	849	885
Algeria	33	34	36	38	40	39	41	45	48	52	55
Egypt	62	65	70	74	76	81	82	86	86	85	86

Source: BP (2016).

countries fare better (Cyprus, Israel, Lebanon, Morocco, and Turkey), efficiency levels are particularly poor in the region's oil-exporting countries.[11]

Along with the rapid rise in energy consumption, CO_2 emissions are increasing in the MENA countries. The region's CO_2 emissions are more than 50 percent higher than the world average per unit of GDP. The situation on a per capita basis is even worse: in comparison to the world average, each individual in the MENA region produces more than twice as much CO_2.[12] Thus, particularly through their energy consumption-related CO_2 emissions, MENA countries contribute substantially to climate change.

Confronted with this steady rise in demand, energy systems in the MENA region are under severe pressure to adapt to the new circumstances. In a sense, all MENA countries benefit from ample global energy supply as they seek to satisfy rising domestic demand. However, there is also a downside. Energy-poor countries must consider expanding import capabilities and options, while exporting countries risk a reduction of exports as increasing proportions of domestic production are utilized to meet domestic demand. Across the region, downstream infrastructure will need to be reinforced. Finally, as energy consumption rises, MENA countries are confronted with the need to adopt climate change mitigation measures.

Challenges from changing international energy

The need to adapt to changing international energy dynamics confronts policymakers with fundamental challenges. These challenges call into question the very role that energy has thus far played in the political economies of the MENA region.

Domestically, the energy-based social contract is at risk, a situation that could have severe consequences for political stability. In the absence of comprehensive public welfare systems (and efficient fiscal regimes), states in the MENA region have traditionally provided social benefits – access to energy and other goods – to their citizens through subsidies. Higher income households typically have greater consumption levels than lower income households, and thus tend to benefit more from subsidies, leading some to argue that subsidies constitute a transfer of public wealth from the bottom to the top. Nevertheless, even if inefficient, unequal, and costly, in absolute terms energy subsidies are improving the living conditions of the people in the MENA region.[13]

MENA governments are thus facing a dilemma. If they continue to provide energy at heavily subsidized prices, domestic demand will continue to increase, with severe negative implications. In both producing and importing countries, artificially low energy prices prevent urgently needed energy infrastructure investments. If prices remain low, efficiency will also remain low, and over time energy systems could become unable to cope with increasing demand. In addition, if prices remain artificially low, public finances will likely come under severe pressure. In energy-producing countries, increased domestic consumption will result in a reduction of export earnings, while importing countries will need to cope with higher import bills.

Reduced export earnings and/or higher import bills as a consequence of rising domestic energy needs could constitute heavy burdens for government budgets in the MENA regions. Beyond households, this could possibly also reduce intra-regional financial support from energy-exporting countries to cash-strapped states, in particular from the GCC monarchies. As a result, governments could be forced to reduce public spending, including on items that have ensured some – albeit modest – degree of legitimacy, such as education, healthcare, and other social services.

In this context, low oil prices are a mixed blessing. In the short term, they reduce pressure to rein in consumption. Importing countries benefit from a smaller import bill while in exporting countries, compared with exports, the relative value of domestic consumption is growing. However, this is not sustainable over the long term. Should prices increase, both the absolute and relative cost of domestic consumption will also rise, potentially exerting severe pressure on public budgets.

In oil-exporting countries, the oil price decline has put governments under extreme budgetary pressures. To finance their budgets, many MENA oil exporters rely on high oil prices (see Table I.3). As prices tumbled to below $30 per barrel at times, many governments were running deficits and, as a consequence, foreign reserves were drawn down (the most prominent example being Saudi Arabia[14]). Even after Brent prices recovered to around $50 to $55 per barrel in late 2016, this is still not sufficient for many government budgets to break even.

In addition to economic and political pressures resulting from changing energy dynamics, MENA countries are also facing fundamental challenges with respect to *climate change*, including rising temperatures and sea levels. Even if the 2015 Paris Agreement were to be fully implemented, now an obsolete prospect with the withdrawal of the USA under President Trump in June 2017, peak temperatures could still reach up to 46 degrees Celsius by the mid-twenty-first

Table I.3 Fiscal break-even oil prices of MENA oil-exporting countries

	2000–2012 (average)	*2013*	*2014*	*2015*	*2016 (projection)*	*2017 (projection)*
Algeria	–	108	135	110	88	85
Bahrain	62	130	123	108	95	93
Iran	49	116	100	84	62	56
Iraq	–	115	113	63	60	60
Kuwait	–	43	56	50	52	53
Libya	47	111	206	197	195	149
Oman	–	98	109	96	73	77
Qatar	42	62	54	52	52	55
Saudi Arabia	–	89	106	95	67	70
UAE	33	70	79	70	72	72

Source: IMF (2016).

century. This could make parts of the MENA region uninhabitable, potentially triggering mass migration. Key economic sectors like agriculture and tourism could also suffer, bringing further economic trouble to a region already suffering from mass unemployment. Climate change is also likely to affect energy systems in the MENA region. As temperatures rise, energy consumption for advanced agricultural methods, providing for more complex and increasingly large water supplies, and greater air-conditioning needs is expected to grow, which would further increase CO_2 emissions and thus reinforce the severity of climate change.[15]

Changes in international energy may also lead to a transformation in the MENA region's *relations to the rest of the word.* As discussed previously, when called upon to respond to the uprisings in the Arab world, the United States, arguably still the world's dominant power, did not intervene to protect the existing regional order. Governments, which have to varying degrees relied on cooperation with the United States to ensure regime survival, perceived this as a warning sign. In response, states like Egypt, Israel, Saudi Arabia, and Turkey have all begun diversifying their foreign relations, including with non-Western powers like China and Russia.[16]

When it comes to oil, US interest in the MENA region has only partly been about actual imports. Far from being dependent on the region, the USA receives only a relatively modest share of its oil needs from the MENA region. In recent years, the share of Middle East imports in total US oil consumption has never exceeded 13 percent. As US unconventional oil production increased, the share of MENA imports fell below 10 percent.[17]

Rather, the MENA region mattered to the USA because of its key role in the overall stability of the global oil market. Ensuring the free flow of oil from the conflict-prone MENA region, home to some 47 percent of proven global oil reserves,[18] has been crucial to avoid economic turbulence. Historically, crises in the Middle East have been accompanied by a rise in oil prices. This was the case during the 1973/1974 OPEC embargo, the 1979 Iranian revolution, the 1990/1991 Gulf War, and the 2010/2011 Arab uprisings.

With the rise of North American unconventional oil and natural gas production, which is increasingly cost competitive, the perception that the USA might continue to lose interest in the MENA region is growing. Some also argue that as more supplies from outside the MENA region become available, the importance of MENA oil to the stability of the global energy system is shrinking – as is US interest in the region.[19]

For the time being, it remains to be seen whether this is how developments will actually play out. At any rate, the likelihood of this possibility is being assessed within and outside the MENA region and, as a result, could lead to shifts in policy. Changes in international energy, therefore, hold the potential to contribute to a transformation in the MENA region's relations with the rest of the world.

This is all happening while there are no effective governance institutions which could address these developments. OPEC proved unable to effectively shape oil market dynamics. Political organizations such as the League of Arab States or the Organisation of Islamic Cooperation have little importance when it comes to policymaking and implementation. To varying degrees, therefore, this leaves the countries of the MENA region alone in dealing with the socio-economic consequences of changes in international energy.

The need for regional and country-level analysis

In short, the *changing dynamics of international energy are confronting the countries in the MENA region with substantial political and economic challenges*. However, while changes in international energy impact countries across the MENA region, there is a large degree of heterogeneity among the various MENA countries. Far from being uniform, the countries of the region vary in many respects.

Geographically, the region spans across vast distances. The distance between Marrakesh and Tehran, for example, is almost 1.5 times as long as the distance between Lisbon and Moscow in Europe. This geographical expanse has exposed the region's countries to a wide variety of cultural and historical influences. The history of Morocco, for example, is not only shaped by the seventh-century Arab–Muslim conquest but also by maritime trade and frequent encounters with Europe, both via the Atlantic and the Mediterranean. Meanwhile, Iran was shaped by a variety of largely land-based exchanges with European, Middle Eastern, and Asian civilizations. But cultural and historic differences are not only to be found at the borderlands of the region. On the Arabian Peninsula, for example, the character of the desert Bedouin tribes from the central Najd differs markedly from the people in the Hejaz at the Red Sea, who for centuries enjoyed trade and exchange with the world.

The different cultural and historical influences have shaped not only these societies, but have also had a lasting impact upon the character of statehood, especially in the context of different experiences with foreign powers. Iran and Turkey have never been colonized, though the former repeatedly experienced foreign interference. Meanwhile, the states of the Arabian Peninsula were founded as a result of a relatively smooth transfer of power from colonial Great Britain (in the case of these states, oil-export revenue has also shaped state structures and state–society relations). The other states of the region – with the exception of Israel, whose foundation represented a state- and nation-building process *sui generis* – achieved independence through struggle, in varying degrees.[20] As a result of these different development trajectories, the MENA region is home to a diverse set of political systems, including absolute and constitutional monarchies, authoritarian revolutionary regimes, and parliamentary democracies.

What is common to most of the countries is the relatively prominent role of the state in the economy. Traditionally, political and economic power in the MENA region have gone hand in hand. At both the local and regional levels, the Ottomans and other rulers discouraged economic activity that took place outside of state control, fearing this could lead to the accumulation of wealth and potential power. In many cases, those granted control over fiefdoms were able to enjoy almost exclusive economic rights in exchange for political loyalty and tribute. While a strong merchant culture with deep historical roots exists in many countries in the region, this does substitute for a full-fledged culture of entrepreneurship. "Free markets" in the Western sense of the term, with states or members of the state bureaucracy typically not engaged in economic activity, have no roots in the region. To some degree, this reflects the fact that, with the exception of Israel and possibly Turkey, there are no Western-style democracies, which were established in Europe and North America in tandem with the liberal economic order.[21] In oil-exporting countries the phenomenon is even more pronounced, as oil revenue has allowed, and perhaps incentivized, states to tighten their grip on politics and the economy.[22]

While the formal state typically assumes predominant roles in most countries of the region, there is nevertheless a large degree of heterogeneity from country to country. In particular, the economic systems are differing degrees of market-based (where the role of the state is indeed rather modest), socialist, or oil revenue based.[23] Even among the oil-exporting countries, there is no single or dominant type of economic system. Substantial differences exist regarding the composition of the political economy, including the amount of oil revenue income, and per capita oil revenue income in particular.[24]

Considering the differences among the various MENA countries, this book sets out to examine changes in international energy as well as political and economic challenges emanating from these changes. Given the heterogeneity among countries, the ways in which MENA countries are challenged by these energy developments vary, and some countries are likely to be more or less affected than others. The differences in degree notwithstanding, the countries in the MENA region *are* all challenged by changes in international energy.

Against this backdrop, there is a need both for regional analyses as well as for country-specific case studies. This book seeks to provide both. In the following chapters, experts working at the crossroads of energy, politics, and economy in the MENA region will engage with these issues.

The first section of the book focuses on *region-wide phenomena*. It begins with a discussion of overall developments in the region, which provide the framework for energy impacts to unfold. The following chapters examine specific developments in the fields of oil, natural gas, and renewable energy, as well as the nexus between water and energy in the MENA region. Finally, the emergence of what may be described as a "new energy region" will be discussed by a comprehensive analysis of the Eastern Mediterranean.

This is followed by three sections of *country-level analyses*, each section exploring one sub-region. In the *Gulf region*,[25] Iran, Iraq, Saudi Arabia, as well as the other Gulf states are examined; in the *Eastern Mediterranean*, Cyprus, Israel, Jordan, and Turkey; and in *North Africa*, Algeria, Egypt, and Morocco.

The book is the outcome of discussions and workshops held in Berlin in 2016. Arguments were presented and discussed among the authors along with experts from academia, the energy industry, and the policy community. The intended purpose of this book is to contribute to debates surrounding politics and economy in the MENA region. Obviously, in such a complex region, energy is far from the sole defining factor. Nevertheless, in crucial ways, energy is affecting politics and economies in the MENA region. We hope this book will advance understanding of how energy, politics, and economies interact in this volatile part of the world.

Notes

1 Bellin, 2004; Pawelka, 2008; Salame, 1994.
2 Perthes, 2015.
3 See, e.g., Achcar, 2013.
4 OECD, 2016.
5 Cooper, 2011.
6 There is no clear-cut definition as to what "unconventional" oil and natural gas production constitutes. Generally, unconventional production requires more advanced and complex technology (e.g., directional drilling and hydraulic fracturing).
7 *The Economist*, 2014.
8 BBC, 2015.
9 During these two years, total world oil production grew by 5.1 mbpd while consumption increased by 3.0 mbpd (see BP, 2016).
10 See Ellinas, Chapter 10, this volume.
11 Authors' calculations based on IEA, 2016.
12 Authors' calculations based on ibid.
13 El-Katiri/Fattouh, 2015; Sdralevich et al., 2014; *Washington Post*, 2011.
14 Bloomberg, 2015.
15 Lelieveld et al., 2016; Klawitter et al., 2011.
16 Rachman, 2016.
17 Authors' calculations based on various years of BP's statistical review. For the latest, see BP, 2016.
18 Ibid.
19 American Interest, 2016; Manning, 2014.
20 Pawelka, 1993; Yapp, 1996.
21 Richards/Waterbury, 1990.
22 The political economies of oil-exporting countries, especially in the MENA region, are discussed by the "rentier state" literature; see Beblawi/Luciani, 1987.
23 Richards/Waterbury, 1990.
24 Jalilvand, 2017.
25 To avoid controversy, the term "Gulf region" is used here. Internationally, including at the United Nations, "Persian Gulf" is the official name. This has been contested in several Arab countries since the rise of Arab nationalism in the twentieth century.

Bibliography

Achcar, Gilbert (2013): *The People Want: A Radical Exploration of the Arab Uprising*. Berkeley and Los Angeles: University of California Press.

American Interest (2016): Why OPEC Fears Donald Trump. November 11. AVAILABLE AT: www.the-american-interest.com/2016/11/11/why-opec-fears-donald-trump/.

BBC (2015): China's Slowdown and Cheap Oil. August 26. Available at: www.bbc.com/news/business-34060921.

Beblawi, Hazem/Giacomo Luciani (Ed.) (1987): *The Rentier State*. London: Croom Helm.

Bellin, Eva (2004): The Robustness of Authoritarianism in the Middle East: Exceptionalism in Comparative Perspective. *Comparative Politics* 36(2), 139–157.

Bloomberg (2015): Saudis Risk Draining Financial Assets in 5 Years, IMF Says. October 21. Available at: www.bloomberg.com/news/articles/2015-10-21/saudis-risk-draining-financial-assets-in-five-years-imf-says.

BP (2016): *BP Statistical Review of World Energy June 2016*. London: BP.

Cooper, Andrew Scott (2011): *The Oil Kings: How the U.S., Iran, and Saudi Arabia Changed the Balance of Power in the Middle East*. Oxford: Oneworld.

Economist (2014): *The New Economics of Oil: Sheikhs v Shale*. December 26. Available at: www.economist.com/news/leaders/21635472-economics-oil-have-changed-some-businesses-will-go-bust-market-will-be.

El-Katiri, Laura/Bassam Fattouh (2015): *A Brief Political Economy of Energy Subsidies in the Middle East and North Africa*. MEP 11. Oxford: Oxford Institute for Energy Studies. Available at: www.oxfordenergy.org/wpcms/wp-content/uploads/2015/02/MEP-11.pdf.

IEA (2016): *Key World Energy Statistics 2016*. Paris: International Energy Agency.

IMF (2016): *Middle East and Central Asia Regional Economic Outlook: Statistical Appendix*. Washington, DC: International Monetary Fund. Available at: www.imf.org/external/pubs/ft/reo/2016/mcd/eng/pdf/mreo0416st.pdf.

Jalilvand, David Ramin (2017): *Transformation des Rentierstaats Iran: Zur Rolle des Energiesektors in der politischen Ökonomie*. Wiesbaden: Springer VS.

Klawitter, Jens/Christine Parthemore/Katarina Hasbani/Adriana M. Valencia/Marcel Viëtor/Ahmed Zahran (2011): *Implications of Climate Change on Energy and Security in the MENA Region*. Washington, DC: Middle East Institute. Available at: www.mei.edu/content/implications-climate-change-energy-and-security-mena-region.

Lelieveld, J./Y. Proestos/P. Hadjinicolaou/M. Tanarhte/E. Tyrlis/GZittis (2016): Strongly Increasing Heat Extremes in the Middle East and North Africa (MENA) in the 21st Century. *Climatic Change* 137(1), 245–260.

Manning, Robert (2014): *The Shale Revolution and the New Geopolitics of Energy*. Washington, DC: Atlantic Council. Available at: www.atlanticcouncil.org/images/publications/Shale_Revolution_and_the_New_Geopolitics_of_Energy.pdf.

OECD (2016): *Youth in the MENA Region: How to Bring Them In*. Paris: OECD Publishing. Available at: www.oecd.org/mena/governance/youth-in-the-mena-region.pdf.

Pawelka, Peter (1993): *Der Vordere Orient und die Internationale Politik*. Stuttgart: Kohlhammer.

Pawelka, Peter (Ed.) (2008): *Der Staat im Vorderen Orient: Konstruktion und Legitimation politischer Herrschaft*. Baden-Baden: Nomos.

Perthes, Volker (2015): *Das Ende des Nahen Ostens, wie wir ihn kennen*. Berlin: Suhrkamp.

Rachman, Gideon (2016): *Easternisation: War and Peace in the Asian Century*. London: The Bodley Head.

Richards, Alan/John Waterbury (1990): *A Political Economy of the Middle East*. Boulder, CO: Westview Press.

Salame, Ghassan (1994): *Democracy without Democrats? The Renewal of Politics in the Muslim World*. London: I.B. Tauris.

Sdralevich, Carlo/Randa Sab/Younes Zouhar/Georgia Albertin (2014): *Subsidy Reform in the Middle East and North Africa: Recent Progress and Challenges Ahead*.

Washington, DC: International Monetary Fund. Available at: www.imf.org/external/pubs/ft/dp/2014/1403mcd.pdf.

Washington Post (2011): Region's Leaders Gamble on Subsidies. February 5. Available at: www.wsj.com/articles/SB10001424052748704570104576124403803198950.

Yapp, Malcolm Edward (1996): *The Near East since the First World War: A History to 1995*. Harlow: Longman.

1 Regional trends after the dissolution of "old orders" in the Middle East and North Africa

Guido Steinberg and Isabelle Werenfels

Introduction

The dynamics unleashed by the Arab uprisings in 2011 form the political backdrop to developments in the field of energy in the Middle East and North Africa.[1] Close to six years after the so-called Arab Spring, the Middle East and North Africa looked like a region falling apart. Previous orders and political arrangements, both national and regional, have been challenged not only by political elites, both old and new, but also by armed insurgents. At the same time, dynamics in the region increasingly reveal new cross-regional linkages among state and non-state actors, such as religious solidarities, ideological rifts, and financial interdependences that appear to be more intricate but also more volatile than previous patterns.

In this chapter the authors identify factors and dynamics that shape the newly emerging patterns of regional order. The authors argue that the weakening of states and state failure is the key dynamic around which the main social and political trends and (new) patterns of cooperation – and potentially more lasting orders in the region – crystallize. These trends and patterns include the following. First, the new power of sub-state actors, ranging from civil protest movements and "traditional" (tribal) leaders, to militant groups of differing ideological persuasions. Second, there is an increase of military interventions by neighbors and/or other regional actors seeking to promote their vision of a regional order. Third, and closely related, is the deepening of sectarian and ethnic rifts, which has resulted in new patterns of solidarity and cooperation across the region. Fourth, state failure has contributed to the resurgence of authoritarian orders and the security state in a number of countries. Finally, the return of great powers, namely Russia, to the region, has important implications for patterns of order and cooperation.

State fragility has strongly affected and in some cases even defined the above trends, while some of these trends have in turn further weakened already fragile states. While these mutually reinforcing dynamics have produced anarchy, they have also unleashed new ambitions, patterns of solidarity, and cooperation, and thus point to possible new emerging suborders in the absence of a larger order. While the above trends and dynamics clearly have an important economic dimension and are affected in multiple ways by oil price volatility, the main focus of this chapter will be on the political and social dimensions.

State weakness and state failure

A defining feature of the era that has followed the Arab uprising is the large number of fragile, failing, or failed states in the MENA region. The 2016 Fragile State Index (FSI) labeled only two Arab countries, Oman and Kuwait, as “stable”, and another two, the United Arab Emirates and Qatar, as “more stable”. Meanwhile, no MENA state was classified as “very stable”, “sustainable”, or “very sustainable”.[2] At the other end of the spectrum, Syria was found in the category of “very high alert”, Iraq of “high alert” and both Egypt and Libya of “alert”. Countries such as Algeria and Morocco, while not in an obvious state of turmoil, were labeled as countries of “elevated warning”. The same is true for Tunisia and Jordan, both bordering the civil war states of Libya and Syria, respectively. Both are bearing the brunt of spillover effects from turmoil in the wider region, including refugee flows, while Tunisia is beset with substantial security and economic challenges due to the presence and return of Jihadi actors from Syria and Libya. The non-Arab states in the region or on its borders did not fare better with regard to stability: Iran was found in the category “high warning”, and both Israel (including Westbank) and Turkey in “elevated warning”. Thus, the key characteristic of regional politics since the uprisings is widespread instability, shaping political developments in the Middle East for years and possibly decades to come.

Prior to 2011, authoritarian states and regimes that appeared stable were the norm. However, under the surface many of the region’s governments and states had become increasingly fragile. Paradoxically, the authoritarian consolidation justified by Arab rulers during the post-9/11 fight against terrorism turned out to be a destabilizing factor, as the ruling elites exploited the situation as an opportunity to repress dissenting actors and legitimize authoritarian rule by presenting Islamist terrorism as the sole alternative to it. This development, in combination with a surge in corruption and a situation in which a small group of elites were the only ones to benefit from liberalization of economies, led to the erosion of regime legitimacy in many states.[3] In the republican systems, including Egypt, Tunisia, Syria, and Libya, the failure of the leadership of post-colonial elites and their developmental models became particularly obvious. Efforts by these regimes to substitute political rights with socioeconomic wealth faltered under pressure from growing populations demanding their share of national wealth.

The post-2011 trajectories of Libya, Syria, and Yemen epitomize the cumulative combined effects of the above-mentioned causes of eroding statehood – and the substantial obstacles for (re-)constructing functioning states.

Libya became the first country to plunge into civil war in 2011. Although the war ended in late 2011, the country fractured in the following years, breaking first into two opposing camps in the east and west, and later further dividing into three competing governments. The post-Gaddafi transition collapsed into renewed civil war in 2014. By the middle of the decade Libya had fragmented into innumerable fiefdoms controlled by militias and local (tribal, familial, city) solidarity groups – with few prospects for quick resolution to the conflict, which was in part a resource-inspired, zero-sum power struggle. Moreover, the absence of statehood provided a perfect breeding ground and regional retreat for Jihadi groups, including local affiliates of the Islamic State (IS).[4]

In Yemen, the events of 2011 did not lead directly into civil war. However, efforts to build a new political system after President Ali Abdallah Salih stepped down in February 2012 faltered in the summer of 2014, when Salih and troops loyal to him joined forces with the Huthi rebels. The Huthis are a Zaidi Shi'a movement from northern Yemen that managed to take Sanaa, the capital, in 2014. Together, the unlikely allies (Salih had previously tried to crush the Huthi rebellion since its inception in 2004) ousted the government of Abdrabboh Mansur Hadi, Salih's successor, which fled first to Aden and then to Saudi Arabia. When the Huthis and Salih threatened to take over Yemen, the United Arab Emirates and Saudi Arabia intervened militarily on behalf of the Hadi government. While the Saudi-led coalition took Aden and advanced northward, the result was a stalemate. The coalition was not strong enough to defeat the Huthis and Salih loyalists in the northern highlands, but the Salih-Huthi forces were unable to advance against the firepower of the Saudi and UAE air forces.

The situation in Syria, where civil war broke out in 2012, was even worse, and Islamist elements of the insurgency quickly gained ground. This was partly due to the lack of external support for the rebels, a consequence of the Obama Administration's palpable reluctance to engage in another war in the Middle East. As a result, the opposition-in-exile, represented by the Syrian National Council and later by the National Coalition, proved unable to provide fighters with money and weapons. Meanwhile, Islamist, Salafist, and Jihadist financiers supported organizations like the Salafist Ahrar al-Sham (The Free Men of Syria), which became the strongest insurgent group in 2013, along with the al-Qaeda-allied Nusra-Front, and other groups, turning the conflict into an increasingly sectarian struggle. This trend was reinforced by the April 2013 appearance of the Islamic State in Iraq and Syria (ISIS), which subsequently conquered large parts of Iraq and Syria. Just when the regime of Bashar al-Assad seemed on the verge of collapse following a string of military defeats in spring 2015, the dictator was saved by the Russian intervention and increasing support from Iran and its Shia proxy forces from Lebanon and Iraq.

Militant sub-state actors profiting from state weakness

While rulers in the Middle East and North Africa struggled to control their populations, some states' increasing inability to provide order and services in combination with severe repression ultimately strengthened numerous sub-state actors. The spectrum of players competing to fill the vacuum left by failing states ranged from civil society activists to local notables and tribal leaders to armed insurgents. The players that have profited most in fragile and failed states like

Tunisia, Egypt, and Iraq are militant groups, including Sunni jihadists connected to al-Qaeda and IS, Shiite militias linked to Iran, and other militant groups fighting in the region's proliferating conflicts.

This abundance of armed groups not only endangers the remnants of the current order(s); it makes future stabilization of the civil war countries highly unlikely and threatens the remaining stable countries in the region. Furthermore, increasing conflict between Sunni jihadist groups (i.e., al-Qaeda against IS) and with their Shiite enemies has further increased already high levels of violence in the MENA region.

The Islamic State (IS)

The organization that profited most from the repercussions of the Arab Spring is likely IS, which emerged from the remnants of the Iraqi al-Qaeda (al-Qaeda in Mesopotamia) following the American withdrawal. IS profited from the Iraqi government's policy to marginalize Sunnis and secularists in the country's political system and the civil war in neighboring Syria, which provided it with strategic depth and thousands of foreign fighters, many of whom left other jihadist organizations following the emergence of IS. The group's success in mobilizing young recruits worldwide is largely due to its promises to make the Salafi utopia of an Islamic state modeled after the early state of the Prophet and his companions come true. IS created a quasi-state in 2014 after conquering large parts of eastern Syria and northern and northwestern Iraq, and the group consequently constructed an affiliate network spreading to Libya, Egypt, Yemen, and other countries outside the region. By broadening the front, IS hoped to ease pressure on its core territory in Iraq and Syria, where the United States and allies (including the Iraqi government) began a campaign to destroy the IS "caliphate" in the fall of 2014.

al-Qaeda

al-Qaeda managed to remain relevant to regional politics in spite of the loss of recruits to IS, with whom it competed for leadership in the jihadist movement. In 2011, it seemed that al-Qaeda had lost all political relevance, as it played no part in the revolutions of the Arab world. However, when the revolts turned into insurgencies and civil wars, groups allied to al-Qaeda began to reassert their presence, despite the losses to IS. The main source of al-Qaeda's continuing strength has been its ability to build alliances and integrate itself into larger insurgencies. This became especially obvious in Syria, where the local al-Nusra-Front became one of the strongest insurgent groups in 2012 and survived the loss of many fighters and sources of funding to IS in 2013. In contrast to IS – which demanded unconditional surrender to its leadership – the al-Nusra-Front (which later changed its name to Jabhat Fath al-Sham) built a strong alliance with Salafist groups like Ahrar al-Sham and others, and even cooperated with ideological adversaries like the Free Syrian Army. For the al-Nusra-Front, success in the struggle against the Assad regime was paramount, and it became increasingly obvious in late 2016 that this pragmatic strategy might be more successful in the long run than IS's attempt to combat all enemies of "true" Islam at the same time.

Shia militias

In contrast to al-Qaeda, which tried to focus on attacks against the United States, IS saw Shiites as a priority target and, since 2003, have tried to provoke the Shiite majority in Iraq into a sectarian civil war. Following the emergence of IS affiliates, from 2014 on these groups attacked Shiite targets in Yemen, Saudi Arabia, Lebanon, Afghanistan, and Pakistan. These assaults galvanized an existing trend toward the establishment of Shia militia that claimed to fight Sunni jihadists, but often attacked Sunni civilians. This was most obvious in Iraq, where an umbrella organization named "Popular Mobilization" (al-Hashd al-Sha'bi) was formed in June 2014 to assist the Iraqi army in fighting IS. The alliance was dominated by militias dependent on Iranian support, like the Badr organization (Munazzamat Badr), the Hizbullah Battalions (Kata'ib Hizbullah), and the League of the Righteous (Asa'ib Ahl al-Haqq), some of which had fought the Americans in Iraq. They became an important force in Iraq and also appeared on the Syrian battlefields, where the Lebanese Hizbullah, Iranian Revolutionary Guards, and militias from Iraq, Afghanistan, and Pakistan supported the Assad regime.

Military interventions by neighbors and fluid new alliances

Meddling by elements of the Iranian security apparatus in the Syrian conflict is just one example of the growing military involvement of North African or Middle Eastern governments in their direct or even peripheral neighborhood. While military interventions in neighboring states by Middle Eastern armies have been a feature of the post-colonial era (Egypt in Yemen in the 1960s, the Iraq–Iran war in 1980–1988, Syrian intervention in the Lebanese civil war from 1976–1990, the Iraqi occupation of Kuwait in 1990), wars between Arab nations and Israel, a perceived outsider in regional politics, were much more common. The number of interventions has risen substantially since 2011, highlighting Middle Eastern governments' perceived need to mitigate the repercussions of instability in neighboring states and desire to check Iranian ambitions by countering its activities in countries with substantial Shiite presence. Saudi Arabia and the United Arab Emirates (UAE) intervened in neighboring Bahrain in March 2011 to help the local government suppress a primarily Shiite protest movement. That same summer, the UAE and Qatar participated in the campaign by the United States and European allies in Libya to topple the regime of Muammar al-Gaddafi. Since 2012, regional powers Turkey, Qatar, and Saudi Arabia have supported different insurgent groups in Syria. They refrained from more aggressive steps until 2016, when Turkey sent troops to prevent the Syrian

Kurds from conquering a land bridge between their territories in northern Syria. Saudi Arabia and the UAE intervened in Yemen in March 2015 to stop the advance of the Huthi–Salih alliance in southern Yemen.

The Saudi–Emirati intervention in Bahrain was the first sign that the 2011 revolutions could trigger military reactions from neighboring powers trying to stem the revolutionary tide or to secure other interests in weak and failing MENA states. When demonstrations in Bahrain threatened to spiral out of control, the government called on the Gulf Cooperation Council (GCC) for help. While modest in scope, the intervention proved that Saudi Arabia and others were prepared to use force to avoid the destabilization of allied regimes, and illustrated that Saudi Arabia had decided to confront Iran and its proxies in a developing regional "cold war" between the two powers.

Saudi Arabia did not play an active role in Libya, although it politically supported the campaign against Muammar al-Gaddafi, while the UAE and Qatar participated in the campaign seeking his ouster. However, the two countries supported different local partners, and thus, when two opposing camps formed in eastern and western Libya and proceeded to engage in civil war, the two Gulf States found themselves on opposing sides of the conflict. The very fact that these rich but relatively small states intervened in a far-off North African country illustrates the extent to which states of the region had weakened. These two countries that aspired to leadership roles could not have envisaged such prominence in the past, when countries like Egypt, Iraq, and Syria were intact.

Saudi Arabia, the UAE, and allied states began their intervention in Yemen in March 2015. The Huthi–Salih alliance was poised to take Aden, the last major city controlled by the Hadi government. Saudi and Emirati leaders feared that a Huthi victory would provide Iran with a bridgehead on Saudi Arabia's southern border, and instead the Saudi–Emirati coalition took Aden and installed the Hadi government before advancing north. While the coalition was not strong enough to battle the Huthis and Salih loyalists in the northern highlands, the Huthi–Salih forces could not advance against the firepower of the Saudi and UAE air forces. This resulted in a stalemate, which did not prevent the Gulf States from continuing airstrikes. As a consequence, Iran stepped up the provision of arms to the Huthi–Salih forces, and tension between the regional rivals escalated over the conflict.[5]

Aside from direct military interventions, Arab states have started to build new alliances to tackle the results of state weakness and the proliferation of militant non-state actors in the region. A few months into the 2011 uprisings, the Gulf Cooperation Council (GCC) launched an initiative to bring Morocco and Jordan into its ranks in an effort to establish a coalition of stable counter-revolutionary monarchies and weather the security challenges in the region.[6] Close financial and security cooperation between Saudi Arabia and these two monarchies is by no means new, and the initiative to expand GCC membership beyond the Gulf has not been realized. However, already close ties between Morocco and Saudi Arabia have deepened further, demonstrated by Morocco's (symbolic) participation in the intervention in Yemen and Saudi Arabia's increasingly overt support for Morocco's position in the Western Sahara.[7]

From the Gulf States' perspective, increasing relations with Jordan and Morocco is important not only in the fight against protest movements and the contagion of state failure, but also in the struggle with Iran. Saudi and Emirati support for the coup d'état in Egypt also served both causes, and even improved relations with Israel. Most importantly, the new al-Sisi government cooperated closely with Israel in the struggle against Islamist militants in Gaza and the Sinai; in fact, cooperation between the two states has not been this close since the days of President Anwar al-Sadat. As a result of overlapping interest in the stability of Egypt and containment of Iran, relations between Saudi Arabia and Israel have improved noticeably, although this has yet to lead to open or formal cooperation.[8]

Thus, in many cases, seemingly fragile coalitions, driven by short-term interests and marked by inherent contradictions, have a profound and possibly endurable logic. This logic lies in the dramatic rise of identity politics amid struggles for regional hegemony across the Middle East and North Africa and the goal of regime maintenance.

The rise of sectarianism and identity politics

Since the Arab uprisings, sectarian, ethnic, and ideological divides have played a larger role in the Middle East than ever before in modern history. State actors, political movements, and armed insurgents all play on existing but hitherto not strongly politicized (minority) identities: Sunni, Shia, Kurdish, and Christian in the Middle East; Berber, Tuareg, and Toubou in North Africa (namely Libya). These identity politics stem from developments that largely pre-date the Arab Spring, from the Iranian revolution and ensuing empowerment of Shia movements across the region, to authoritarian regimes' instrumentalization of minority groups or repressive minority rule, to the US intervention in Iraq and resulting state failure that unleashed sectarian dynamics and led to increased involvement by neighboring states in Iraqi affairs. Across the MENA region, state weakness and state failure are a key factor for the surge in sectarianism post-2011.[9] Long-standing rivalries and ambitions by Saudi Arabia and Iran constitute a further factor.

The Shia–Sunni divide

Sectarian conflict between Sunnis and Shiites has become a constant feature of regional politics since the 1979 Islamic Revolution in Iran. Tensions escalated after 2003, as the US invasion of Iraq has allowed the Shiite majority to win elections and dominate Iraqi governments since 2005. The insurgency that developed in the following years took on an increasingly pronounced anti-Shiite stance, culminating in a short but bloody civil war from 2005 to 2007. Although US forces managed to bring the situation under control, sectarian tensions and violence have been a standard feature of Iraqi politics ever since, contributing to the increase in sectarian strife across the region since 2011. This escalation of tensions is related in part to the struggle between Saudi Arabia and Iran over hegemony in the Gulf, undergirded by two competing religious-political ideologies. Eager to counter perceived or real Iranian gains as a result of the Arab Spring, the Saudi regime largely supported Sunni political actors or proxy forces, whereas Iran relied on its time-honored strategy of cooperating with Shiite militant groups like the Lebanese Hizbullah and Iraqi militias, and also relied on Shia Islamist political parties in Baghdad. The civil war in Syria became one of the most important battlefields of this conflict, as parties interpreted events along sectarian lines.

Aside from regional powers, forces on the ground also participated in the unfolding sectarian conflict. Non-state actors like IS propagated an anti-Shiite agenda and perpetrated numerous attacks and crimes against prisoners and civilians, provoking retaliation in kind by Shiite militias in Iraq. This violence was accompanied by a regional propaganda war in which the Sunnis seemed to have the upper hand. Importantly, the rise of Salafist ideology in recent years appears to have contributed to anti-Shiite sentiment in the region.

The Sunna–Shia divide also resonated in North Africa, a region without a meaningful Shia presence. Morocco severed diplomatic ties with Iran in 2009 due to the latter's alleged proselytizing among Moroccan Sunnis, and while diplomatic relations were restored in 2014, Morocco remains firmly aligned with the anti-Shia camp. Tunisia also participates in the Sunni "coalition", if less conspicuously. Algeria remained the odd one out in North Africa, and appeared to lean closer to Iran though claiming neutrality, as illustrated by its 2016 refusal to agree with Saudi Arabia's designation of Hizbullah as a terrorist organization. After initial alignment with the "anti-Iran front" under al-Sisi, Egypt, without a Shia population of its own, also began to waiver in 2016. Egyptian overtures toward Iran were driven largely by three factors: Saudi *rapprochement*, even if limited, with the Muslim Brotherhood, which the Egyptian government frames as the nation's and region's greatest enemy, in early 2015; Sisi's siding with Assad in the Syria conflict, and the threat of Saudi curbing its financial backing.[10] This demonstrates the limits of viewing regional relations mainly through a sectarian prism.

The Kurdish question

The rise of sectarianism occurred in parallel with the Kurds' renewed quest for their own state, this time in Syria. The war in Iraq allowed Iraqi Kurds, under the leadership of Masud Barzani and Jalal Talabani, to consolidate control over the Kurdish areas of northern Iraq and establish the federal region of Iraqi Kurdistan in 2005. When civil war broke out in neighboring Syria, Syrian Kurds made a similar effort to establish a zone of control in the largely Kurdish inhabited areas in the north. Following the Syrian regime's July 2012 withdrawal from most of the Kurdish areas, the Party of Democratic Union (PYD) eclipsed its rivals and took control of the zone it called "Rojava". In the following years, the Kurdish forces became a strong local adversary of IS, and when the US intervened against IS, the PYD quickly became their strongest and most reliable ally on the ground, scoring important victories. This provoked Turkey, as the PYD is the Syrian wing of the Turkish Kurdistan Workers Party (PKK), considered by the Turkish government as the biggest threat to domestic security. Although the Turkish government started negotiations with the Kurds in late 2012, the peace process broke down in July 2015, with both sides blaming the other. Thus, when Syrian Kurds threatened to unify the scattered areas under their control with an advance north of Aleppo in 2016, Turkey intervened. The Kurdish question threatens to remain one of the most important drivers of conflict in the Middle East.

The return of the security paradigm and the consolidation of the authoritarian state

Against the backdrop of civil wars and failing states and fueled by militant ascendancy and military interventions, an important trend emerged in countries where regimes were not toppled: the consolidation of the authoritarian state.

With few exceptions, states in the Middle East and North Africa in 2011 experienced popular contestation, even if in differing degrees. In most cases, protests united Islamist and (left-wing) secular opposition actors. In the first weeks of protests in Bahrain, the oppressed Shiite minority (under Islamist leadership) together with civil society actors demonstrated against Sunni minority misrule.

Rulers across the region displayed similar patterns in reacting to popular contestation. Seeing the fall of regimes in Tunisia, Egypt, Yemen, and Libya and experiencing domestic pressure for reform, Arab rulers quickly turned to socio-economic measures. Oil-rich states like Saudi Arabia and Algeria were not the only ones which sought to appease contesting actors with drastic increases in subsidies and salaries. With few exceptions, rulers also announced political reforms, which turned out to be minor and symbolic at best in most cases. In Morocco, King Mohammed VI engaged in partly substantial reforms, but stopped short of ceding his near-absolute *de jure* powers. Most authoritarian leaders in the region used a mixture of cooptation and repression to successfully divide movements that contested their authority. However, a number of states, most notably Syria, Egypt (after 2013), Iran, and Saudi Arabia, no longer pursued a mixed bag of sophisticated strategies to upgrade their authoritarian systems, but rather engaged in "narrowly-nationalist and exclusionary-repressive" agendas to suppress contestation against the regime.[11]

As violence in Syria, Libya, and Yemen escalated and Jihadi groups quickly rose out of the post-Arab Spring turmoil, authoritarian leaders across the region began to play strongly on their populations' growing fear of destabilization and anarchy to discourage protests and "legitimately" strengthen their security apparatuses. These strategies fell on even more fertile ground as developments in Egypt turned violent following the 2013 removal of President Mohammed Morsi (belonging to the Muslim Brotherhood) from power by the military. Egypt's return to the authoritarian fold garnered substantial financial support from Saudi

Arabia and the UAE, two of the region's most authoritarian and important "counter-revolutionary" players.[12]

Unsurprisingly, between 2010 and 2015 only one Arab state was able to shed the Freedom House designation of "not free".[13] Despite the hopes and expectations of Western observers and Arab civil societies, the odd one out in this landscape, democratizing Tunisia, did not develop into a model transposed throughout the region. This was prevented by profound structural differences between countries, along with widespread fear actively fueled by ruling elites of destabilization and ensuing external intervention. In this context, Tunisia was not perceived as a successful nascent democracy but as an increasingly fragile state beset with substantial economic problems and Jihadi activity, and strongly dependent on external support.[14]

In 2017, authoritarian Arab regimes appeared as apt at fending off contestation as they were pre-2011 thanks to accumulated experience, learning from neighbors' mistakes or "best authoritarian practices", and profiting from "revolutions" turned violent.[15] Authoritarian resurgence was supported, voluntarily or involuntarily, by external actors. This included the USA, the EU, and individual European member states, as well as international financial institutions, which feared migration waves and the export of terrorism as consequences of failing states.[16] As a result, support for the region's most authoritarian regimes, like the al-Sisi government, grew, and by 2017 the international rehabilitation of Syrian dictator Bashar al-Assad appeared to be a possible scenario. Only a few years after the so-called Arab Spring, external actors had come full circle, resorting to the security and (short-term) stabilization paradigm that dominated cooperation with these countries pre-2011. At the same time, key triggers of the uprisings, such as lack of inclusion and socioeconomic imbalances, persisted and continued to call the sustainability and stability of non-inclusive, non-equitable political and socioeconomic systems into question – particularly in an era of persistently lower oil prices as compared to the previous decade.

The authoritarian and security states across the region demonstrate a profound lack of stability. With oil prices predicted to remain below the fiscal break-even in 2017, countries like Algeria and Saudi Arabia run the risk of potential periods of growing domestic upheaval. The increasing political and financial interdependencies of oil-rich monarchies and fragile republics like Egypt, Lebanon, and Tunisia have also heightened the vulnerability of both the authoritarian donors and the authoritarian, hybrid, or democratizing recipients.

International powers and new regional alignments

When the Arab Spring unleashed the previously described dynamics, the United States and Russia, two of the world's great powers, were absent from the stage. The Obama Administration's so-called pivot to Asia diverted US attention from the region, including the Israeli–Palestinian conflict, while for its part Russia had not maintained special relationships in the region, except with Syria to a limited degree. This vacuum opened the door for regional powers, namely Iran and

Turkey, the two-non Arab countries, as well as Saudi Arabia. These countries are seeking to shape the post-2011 regional order to serve their domestic political status quos and ideological underpinnings, to consolidate or expand influence on regional developments, and, most importantly, to constrain political foes – the "Shiite", "the Sunni", or the "Kurdish enemy". Fear appears as much a driving force as ambition to (re-)shape the region. For example, the 2015 nuclear deal with Iran fueled Saudi fears of a *rapprochement* in economic, political, and security terms between its Western partners and rival Iran.

At the same time, regional developments, namely the war in Syria, drew world powers back to the Middle East. The USA and the European countries had supported the outcome of revolutions in Tunisia and Egypt, and had some hope of regime change in Yemen and Syria. Russian distrust of Western post-Arab Spring activity was evoked not only by Western cooperation with Islamist governments in Egypt and Tunisia, which Russia viewed skeptically given its domestic fight against political Islam, but also stemmed from the perceived abuse of its UN–Security Council consent (by abstention) to a seemingly limited and punctual NATO intervention in Libya that de facto became a regime change mission. Finally, and most importantly, geopolitical rivalries between the USA and Russia that re-emerged in the 2014 Ukraine crisis were conflated in Syria, where one of Russia's last remaining client states and allies in the region, the Assad regime, appeared to be endangered.[17]

The 2016 Russian intervention in Syria deepened not only existing rifts with Europe and the United States, but also exacerbated sectarian cleavages across the region. The Russian reshuffling of the cards initially produced two axes: the Russia–Iran–Syria–Hizbullah axis, and the "Sunni axis" consisting of most Arab states and Turkey. For different reasons, Iraq, Lebanon, and Algeria remained neutral or showed a bias for the first axis. Regional powers like Saudi Arabia and Turkey with vested interests in Syria grappled to maintain leverage in the conflict, and the latter slipped into open conflict with Russia in 2015 after Turkey shot down a Russian warplane which Ankara claimed had entered Turkish airspace. Over time the lure of those gaining the upper hand in the conflict, namely the Assad regime and its Russian and Iranian backers, became attractive, as Turkey and to a lesser degree Egypt made substantial efforts to improve ties with Russia and Iran in 2016.

Ironically, on the basis of ongoing conflicts in civil war-ridden Syria, Yemen, and Libya, alignments based on identity politics as well as new international and regional cooperation patterns began to crystallize. The future of some of these new alignments (e.g., Russian–Iranian cooperation) remains open. At the same time, the increasingly strained US–Russian relations coupled with an unprecedented intensity of US–Saudi relations under the new Trump Administration dims the perspectives for any US–Iranian *rapprochement*. Against this backdrop the possibility of a cessation of identity politics across the Middle East and North Africa remains slim. The resulting political solidarities and the damage done to societies that formerly handled their diversity relatively well appears to be profound and lasting.[18]

Conclusion

The Middle East and North Africa is clearly a region in turmoil. It suffers from the failure and weakness of states, the resulting strength of non-state militant groups, sectarian and ethnic conflicts, and military interventions by regional and outside powers. Although it may appear as though we are witnessing a complete breakdown of the old regional order, it is also possible to identify new trends that hint at what the region will look like in the years to come. First is the realignment of forces, with Saudi Arabia, the leader of the counter-revolution, at its core. Saudi Arabia has undertaken strenuous efforts to build an alliance of status quo forces (the GCC states, Egypt, Morocco, and Jordan), which also form the core of the Saudi-led front against Iran and its allies. Leaders in most of these states have tried to strengthen their rule after the protests of the Arab Spring, arguing that the alternative to their survival is civil war, sectarian and/or ethnic strife, and takeover by Islamist terrorists. Against the backdrop of increasing sectarian and ethnic tensions across the region, this narrative has convinced key segments of domestic populations and many Western governments alike.

The return of Russia (as the successor to the Soviet Union) to the Middle East, the withdrawal of the USA from Iraq (and some would say from the Middle East), and Iran's increasing influence could herald the emergence of a camp that may confront the Saudi-led alliance in the coming years. Although it is far from clear whether Russia is able and ready to remain in Syria for the long term and whether Russian–Iranian cooperation will become more strategic, the outline for the coming years is clearly visible. What remains to be seen is the role the United States – which remains closely allied with Saudi Arabia and its allies – will play in the coming years. Last but not least, national and regional stability, as well as the future of the emerging alliances, will be strongly determined by both economic ambitions and capacities of the key oil producers in the region. Thus, changes in international energy markets and energy policies could have a lasting impact upon the course of developments in the MENA region in the years to come.

Notes

1 It is important to note that important dynamics, such as the rise of sectarianism or the spread of Jihadism in Syria attributed to the Arab uprisings of 2011, have their roots in developments that began a decade earlier.
2 The Fund for Peace, 2016.
3 For (long-term) social costs of strategies prior to 2011, see Heydemann, 2015.
4 For the perspectives of conflict resolution in Libya, see International Crisis Group (ICG), 2016.
5 Juneau, 2016, p. 660.
6 Boukhares, 2011.
7 See Tout Sur l'Algérie, November 22, 2016a; March 10, 2016b.
8 An Israeli official from the security establishment in 2016 (off the record) used the metaphor of a double-decker bus to describe these relations: "Empty on the upper deck, very busy on the lower deck."
9 See Hinnebusch, 2016.

10 The Economist, 2016.
11 Heydemann, 2015.
12 See, e.g., *Financial Times*, 2015.
13 See: Freedom House, 2011, 2016.
14 This was particularly true for populations in more pluralist authoritarian countries, such as Morocco, Jordan, or Algeria (interviews between 2011 and 2015 in Algeria and Morocco with oppositional and civil society actors).
15 For "authoritarian diffusion and learning" see Washington Post, 2016.
16 Leenders, 2016, pp. 18–22.
17 Oweis, 2016.
18 This was mirrored, for instance, in the profound hostility toward "the other" found on social media; see Werenfelds/Transfeld, 2016.

Bibliography

Boukhares, Anouar (2011): *Does Morocco Have a Place in the GCC?* Carnegie Endowment for International Peace.

Financial Times (2015): Gulf States Put Their Money on Sisi's Egypt with Pledges Worth $12bn. March 13. Available at: www.ft.com/content/85c2b3cc-c9a0-11e4-a2d9-00144feab7de.

Freedom House (2011): *Freedom in the World.* The Authoritarian Challenge to Democracy. Washington, DC: Freedom House. Available at: http://reliefweb.int/sites/reliefweb.int/files/resources/EFA28E3670B830004925781E000EA6EA-Full_Report.pdf.

Freedom House (2016): *Freedom in the World.* Anxious Dictators, Wavering Democracies: Global Freedom under Pressure. Washington, DC: Freedom House. Available at: https://freedomhouse.org/sites/default/files/FH_FITW_Report_2016.pdf.

Heydemann, Steven (2015): Mass Politics and the Future of Authoritarian Governance in the Arab World. In Lynch, Marc (Ed.): *The Arab Thermidor: The Resurgence of the Security State*. Washington, DC: POMEPS.

Hinnebusch, Raymond (2016): The Sectarianization of the Middle East. In Lynch, Marc (Ed.): *Transnational Diffusion and Cooperation in the Middle East*. POMEPS.

International Crisis Group (ICG) (2016): *The Libyan Political Agreement: Time for a Reset*. Middle East and North Africa Report No. 170. Brussels: International Crisis Group (ICG). Available at: https://d2071andvip0wj.cloudfront.net/170-the-libyan-political-agreement.pdf.

Juneau, Thomas (2016): Iran's Policy towards the Houthis in Yemen: A Limited Return on a Modest Investment. *International Affairs* 92(3), 647–663.

Leenders, Reinoud (2016): Arab Regimes' International Linkages and Authoritarian Learning. In Lynch, Marc (Ed.): *Transnational Diffusion and Cooperation in the Middle East*. POMEPS.

Oweis, Khaled Yacoub (2016): Syria after the Russian Intervention. *SWP Comments* 16.

The Economist (2016): Shifting Sands: As Egypt Quarrels with Saudi Arabia, It Is Finding New Friends. November 25. Available at: www.economist.com/news/middle-east-and-africa/21710912-series-incidents-has-disrupted-relationship-between-arab-worlds.

The Fund for Peace (2016): *The Fragile States Index*. Washington, DC: The Fund for Peace.

Tout Sur l'Algérie (2016a): Conflit au Sahara occidental: le Maroc et neuf pays arabes se retirent du Sommet afro-arabe. November 22. Available at: www.tsa-algerie.

com/20161122/conflit-sahara-occidental-maroc-pays-golfe-se-retirent-sommet-afro-arabe/.

Tout sur l'Algérie (2016b): Sahara occidental: les monarchies du Golfe soutiennent le Maroc. March 10. Available at: www.tsa-algerie.com/20160310/sahara-occidental-monarchies-golfe-soutiennent-maroc/.

Washington Post (2016): How Arab Authoritarian Regimes Learned to Defeat Popular Protests. August 25. Available at: www.washingtonpost.com/news/monkey-cage/wp/2016/08/25/how-arab-authoritarian-regimes-learned-to-defeat-popular-protests/?utm_term=.0ad4d1a1dac9.

Werenfelds, Isabelle/Mareike Transfeld (2016): *#HashtagSolidarities: Twitter Debates and Networks in the MENA Region*. Research Paper 5. Berlin: Stiftung Wissenschaft und Politik (SWP). Available at: www.swp-berlin.org/fileadmin/contents/products/research_papers/2016RP05_trs_wrf.pdf.

2 The price war, OPEC, and the future of the MENA region

Giacomo Luciani

Introduction

The international relevance and political economy of the Middle East and North Africa (MENA) region is primarily related to its vast oil and gas resources. Following a period of approximately 15 years (2000–2014) during which oil and gas prices tended to increase rapidly and the world became accustomed to crude oil commanding a price in excess of $100 per barrel, the market suddenly turned around and prices collapsed. This chapter examines the causes of this sudden shift in market equilibrium, the role of OPEC (or lack thereof), and the implications that the new situation may have on political stability in the MENA region.

The chapter begins with a theoretical discussion, which aims to clarify why the oil market is subject to sudden and large changes in prices, and the role of limited information. This is necessary to properly understand the root causes of the current price war, the role of OPEC, and the shift in the strategic outlook of major oil-exporting countries since about 2011. The final section examines the implications of these developments for the future of the MENA region, arguing in particular that high oil prices had a destabilizing effect on the region and led to the eruption of a regional civil war. It is the outcome of this civil war that will define the future of the region.

Oligopoly equilibrium in global oil: a theoretical reflection

In an oligopolistic market – which is the most common market structure for manufactured products and main raw materials, including oil – price is determined by the few producers with the largest market shares (price leaders or makers). In most cases, a producer whose market share is large has no interest in competing on price, because lower prices will apply to larger volumes, resulting in a greater revenue loss than its competitors. Smaller producers are price takers, meaning that their individual influence on prices is limited; their market share is constrained by production capacity or difficult market access; consequently, in most cases they prefer to align themselves with the prices offered by larger producers who are the price leaders. The key to the stability of an oligopolistic market equilibrium of this kind is the presence of barriers to entry, which limit the possibility of new producers increasing production beyond what the market can absorb.

Normally, oligopolistic equilibria do not last long. Exogenous developments – whether some form of technological progress or new product development, or a reduction in the cost of production, or in entry barriers for technical or institutional reasons – emerge to upset the existing equilibrium. The existing allocations of market shares are then challenged, either by advantages acquired by some participants, or by increases in production capacity whereby the market can no longer sustain all existing capacity. In these instances a price war becomes inevitable, even if all participants lose out for as long as the war lasts. A price war is a fight for survival – some contenders will disappear or lose market share, until a redistribution of market shares obtains and a new equilibrium is found and accepted by all.

Price wars are thus part and parcel of the normal functioning of oligopolistic markets. In the absence of an explicit agreement to limit supply – which is generally illegal or difficult to achieve – oligopolistic markets can maintain stable prices as long as market shares change only marginally. However, when a fundamental change in technology or production capacity intervenes, which threatens to result in a major reshuffle of market shares, a price war is the only way to find what the shape of a new stable equilibrium might be.

In some industries, including oil, the gestation period for investment is lengthy; current production reflects decisions made several years earlier, frequently in a totally different pricing environment. Furthermore, the most important component of production costs in the oil industry is investment (CAPEX), while direct or operating costs (OPEX) are relatively less important. Companies will find it convenient to continue producing as long as they are able to cover operating costs, even if prices do not allow for the full recovery of capital costs. Producers will lose money, but less than they would lose if capacity were left unused, as investment costs are sunk and cannot otherwise be recovered.

Therefore, due to its intrinsically oligopolistic nature, high capital costs, and long gestation periods for new projects, the oil industry was always characterized by widely fluctuating prices. In other words, the oil supply curve is very inelastic, meaning that changes in prices will not be reflected in equivalent changes in the volumes produced – or, reversing the causality, changes in volumes produced will cause more than proportional changes in prices.

This is all the more so because demand for oil products is also highly inelastic in the short term. Demand for oil products is determined by choices about residence, size, and quality of housing, and transportation mode and vehicles, none of which can easily be changed in the short term. Hence even large increases in prices will cause only minimal changes in demand, and conversely, demand will not increase much when prices decline.

Ultimately, this means that at any moment in time price is not clearly identified by so-called fundamentals of demand and supply, as the latter can be close to equilibrium at very different levels of price, with some relatively minor addition or subtraction from storage along the logistics from the well to the pump.

Lack of information about fundamentals

Insufficient information about investment, production, exports, and stocks at the global level increases uncertainty, as fundamentals are only very imperfectly known. In other energy markets, notably gas and even more so electricity, fundamentals are well known day by day (minute by minute for electricity), and demand, and supply must match quickly (or in real time for electricity). This is not the case for oil, as the lack of information and the complexity of the logistics chain from well to pump allow demand and supply to diverge to some extent even for relatively long periods of time.

In the short term, physical transactions for oil are difficult to observe, as they take place bilaterally and are not standardized for volume, quality of the oil, or contractual conditions. In contrast, the market for futures (paper barrels) is standardized and takes place throughout the day, generating a new price signal every few seconds. Consequently, although in theory it is the price of futures that should eventually converge to the price for physical transactions (supposedly dictated by fundamentals), in practice it is the price for physical transactions that converges to the price of futures. The price that is so discovered reflects the equilibrium of demand and supply for paper, rather than physical, barrels and may diverge from the equilibrium price for wet barrels over several months or even years. During this time, while oil in storage will increase or decrease depending on the sign (+ or –) of the imbalance, the price will not necessarily be affected. The market for wet barrels has in fact been out of equilibrium since at least 2010 and oil in storage increased year after year, but the price for paper barrels remained high as investors expected supply to be affected by the Arab Spring and political turmoil in the Middle East, an expectation that persisted until the summer of 2014.

Given that expectations and "market sentiment" are more important than fundamentals in determining the oil price, price wars are likely to be long and bitter. The excess of supply over demand will begin correcting only when expectations are reversed and the price starts to fall. The reversal of expectations, particularly under conditions where it is unclear how far the price must decrease before a new equilibrium is established, will likely lead to a larger correction than would otherwise be the case. Moreover, investors will look to profit from shorting oil futures, thereby causing the price to fall even further.

The current price war

An oil price war has been underway since 2014. This price war was caused by excess production and increasing volumes of oil in storage since at least 2011, and was sanctioned by OPEC's and Saudi Arabia's decision in November 2014 not to cut production. Several major producers even increased production in subsequent months, thus moving against prevailing market expectations. Saudi officials have since acknowledged that they have been taken by surprise by the extent of the price reaction to their refusal to act as the "swing producer", i.e., the producer that takes upon itself the task of equilibrating the market. This is a role which Saudi Arabia played in the early 1980s, when it allowed its production to decline from 10.3 million barrels per day in 1980 and 1981 to 3.5 million in 1985, in the futile attempt to defend the OPEC-sanctioned price of Arabian Light. However, the Kingdom abandoned this policy in 1985,[1] initiating the first price war, and has declined to resume the role of swing producer ever since. A second price war took place in 1998/1999, with prices dropping below $10 per barrel. Prices recovered only after some non-OPEC producers (notably Russia, Norway, and Mexico) agreed to cooperate with OPEC in curbing production.

Over the past decade, market sentiment was primarily influenced by the so-called "peak oil" theory,[2] which maintained that oil demand was constantly and inevitably growing, while supply would inevitably be constrained by declining resources. Between 2004 and 2008, prices did increase exponentially, as the market sought the upper limit beyond which demand would start to significantly decline. This so-called "tipping point", which we may more rigorously define as the price beyond which the elasticity of demand equals or surpasses unity, was in fact never reached. Elasticity of demand remained stubbornly below unity, meaning that the quantities demanded decreased much less than the price increased, even when, after 2011, prices surpassed $100 per barrel.

Rigidity of demand supported the formation of a speculative bubble, which burst in the summer of 2008 owing to the financial crisis, as liquidity was temporarily drained from the paper barrels market. Absent the financial crisis, the exponential price increase could have continued. Indeed, as central banks moved to provide liquidity to markets and avoid financial implosion, the price of oil quickly recovered in 2009 and early 2010. By the end of 2010, the eruption of the Arab Spring convinced the market that a physical shortage could happen at any moment, sustaining what was at the time called a "risk premium", and resulting in a period of stable prices of between $110 and $120 per barrel.

The problem is that the "peak oil" theory turned out to be wrong; it would have been correct if only conventional oil resources were available, but so-called "unconventional" resources are vast, and almost all are commercially viable at price levels that existed between 2011 and 2014.

For years, the International Energy Agency has been updating a chart ordering all available resources according to their cost of production. The message of Chart 1, reproduced in Figure 2.1, is quite clear: at a price of $120 per barrel, as was the case in 2013, even the most expensive unconventional resources are commercially viable. While about 1200 billion barrels have already been produced, remaining resources total approximately 7000 billion barrels, all of which are commercially viable at prices exceeding $100. It was clear that it would be only a matter of time before needed investment would be made to bring this oil to the market, a development that would inevitably cause a decline in prices.

In 2013,[3] the IEA proposed another chart (Chart 2: see Figure 2.2) which also has a clear message: the oil necessary to satisfy global demand up until 2035 can be produced at a cost of less than $50 per barrel. If the price is $120, much more

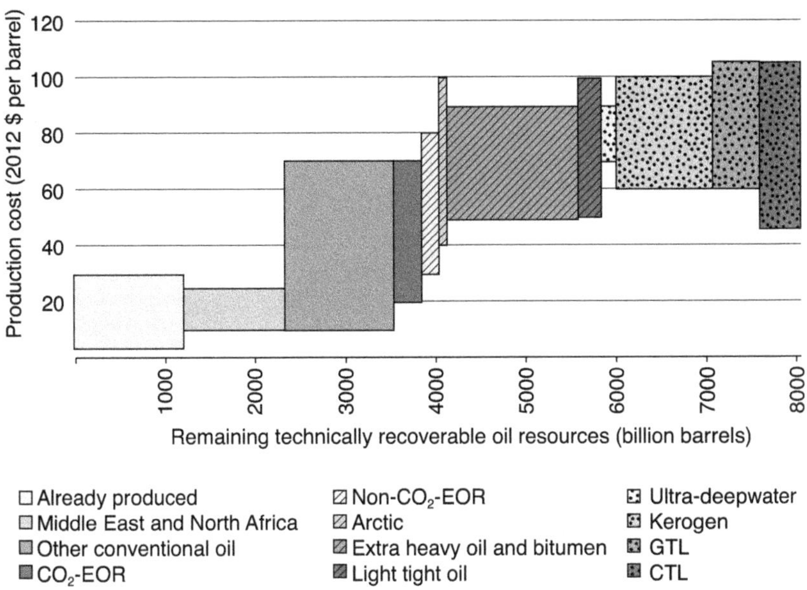

Figure 2.1 Supply costs of liquid fuels.

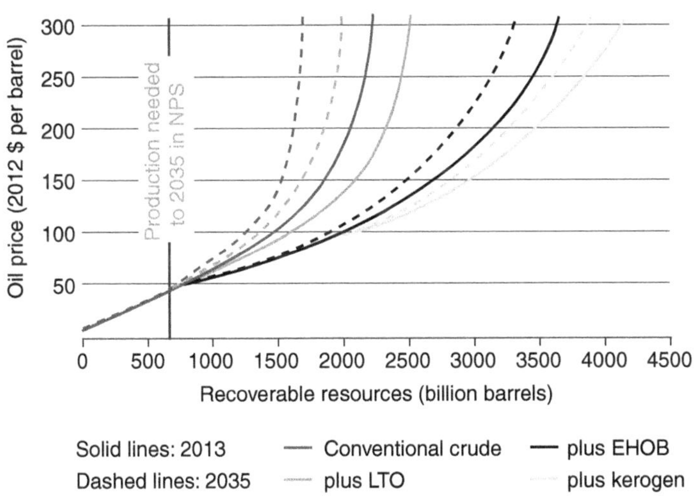

Figure 2.2 World supply cost curves for 2013 and 2035 in the New Policies Scenario.

Notes

The supply curves are cumulative, i.e., the "plus LTO" line includes conventional crude and LTO; the "plus EHOB" includes conventional crude, LTO and EHOB, and so on. The vertical line indicates the amount of production required between 2013 and 2035 in the New Policies Scenario (NPS).

oil will be produced than is needed. And so this has happened since 2011: companies increased investment in the expectation that prices would remain high. Several projects launched after 2000 and more recently have yet to be completed; however, companies have already sunk significant sums, and thus will not simply abort the projects. Therefore, production may well continue to increase until the pipeline of unfinished projects is exhausted, while some new projects will still be profitable at the lower prices, and will be sanctioned.

In the meantime, production from shale oil, where projects have a short gestation period, has exploded. As Chart 3 clearly illustrates (see Figure 2.3), the increase in US oil production was very gradual up until about 2011, then increased exponentially. Between the summer of 2011 and the spring of 2015, US production increased from 5.5 to 9.5 million barrels per day, an increase of four million barrels per day, equivalent to the total production of Iraq. This clearly represents the largest single contribution to excess production. However,

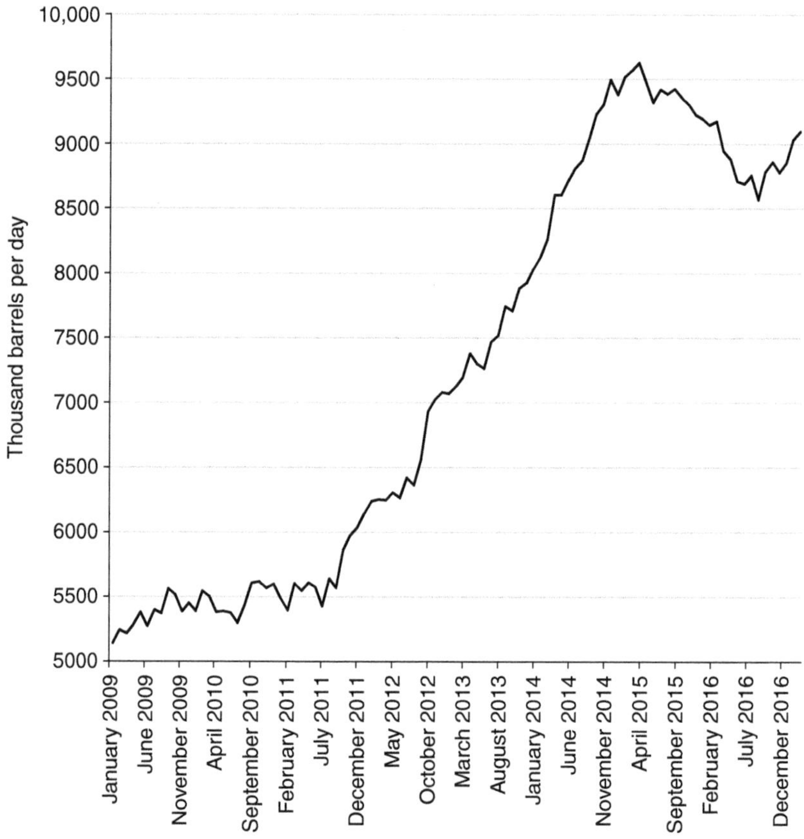

Figure 2.3 US crude oil production (monthly).

Source: EIA.

it would be a mistake to believe that US shale oil is the sole culprit, as the problem is in fact much bigger.

It was expected that as soon as prices turned around, US shale oil production would decline as rapidly as it had increased, leading to a rapid rebalancing of the market. However, this was not the case. Shale oil production instead demonstrated unexpected resiliency, and total US production remained at above 9.5 million barrels per day up until April 2015.[4] After that date, production declined by approximately one million barrels until September 2016, but it started to climb again thereafter.

In the meantime, Iran increased its production following the lifting of sanctions linked to the country's uranium-enrichment program; Iraq increased production notwithstanding continuing civil war; and Russian companies increased production to post-Soviet peak levels in 2016; in short, the world remained awash with oil.

The role of OPEC

As the previous sections make clear, OPEC has very limited control over oil pricing. In the 1970s, OPEC member countries collectively controlled a 51 percent share of the oil market, which allowed them to play the role of price leaders, or at least gave the impression that this was the case. OPEC tried to consolidate the increase in prices that followed the 1973 Yom Kippur war and the 1979 Iranian Revolution, but in so doing encouraged production increases from outside OPEC, notably from Alaska, the North Sea, Mexico, West Africa, and the Soviet Union. As a result, OPEC's share of global oil production declined rapidly, hitting a low of 27.6 percent in 1985.[5]

To defend the high prices, OPEC inaugurated production quotas, but not all member countries respected agreed limits, and the burden of defending prices fell disproportionately on Saudi Arabia, whose production declined from a peak of 11.5 million barrels per day in 1981 to 3.5 barrels in 1985. At that point, Saudi Arabia officially abandoned the role of swing producer, setting the first price war in motion.

From that moment, OPEC member countries have been price takers. The price is fixed on markets for crude oils not produced by OPEC, notably Brent and WTI, and the OPEC member countries have linked their prices to those two benchmarks through various formulas. The largest-volume OPEC crude oils are not freely tradable because the producers do not want them to be traded; hence, no independent price signal is generated by their demand and supply.[6]

Benchmark prices are, as explained, determined by trading in paper barrels and market sentiment, and all OPEC can do is try to influence this sentiment through public statements from influential ministers, through the concluding statements from OPEC meetings and conferences, or by changes in quotas, which, however, have become increasingly rare. The impact of these tactics upon market sentiment may be significant or insignificant, depending on circumstances. For example, the fact that OPEC could not agree on a cut of production in November 2014 certainly accelerated the fall in prices; however, had a cut been agreed upon, the market would most likely have shrugged it off, only delaying the decline in prices. Within OPEC, Saudi Arabia enjoys the greatest signaling power, as the market pays close attention to every word uttered by the Saudi Oil Minister. Unfortunately, however, the Minister finds it politically difficult to intervene when prices are too high in order to bring them down.

In 2008, the King of Saudi Arabia took the very unusual step of officially declaring that an oil price of between $75 and $80 per barrel would be "fair" for both exporters and importers.[7] This was a very important statement, much more so than similar statements that journalists extract regularly from the Oil Minister when he appears in public. The price band indicated by the King was also strikingly close to the price level advocated by major political leaders in industrial countries at the time.

However, the market remained unimpressed. Prices climbed well beyond the upper limit of the band indicated by the King and nothing much happened; no attempt was made to enforce the upper limit that he had fixed. On several occasions, the Minister declared whatever price was prevailing at the time as "perfect", thus ratifying the collective wisdom of "the market" and implicitly acknowledging that the Kingdom was powerless to steer prices in the desired direction.

Major Gulf exporters (Saudi Arabia, Abu Dhabi, and Kuwait) did not expect prices to fall as low as they did at the beginning of 2016. Although Ali Naimi declared in 2014 that the Kingdom was ready to see prices fall as low as $20 a barrel (or lower: he just said that how low they would go was "irrelevant"),[8] by the spring of 2016 he had been replaced with Khalid al Faleh and the Saudi government was becoming distinctly nervous.

Hence the search for an agreement to stabilize the market started, one which necessarily involved not just OPEC but also the major non-OPEC producers – Russia first and foremost – and only left out OECD producers such as the USA, Canada, and Norway. The sought-for agreement was reached at the end of November 2016, when OPEC decided to cut production by 1.2 million barrels per day, and the non-OPEC producers pledged to cut a further 600,000 barrels per day. OPEC's new set of quotas in fact allowed Iran to somewhat further increase production – to come closer to recovering the production level it had before the sanctions – and imposed no limitation on either Libya or Nigeria, in recognition of their unusually low level of production due to security issues. In the end, the bulk of cuts were absorbed by Saudi Arabia within OPEC and Russia outside, so that in fact the agreement was a Saudi–Russian pact, which inaugurated a new joint venture aimed at moderating the global oil market.

Prices did respond, returning to a level of between $50 and $60 per barrel, but more frequently closer or even lower than the lower margin of the band. It soon became clear that the agreement, albeit it achieved an unusually high level of compliance on the part of the participating producers, would not be sufficient to rebalance the market. US crude oil production, which had started climbing again already in September 2016, further recovered. By the end of May 2017, when the original OPEC–non-OPEC pact came to the end of its first period of validity and was extended, US crude oil production had gained back fully half of the million barrels per day that it had lost since May 2015.

In the process, market sentiment evolved considerably: while at the end of 2014 many commentators still expected prices to climb back to $100 per barrel or thereabouts, by the spring of 2017 the most bullish views were of prices possibly passing the $60 mark and coming closer to $70 by the end of the decade.

Evolving strategic outlook

At a more structural level, OPEC's credibility has been undermined because the strategic perspective of its key member countries has changed. Since the late 1960s, OPEC has articulated a conservationist approach to the management of oil resources, whereby the latter should be exploited slowly so that they would last longer and serve the needs of future generations.[9] Although some OPEC members were quite happy to draw down their reserves rapidly, others, including Arab Gulf producers and Iran in the early years after the Revolution, have deliberately restricted production in order to extend their production horizon.

This stance has progressively weakened and may be on the verge of being abandoned altogether. In particular, the Arab Gulf producers are increasingly worried about climate change, which they now accept as an imminent global threat.

Although oil will remain an important primary source of energy for decades to come, its outlook is increasingly influenced by the theory that fossil fuels will become stranded assets. "Peak oil" has given way to "unburnable carbon", the idea that if the international community is serious about decarbonization, demand for oil may soon stagnate or even peak and then decline. This perception was greatly reinforced by the successful conclusion of the Paris Climate Accord at the end of 2015, when all countries agreed to a very ambitious target of keeping global warming "well below" 2° centigrade. Although the election of Donald Trump and his decision to withdraw from the Paris Accord somewhat undermined the credibility of the latter, it solicited strong support from some unexpected critical energy consumers, such as China and India.

Meeting the target agreed in Paris may require globally declining oil demand already in the 2020s. Under such a scenario, oil prices are bound to remain low. Producers will then conclude that it is in their best interest to speed up the exploitation of their reserves, and extract their oil, rather than leaving it in the ground.

Oil prices and political stability in the MENA region

The impact of oil prices upon individual MENA countries clearly depends on whether they are net exporters or importers. The frequently heard, yet simplistic, take on the impact of low oil prices upon political stability in major MENA oil exporters, the GCC members in particular, maintains that domestic stability is based on an immutable bargain with their people, whereby acquiescence to the patrimonial monarchies' monopoly on power is exchanged for income and material benefits. Therefore, political instability must be expected if oil prices do not recover soon.

However, there are multiple reasons why low prices, per se, are not likely to cause political instability in the Gulf monarchies.[10] The major Gulf producers (Kuwait, Qatar, Saudi Arabia, and UAE) have accumulated large financial reserves, have essentially no debt, enjoy a flexible structure of expenditure that allows for large incremental cuts, and own large real assets that can be divested. The room for maneuver that Gulf governments enjoy relative to any other government in the world is significant. Of course, should the Gulf monarchies sit back and do nothing, the situation may eventually become critical – but "eventually" is neither tomorrow nor the day after.

Other producers are suffering far more than the Gulf countries. They must all cut back on expenditure and/or (as many have done) allow their currencies to depreciate in order to reduce budget deficits (oil revenue is in dollars, while expenditure is mostly in the national currency), thus shifting the pain of adjustment to all earners of incomes in national currency. In contrast, the purchasing power of salaries paid in national Gulf currencies is protected by the dollar peg, and indeed may increase if other currencies lose value relative to the dollar. We may see governments losing legitimacy and facing political turmoil, but the Gulf governments will not be the first in line.

Thus, if we consider the situation from the point of view of the political stability of individual countries, it is likely that the Gulf monarchies will remain the most stable in the region, and more stable than other important producers such as Venezuela, Nigeria, Kazakhstan, Azerbaijan, or even Russia. However, we should consider not only the stability of individual countries, but also regional stability in the Middle East as a whole.

In this respect, it is important to understand that high oil prices, far from being a stabilizing factor in regional Middle East politics, have rather been a key determinant of rapidly growing instability throughout the region. Since the turn of the century, political instability and high oil prices have reinforced one another in a tightening vicious circle. There is a close connection between regime change in Iraq and the onset of the oil price cycle that began in 2004. In the run-up to the allied intervention in Iraq, it was expected that the demise of Saddam's regime would open up the country to international oil companies' investment, followed by rapid increase in oil production. In contrast, it soon became apparent that the outcome was entirely different, as oil prices started increasing gradually. The outbreak of the Arab Spring further stoked fears that oil supplies from the Middle East might be seriously disrupted, although this never came to pass. Since 2004, the Middle East has progressively precipitated into a regional civil war, engulfing all countries and all political forces. At the time of writing, this war is actively fought in four counties (Iraq, Syria, Yemen, and Libya), but in fact all countries are involved, and all will be affected by the eventual outcome.

It is clear that the period of very high prices led to greater regional instability rather than the opposite. High prices enhanced the income gap between major oil exporters and the rest of the region, as well as income concentration within each country. The Arab Spring and its regional dimension cannot be easily explained unless we take into account the dynamics of income distribution at the regional level, rather than just within each country in the region. Although national statistics show that income distribution did not worsen appreciably, the extreme concentration of income and wealth in the hands of the top 1 percent of the distribution is underestimated. Furthermore, income inequality is extremely large when considered at the regional level. It is the perception of growing inequality, further fueled by the growing role of regional media and the constant images of Dubai-style success which they project, that has ignited resentment and revolt against incumbent authoritarian regimes.

In the major oil-exporting countries, governments continued to rely on old and ineffective redistribution policies, which further benefitted the haves without offering significant improvement to the have-nots: low prices for energy products (energy subsidies) have a regressive impact upon income distribution; infrastructure expenditure benefits local contractors; increased spending leads to higher prices for housing, benefitting real estate investors and damaging poorer nationals for whom cheap housing is not provided; even the very generous schemes to support nationals studying abroad only accrue to a minority, while the majority of adolescents receive only mediocre education that fails to prepare them for gainful employment. Youth unemployment climbed, as nationals were squeezed out of the market by unskilled expatriates from low-wage South Asian countries (the bottom wages showed no signs of increasing, notwithstanding the spending boom, as the supply of immigrant labor is essentially infinite).

In the non-rentier Middle Eastern states, the development model of Dubai and the other Gulf countries became hegemonic: political elites nurtured cronies whose role was to attract investment from the Gulf, offering opportunities to invest in real estate, luxury tourism, and financial speculation. The economies of the non-rentier countries experienced satisfactory growth from 2000 to 2010, but the quality of increased investment and value added did not allow for trickle-down to occur.

At the same time, the period of high prices allowed for the continuation of adventurist and anachronistic policies, from the Iranian uranium enrichment program, to the support of the genocidal regime of Bashar al Assad or the rearmament programs of Saudi Arabia and the UAE. The oil rent, recycled through multiple channels, found ways of ending up in the hands of al-Qaeda first and

Daesh or other extremist groups later, as well as the Houthis in Yemen. There is no clear line between guilty and innocent, since the lack of any sort of budget constraint encouraged all parties to act imprudently and to engage in conflicts with uncertain outcomes, in which "victory" would hardly have any meaning at all.

Will tensions decrease now that the tide of oil prices has turned? Unfortunately, history cannot run in reverse and omelettes cannot be turned back into eggs. While increasingly limited financial resources may encourage a speedier resolution of the regional civil war, political stabilization will require the shaping of a regional economic order that promises opportunities for all and allows for reducing economic disparities.

Low oil prices are a challenge for all countries in the region, including those that are not major oil exporters. Syria is in ruins, and even if the civil war were to come to an end soon, the state and security apparatus will need external support for years, if not decades. In Egypt, al Sisi's repressive police state is unable to control large sections of the territory and continues to rely on the same policies of the Mubarak years, repeating all of the same mistakes. The regime maintains power thanks to ferocious repression, sadly illustrated by the assassination of Italian student Giulio Regeni on top of many Egyptians. Were it not for the (dwindling) financial support of Saudi Arabia and the UAE, Egypt's economic crisis would be even worse than it is already.

In the meantime, and if direct involvement in hostilities is minimized, the citizens of the Gulf will certainly appreciate the benefits of relative security and stability, in contrast to the chaos and destruction in neighboring countries. Under these conditions, the vast majority of citizens may be expected to accept a reduction in material benefits received from the state in line with reduced oil revenue.

Still, the regional civil war may turn against the Gulf monarchies, since they appear to be fighting too many enemies simultaneously (Iran and its proxies, Daesh, the Muslim Brotherhood). But the fight cannot be stopped unilaterally, and if it is lost, the stability of the monarchies will be affected. The UAE or Qatar could potentially isolate themselves from the regional context but have chosen not to do so: both are deeply involved in regional conflicts. As their attitude towards Iran is also divergent, the civil war is now within the GCC, and is attracting interference from outside actors, which guarantees that it will not end any time soon.[11]

Conclusion

Oil developments are central to the understanding of MENA political and economic dynamics, but one should be wary of simplifications. While in theory an abundance of oil rent is a stabilizing factor for incumbent regimes, issues related to the regional and domestic distribution of benefits in combination with the regional character of all MENA domestic politics may lead, and indeed has led, to the opposite result. There are times or circumstances in which oil may shape politics, but there are also times and circumstances when politics shape oil industry developments. Currently the international oil market is characterized by the shared sentiment that resources are abundant and the economic value of oil may decrease in a world bent upon decarbonization. At the same time, a regional civil war in the Middle East is underway, one whose outcome is extremely difficult to predict. High oil prices contributed to triggering the regional civil war, but low oil prices are unlikely to bring this war to an end.

Notes

1 See the speech by the then-Minister of Petroleum and Minerals of Saudi Arabia, Zaki Yamani, at the Oxford Energy Seminar on September 13, 1985, about which Robert Mabro commented as follows:

> The message, which is also the key to a correct assessment of Saudi Arabia's position was simply that Saudi Arabia is no longer willing or able to take that heavy burden and duty, and therefore cannot be taken for granted. The burden was placed by "the non-OPEC producers relying on OPEC to protect the price of oil" and by "most of the OPEC member countries [which] depend on Saudi Arabia to [...] protect the price of oil.
>
> (Mabro, 1986, p. 8; see also Luciani, 2015, pp. 16–19)

2 For an early formulation see Campbell, 1997.
3 IEA, 2013, pp. 473–474.
4 EIA, 2016.
5 It has since recovered and hit a new peak at 43.8 percent in 2008, slightly declining thereafter (calculations based on data from BP, 2015).
6 Major exporters like Saudi Arabia will only sell to customers accepting destination limitations to designated refineries. Consequently, a cargo of crude oil cannot change hands, preventing the emergence of a forward market. The rationale for this policy is the desire to differentiate prices to different destinations (the Far East pays more, the USA pay less) and maximize revenue.
7 Reuters, 2008. This was reiterated in May 2009. See Luciani, 2015.
8 Reuters, 2014.
9 In the late 1960s the issue of conservation was very much at the center of OPEC's preoccupations. See Parra, 2004, pp. 122–125.
10 The two major Arab oil exporters outside of the GCC, namely Iraq and Libya, have been in the throes of civil war since well before the collapse in prices.
11 The differences lie at the base of the rift between Qatar on one side and the UAE, Bahrain and Saudi Arabia on the other, while Kuwait attempts a difficult mediation and Oman increasingly distances itself from the rest of the GCC. The Gulf States are on opposite sides, because Qatar has supported the Moslem Brotherhood, while the UAE and Saudi Arabia brand the same as terrorists.

Bibliography

BP (2015): *Statistical Review of World Energy 2015*. London: BP.

Campbell, Colin J. (1997): *The Coming Oil Crisis*. Essex: Multi-Science Publishing and Petroconsultants S.A.

EIA (2016): *Crude Oil Production*. Washington, DC: U.S. Energy Information Administration.

IEA (2013): *World Energy Outlook 2013*. Paris: International Energy Agency.

Luciani, Giacomo (2015): Saudi Arabia and the Limits of Signalling. *Oxford Energy Forum*, May(100), 16–19.

Mabro, Robert (1986): *OPEC and the World Oil Market: The Genesis of the 1986 Oil Price Crisis*. Oxford: Oxford Institute for Energy Studies/Oxford University Press.

Parra, Francisco (2004): *Oil Politics: A Modern History of Petroleum*. London: I.B. Tauris.

Reuters (2008): Saudi Targets "Fair" Oil Price at $75. November 29. Available at: www.reuters.com/article/us-saudi-oil-idUSTRE4AS25R20081129.

Reuters (2014): Saudi's Naimi Says OPEC Will Not Cut Output However far Oil Falls: MEES. December 22. Available at: www.reuters.com/article/us-saudi-opec-idUSKBN0K012K20141222.

3 Global gas and LNG markets

The role for MENA countries

Anne-Sophie Corbeau

Introduction

The development of global gas markets, and LNG markets in particular, has political and economic implications for the Middle East and North Africa (MENA) region. This region is highly dependent on gas, which accounts for 51 percent of its primary energy mix as compared to a world average of 22 percent. Gas demand in the MENA region has grown faster than in the rest of the world: around 6 percent annually between 2000 and 2015.[1] Increasing demand has been supported by rising domestic production and low gas prices, and the region represents 17 percent of global gas demand and 21 percent of production, making it a net exporter.

Many institutions and energy companies predict a bright future for natural gas. However, these optimistic perspectives collide with a harsh reality: in many regions outside MENA, gas is not competitive against cheap coal, or does not enjoy the same policy support as renewables, whose costs have plummeted.[2] The IEA estimates that the Middle East's gas demand will grow by 83 percent by 2040.[3] From a gas perspective, the region is a paradox. It holds significant gas reserves, but many countries are importers. Rapidly increasing demand combined with slower production growth means that most MENA countries are short of gas. The next generation of gas fields is likely to be more expensive to develop, raising questions of how to meet increasing gas needs and whether energy alternatives and energy efficiency could dampen demand growth.

The region has traditionally exported gas, notably LNG. In 2015, the MENA region exported around 140 bcm of LNG and 60 bcm of pipeline gas, including 24 bcm of pipeline gas traded within the region.[4] Regional geopolitical dynamics and low prices have limited intra-regional pipeline trade, forcing five countries to turn to LNG imports and others to consider the option. Increasing LNG imports could place financial stress on national oil and gas companies and governments, as domestic prices remain low despite recent price reforms.[5] Meanwhile, higher prices could dampen future demand growth. Recently, the MENA region's participation in global gas trade has declined, as three out of seven LNG exporters have ceased exports (Egypt, Libya, and Yemen). However, there are exceptions. Qatar, the world's largest LNG exporter and a low-cost gas producer with ample resources, could increase LNG exports. Iran and Iraq also have LNG exports plans, while Iran is the only country in the region considering new export pipelines.

This chapter begins with a global perspective on gas and LNG markets before focusing on MENA countries. It analyzes how a series of factors – slow-down of production growth, rapidly increasing demand, low domestic gas prices, and limited build-up of energy alternatives – have caused the region to go from a significant source of LNG exports to a LNG-importing region. It concludes with an assessment of the region's evolving role in global LNG markets.

A global perspective on gas markets

In 2015, the world consumed around 3500 bcm of natural gas. Of this total, 960 bcm was consumed in North America, 670 bcm in Asia, 590 bcm in the MENA region, and 470 bcm in Europe.[6] Regions witnessed significant demand variations. In North America, low gas prices increased demand in the power sector, while in Europe gas demand declined due to a sluggish electricity growth, strong renewables deployment, and competition from cheap coal. In Asia, gas demand fell in Japan and Korea after peaking in 2013 due to the restart of nuclear power plants and competition from coal-fired plants.[7]

In China, lower economic growth affected gas consumption, while many Southeast Asian countries such as India, Bangladesh, the Philippines, Indonesia, Malaysia, and Vietnam prioritize coal-fired capacity expansions over gas. Demand in Africa, the Middle East, and Latin America remains constrained by the availability of gas supply, whether domestic or imported. Low domestic gas prices in these countries often do not provide sufficient incentives to develop non-associated gas production. However, governments have started to increase regulated gas prices.[8]

Despite its significance as a demand region, Asia does not have its own trading hub and relies on oil-indexed LNG.[9] Between 2011 and 2014, high contract prices led many Asian consumers to ask for a move away from oil indexation or to seek LNG supply sources priced according to an alternative indexation (such as US LNG pricing based on the Henry Hub cost-plus approach). Developing a trading hub will take time, particularly as the state of liberalization in Asian countries (with the exception of Singapore) is not very advanced, but Asian importers continue to promote the idea to increase portfolio diversification and flexibility. Since 2015, global prices have converged due to the decline in oil prices and global oversupply. Japanese LNG import prices dropped from around \$16/MMBtu in 2013 to \$6/MMBtu in mid-2016, before increasing again to \$8/MMBtu in 2017, while Asian spot LNG prices plummeted to \$4 to \$10/MMBtu from \$19/MMBtu in January 2014, bringing Asian LNG prices close to parity with European spot prices. This low spot price environment will likely continue as markets absorb the anticipated wave of LNG. However, while lower prices incentivize countries to import gas, the current low price environment has postponed or even canceled upstream and LNG investments, sparking concerns that the gas industry may be unable to ensure the timely delivery of gas supplies when demand rebounds.

Amid changing global energy dynamics, the Paris Agreement has provided a new blueprint for a low-carbon energy future. However, despite forecasts of a bright future for natural gas, COP21 failed to recognize natural gas as an alternative fuel source in a carbon-constrained world. Natural gas demand is only increasing in areas where gas supply is available and lacks significant competition from coal and renewables. This includes the MENA region, places like the United Kingdom and the USA where policy measures have been taken to decommission coal-fired plants and/or to add a carbon price, or places like China where environmental policy could enhance the role of gas – if the price is right.

Gas developments in the MENA region

Gas demand is growing in the MENA countries, which hold around 90 tcm of proven gas reserves.[10] Most MENA countries are short of gas, as gas demand growth has outpaced domestic production. In 1990, the Middle East's gas demand was only 97 bcm (5 percent of the global total); this rose to 187 bcm in 2000 and to 490 bcm by 2015, accounting for 14 percent of global demand. Algerian demand nearly doubled between 2000 and 2015, from 20 to 29 bcm, while Egyptian gas demand more than doubled, from 20 to 48 bcm, peaking at 53 bcm in 2012 before being curtailed by shortages.[11]

Low domestic gas prices, rapid population growth, and economic and industrial growth have spurred a rapid increase in energy demand. Gas demand growth in particular has been driven by the power sector. Between 2000 and 2015, electricity demand in the Middle East quadrupled thanks in part to strong GDP growth. Gas accounted for two-thirds of the additional power generation, bringing its power sector share to 64 percent in 2013. The IEA expects the region's power demand to double by 2040, with 80 percent of the gains met by gas.[12] Low gas prices have also provided a competitive edge for MENA petrochemical, aluminum, and cement industries. There is some limited residential and commercial consumption in Iran, Egypt, and Algeria while Iran consumes gas in the transport sector. Finally, some oil exporters have privileged exporting oil and consuming gas.

While MENA gas demand is increasing, production growth has slowed down. Iran and Qatar are exceptions, whereas gas output has been declining in Algeria and Egypt since the end of the 2000s. Furthermore, most of the region's gas production is associated gas, and is thus influenced by oil production and therefore OPEC decisions. New gas fields are more likely to be non-associated gas, which is more expensive to produce, while some fields like Khazzan in Oman are tight or sour, such as Bab in the United Arab Emirates (UAE).

The MENA region accounted for 43 percent of global LNG exports in 2015 (40 percent in 2016), and is a growing LNG importer (4 and 7 percent of global trade in 2015 and 2016). The region exported approximately 2.4 times more LNG than pipeline gas in 2015, a ratio that increases to nearly four times if intra-regional trade is excluded. Despite these statistics, the region's role as a source of LNG exports is under pressure, while growing LNG imports will expose the region's gas markets to global LNG market developments (see Table 3.1).

LNG trade has surged: from 102 mtpa in 2000 to 263 mtpa in 2016. Asia remains the dominant market, accounting for 73 percent of LNG imports in 2016, while Qatar alone exports 30 percent of global LNG trade.[13] Many developing markets, including MENA countries, are increasingly turning to LNG thanks to floating storage and regasification units (FSRUs). LNG has also become more flexible, with spot and short-term LNG trade reaching 28 percent of the global total in 2016.[14]

In short, the global LNG market is transforming. Prospects of high LNG demand in Asia combined with the view that the region would continue to pay a premium have incentivized many LNG export projects to move forward. From 2015 to 2020, around 150 mtpa in new LNG export capacity is expected to come online, predominantly from Australia and the USA, with Australia expected to overtake Qatar as the world's largest LNG exporter by 2020. Nine countries could also become new LNG importers by 2020, while some traditional LNG importers are becoming exporters, and vice versa.

There is around 1000 mtpa of proposed export capacity. Most projects are located in North America, Australia, Russia, and Eastern Africa, while Indonesia, Iran, Papua New Guinea, and Qatar could add new capacity. Each region has its own challenges to overcome. However, the oversupply situation, uncertainty

Table 3.1 Import/export status of MENA countries

	Exporter (as of 2016)	*Planned exporter*	*Importer (as of 2016)*		*Planned imports*	
			LNG	*Pipeline*	*LNG*	*Pipeline*
Algeria	X					
Egypt	X		X		X	
Libya	X					
Morocco				X	X	
Tunisia				X		
Bahrain					X	
Iraq		X (LNG)		X		X
Iran	X	X		X		
Israel		X?	X	Stopped		
Jordan			X	Stopped		X
Kuwait			X		X	
Oman	X			X	X	
Qatar	X					
Saudi Arabia					X	
UAE	X		X	X	X	
Yemen	Stopped					

Sources: GIIGNL (2016); author's assumptions.

about future LNG demand, and low oil prices could create a dearth of final investment decisions (FIDs). Key questions for LNG potential include when LNG markets will rebalance, where LNG will be needed, and whether oil prices will be high enough to support capital-intensive projects. Companies will also need to reduce costs to make LNG affordable and a credible option against cheap coal.

The role of LNG in MENA countries

MENA: once a key source of LNG exports

MENA countries have been a major source of LNG exports. Algeria became the first exporter in 1964, followed by Libya in 1970, and Abu Dhabi in 1977, after which time MENA became the largest LNG exporting region in the world. However, its dominance was eroded over the course of the 1980s and 1990s as new exporters like Malaysia, Indonesia, and Australia emerged. The region regained its significance thanks to the emergence of Egypt and Yemen as exporters in the 2000s and the decisive role of Qatar, which began exporting in 1996 and expanded exports dramatically from 2009 to 2011 (see Figure 3.1).

However, LNG exports from the region are waning, totaling 105 mtpa in 2015, down from 115 mtpa in 2011. Qatar remains dominant, and represents three-quarters of the region's LNG exports, while exports were halted in Libya (2011), and Yemen (2015), considerably reduced in Egypt, and declined in Oman, Abu Dhabi, and Algeria. Looking forward, while global LNG export capacity is expected to increase by 150 mtpa from 2015 to 2020, there are no firm plans to build LNG export facilities in the MENA region. Only Qatar could potentially do so following the lifting of the moratorium in 2017.

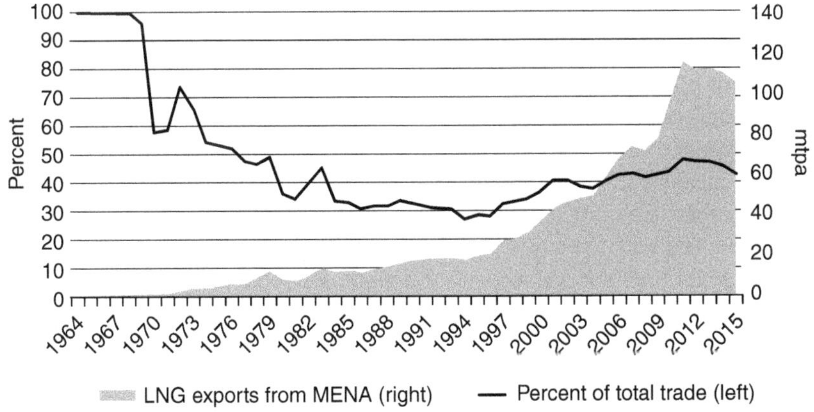

Figure 3.1 LNG exports from MENA countries.

Source: GIIGNL (2016).

The LNG pioneers

The discovery of Algeria's massive natural gas resources coincided with the development of LNG cargoes and the United Kingdom's search for cleaner fuels following London's Great Smog in 1952. Algeria began exporting LNG in 1964, and dominated the global LNG trade for the next ten years before being overtaken by Brunei. Algeria continued to expand its LNG export infrastructure over the following decades, but suffered major setbacks due to pricing disputes with key European customers and the liberalization in the US market. Boosted by growing European demand, Algerian LNG exports reached 20 mtpa in 1998. However, difficulties developing upstream assets and meeting rising domestic demand made the government's export targets, set at 85 bcm by 2013 and 100 bcm thereafter, unrealistic. Despite the addition of two new export plants (Skikda and Gassi Touil), by 2015 LNG exports had reached just 12 mtpa. Due to rapid demand growth and dwindling production, exports dropped from 60 bcm in 2008 to 44 bcm in 2015, and facilities remain underutilized at around 43 percent.[15] Demand may range between 48 bcm and 67 bcm by 2023; the high demand scenario will likely result in a further drop in exports.[16]

Libya is also an early LNG pioneer. Libya's 3.2 mpta Marsa El Brega LNG plant was third in the world after Algeria's Arzew and Alaska's Kenai, and became operational in 1970 just a few months after Gaddafi came to power. The plant operated at capacity during the first decade of operations, exporting mainly to Spain and Italy, but following the imposition of sanctions upon Libya in the 1980s and the withdrawal of Esso, LNG exports dropped to around 0.7 mtpa.[17] In 2005, an agreement to rejuvenate the Brega plant and restore it to its nameplate capacity was concluded.[18] There were also plans to build an additional LNG export plant should new discoveries exceed the needs of the domestic market and Marsa El Brega. However, construction never took place and Libya has not exported LNG since 2011. The rejuvenation of the LNG plant appears increasingly unlikely following the 2011 Arab Spring and subsequent civil war.

While Algeria was the first MENA country to export LNG, Abu Dhabi became the first and unique Middle Eastern exporter from 1977 until 1996. The development of gas in the UAE was initiated to reduce flaring of associated gas. The construction of the two-train 2.06 mtpa ADGAS plant began in 1973, and the first shipment was loaded in April 1977 and sent to the Tokyo Electric Power Company. Japanese company Mitsui, a project partner with BP, Total, ADNOC, and Bridgestone, was instrumental in reaching the agreement with TEPCO due to its relationship with the buyer. A third train was commissioned in 1994, bringing Abu Dhabi's export capacity to 5.8 mtpa. Between 1998 and 2015, the ADGAS plant delivered a remarkable average 5.5 mtpa.[19] The key question is what will happen after the contract expires in 2019 and whether the UAE can continue to deliver or have to import more LNG and pipeline gas (from Qatar). Imports from Qatar now appear less likely after the UAE broke off relations with Qatar in June 2017.

The heavyweight: Qatar

Qatar is a regional and global LNG giant, thanks in part to Shell's discovery of the giant North Field in 1971. As of the end of 2015, Qatar's proven reserves amounted to 24.5 tcm, making it the third-largest gas reserves holder after Iran and Russia.[20] LNG exports developments took around 25 years, even though Qatar Petroleum (QP) first invited proposals from IOCs to develop the North Field in 1981. Progress was hampered by slow progress on LNG marketing and difficult discussions about fiscal and gas supply agreements.

Similar to ADGAS, Japan played a key role in the development of Qatari LNG. Indeed, a breakthrough came when Mitsui became the fourth foreign partner in Qatargas, bringing along Chubu Electric as a potential buyer. Shortly afterwards, Qatargas took FID in 1993 on the first two trains (Qatargas 1) and the first LNG cargo was loaded in December 1996, while the second train started in 1997. The EPC contractor and shipowners were Japanese firms, while the financing came from Japanese commercial banks as well as export credit agencies. The development of Qatargas 1's third train was also supported by a consortium of Japanese utilities. When Mobil joined the development of Qatari gas in 1992, it was agreed that a second liquefaction company, RasGas, would be created, where Mobil (later ExxonMobil) took 30 percent. The two-train RasGas 1 was developed with Korea as a main market, and started exporting in 1999.

Between 2009 and 2011, Qatar's profile as a LNG exporter took off. During this period, six mega-trains of 7.8 mtpa – the largest ever built – came online, making Qatar the largest LNG exporter in the world at 77 mtpa by 2011. This expansion was completed by the construction of a fleet of larger LNG cargoes, the Q-flex and Q-max. During that time, Qatar faced a significant challenge: when the FIDs for these trains were taken, approximately one-third of the LNG was expected to be sold to Europe, Asia, and the USA. However, the rise in US shale gas production meant that Qatar had to rely even more on European and Asian markets to market its gas, as the USA would increasingly meet domestic needs with domestic production.[21]

While Qatar will remain the largest LNG exporter until all Australian LNG plants come online and reach full capacity around 2019/2020, the key question is whether the lifting of the moratorium on additional North Field developments in 2017 will translate into LNG, pipeline, or GTL exports. Given current market conditions, Qatar would have an advantage as a low-cost producer and could easily debottleneck existing capacity before adding new trains.

New exporters

Oman became a LNG exporter in 2000 with the opening of the Oman LNG plant, followed by Qalhat LNG in 2006. Oman's total export capacity is 10.4 mtpa, and its main customers are KOGAS and Osaka Gas, while Qalhat has contracts with Union Fenosa, Mitsubishi, and Osaka Gas. Most contracts will expire around 2024/2025. LNG exports peaked in 2007 before falling due to a shortage in feedgas, and most plants are currently operating below capacity (76 percent on average in 2016). Oman must also contend with rising domestic demand, which tripled from 2000 to 2014 to reach 23 bcm.[22] Oman imports pipeline gas from Qatar through the Dolphin pipeline, but the future of this supply may be uncertain, as Qatar signed a supply deal to increase exports to the UAE in October 2016. However, Oman may have other alternatives, including a potential pipeline link from Iran, a project that received a boost following the lifting of sanctions against Iran. The project would also allow Iran to export LNG through Oman's existing plants.

Egypt also has LNG export capacity, including two liquefaction plants, the 5 mtpa Damietta, and the two-train 7.2 mtpa Idku, which became operational in 2005. However, exports ceased and the plants were mothballed in 2013 and 2014 despite initial plans to add another train. Egypt exported a few cargoes in 2016. To meet domestic needs, Egypt became a LNG importer in 2015 (see below), and while there has been discussion about reviving the plants, including by using Israeli gas, these plans have been stymied by geopolitical issues.

Egypt also began exporting pipeline gas via the Arab Gas Pipeline to Israel and Jordan in 2007, and planned to export gas to Europe via Turkey. However, many of these pipeline exports ceased or became intermittent and unreliable following the Arab Spring and subsequent attacks on the pipeline. The shortage of gas for Egypt's domestic market resulted in the suspension of gas supplies to Israel and reduction of flows to Jordan. However, the August 2015 discovery of the large Zohr gas field by ENI will change the supply picture in Egypt considerably, providing the gas to meet Egypt's domestic needs.

Yemen is a relative latecomer to LNG, and only started exporting in 2009. The Yemen LNG liquefaction plant is the country's largest industrial investment, at $4.5 billion, and the output of the two-train 6.7 mtpa facility was contracted by GDF-Suez (now Engie), KOGAS, and Total. While some of this gas was originally intended for the US market, the growth of domestic US gas production caused Yemeni LNG to be diverted mostly to Asia. Since 2011, Yemeni LNG exports have been frequently disrupted by instability in the country. Following the outbreak of the Yemeni civil war in 2015, Yemen LNG declared *force majeure* and the plant was subsequently mothballed. However, unlike in Libya where the LNG plant has been damaged, Yemen LNG could restart if the geopolitical situation improves.

Potential exporters

Iran is a major wildcard for the LNG industry. Iran possesses the world's largest gas reserves, but international sanctions have thus far prevented the development of these resources for export. Sanctions have restricted access to international finance and made key technology (namely liquefaction technology) and expertise unavailable. There have been several planned LNG export projects, such as Iran LNG, Pars LNG, Persian LNG, and Qeshm LNG, and while none have come to fruition the lifting of sanctions following the 2015 nuclear deal could enable Iran to return to the LNG scene, albeit with uncertainty on the timeframe and the projects due to the US new stance on Iran. However, several hurdles to LNG exports remain, including increasing global LNG supplies, low market prices, and domestic demand. While reserves are not an issue, rapidly increasing gas demand could compete with export projects as large volumes of gas are needed for the domestic market and reinjection.

The quicker option to begin exporting LNG is to build a pipeline to Oman and export from its existing facilities, a project which the National Iranian Gas Company (NIGC) estimates could be completed in two years. Another option is to continue work on and complete the country's most advanced LNG facilities, Iran LNG, which, according to Iranian facilities, would take three to four years to complete.[23] Iran is also exploring options to export gas by pipeline, and completed a 9 bcm/y pipeline to Iraq in 2016.[24] Iran is also looking to export gas to Pakistan and India, while other pipeline options to the UAE and Kuwait are less advanced.

Iraq is another country previously included in discussions of potential LNG exports. Iraqi LNG exports were under consideration in 2013, when the Iraqi government approved the creation of the Basrah Gas Company joint venture to develop LNG facilities to utilize flared associated gas and develop non-associated gas. As of 2014, Iraq was the fourth-largest natural gas flaring country in the world. Under the joint venture, Shell and Mitsubishi also proposed a 4 mtpa plant to capture associated and flared gas, and the construction of a LNG exporting facility was a long-term consideration. However, gas projects have been hit by delays, and production is unlikely to increase as planned, while any plan to develop exports comes second to fulfilling domestic demand, as there is a shortage of gas for Iraqi power plants.

The paradox of LNG imports

While the MENA region is rich in gas, reserves are concentrated in Iran and Qatar, leaving most countries short of gas. The previously described combination of rapidly increasing gas demand for power and industry, slower gas production growth, and low domestic gas prices has caused many countries to turn to imports. While Oman and the UAE receive gas imports via pipeline from Qatar, other countries (including Dubai in the UAE) have looked to LNG imports.

MENA countries aside from Iran and Qatar face challenges in developing domestic supply. Low domestic gas prices have also made the development of new tight or non-associated gas fields economically unattractive unless project developers are able to secure higher prices or subsidies. Gas shortages are therefore expected to continue, as domestic production cannot keep pace with gas demand. The IEA expects gas consumption in the Middle East to increase by 363 bcm between 2014 and 2040. Under this scenario, gas would represent 54 percent of the primary energy mix, while renewables and nuclear combined would only account for 7 percent of primary energy demand by 2040.

Pipeline gas from Qatar and Iran could help meet regional demand, but intra-regional trade has failed to take off. Iran does not export to any GCC country, while Qatar's announced increase in the volumes to the UAE through the Dolphin Pipeline now appears less likely. Net exports from the MENA region (excluding Qatar) have been declining substantially from their peak in 2006 (see Figure 3.2). Meanwhile, five MENA countries have turned to LNG to meet rising gas demand, relying on new and planned FSRUs, which are less expensive and can be developed in around two years.

Kuwait and Dubai: the first MENA LNG importers

Kuwait and Dubai were the region's first LNG importers. Kuwait has significant associated gas, the production of which is limited by OPEC oil production quotas, while the development of Jurassic gas fields has proved challenging. Kuwait must also address rising natural gas demand and a struggling electricity sector that relies on both oil and gas-fired power plants. Significant gas shortages took place in the summer of 2007, leading to power cuts. As burning fuel oil or diesel is inefficient, expensive, and less environmentally friendly than gas, Kuwait has increasingly turned to natural gas in the power sector, and in 2009 a FSRU went into operation, enabling Kuwait to import 0.6 bcf/d during the peak summer months. A larger FSRU enabled imports to reach 3 mtpa in 2015, the lease for which expires in 2019 (although it may be extended).[25] KPC signed LNG supply deals with Shell and BP for the existing FSRU. Kuwait is also planning to build a new land-based terminal that would be operational by the end of 2020 to meet increasing power sector demand.

The UAE is also facing an important gas deficit, as gas demand doubled since 2000 to 69 bcm in 2015. In terms of gas production, most of the gas in the UAE

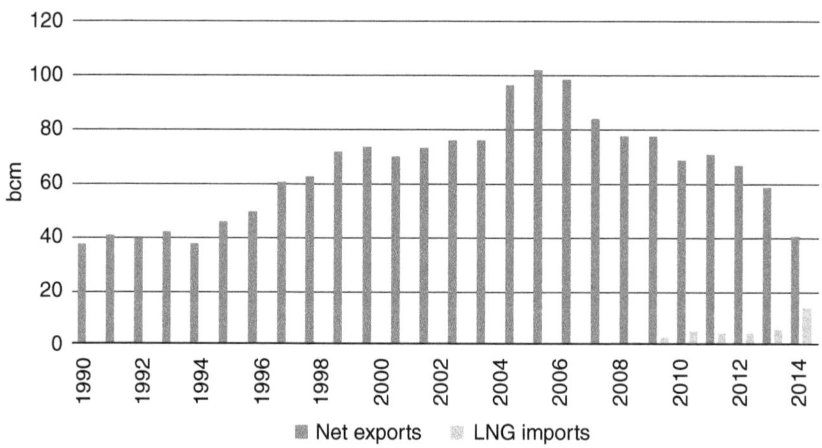

Figure 3.2 Net exports from the MENA region (excluding Qatar).

Sources: GIIGNL (2016); BP (2016).

is associated and thus subject to production limitations imposed by OPEC. Gas in non-associated fields is sour and the development of the Bab field has been postponed due to low oil prices. To meet demand, in 2010 Dubai opted for a FSRU to meet summer air-conditioning needs. The UAE imported 3.1 mtpa in 2016.[26] Abu Dhabi also commissioned a FSRU in late 2016, while Sharjah signed a MOU to import LNG from Uniper.

Egypt's gas shortages force Israel, Jordan, and Egypt to import LNG

Egypt went from an exporter of pipeline gas and LNG (18 bcm in 2009) to an LNG importer in 2015 due to collapsing domestic production (from 61 bcm in 2012 to 46 bcm in 2015) and rising domestic demand.[27] Following the 2011 Arab Spring, Egypt cut exports to Israel and progressively reduced exports to Jordan, but despite halting gas exports completely in 2014, power blackouts demonstrated that Egypt remained unable to meet its domestic needs. To address the problem, two FSRUs contracted from Höegh and BW Shipping started operating in 2015 with a combined import capacity of 13 bcm/y.[28] Both are located in Ain Sokhna. Egypt imported 7.5 mtpa in 2016. Development of the Zohr field, anticipated in late 2017, and other fields, could increase production to above peak production levels (even though existing fields are likely to decline).[29] However, gas demand has been constrained by lack of supply availability and could rebound as supply becomes available. Depending on future demand growth, timeliness of production, and affordability of LNG, LNG imports may continue beyond 2020.

Israel started importing LNG in 2013 after Egypt stopped gas deliveries through the Arab Gas Pipeline (formerly around 2 bcm). The Public Utilities Authority has approved the continued use by IEC of the FSRU to import LNG until 2019.[30] However, Israel's import needs are limited thanks to the development of the Tamar field, and it could export LNG itself or through Egyptian facilities.

Egypt's disruptions hit Jordan, which formerly relied in particular on Egypt for most of its gas (>3 bcm). Plans to construct a LNG terminal began in 2011 and, following lengthy negotiations, the terminal was commissioned in May 2015. The project's economics were improved by the existence of the pipeline infrastructure and CCGTs, and Jordan imported 3.1 mtpa in 2016.[31]

Potential LNG importers

Bahrain, Morocco, and potentially Saudi Arabia may also become LNG importers. Bahrain's gas demand doubled from 9 to 16 bcm between 2000 and 2015, driven by the power and industry sectors,[32] and the country plans to add 1.5 GW of generating capacity at the Al Dur power and desalination plant, while aluminum producer Alba plans to build a 1.35 GW plant. While Bahrain aims to expand associated gas production from the Tatweer oilfield by around 3.5 bcm,[33] it is also considering LNG imports and planning to develop a FSU in 2019.[34]

Morocco is considering building a LNG terminal to diversify or replace Algerian pipeline imports after the transit contract expires in 2021. The terminal, located in Jorf Lasfar, will be connected to the existing pipeline system, and Morocco plans to import 2 mtpa starting in 2020, and 3.5–4 mtpa by 2025. This is part of a wider plan to increase power capacity by deploying renewables and adding 2.4 GW of gas-fired capacity, while another 6.3 GW of gas-fired capacity may be installed in the longer term.[35] Unlike in most MENA countries where LNG supplements domestic production, LNG imports would replace Algerian pipeline imports in Morocco.

Saudi Arabian Energy Minister Khalid al-Falih has also indicated that Saudi Arabia may start importing gas, while the share of gas in the primary energy mix would increase from 50 to 70 percent in the future.[36]

Implication of gas market dynamics for MENA countries

The current environment is clearly a buyers' market and is expected to remain so until the early 2020s. Even if oil prices recover, spot prices will likely remain low as long as the oversupply persists, and future LNG importers find themselves at an advantage thanks to the current low gas price environment. The evolution of LNG import prices is key for MENA countries with low wholesale prices. Buyers are in a better position to negotiate prices and contractual terms and, due to the uncertainty of future demand, prefer to import spot cargoes or to use short-term contracts complementing existing long-term contracts. While this behavior exists in the MENA region, the MENA buyers' position is quite different from European and Asian buyers, which face competition from cheap coal and new entrants. In MENA countries, uncertainties stem from the development of renewables and the strong push on energy efficiency.

Meanwhile, suppliers (notably Qatar) have been adapting to new market realities and increasing pressure on long-term contracts. Qatar signed several shorter term contracts with European buyers in 2013 and 2014, and provided commissioning cargoes for all new LNG importers in 2015, namely Jordan, Egypt, and Pakistan, and concluded a 15-year contract with Pakistan. Qatar also deals with new players, such as independent Chinese LNG importer JOVO,[37] and several contracts were renegotiated due to buyers' pressure (PetroChina, Petronet).

The evolution of LNG trade is crucial for the region. While global LNG export capacity will increase by 50 percent (+150 mtpa) between 2015 and 2020, none of this new capacity will be in the MENA region, and it is difficult to foresee new export projects being sanctioned in the current environment. However, depending on when LNG markets rebalance, new projects may need to be approved to avoid a rapid tightening of global gas markets after 2020. Should the oversupply extend beyond 2020, there could be a dearth in FIDs and a lasting low gas price environment until markets rebalance. Like all producers, MENA producers are affected by the current low oil and gas environment, delaying upstream investments. This situation could exacerbate the gas deficit and make imports increasingly necessary.

What role for MENA countries and the GECF?

The Gas Exporting Countries Forum (GECF) is quite different from OPEC. This is due to differences between oil and gas markets (oil is a global commodity, while gas markets are more regionalized), as well as different positions of leading gas-producing countries. For example, Iran's exports are limited, Russia is mostly a pipeline exporter to Europe, and Qatar is a LNG exporter.

The GECF was formally established in 2008 following the seventh Ministerial, while discussions date back to the first Ministerial in 2001. The GECF's official purpose is:

> [T]o support the sovereign rights of its Member Countries over their natural gas resources and their ability to independently plan and manage the sustainable, efficient and environmentally conscious development, use and conservation of natural gas resources for the benefit of their people.[38]

However, despite ministerial meetings and occasional calls to sustain gas prices in international markets (for example, from Nigeria's President Muhammadu Buhari in November 2015), the GECF is yet to take concerted action. In practice, there are no quotas on gas exports, and members compete in Europe and in global LNG markets. Iranian Oil Minister Bijan Zanganeh reportedly said that the growth of global spot LNG trade coupled with a shift away from long-term gas supply contracts could raise the possibility of concerted GECF action, an interesting statement from a non-LNG-exporting country that is certainly at odds with the position of GECF members like Qatar, which rely heavily on long-term contracts while using spot trade to optimize their portfolio.

The lack of concerted action does not mean that individual GECF countries cannot use market power. In global gas markets, Russia is the swing producer with an estimated 200 bcm of spare capacity. However, Russia may have to defend its market share in Europe against an influx of LNG, particularly if the current oversupply continues and LNG exporters look to dump excess supply in Europe. This increasing competition between LNG and pipeline gas involves three GECF countries (Algeria, Qatar, and Russia), one observer (Norway), and the USA. Should Russia decide to aggressively maintain market share, this could raise the potential of a price war, a development unlikely to be welcomed by Qatar and Norway.

Conclusions

The role of the MENA region in global gas markets is bound to change. Its position as the largest LNG exporter is challenged by Australia and the USA as some regional exporters struggle to maintain exports at current levels. MENA region LNG exports are likely to remain flat until 2020, resulting in a decrease from 43 percent in 2015, to 28 to 30 percent of the global total by 2020. A significant restart of Egyptian LNG is unlikely to happen before 2025, while exports in Abu

Dhabi and Oman will likely be constrained by growing domestic demand. Oman's LNG plant may remain operational if a pipeline from Iran to Oman is built. If Algeria's total exports are reduced, the country could still decide whether to reduce pipeline gas or LNG.

Ultimately, the post-2020 LNG export outlook hinges on Qatar, and how fast and whether Iran builds LNG export facilities or exports through Oman. Iraq is also a source of LNG export potential. Depending on these developments, the region could retain a steady share of global LNG exports beyond 2020. Nevertheless, in the case where global LNG demand triples by 2040, that would require a massive expansion of Qatar's and Iran's capacity to double MENA LNG exports from 106 mtpa in 2016. Meanwhile, the evolution of LNG export volumes combined with the potential evolution of LNG pricing formulas from oil linkage to a spot-indexed formula will impact future LNG export revenues.

MENA LNG imports are likely to increase, since this is a flexible way to source natural gas. Import volumes depend on the evolution of natural gas demand and the role of gas in a decarbonized world. While many foresee a rapid increase in the region's gas consumption, the development of alternatives, the impact of increasing gas prices, and the availability of supply (domestic or imported) are major uncertainties. LNG imports expose MENA countries to the evolution of global LNG markets and put them in competition with other regions. This will also impact the country's finances and possibly its future energy mix depending on the cost of future LNG supplies against developing alternatives. The current oversupply environment is favorable for those hoping to increase their imports as LNG suppliers are looking for new markets, an opportunity for would-be importers to obtain more favorable contractual conditions.

Notes

1 BP, 2016.
2 KAPSARC, 2015.
3 IEA, 2016b.
4 BP, 2016.
5 Corbeau et al., 2016.
6 BP, 2016.
7 Corbeau et al., 2016.
8 Ibid.
9 Corbeau et al., 2014.
10 BP, 2016.
11 Ibid.
12 IEA, 2016b.
13 GIIGNL, 2017.
14 Corbeau, 2016.
15 GIIGNL, 2017.
16 CREG, 2015.
17 GIIGNL, 2017.
18 Bouaziz et al., 2007.
19 GIIGNL, 2017.

20 BP, 2016.
21 Corbeau/Flower, 2016.
22 IEA, 2016a.
23 Harder, 2016.
24 The Iran Project, 2016.
25 GIIGNL, 2017.
26 Ibid.
27 BP, 2016.
28 GIIGNL, 2017.
29 BP, 2016.
30 Globes, 2015.
31 GIIGNL, 2017.
32 BP, 2016.
33 MEES, 2015a.
34 Ibid.
35 MEES, 2015b.
36 Interfax, 2016.
37 Corbeau, 2016.
38 GECF, 2016.

Bibliography

Bouaziz, Mounir/Bashir Ashahab/Abdelsalam Y. Hussein/Mark Hope (2007): *Libya LNG – Rejuvenating Brega and Developing New LNG*. International Conference on Liquefied Natural Gas: PS5–4.1. Des Plaines: Gas Technology Institute. Available at: www.ivt.ntnu.no/ept/fag/tep4215/innhold/LNG%20Conferences/2007/fscommand/PS5_4_Bouaziz_s.pdf.

BP (2016): *Statistical Review of World Energy 2016*. London: BP.

Corbeau, Anne-Sophie (2016): LNG Contracts and Flexibility. In Corbeau, Anne-Sophie/David Ledesma (Ed.): *LNG Markets in Transition: The Great Reconfiguration*. Oxford: Oxford University Press.

Corbeau, Anne-Sophie/Andy Flower (2016): The Maturing of the LNG Business. In Corbeau, Anne-Sophie/David Ledesma (Ed.): *LNG Markets in Transition: The Great Reconfiguration*. Oxford: Oxford University Press.

Corbeau, Anne-Sophie/Anne Braaksma/Farid Hussin/Yayoi Yagoto/Takuro Yamamoto (2014): *The Asian Quest for LNG in a Globalising Market*. Partner Country Series. Paris: IEA/OECD. Available at: www.iea.org/publications/freepublications/publication/PartnerCountrySeriesTheAsianQuestforLNGinaGlobalisingMarket.pdf.

Corbeau, Anne-Sophie/Rami Shabaneh/Sammy Six (2016): *The Impact of Low Oil and Gas Prices on Gas Markets: A Retrospective Look at 2014–15*. KS-1634-DP028. Riyadh: King Abdullah Petroleum Studies and Research Center (KAPSARC). Available at: www.kapsarc.org/wp-content/uploads/2016/05/KS-1634-DP028-The-Impact-of-Low-Oil-and-Gas-Prices-on-Gas-Markets-A-Retrospective-Look-at-2014-15_1-5-16web1.pdf.

CREG (2015): *Programme indicatif d'approvisionnement du marché national en gaz naturel, 2014–2023*. Programmes indicatifs d'approvisionnement du marché national en gaz, République algérienne Démocratique et Populaire, Ministère de l'Energie. Available at: www.creg.gov.dz/images/stories/PDF/PIG_2014_2023.pdf.

GECF (2016): *Mission and Objectives*. Doha: Gas Exporting Countries Forum (GECF). Available at: www.gecf.org/about/mission-objectives.aspx.

GIIGNL (2017): *The LNG Industry in 2016*. Neuilly-sur-Seine: Groupe International des Importateurs de Gaz Naturel Liquéfié (GIIGNL). Available at: www.giignl.org/sites/default/files/PUBLIC_AREA/Publications/giignl_2017_annual_report_0.pdf.

Globes (2015): IEC Extends LNG Floating Tanker Contract. November 3. Available at: www.globes.co.il/en/article-iec-extends-lng-ship-contract-1001078472.

Harder, Christopher (2016): Iran Seeks Rapid Reboot for Natural Gas Exports – Energy Journal, Moneybeat. *Wall Street Journal*, January 27. Available at: http://blogs.wsj.com/moneybeat/2016/01/27/iran-seeks-rapid-reboot-for-natural-gas-exports-energy-journal/.

IEA (2016a): *Natural Gas Information: Database Documentation (2016 Edition)*. Paris: International Energy Agency. Available at: http://wds.iea.org.

IEA (2016b): *World Energy Outlook 2016*. Paris: International Energy Agency.

Interfax (2016): Saudi Arabia Considers Importing Gas. June 9. Available at: http://interfaxenergy.com/gasdaily/article/20608/saudi-arabia-considers-importing-gas.

KAPSARC (2015): *Natural Gas: Entering a New Dark Age?* KAPSARC Energy Workshop Series: KS-1519-WB16A. Riyadh: King Abdullah Petroleum Studies and Research Center (KAPSARC). Available at: www.kapsarc.org/wp-content/uploads/2015/10/KS-1519-WB17A-Natural-Gas_-Entering-the-New-Dark-Age.pdf.

MEES (2015a): Bahrain LNG Plans. 11 December. *MEES* 58(50). Available at: www.mees.com?2015/12/11/transportation/bahrain-lng-plans/e32dc4d0-4932-11e7-b342-e97b4a7b08d9.

MEES (2015b): Morocco's $4.6bn LNG Scheme Continues To Drum Up Interest. May 15. *MEES* 58(20). Available at: www.mees.com/2015/5/15/transportation/moroccos-46bn-lng-scheme-continues-to-drum-up-interest/e429c660-4932-11e7-9a71-ed20433d86bf.

The Iran Project (2016): Iran Starts Injecting Gas in Export Pipeline to Iraq. April 10. Available at: http://blogs.wsj.com/moneybeat/2016/01/27/iran-seeks-rapid-reboot-for-natural-gas-exports-energy-journal/.

4 Renewable energy

A recent but dynamic trend in the MENA region

Sybille Roehrkasten and Mohammed Qader

Introduction

During the past decade, the deployment of renewables in the MENA region has expanded significantly.[1] The expansion started from a very low base while the energy supply in the region remains dominated by fossil fuels. However, almost all MENA countries have adopted national renewables targets. Should these targets be realized, they will have a significant impact upon the region's electricity mix.

This chapter outlines the major drivers and trends of renewable energy deployment in the region. It sheds light on the status quo and future plans – both in the region as a whole and in selected countries. Furthermore, it analyzes major barriers that need to be overcome to increase the deployment of renewables. Finally, it examines a very interesting development that has accompanied the recent expansion of renewables in the region: the changing stance of MENA countries with respect to international cooperation. While MENA countries long opposed global action to promote renewables, this is changing, and today the region is even the home of the International Renewable Energy Agency (IRENA).

Why are MENA countries increasingly investing in renewables?

Energy security concerns are a major driver for the recent uptick in renewable energy investments in the region.[2] Meeting rapidly rising domestic energy demand, a result of population and economic growth, is a major challenge for all MENA countries, while water scarcity further augments energy demand growth. Satisfying fresh water needs in the region relies increasingly on desalination, a highly energy-intensive technology.[3] Between 1990 and 2012, total primary energy demand in the MENA region almost tripled: from 289 Mtoe to 849 Mtoe. Until 2030, it is expected to grow by more than 45 percent to reach 1232 Mtoe. In the electricity sector, demand growth is even more pronounced: electricity generation experienced an almost fourfold increase: from 308 TWh in 1990 to 1206 TWh in 2012. By 2030, electricity generation is expected to reach 2084 TWh, representing growth of more than 70 percent.[4] Investments in renewable energy capacities are considered as an instrument to meet rising demand and to diversify the electricity mix. In this context, it is important to note that in contrast to the situation in more saturated markets, renewable energy investments in the MENA region are seen as an addition to investments in conventional energy rather than a replacement.

While all MENA countries are confronted with rising domestic energy demand, energy security concerns differ between countries that are energy-exporting versus -importing countries. For countries lacking significant domestic fossil fuel reserves, reducing import dependency is an obvious and long-lasting concern. For these countries, investments in renewables offer the opportunity to deploy domestically available energy sources and reduce spending on imports. For fossil fuel-rich and exporting countries, securing long-term export strength is a major challenge. For these countries, rising domestic energy demand leads to decreasing export shares, while fluctuating oil prices and changes in global oil and gas market dynamics increase the risks associated with their dependence on fossil fuel revenues. While the growth of unconventional production, especially in North America, has expanded the global fossil fuel supply and increased competition among fossil fuel exporters,[5] global ambitions to combat climate change increasingly challenge the long-term demand security for fossil energy. These developments have the potential to significantly weaken the mono-economies of fossil fuel-exporting countries. For exporters, investments in renewables not only contribute to reducing domestic fossil fuel consumption and thus free up resources for export, but could also help these countries maintain their energy leadership by diversifying business models.

Major improvements in the cost competitiveness of solar and wind energy are another important driver for the increased deployment of renewables in the region. Thanks to global scaling up of solar and wind energy and recent technical breakthroughs, prices for solar and wind energy are dropping around the globe. The price drops for solar PV have been most pronounced, as the levelized cost of electricity (LCOE) decreased by 58 percent between 2010 and 2015. In 2015, solar PV module prices were 80 percent lower than in 2009, while wind turbines experienced a 30 to 40 percent price drop from 2008/2009 to 2015.[6] These developments have been particularly favorable for the MENA region, which boasts huge solar and wind potential that can be capitalized on as solar and wind energy costs have become competitive with fossil fuel-fired power plants. The countries of the Gulf Cooperation Council (GCC) are a particularly interesting case, as they are not only rich in fossil fuels but also enjoy high levels of solar radiation and thus very low costs for solar energy by international comparison. A solar PV tender in Dubai in 2016 set the worldwide price record at 2.99 US cents per kWh, half the price of the previous year's record and one-third lower than electricity prices for electricity from a newly constructed coal-fired power plant in Dubai.[7] Solar energy in the Gulf region is currently cost competitive with conventional sources of oil, gas, and coal, which still dominate MENA countries' electricity supply. Against this backdrop, it is not surprising that the GCC countries are emerging as major investors in solar and wind projects around the globe, with ACWA Power (Saudi Arabia), Abdul Latif Jameel (Saudi Arabia), and Masdar (UAE) taking the lead.[8]

Thus far, climate change mitigation has not been a major motivation driving MENA countries' investments in renewables. However, in some countries, like the UAE and Morocco, domestic climate change mitigation is starting to play a role. International climate finance has been an important enabler of renewable energy projects in the region. Meanwhile, climate mitigation efforts undertaken in other parts of the world are already affecting the future export prospects for fossil fuel-rich MENA countries, as outlined above

Renewable energy deployment: state of the art

Although renewables are gaining momentum in the MENA region, it is important to emphasize that the energy supply remains almost exclusively dependent on fossil energy. In 2012, renewable energy provided only 1.2 percent of total primary energy demand in the region, while in the electricity sector renewables accounted for 3.3 percent of electricity generation and 6.2 percent of installed capacity. Hydropower is by far the largest share (3.2 percent of electricity generation and 5.6 percent of installed capacity), while non-hydro renewables remain a minor contribution to the region's electricity mix.[9]

Hydropower has been used in the MENA region for decades, with installed capacity totaling more than 20,000 MW in 2015,[10] accounting for 86 percent of total installed renewable energy capacity. Hydropower capacity has grown by almost 40 percent over the past decade, with about half of the new growth taking place in Iran, followed by Egypt, Iraq, Syria, and Morocco. Not all the countries in the region have the geographic ability to utilize hydropower, and only Morocco and Iran have plans to add new hydropower capacities in the future.

Over the past ten years, non-hydro renewables in the MENA region have experienced significant growth (see Figure 4.1). In 2007, renewables passed the 500 MW mark for the first time, up from just 154 MW of installed capacity in 2000. By 2015 renewables had reached 3329 MW, representing a more than twentyfold increase since 2000.

Wind energy and solar PV dominate the non-hydro-renewable landscape in the region. Wind capacities have steadily increased over the past ten years, reaching 1896 MW in 2015 and accounting for nearly 57 percent of the total installed non-hydro-renewables capacity. Most of this capacity is located in Morocco and Egypt. Solar PV was negligible in the region prior to 2008, but expanded rapidly afterwards. In 2015, there was 1199 MW of solar PV, accounting for 36 percent of installed non-hydro-renewables capacity in the region. More than 60 percent of this is in Israel. CSP installation began in 2008, and by 2015, 191 MW had been installed (6 percent of non-hydro capacities), more than the half located in the UAE. Meanwhile, bioenergy remains negligible (43 MW in 2015).

Beyond the electricity sector, in the MENA region solar water heating has become a major renewable energy application. As of 2013, the energy equivalent of the region's installed solar water-heating capacity was over three times higher

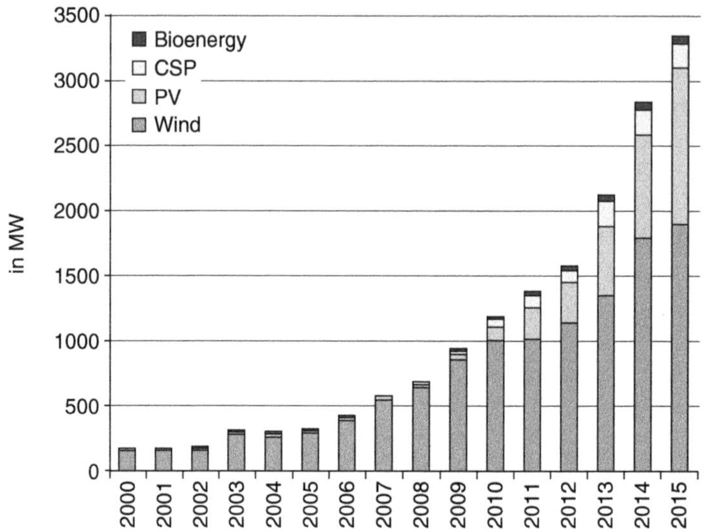

Figure 4.1 Expansion of non-hydro renewable energy capacities between 2000 and 2015.
Source: Own calculation based on IRENA data (2016c).

than the installed capacities of all other non-hydro renewables.[11] Solar water heating exists in Egypt, Israel, Jordan, Lebanon, the Palestinian Territories, and Tunisia. Notably, solar water heating's simplicity allows much of the needed equipment to be locally manufactured, increasing the economic benefits.[12]

Solar water desalination is another relevant application for non-electricity renewables, using solar power (mainly CSP) to desalinate and process brackish and sea water to produce fresh water. The economics of this integrated technology varies significantly depending on location, salinity of water, and the specific desalination technology in use. Currently, this is not yet cost-competitive and progress is therefore limited to a few commercial and pilot projects. However, it is expected to take off gradually, especially in the GCC countries, which have the lowest levels of renewable fresh water resources in the region and would benefit dramatically from moving away from existing conventional water-desalination facilities that consume huge amounts of fossil fuel, which could be freed up for export.

Morocco is leading the MENA region in installed non-hydro-renewable energy capacities (see Figure 4.2), with 829 MW of installed capacity in 2015.[13] In 2014, non-hydro renewables accounted for 10.9 percent of total installed capacity, the highest renewable energy share in the Arab region.[14] Since 90 percent of its energy supply is imported, reducing import dependency is a major driver of renewables deployment in Morocco.[15] By 2020, the country aims for renewables to account for 42 percent of electricity capacity, comprising 2 GW of solar, 2 GW of wind and 2 GW of hydropower.

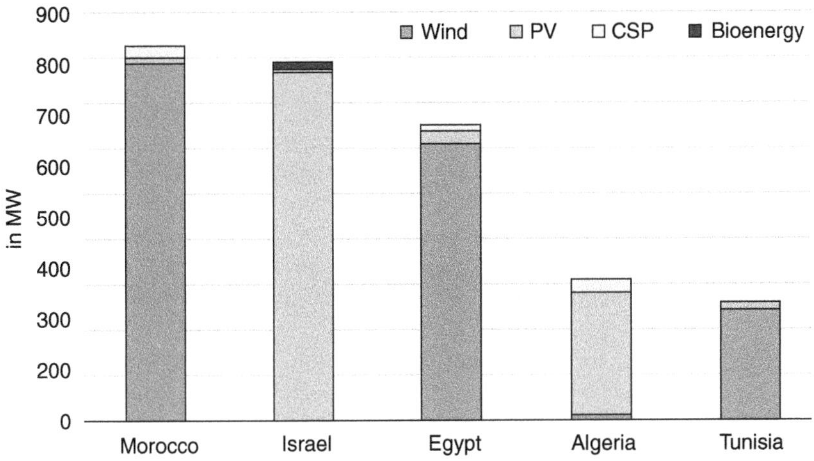

Figure 4.2 Top five countries in non-hydro renewables capacities in 2015.

Source: Own calculation based on IRENA (2016c).

Israel has the second-largest non-hydro-renewables capacities in the region: at 789 MW in 2015. Solar PV, at 766 MW, is clearly dominant, and accounts for 97 percent of installed renewables. Israel leads the region in solar PV, with more than 60 percent of all installed solar PV capacities in the MENA region.[16] Israel aims for a 10 percent renewables share in electricity generation by 2020, equaling 4 GW of installed capacities. Electricity generated from wind and solar PV has been subsidized since 2004, while feed-in tariffs were introduced in 2009, and all new buildings have been required to install solar water heating systems since 1980.[17]

Egypt has the third-largest installed non-hydro-renewable energy capacities, totaling 655 MW in 2015. However, compared to Morocco the share of installed renewables is much smaller, with only 2 percent in 2014. Egypt has ambitious renewables plans looking forward to 2020, when it aims to reach 8.5 GW of installed renewable energy capacities.[18] These plans are accompanied by policy reforms designed to boost renewable deployment, including the introduction of net metering, feed-in tariffs, and auctions.[19] Meeting increasing energy demand driven by population growth is a major driver of Egypt's renewable energy expansion.

Tunisia has the second largest share of non-hydro-renewable capacities in the Arab world: at 6.63 percent or 265 MW in 2014.[20] As a net energy importer, Tunisia aims to further exploit its solar and wind potential to meet domestic energy demand and export electricity to Europe. One of the biggest renewables projects is the anticipated 2.25 GW CSP tower technology plant TUNUR. It is furthermore planned to transmit electricity to Europe through a cable running between Tunisia and Italy. Tunisia was also one of the earliest countries in the region to implement renewables policies, including import tax exemptions for raw materials needed for renewables and energy-efficiency projects issued in 1995.[21]

Future plans

Governments in the MENA region have set very ambitious plans for the future expansion of renewable energies (see Table 4.1), and all MENA countries, with the exception of Bahrain and Oman, have adopted national renewable energy targets.[22] According to these plans, the Arab countries will add 75,000 MW of new renewables capacities by 2030 in addition to the 12,000 MW installed by 2015.

According to plans leading up to 2030, CSP will be the most prevalent renewable technology in the region, with planned capacity additions amounting to over 41,000 MW.[23] Compared to less than 200 MW of installed capacity in 2015, the realization of these plans would increase CSP capacities by a factor of over 200. Similarly, solar PV plans anticipate additions of over 29,000 MW to the 1199 MW existing in 2015. Plans for wind energy similarly envisage 26,000 MW in new capacity on top of the 1896 MW of installed capacity in 2015. In addition to these three major technologies, there are also plans to expand bioenergy and geothermal deployment in the region by 3700 MW and 1200 MW respectively, more than 80 percent of which will be in the Kingdom of Saudi Arabia (KSA). The expansion plans also comprise hydropower, which is the only technology where plans for future capacity additions are less than the current installed capacity, since most of its potential has already been exploited.

According to the authors' calculations based on IEA estimates, the share of renewable energy in the region's installed electrical capacity will increase significantly: from 6.2 percent in 2012 to almost 16 percent in 2030. While the IEA estimates the share of gas in electrical capacity will remain almost stable (from

Table 4.1 Technology-specific renewable energy installed capacities vs. plans of MENA countries for 2030

Technology	*Installed capacities 2015 (MW)*	*Planned additional capacities by 2030 (MW)*
CSP	191	>41,000
PV	1,199	>29,000
Wind	1,896	>26,000
Bioenergy	43	>3,000
Geothermal	0	>1,200
Hydropower	21,125	>4,000

Source: Own calculations based on various sources.*

Note

* For the 2015 capacities, see IRENA (2016c); for the 2030 plans based on League of Arab States et al. (2014) and REN21 (2013).

66 percent in 2012 to 67 percent in 2030), it predicts a strong relative (and absolute) decline in oil capacities (from 26.5 percent in 2012 to 15% percent in 2030).[24]

In the region, Saudi Arabia has the boldest plans for the future expansion of renewables. This is a very notable development for Saudi Arabia, the world's leading oil exporter and a country whose energy mix still relies exclusively on fossil fuels. Future plans include installing 25 GW of CSP, 16 GW of solar PV, 9 GW of wind energy, 3 GW of waste-to-energy, and 1 GW of geothermal by 2032, a significant increase compared to 25 MW of installed renewable capacities in 2015.[25] Saudi Arabia's solar plans account for more than 50 percent of the planned solar capacities in the MENA region. However, experts question the viability of these plans, and the Saudi government has already postponed the timeframe from 2032 to 2040.[26] At the beginning of 2016 Saudi Arabia announced "Vision 2030", which sets the goal of 9.5 GW of renewables by 2030, significantly lower than the previously announced targets.[27]

Barriers to renewable proliferation

The big question is whether these ambitious plans will actually be realized. Recent analysis by the Regional Center for Renewable Energy and Energy Efficiency (RCREEE)[28] shows that thus far, installed renewables capacities in the Arab region lag far behind the targets. RCREEE emphasizes that strengthening institutional capacities is critical to enforce and implement renewable energy measures. In its renewable energy market analysis of the GCC region, the International Renewable Energy Agency (IRENA) reached a similar conclusion, asserting that targets alone are insufficient, and instead need to be backed by dedicated policies and regulatory frameworks to be effective. IRENA argues that such policies are often missing, and calls for long-term policy planning in the region to create a stable and transparent regulatory and investment climate.[29]

Leveling the playing field between renewables and fossil fuels is particularly challenging in the Arab world, where fossil fuels are still heavily subsidized. Energy subsidies are an important part of the social contract in the region, and citizens have grown accustomed to very cheap electricity and fuels. According to the International Monetary Fund,[30] almost 50 percent of spending on global fossil fuels subsidies occurs in the MENA region, while the renewable energy industry still receives very little support from governments. Thus, gradually reducing fossil fuel subsidies is of the utmost importance if renewables are to become cost-competitive.

The difficult investment climate in the region further hampers investments in renewables. Ongoing conflicts and political and economic instability stymie investments – not only in renewable energies but also in the energy sector as a whole. Overall, private investment in renewable energies in the Arab world remains low. Insufficient grid infrastructure, and limited grid capacity and grid access pose additional barriers to privately developed projects.[31]

The changing stance of MENA countries in international renewables cooperation

The recent uptick in renewables in the region has been mirrored by the changing approach of MENA countries to international cooperation for renewables promotion. This shift has already had far-reaching implications for global energy governance. While the long silence of the United Nations (UN) on renewable energies was due to opposition from MENA countries, the MENA region is currently host to IRENA, an intergovernmental organization dedicated exclusively to renewables. MENA countries have also increased regional cooperation on renewables, including the establishment of the RCREEE in 2008, which collaborates closely with the Arab League.

IRENA was founded in 2010 to promote renewables around the world. The headquarters of the 145-member-strong organization are located in Abu Dhabi in the UAE.[32] The decision to establish IRENA in a member state of the Organization of the Petroleum Exporting Countries (OPEC) was met with surprise and skepticism. In the initial years of IRENA's existence, some renewable energy advocates were concerned that IRENA had been captured by an OPEC country in order to prevent the organization from assuming a major role in global energy governance. However, the opposite has been true. The fact that IRENA is located in an OPEC country illustrates that energy policies within OPEC are also shifting. Today, OPEC countries no longer concentrate exclusively on fossil fuels; rather, in their search for alternative business models they are increasingly investing in renewable energies.[33]

MENA countries also played a crucial role in IRENA's creation. When the German government took the initiative to found IRENA, several MENA countries – such as Egypt, Jordan, Morocco, and the UAE – expressed their political support early on. Serving as IRENA's headquarters became a clear priority for UAE foreign policy and a question of national pride, and the UAE mounted an active diplomatic campaign in which it pointed out that most international organizations were located in industrialized countries while no international organizations were located in the Arab world. During this campaign, the UAE further emphasized its commitment to expanding renewable energy, referring to plans to build a 100 percent renewables city, Masdar City. In addition, the UAE promised generous funds for IRENA and financing for renewables projects in developing countries. This diplomatic campaign proved to be very successful, and when the decision on IRENA's headquarters was made, Abu Dhabi was selected over competitors Bonn and Vienna.[34]

All MENA countries are either members of IRENA or in the accession process,[35] and the UAE is a major financier of IRENA's activities. In 2014 and 2015, the UAE provided IRENA with $7.4 million in annual voluntary contributions, accounting for nearly 40 percent of IRENA's core budget and around 23 percent of IRENA's total grand volume. The UAE has also offered to provide $350 million in concessional loans to finance renewable energy projects in developing countries through the IRENA/Abu Dhabi Fund for Development

(ADFD) Facility.[36] Some of IRENA's activities have focused explicitly on the MENA region, including collaboration with RCREEE and the Arab League to implement the Pan Arab Renewable Energy Strategy 2030,[37] participation in the creation of the MENA Renewables Status Report,[38] and the release of a renewable energy market analysis of the GCC region.[39] In addition, the UAE was one of the first countries covered by IRENA in its Remap assessment, which explored options to double the worldwide share of renewable energy by 2030,[40] and in 2014 IRENA also published a Renewables Readiness Assessment of Oman.[41]

The Arab countries enhanced regional cooperation in 2008 with the establishment of RCREEE in Cairo. RCREEE's founding document, the Cairo Declaration, was signed by ten Arab states: Algeria, Egypt, Jordan, Lebanon, Libya, Morocco, Palestine, Syria, Tunisia, and Yemen; in addition, the European Commission and the Governments of Germany and Denmark also joined. The Cairo Declaration articulates the major objectives of RCREEE as follows: first, to increase the implementation of cost-effective renewables and energy-efficiency policies, strategies, and technologies in the Arab region; and second, to increase the share of renewables and energy-efficiency products and services in Arab countries and from Arab countries on the global market.[42] Following its creation, seven additional countries have joined RCREEE: Bahrain, Djibouti, Iraq, Kuwait, Mauritania, Somalia, and Sudan.[43] Financial support is provided by the German and Danish development cooperation and the New and Renewable Energy Authority of Egypt.[44]

RCREEE collaborates closely with the Arab League, particularly when it comes to energy efficiency. In terms of renewables, RCREEE has focused on implementing the Pan Arab Renewable Energy Strategy 2030, adopted by Heads of State at the 2013 Arab Economic and Social Development Summit. According to IRENA, this strategy signifies the first time that the Arab region has achieved a broad political consensus on long-term renewables goals. Following its adoption, IRENA and the Arab League commissioned RCREEE to prepare a report on the strategy and identify priorities for implementation.[45] RCREEE monitors and ranks its member states in their progress on expanding renewable energy[46] and improving energy efficiency[47] through the Arab Future Energy Index (AFEX). Thus far, the major message of AFEX is clear: improvements in the deployment of renewable energies in the MENA region have been impressive. However, if the countries want to achieve their ambitious plans for the future, setting targets alone will not suffice; rather, these targets must be backed by appropriate market structures and policy frameworks.

Conclusion

The recent expansion of renewable energies in the MENA region is driven by energy security concerns and global price decreases in solar and wind energy. For all countries in the region, investments in renewables are seen as an instrument to meet rising domestic energy demand and to diversify the electricity mix.

For energy-importing countries, the deployment of domestically available renewable energy sources contributes to reduced import dependency. For energy-exporting countries, investments in renewables are a means to secure long-term export strength. Due to huge wind and solar potential, the MENA region strongly benefits from lower global prices for solar and wind energy, which have made solar PV and wind competitive with fossil fuel-fired power plants.

While the region has relied on hydropower for decades, in the past ten years non-hydro renewables have taken off, dominated by wind energy and solar PV. Plans projected to 2030 predict a massive expansion of CSP, solar PV, and wind energy. Morocco, Israel, and Egypt are currently at the forefront of non-hydro-renewable deployment in the region, while the Kingdom of Saudi Arabia has the boldest plans for future expansion. However, whether these plans will actually become a reality remains an open question, as targets are thus for insufficiently supported by dedicated policies and regulatory frameworks. In particular, leveling the playing field between renewables and fossil fuels will be challenging in a region known for substantial fossil fuel subsidies. The region's difficult investment climate poses an additional barrier not only for expanding renewables capacities but also for overall energy sector development.

To the surprise of many, MENA countries are actively engaging in international renewables cooperation. The UAE is the proud host of the IRENA – the first international organization located in the Arab world – while several MENA countries played a crucial role in IRENA's creation and all MENA countries are either IRENA members or in the accession process. With the establishment of RCREEE, Arab countries have furthermore intensified regional cooperation. Ultimately, the creation of IRENA resulted in two major developments previously assumed impossible: Israel opened an office in the UAE, and an OPEC state became the home of the global voice for renewables.

Notes

1 The MENA region is defined as comprising the following countries: Bahrain, the Islamic Republic of Iran, Iraq, Jordan, Kuwait, Lebanon, Oman, Qatar, Saudi Arabia, Syrian Arab Republic, United Arab Emirates and Yemen, Algeria, Egypt, Libya, Morocco, Tunisia, and Western Sahara (under UN mandate). See also IEA (2014b) for this definition.
2 REN21, 2013; RCREEE, 2015b; IRENA, 2016d.
3 In the countries of the GCC, desalination already provides large shares of fresh water supply, ranging from 27 percent in Oman to 87 percent in Qatar. In Qatar, desalination accounts for 30 percent of total energy consumption. See IRENA, 2016d.
4 Own calculations based on data of the World Energy Outlook (IEA, 2014b). In contrast to the WEO (IEA, 2015), the WEO (2014) contains data on sub-Saharan Africa, so that numbers for the MENA region can easily be calculated (Africa – sub-Saharan Africa + Middle East).
5 Droege et al., 2016.
6 IRENA, 2015b, 2016b.
7 Bloomberg, 2016.
8 IRENA, 2016d.

9 Own calculations based on IEA, 2014b.
10 Own calculations based on IRENA, 2016c.
11 REN21, 2013.
12 League of Arab States et al., 2014.
13 Own calculation based on ibid.
14 RCREEE, 2015b.
15 IEA, 2014a.
16 Own calculations based on IRENA, 2016c.
17 IEA, 2016a.
18 RCREEE, 2015b.
19 REN21, 2015.
20 RCREEE, 2015b.
21 IEA, 2016b.
22 In the case of the UAE, targets do not apply to the UAE as a whole but to individual emirates (IRENA, 2015a).
23 The numbers cited in this section are based on League of Arab States et al., 2014. Data for Israel are taken from REN21, 2013.
24 The estimates for the renewables capacities in 2030 based on the World Energy Outlook 2014 are much more conservative than the estimates based on League of Arab States et al. (2014) and REN21 (2013). The only exception is hydropower. Here, calculations based on IEA data reveal higher numbers.
25 IRENA, 2015a.
26 Reuters, 2015.
27 The numbers mentioned in Table 4.1 do not comprise the adjusted numbers announced in 2016, as the 2016 adjustment only refers to overall renewable energy capacities without giving technology-specific targets.
28 RCREEE, 2015b.
29 IRENA, 2016d.
30 IMF, 2014.
31 RCREEE, 2015b.
32 IRENA, 2016a.
33 Roehrkasten/Westphal, 2013.
34 Ibid.; Roehrkasten, 2015.
35 Lebanon, Libya, and Syria are not yet member states but are in the accession process.
36 IRENA/Abu Dhabi Fund For Development, 2016.
37 League of Arab States et al., 2014.
38 REN21, 2013.
39 IRENA, 2016d.
40 IRENA/Masdar Institute, 2015.
41 IRENA, 2014.
42 Cairo Declaration, 2008.
43 RCREEE, 2016a.
44 RCREEE, 2016b.
45 League of Arab States et al., 2014.
46 RCREEE, 2015b.
47 RCREEE, 2015a.

Bibliography

Bloomberg (2016): New Record Set for World's Cheapest Solar, Now Undercutting Coal. May 3. Available at: www.bloomberg.com/news/articles/2016-05-03/solar-developers-undercut-coal-with-another-record-set-in-dubai.

Cairo Declaration of Intentions on Establishment of Regional Center for Renewable Energy and Energy Efficiency (RCREEE) (2008): June 25. Available at: www.rcreee.org/sites/default/files/legal_cairodeclaration_2008_en.pdf.

Droege, Susanne/Hanns Günther Hilpert/Kirsten Westphal (2016): *Ölpreisbaisse – Folgen für Weltwirtschaft, Klimapolitik und politische Stabilität*. SWP-Aktuell. Berlin: SWP. Available at: www.swp-berlin.org/fileadmin/contents/products/aktuell/2016A18_dge_hlp_wep.pdf.

IEA (2014a): *Morocco 2014: Energy Policies beyond IEA Countries*. Paris: International Energy Agency.

IEA (2014b): *World Energy Outlook 2014*. Paris: International Energy Agency.

IEA (2015): *World Energy Outlook 2015*. Paris: International Energy Agency.

IEA (2016a): *Policies and Measures – Renewable Energy: Israel*. Paris: International Energy Agency.

IEA (2016b): *Policies and Measures – Renewable Energy: Tunisia*. Paris: International Energy Agency.

IMF (2014): *Subsidy Reform in the Middle East and North Africa: Recent Progress and Challenges Ahead*. Middle East and Central Asia Departmental Paper 14/3. Washington, DC: International Monetary Fund. Available at: www.imf.org/external/pubs/ft/dp/2014/1403mcd.pdf.

IRENA (2014): *Renewables Readiness Assessment Oman*. Abu Dhabi: International Renewable Energy Agency.

IRENA (2015a): *Renewable Energy Target Setting*. Abu Dhabi: International Renewable Energy Agency.

IRENA (2015b): *Renewable Power Generation Costs in 2014*. Abu Dhabi: International Renewable Energy Agency.

IRENA (2016a): *IRENA Members*. Abu Dhabi: International Renewable Energy Agency.

IRENA (2016b): *The Power to Change. Solar and Wind Cost Reduction Potential to 2025*. Abu Dhabi: International Renewable Energy Agency. Available at: www.irena.org/DocumentDownloads/Publications/IRENA_Power_to_Change_2016.pdf.

IRENA (2016c): *Renewable Energy Capacity Statistics*. Abu Dhabi: The International Renewable Energy Agency.

IRENA (2016d): *Renewable Energy Market Analysis: The GCC Region*. Abu Dhabi: International Renewable Energy Agency.

IRENA/Abu Dhabi Fund For Development (2016): *Frequently Asked Questions*. Abu Dhabi: International Renewable Energy Agency.

IRENA/Masdar Institute (2015): *Renewable Energy Prospects – United Arab Emirates*. Abu Dhabi: International Renewable Energy Agency.

League of Arab States/IRENA/RCREEE (2014): *Pan-Arab Renewable Energy Strategy 2030: Roadmap of Actions for Implementation*. Abu Dhabi: International Renewable Energy Agency.

RCREEE (2015a): *Arab Future Energy Index 2015: Energy Efficiency*. Cairo: Regional Center for Renewable Energy and Energy Efficiency.

RCREEE (2015b): *Arab Future Energy Index 2015: Renewable Energy*. Cairo: Regional Center for Renewable Energy and Energy Efficiency.

RCREEE (2016a): *Member States*. Cairo: Regional Center for Renewable Energy and Energy Efficiency.

RCREEE (2016b): *Partners*. Cairo: Regional Center for Renewable Energy and Energy Efficiency.

REN21 (2013): *MENA Renewable Status Report*. Paris: Renewable Energy Policy Network for the 21st Century.

REN21 (2015): *Renewables 2015 Global Status Report*. Paris: Renewable Energy Policy Network for the 21st Century.

Reuters (2015): Saudi Arabia's Nuclear, Renewable Energy Plans Pushed Back. January 19. Available at: www.reuters.com/article/saudi-nuclear-energy-idUSL6N0UY2LS20150119.

Roehrkasten, Sybille (2015): Global Governance on Renewable Energy. In *Global Governance on Renewable Energy: Contrasting the Ideas of the German and the Brazilian Governments*. Wiesbaden: Springer Fachmedien Wiesbaden.

Roehrkasten, Sybille/Kirsten Westphal (2013): *IRENA and Germany's Foreign Renewable Energy Policy*. Working Paper Global Issues Division. Berlin: Stiftung Wissenschaft und Politik. Available at: www.swp-berlin.org/fileadmin/contents/products/arbeitspapiere/Rks_Wep_FG08WorkingPaper_2013.pdf.

5 The energy–climate–water nexus in the MENA region and the need for an integrated approach

Thomas Fink and Manfred Fischedick

Introduction

The global power system is one of the main emitters of greenhouse gas (GHG) emissions, which are responsible for climate change, including global warming. Worldwide electricity demand is also increasingly driving growing water needs, while both electricity and water are underwriting economic growth and prosperity. Population growth and changing consumption patterns are among the socioeconomic trends driving increases in electricity and water. The provision of electricity and water is, therefore, crucial to sustainable economic growth.

The linkages between the global power system and climate change play a central role in political discussions and have been intensively addressed in the scientific literature.[1] However, an understanding of the mutual dependencies and trade-offs between power and water supply is still in the early stages of development when it comes to decisions about future power systems.

The Middle East and North Africa (MENA) region is particularly affected by the energy–climate–water nexus, as it is experiencing a rapid increase in electricity demand, growing water scarcity, and significant climate change effects. Indeed, in the MENA region, electricity production requires water, while water production requires electricity, an interdependency that exacerbates the problem of emissions and water scarcity. In order to transition to a more sustainable development for the region, a wider understanding of the linkages and dependencies between climate change and the power and water supply is needed to identify trade-offs and design a comprehensive and integrated approach.

The political turmoil afflicting several MENA countries over recent years has underscored the need for political reforms, social participation, and increasing socioeconomic development. Political discussions in many countries have identified the need for secure energy supplies at an economically competitive price as a prerequisite for economic development. However, due to limited public budgets in many MENA countries, the development of adequate decision-making processes and planning institutions to shape the future power system has been limited. Moreover, there is not yet sufficient consideration of issues like the water consumption of energy technologies, their contribution to the mitigation of GHG emissions and decarbonization, and their contribution to the region's socioeconomic development. This is despite the fact that power systems in the region are anticipated to experience rapid growth in the coming years, due in part to growing water demand. Absent such considerations, there is a danger that the region will fail to include important decision-making criteria to address the various challenges at hand, and thus will make decisions that ignore these challenges and create lock-in effects.

This issue requires particular attention, as several countries in the region are currently highly dependent on energy imports for their power systems, which in turn are often characterized by subsidized consumer prices. Public spending on energy subsidies has increased rapidly over recent years as energy subsidies have become a leading instrument of social largesse, surpassing education-related expenses in most countries in the region.[2]

However, the region also boasts prolific solar and wind resources and the potential to develop renewable energy,[3] which could enable the provision of electricity at stable and competitive prices. Despite this endowment of sustainable resources, fossil fuels continue to dominate the power systems of the MENA region, although the installment of wind power and innovative concentrating solar power (CSP) plants and photovoltaic units is increasing.

Against this backdrop, this chapter discusses global climate change as an overall framework to introduce linkages and interconnections between energy and climate change, taking into account water issues and the energy–water–climate nexus. The concept of the nexus is then applied and analyzed in the MENA regional context. Finally, this chapter concludes that a holistic approach is necessary to address the energy–climate–water nexus appropriately in planning institutions.

The overall framework: global climate change

Over the past decade, the global concentration of GHG in the atmosphere has been increasing and is approaching 400 ppm, a level which makes it increasingly difficult to meet the critical 2-degree global-warming target. Between 2002 and 2011, GHG emission growth averaged 2.0 ppm per year, faster than in any previous decade since 1958.[4] The World Meteorological Organization observed that the Earth is already 1° Celsius warmer today than at the beginning of the twentieth century, while 2014 and 2015 have furthermore been extremely warm years globally.[5] If these trends continue, climate change will likely accelerate, bringing with it increasing droughts, floods, and rising sea water levels.

However, more promising trends have also emerged in recent years. For example, global CO_2 emissions stagnated in 2014 and 2015 even as the global economy continued to grow. The market penetration of renewable energies, which have become increasingly competitive in countries around the world,[6] played a critical role in this development, weakening the link between economic growth and emissions growth.[7]

At the political level, decarbonization has become a key policy goal, one that was quite visible at the 2015 G7 summit in Germany. Moreover, the COP21 UN climate change conference in Paris in 2015 represents a milestone in international climate. In Paris, 195 nations agreed to limit temperature increase below 2° Celsius compared to preindustrial levels and to work toward limiting the increase to 1.5°. For the first time, developing and industrialized countries promised to contribute to greenhouse gas mitigation efforts. The outcome of the Paris conference, based on the so-called Intended National Determined Contributions (INDCs) that were submitted on a voluntary basis and agreed upon prior to COP21, included a ratcheting mechanism requiring countries to submit updated climate plans with higher ambitions every five years and to develop long-term plans for full decarbonization. To achieve this, scaled-up financial support from developed countries will support the efforts of developing countries in building their own clean and sustainable futures. However, despite these promises and agreements, there is no formal enforcement requirement should countries fail to reach designated targets.

Achieving the 2-degree target requires a reversal of current trends until 2020, a reduction of GHG emissions of 40 to 70 percent compared to 2010 levels by 2050, and full decarbonization at the latest by 2080.[8] In this context, the activities formulated at COP21 should be seen as a first step, since the cumulative nationally determined contributions do not provide sufficient reductions to achieve the 2-degree target.[9] Ambitious efforts to deploy renewable energy and increase energy efficiency until 2030 could enable significant reductions in CO_2 emissions and provide the baseline for a 2-degree pathway. However, compared to a reference case scenario, substantially more efforts are necessary even before 2030,[10] which will require the adoption of adequate GHG mitigation pathways in each country. For some countries, GHG mitigation strategies that lead to a more or less decarbonized world over time have already been developed. Although no general decarbonization strategy exists thus far, several countries have developed strategies that incorporate key elements in the development of GHG mitigation pathways, namely energy efficiency and power sector decarbonization.

The electricity sector in particular has to play a key role in decarbonization, and existing national strategies confirm that the GHG mitigation potential in electricity generation is substantial, with opportunities to reduce CO_2 emissions by 93 percent per kWh on average until 2050.[11]

Understanding the broader energy–climate–water nexus

While electricity generation has strong linkages with climate mitigation, water has strong dependencies and linkages with electricity generation. The intensity of these linkages varies among countries, regions, and production systems, but on the whole, global trends like urbanization and population growth are reinforcing these dependencies and linkages. At the same time, climate change impacts water supply security and water scarcity,[12] which in turn affects electricity generation.

Against this backdrop, the water–energy nexus has come increasingly to the fore in recent years.[13] The concept describes the interactions and interdependencies between energy and water resources, emphasizes the link between water for energy, and energy for water, and a systemic link to climate.[14] The approach may also be expanded to include agriculture, commonly referred to as the water–energy–food nexus, which is increasingly addressed in literature.[15]

Despite several dependencies and linkages between energy, water, and climate, an integrated approach to planning in electricity and water sectors remains largely lacking. This is surprising given that the electricity–water value chain is not only necessary for hydropower and thermoelectric systems (as a medium for cooling) but also for fossil fuel extraction, refining and production of petroleum products, and the irrigation of bioenergy crops.

Based on estimates of the amount of water consumed by different electricity-generation technologies, technologies such as nuclear power and centralized fossil fuel-based power plants require large volumes of water for electricity generation, whereas renewable energy technologies such as wind power and solar photovoltaic have only modest water needs.[16]

During the past decade, water constraints have already been a risk to electricity supply in several countries. Water-induced cuts in hydro, coal, and nuclear power production have increased in many parts of the world as a consequence of droughts and heatwaves, and many countries experience cuts on a regular basis due to limited water availability during the summer.[17] Focusing on the entire value chain of energy resources, including exploitation and treatment, the energy carrier coal, for instance, already accounts for 7 percent of total water withdrawal globally. This number is set to double in the next 20 years, as countries like India and China intend to invest significantly in coal power plants.[18]

Thus, future water demand for electricity generation depends not only on electricity demand growth, but also to a large extent on the portfolio of electricity-generation technologies. This makes necessary the assessment of different electricity-generation technologies based on a more holistic set of characteristics.

Energy also plays a significant role in the water supply value chain. Energy (particularly electricity) is needed for water extraction, treatment, transportation, and waste water disposal. Desalination and the transportation of water over long distances in particular can be highly energy-intensive processes.[19] This interrelationship illustrates the need for a cross-sectoral approach to electricity and water infrastructure planning, and the utilization of relevant supply technologies (see Figure 5.1).

Renewable energies can address water resource challenges while also contributing to CO_2 emissions reductions. In China, for instance, an estimated 20 percent increase in renewables for electricity generation to reach 30 percent in 2030 would result in an approximately 30 percent reduction in water consumption for electricity.[20] This illustrates the potential for renewable energies in electricity generation to address water scarcity. Meanwhile, improved cooling technologies (e.g., dry cooling tower) for nuclear power or fossil fuel plants could help significantly to reduce water demand; however, this would also reduce overall plant efficiency and consequently increase GHG emissions.

An integrated planning approach would help to understand and address linkages, dependencies, synergies, and trade-offs between both sectors. Such an approach is needed to formulate and implement mutually beneficial strategies, and to improve

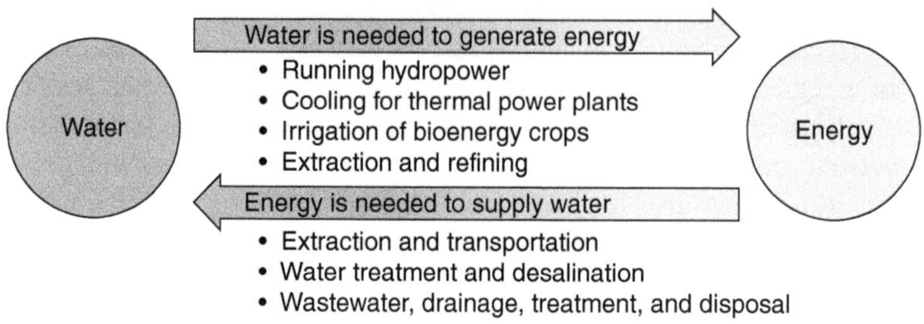

Figure 5.1 Linkages and dependencies of energy and water as part of the energy–water nexus.

Source: Own representation with regard to World Bank (2014).

management and governance of strategies across sectors.[21] The adoption of a more holistic and integrated approach would take into account various interrelated issues, including the contribution of electricity and water infrastructure to improving socio-economic development, the potential for improvements in energy and water to mitigate climate change (and links to food production processes), and geopolitical issues in water-scarce regions. An approach based on multiple interlocking criteria is also necessary to achieve the United Nations Sustainable Development Goals (SDGs), which have strong linkages to nexus challenges. An overview of SDGs directly related to energy and water is illustrated in Figure 5.2.

United Nations Sustainable Development Goals

17 goals to transform our world

1 No poverty
2 Zero hunger
3 Good health and well-being
4 Quality education
5 Gender equality
6 Clean water and sanitation
7 Affordable and clean energy
8 Decent work and economic growth
9 Industry, innovation, and infrastructure
10 Reduced inequalities
11 Sustainable cities and communities
12 Responsive consumption and production
13 Climate action
14 Life below water
15 Life on land
16 Peace, justice and strong institutions
17 Partnerships for the goals

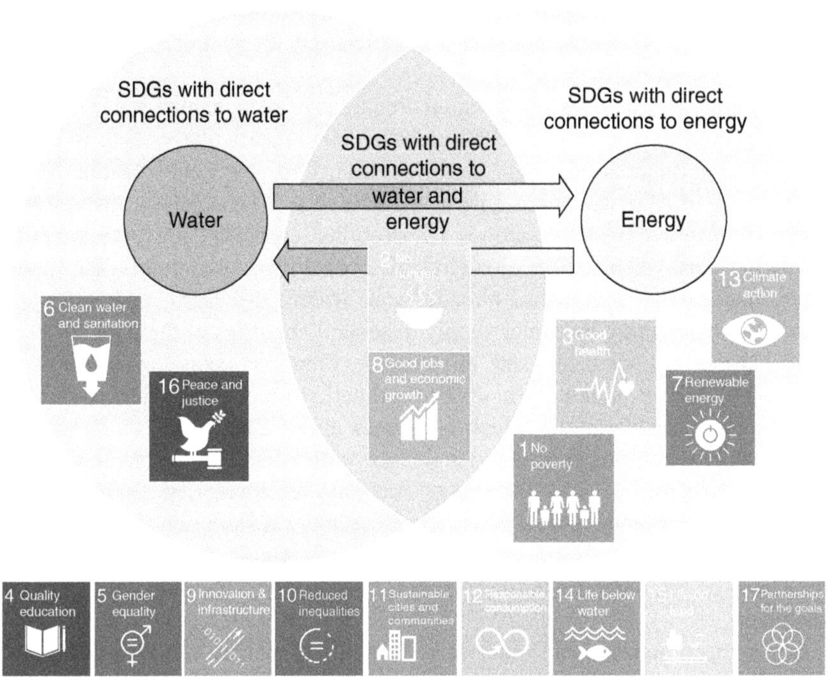

Figure 5.2 Energy–water nexus against the background of relevant United Nations Sustainable Development Goals (SDGs).

Source: Own representation with regard to UN (2015).

The energy–climate–water nexus in the MENA region

If current trends continue, the MENA region will experience a rapid increase in electricity demand, which will require the installation of additional electricity-generation capacity. According to existing scenarios, while the consumption of renewables will increase, this will be accompanied by an even steeper rise in conventional electricity generation from gas and oil, and the installation of additional nuclear and coal-fired power plants in several MENA countries by 2030.[22] These conventional power-generation technologies are characterized by higher water consumption as compared to most renewable energies technologies.[23] In addition, many non-conventional energy sources under discussion in the region, including shale oil and gas and solar thermal power plants, also require water for extraction and/or operation. Given that traditional water resources in the region are depleting rapidly, this is an alarming development. The MENA region is currently among the most water-scarce and arid regions in the world, and is expected to become even hotter and drier in future.[24] Water resources like the river Nile and the river Jordan, which serve as the primary source of water for populations in Egypt and Jordan, are increasingly suffering from extensive water withdrawal.[25] Thus strategies are needed not only to respond to water scarcity, but also to make decisions about the future electricity system according to water demand and sustainable growth.

Many countries in the MENA region are already facing annual water demand gaps, expected to worsen until 2050 at least. This is particularly acute in counties with large populations, such as Egypt, Iran, Iraq, and Saudi Arabia, but is also the case in Algeria, Jordan, Libya, and Morocco.[26] To satisfy growing water demand and to avoid socioeconomic vulnerability, especially for rural and poor populations, sea water desalination strategies could play a key role in the future water supply. This option has already been widely discussed, and indeed is already supplementing the water supply in several countries of the Arabian Peninsula. However, advanced and efficient desalination technologies consume around 2.9 kWh/m^3, making sea water desalination more energy intensive than long-distance transportation, which consumes about 2.5 kWh/m^3 on average.[27] The electricity consumption of a single sea water desalination plant, with an average production of 200,000 m^3/day, accounts for more than 200 GWh per year. Given that average global per-capita electricity consumption was 3353 kWh in 2014,[28] the annual electricity consumption of a single desalination plant is equivalent to the annual electricity demand of a city with more than 62,000 inhabitants.

For energy-importing and water-scarce countries, such as Morocco or Jordan, the provision of an appropriate and economically feasible water supply structure is a challenge. The combination of sea water desalination and renewable energies such as CSP could defuse the dependency on energy imports by utilizing local solar resources. Indeed, the combination of CSP power plants and thermal sea water desalination is a potentially promising option for MENA countries given the high levels of direct solar radiation conditions and the increasing demand for water.[29] Sea water desalination processes that rely on electricity directly can also be combined with wind and solar photovoltaic technologies. These options are attractive not only for import-dependent MENA countries, but also for any MENA countries relying on fossil fuels for electricity generation, as this would help reduce GHG emissions. This is significant as, for instance, the amount of electricity required to secure water supply is expected to increase by up to 40 percent in the Middle East, along with generally increasing electricity consumption. The implementation of strategies that incorporate renewable energy and efficiency gains in irrigation could help limit this demand increase to 22 percent, accompanied by significantly lower CO_2 emissions from electricity generation.[30] Regardless of the use of renewable energies and efficiency gains, there will still be a substantial additional electricity demand for the supply of water. This reality is not yet acknowledged in most electricity scenarios and needs to be taken into account by decision-makers in the Middle East.

The currently operational electricity-generation capacity in most MENA countries is mainly based on steam turbine and gas turbine systems, which require significant water volumes in operation. In most MENA countries, with the exception of Egypt where around 25 percent of the installed electricity-generation capacity uses fresh water cooling systems, sea water is used for cooling,[31] which makes electricity generation less vulnerable to water shortages.

In considering the future electricity-generation needs of the MENA region, planners should avoid the continuance of current trends in electricity generation, namely the addition of conventional electricity-generation capacities such as gas power plants. In particular, the pursuit of existing plans for new coal and nuclear plants, along with the extraction of shale oil and gas, would likely reinforce the link between water consumption and electricity generation, and could lead to long-term path dependencies in the electricity systems of the MENA region. Rapid increases in electricity demand will likely by reinforced by the increasing demand for water, while electricity-generation technologies such as coal power plants would significantly increase CO_2 emissions in electricity generation, whereas coal and nuclear power would do little to alleviate energy-import dependencies.

Thus, the linkages between water security and increasing electricity consumption in the MENA region are clear, as if the fact that additional electricity production can lead to rapid increases in water consumption. These issues should be taken into account in planning future electricity and water infrastructure in the MENA region and in climate change mitigation strategies.

Conclusion: an integrated planning approach to address the energy–water–climate nexus

The previous section described the various interactions and interdependencies of climate change, electricity generation, and water resources, while it is clear that the global electricity system is a key contributor of GHG emissions that drives climate change, necessitating national and international mitigation strategies. Renewable energies can address several of these challenges, including challenges with water consumption, and should be included in strategies addressing linkages and interdependencies of the nexus.

It is clear that a more holistic and integrated assessment of electricity-generation technologies, which takes climate change policies into account, is required for electricity sector planning. Furthermore, the role of water consumption and the provision of water supply should also be taken into account, as should the potential for different energy technologies to contribute to a sustainable economic growth path.

Amid the challenges facing the MENA region, the reality of rising current and future electricity demand is both apparent and important, not just in its own right, but also in relation to water supply. However, regional planning in the electricity and water sectors still occurs independently of one another, and increased awareness of the relationship between the two among decision-makers is crucial. This will require a comprehensive understanding of the water value chain, including the need for electricity for water extraction, treatment, and transport. In assessing electricity-generation technologies, technology-specific water consumption totals and overall water consumption throughout the energy resource value chain should be key considerations. This is particularly true for the implementation of electricity-generation technologies such as coal and nuclear power, but also non-conventional energy resources like shale oil and gas, which are part of the political discussions in especially water-scarce countries such as Morocco and Jordan.

Electricity-generation technologies should also be assessed according to climate change mitigation standards and policies, including mitigation of CO_2 emissions. This is particularly relevant in the MENA region, where CO_2 emissions from electricity generation are increasing. The region could be significantly impacted by a changing climate, becoming even hotter and dryer as a consequence. The MENA region should formulate the necessary climate change mitigation strategies to obtain a higher creditability in international climate debates, and develop strong and overarching (holistic) strategies at the national level to overcome trade-offs between ministries and institutions.

Last but not least, the future electricity system in the region will necessarily need to be economically competitive, support sustainable economic growth, and provide opportunities for a local value generation. This is particularly important for the region's young and growing population, and could be a strategic pillar for political stability in the future.

Overall, this argues for a more holistic and integrated planning approach accompanied by a strong climate change policy that accounts for the various challenges facing the region. Key considerations should include the electricity system and its linkages to climate change and securing the future water supply. As decarbonization strategies in other countries have illustrated, in addition to the development of renewable energies, energy efficiency is part of effective climate mitigation, and the strategy becomes even more important when taking water demand into account. Efficient irrigation methods and electricity and water pricing which reflects the real costs could foster awareness of the challenges and linkages between climate change and the electricity and water system.

Including multi-criteria assessments of the future electricity system in the decision-making process could provide a valuable instrument for planning institutions in assessing technologies and determining their shares in the future electricity system. Such assessments could include considerations of different stakeholder groups and their needs, and using such a participatory instrument could help decision-makers not only to raise the awareness of the various challenges faced in the region, but also to reduce complexity and provide a transparent way to legitimize decision-making processes. Strong climate change policies, including concrete targets for renewable energies and efficiency improvements as well as a clear allocation of responsibilities among different ministries and institutions, are also crucial for sustainable development in the MENA region.

Notes

1 IPCC, 2014.
2 IMF, 2014.
3 DLR, 2005.
4 Ciais et al., 2013.
5 WMO, 2016.
6 Philibert, 2015.
7 IEA, 2016.
8 IPCC, 2014.
9 UNFCCC, 2016.
10 IRENA, 2016.
11 DDPD, 2015.
12 IPCC, 2014.
13 Siddiqi/Anadon, 2011; Cheng/Lammi, 2016; Roehrkasten et al., 2016.
14 Dubreuil et al., 2013.
15 Hoff, 2011; FAO, 2014; WWAP, 2014; IRENA, 2015.
16 Siddiqi/Anadon, 2011.
17 Roehrkasten et al., 2016.
18 Cheng/Lammi, 2016.
19 Siddiqi/Anadon, 2011.
20 IRENA, 2015.
21 Hoff, 2011.
22 Brand/Blok, 2015.
23 Siddiqi/Anadon, 2011.
24 Niang et al., 2014.
25 Kameri-Mbote, 2007; Hadadin et al., 2010.
26 World Bank, 2012.
27 WWAP, 2014.
28 WEC, 2016.
29 DLR, 2007.
30 Dubreuil et al., 2013.
31 Siddiqi/Anadon, 2011.

Bibliography

Brand, Bernhard/Kornelis Blok (2015): Renewable Energy Perspectives for the North African Electricity Systems: A Comparative Analysis of Model-based Scenario Studies. *Energy Strategy Reviews* 6, 1–11.

Cheng, Iris/Harri Lammi (2016): *The Great Water Grab. How the Coal Industry is Deepening the Global Water Crisis*. Greenpeace International. Available at: www.greenpeace.org/international/Global/international/publications/climate/2016/The-Great-Water-Grab.pdf.

Ciais, Philippe/Christopher Sabine/Govindasamy Bala/Laurent Bopp/Victor Brovkin et al. (2013): Carbon and Other Biogeochemical Cycles. In Stocker, T.F. et al. (Eds): *Climate Change 2013: The Physical Science Basis. Contribution of Working Group I to the Fifth Assessment Report of the Intergovernmental Panel on Climate Change* (pp. 465–470). Cambridge and New York: Cambridge University Press.

DDPD (2015): *Pathways to Deep Decarbonization 2015 Report*. Sustainable Development Solutions Network (SDSN) and Sustainable Development and International Relations (IDDRI).

DLR (2005): *Concentrating Solar Power for the Mediterranean Region*. Stuttgart: German Aerospace Center.

DLR (2007): *Concentrating Solar Power for Seawater Desalination*. Stuttgart: German Aerospace Center.

Dubreuil, Aurelie/Edi Assoumou/Stephanie Bouckaert/Sandrine Selosse/Nadia Maı¨zi (2013): Water Modeling in an Energy Optimization Framework – The Water-scarce Middle East Context. *Applied Energy* 101(C), 268–279.

FAO (2014): *The Water–Energy–Food Nexus – A New Approach in Supporting of Food Security and Sustainable Agriculture*. Rome: Food and Agriculture Organization of United Nations. Available at: www.fao.org/nr/water/docs/FAO_nexus_concept.pdf.

Hadadin, Nidal/Maher Qaqish/Emad Akawwi/Ahmed Bdour (2010): Water Shortage in Jordan – Sustainable Solutions. *Desalination* 250(1), 197–202.

Hoff, Holger (2011): *Understanding the Nexus. Background Paper or the Bonn 2011 Nexus Conference: The Water, Energy and Food Security Nexus – Solutions for the Green Economy*. Stockholm: Stockholm Environment Institute.

IEA (2016): *Decoupling of Global Emissions and Economic Growth Confirmed*. Paris: International Energy Agency.

IMF (2014): *Energy Subsidies in the Middle East and North Africa: Lessons for Reform*. Washington, DC: International Monetary Fund. Available at: www.imf.org/external/np/fad/subsidies/pdf/menanote.pdf.

IPCC (2014): *Climate Change 2014. Synthesis Report. Contribution of Working Groups I, II and III to the Fifth Assessment Report of the Intergovernmental Panel on Climate Change (IPCC)*. Geneva: Intergovernmental Panel on Climate Change.

IRENA (2015): *Renewable Energy in the Water, Energy and Food Nexus*. Abu Dhabi: International Renewable Energy Agency (IRENA).

IRENA (2016): *Remap – Roadmap for a rRenewable Energy Future, 2016 Edition*. Abu Dhabi: International Renewable Energy Agency.

Kameri-Mbote, Patricia G. (2007): *Water, Conflict, and Cooperation: Lessons from the Nile River Basin*. Washington, DC: Woodrow Wilson International Center for Scholars.

Niang, Isabelle/Oliver Ruppel/Mohamed Abdrabo/Amal Essel/Christopher Lennard/Jonathan Padgham/Penny Urquhart (2014): Africa. In Barros, V.R. Christopher Field/David Jon Dokken/Michael Mastrandrea/Katharine Mach (Eds): *Climate Change 2014: Impacts, Adaptation, and Vulnerability. Part B: Regional Aspects. Contribution of Working Group II to the Fifth Assessment Report of the Intergovernmental Panel of Climate Change*. Cambridge and New York: Cambridge University Press.

Philibert, Cédric (2015): *Renewables in the MENA Region. Presentation at COP 21*. Paris: International Energy Agency.

Siddiqi, Afreen/Laura Diaz Anadon (2011): The Water–Energy Nexus in Middle East and North Africa. *Energy Policy* 39(8), 4529–4540.

UN (2015): *Sustainable Development Goals. 17 Goals to Transform our World*. Geneva: United Nations.

UNFCCC (2016): *Aggregate Effect of the Intended Nationally Determined Contributions: An Update. Synthesis Report by the Secretariat*. FCCC/CP/2016/2. Marrakech: United Nations Framework Convention on Climate Change. Available at: http://unfccc.int/resource/docs/2016/cop22/eng/02.pdf.

WEC (2016): *Average Electricity Consumption per Electricified Household. May 2016*. World Energy Council. Available at: www.wec-indicators.enerdata.eu/household-electricity-use.htm.

WMO (2016): *WMO Statement on the Status of the Global Climate Change in 2015*. Geneva: World Meteorological Organization (WMO). Available at: https://wedocs.unep.org/rest/bitstreams/11935/retrieve.

World Bank (2012): *Renewable Energy Desalination: An Emerging Solution to Close the Water Gap in the Middle East and North Africa*. Washington, DC: International Bank for Reconstruction and Development/World Bank.

World Bank (2014): *Infographic: Thirsty Energy – Energy and Water's Interdependencies. The World Bank Group, January 16, 2014*. Washington, DC: The World Bank Group.

WWAP (2014): *The United Nations World Water Development Report 2014: Water and Energy*. United Nations World Water Assessment Program. Paris: UNESCO. Available at: http://unesdoc.unesco.org/images/0022/002257/225741E.pdf.

6 Oil and resilience

Changing energy dynamics and the smaller Gulf States

Laura El-Katiri

Introduction

Energy has fundamentally shaped the economies of the Gulf oil and gas producers. While Saudi Arabia remains the region's largest oil producer by far, the five smaller Gulf States, namely Bahrain, Kuwait, Oman, Qatar, and the United Arab Emirates (UAE), are an important energy trade bloc in their own right, accounting for around one-fifth of total world oil and natural gas reserves. Like their larger Gulf neighbors, Saudi Arabia, Iraq, and Iran, the smaller Gulf countries are also highly dependent on fossil fuel export revenues for their fiscal stability, as the historical ruling bargain in these countries has meant that the state does not derive the majority of its income from taxes on local incomes and business, but from the sale of oil and to a lesser extent natural gas on international markets.

Following a period of relatively high and stable global oil prices during the late 2000s up until mid-2014, the low oil price environment that has since prevailed has considerably challenged business-as-usual in the smaller Gulf States. This is not because the oil price collapse that occurred in mid-2014 is unprecedented in history – it is not, as the 1980s and 1990s amply illustrate – but because the wider transformation of the global energy landscape makes structural reform inside the Gulf kingdoms and emirates increasingly critical. A number of additional factors add to this development: the rapid rise in domestic population and education levels, coupled with some of the world's highest per-capita wealth in Kuwait, the UAE, and Qatar, and high living standards which contribute to heightened expectations for the future. External events, particularly the Arab Spring in parts of North Africa and the Levant earlier this decade, have also raised Gulf governments' awareness of the transformative power of unsatisfied popular expectations.

In this context, the post-July 2014 decline in global oil prices has added an important catalyst to developments already underway, though in some of the smaller Gulf States more than in others, which raises questions of how to satisfy future generations' socioeconomic aspirations at a time when high oil export revenues can no longer be taken as a given. While many of the current reform efforts in the region are primarily economic – involving structural reform to fiscal expenditure, labor market policies, and the promotion of more private sector activity – they are also intrinsically political. After all, political stability in the region is linked to economic resilience, and ultimately to building stable and increasingly self-sustaining economies that can generate growth without the region's historical reliance on external oil prices.

To achieve this, much work remains to be done. In the short term, some of the Gulf's smaller economies have demonstrated considerably more economic and political resilience than most of the region's larger economies, not only in the face of falling oil prices and governmental revenues, but also in view of an otherwise bleak political and economic outlook in many other parts of the Middle East and North Africa. Five years on from the Arab Spring, none of the Arab monarchies, including the small Gulf economies, is in serious danger of facing political upheaval similar to that seen in a number of Arab republics since December 2010. Given that this time period includes the past few years of lower oil prices and thus lower state revenues illustrates these countries' considerable political resilience, which is based also on their ability to maneuver their economies through challenging economic times.

Indeed, their comparably small size, both in land and population, along with significant fiscal resources, including historically low levels of debt and the accumulation of savings in the form of foreign assets, have placed this chapter's five Gulf monarchies in a somewhat unique position to weather political and economic upheaval with comparably more ease than many other countries in the region. This is particularly true for the three wealthy states of Kuwait, the UAE, and Qatar. Indeed, the UAE and Qatar have also been among the region's most proactive reformers alongside their larger neighbor, Saudi Arabia.

This chapter looks at the implications of shifting global energy dynamics for a set of economies that are themselves in the midst of a long-term transformation. The chapter first explores the short-term effects of shifting energy dynamics, with a particular focus on fiscal dynamics, including increased pressure on Gulf governments to reduce long-term spending commitments. It then discusses the likely long-term implications and policy imperatives that follow current changes in the global and regional energy landscape.

Fiscal resilience and structural economic reform

Global energy market dynamics in recent years have not made for an easy ride for Gulf oil and gas producers. The oil price collapse since mid-2014 has affected the region at its core, impacting financial revenues, while the near-term outlook promises little immediate prospects for a substantial oil price recovery. For the Gulf producers, structural changes in global oil market dynamics, namely the current and expected near-term growth of both OPEC and non-OPEC production triggered by the recent market re-entry of Iran, planned output increases in Iraq, and the prospect of expanding unconventional oil and gas production from North America, imply that the current short-term outlook may indeed become at least a medium-term scenario.

For the Gulf's smaller economies, this is a priori no minor challenge. Oil and gas export revenues are the principal source of export income in the GCC, accounting for over 90 percent of total export revenues in countries such as Qatar and Kuwait. These oil and gas revenues also account for well over 80 percent of total government revenues (Table 6.1), and the hydrocarbon industry is also a major factor driving regional economic growth. A substantial share of GDP is directly linked to the sector, not including the indirect impact of oil and gas upon regional value-added products such as steel, aluminum, and petrochemicals. Meanwhile, government spending is a critical factor in driving demand for popular non-oil sectors, including construction, hospitality, and services.

Thanks to the large increase in the value of crude and natural gas exports from the late 2000s up until mid-2014, the massive inflow of export revenues from the previous decade has had the marked effect of reducing the pressure for structural reform in the GCC economies. The 2000s saw expanding state budgets and welfare payments, which in many cases were further increased in the aftermath of the outbreak of political uprisings in many parts of the Arab world in what came to be called the Arab Spring.[1] The GCC countries' heavy reliance on oil revenues implies that their economies are highly exposed to developments in the global oil market. This is further reflected in these economies' relatively high fiscal break-even oil price to balance their budgets.

The sharp oil price decline has undoubtedly altered the economic outlook for the GCC economies as a whole (see Table 6.2). Following a period of sustained real GDP growth averaging 5.8 percent from 2000 to 2011, the IMF projects that growth rates will slow to 3.4 percent in 2015 and to 3.2 percent in 2016. In addition, after achieving large fiscal surpluses that averaged 12.4 percent of GDP between 2000 and 2011, the GCC countries are projected to run fiscal deficits of 7.9 percent and 3.6 percent of GDP in 2015 and 2016. Under the current oil price assumptions, the IMF estimates that the fall in anticipated oil export earnings will amount to $287 billion or 21 percent of GDP in the GCC in 2015. This change in the macroeconomic outlook is already impacting key sectors. The region's stock markets have fallen from the high levels reached in the first half

Table 6.1 GCC hydrocarbon vulnerability, 2014

	Fossil fuels % of GDP	*Fossil fuels % of exports*	*Fossil fuels % of government revenue*	*R/P* (years)*
Bahrain	26.2	73.1	85	11
Oman	49.7	66.1	87	21
Saudi Arabia	45.1	85.7	78	66
Kuwait	62.6	94.3	80	91
Qatar	54.4	91.7	80	106
UAE	38.9	31.1	65	81

Sources: MEES (2014); IMF (2016).

Note

* Includes gas on BOE basis.

Table 6.2 Fiscal break-even oil prices for the GCC states (US$/billion)

	Average 2008–2012	*2013*	*2014*	*2015 projected**	*2016 projected**
Bahrain	99	125.3	122.5	107	105
Kuwait	41.4	43.6	56	49.1	51.8
Oman	69.4	98.3	108.2	94.7	97.5
Qatar	58.5	60	56.3	55.5	57.8
Saudi Arabia	67.4	89	105.7	105.6	95.8
United Arab Emirates	67.4	69.4	78.4	72.6	67.5

Source: IMF (2015b).

Note
* IMF staff projections, October 2015.

of 2014, local banks are reining in lending activities, and the confidence of the private sector has taken a hit. Recent EIA estimates suggest that between 2014 and 2015, real oil export revenue fell by nearly half in Kuwait, the UAE, and Qatar.[2]

Nevertheless, it is important to qualify the outlook for the region given the countries' relative financial strength. Among the Gulf economies, some of the smaller GCC states are undoubtedly better positioned than the larger economies, including Saudi Arabia with its vast foreign currency reserves. Kuwait and the UAE, for instance, have low levels of existing foreign and domestic debt (see Table 6.3) and have accumulated large foreign assets, including some of the world's largest sovereign wealth funds (SWFs). This is the result of a relatively prudent and sustained savings policy, bolstered by the period of oil revenue windfalls since 2003.

The UAE holds an estimated total of US$1.2 trillion in foreign assets, spread among different SWFs and a total population of around nine million (only around 10 percent of whom are Emirati nationals). This is a sizable amount that provides a comfortable fiscal buffer and basis against which to borrow from international capital markets. Kuwait and Qatar, with only a few million people each, are similarly positioned – at least theoretically – to fiscally sustain prolonged periods of lower government revenues. These comparably vast fiscal

Table 6.3 Selected macroeconomic indicators for the GCC economies

	Average 2000–2011	*2012*	*2013*	*2014*	*2015 (projected)*	*2016 (projected)*
Real GDP (annual growth)	5.8	5.4	3.6	3.6	3.4	3.2
Current account balance	16.5	24.4	20.6	16.5	2.8	5.4
Overall fiscal balance	12.4	15.1	12.1	4.6	–7.9	–3.6
Inflation p.a. (annual growth)	2.9	2.4	2.8	2.6	2.1	2.5

Source: IMF (2015a).

resources are also reflected in the large GDP per capita in the UAE, Kuwait, and Qatar, a measure of income indicating the enormous wealth the countries hold both in regional and international comparison (Table 6.4).

When considering how long it would take to exhaust these fiscal buffers relative to the size of these countries' domestic economies, small countries such as Kuwait, Qatar, and the UAE are clearly better positioned than Saudi Arabia (Table 6.5). While Saudi Arabia's foreign assets are vast, the country's economic size and annual expenditure mean that those resources are much more quickly consumed than in smaller sized economies.

Bahrain, whose fiscal position is considerably more precarious than that of all other GCC members due mainly to significantly lower oil income, is an outlier (Table 6.6). Oman, too, is more vulnerable than its wealthier neighbors, as the country is a relatively small-scale producer and exporter of oil and the volume of its liquefied natural gas (LNG) exports remains small. Both Bahrain and Oman's fossil fuel resources have a much shorter time horizon than those of other Gulf producers, and will last for no more than a few decades at most. Along with the wider region, however, both countries have fairly easy access to capital and borrowing from international financial markets, and Saudi Arabia in addition can borrow domestically. Thus, even though structural economic reform is in principle most urgent in these two more vulnerable countries, their capacity to borrow will likely protect them from radical reform beyond what domestic policymakers deem politically supportable.

The regional energy transition

Beyond short-term considerations of immediate fiscal liquidity, the Gulf States' long-term resilience to changing market conditions rests on a far broader spectrum of policy choices. Their comparable prosperity, even following two years of low oil prices, offers these economies a somewhat unique opportunity to

Table 6.4 Total government gross debt (% of GDP) and GDP per capita (PPP)

	Average 2000–2011	*2012*	*2013*	*2014*	*2015 (projected)*	*2016 (projected)*	*GDP per capita (PPP) (constant 2011 international $)*
UAE	9.8	17.1	11.7	12.1	14.7	15.1	64,563
Kuwait*	15.8	3.6	3.2	3.4	4.4	4.0	69,878
Qatar	31.2	36.0	32.1	31.5	28.9	26.1	134,182
For comparison:							
Saudi Arabia	45.1	3.6	2.2	1.6	1.8	1.7	49,619

Source: IMF (2015a).

Note

* Banking system claims only. Excludes debt raised by federal and Emirati governments in the international markets.

Table 6.5 Foreign assets in GCC Sovereign Wealth Funds (SWFs), March 2016

	Fund name	*Inception*	*Value (US$ billion)*
UAE (Abu Dhabi)	Abu Dhabi Investment Authority (ADIA)	1976	792
	Abu Dhabi Investment Council	2007	110
	International Petroleum Investment Company (IPIC)	1984	66.3
	Mubadala Development Company	2002	66.3
UAE (Dubai)	Investment Corporation of Dubai	2006	183
UAE (Ras Al Khaimah)	RAK Investment Authority	2005	1.2
UAE Total 1218.8			
Saudi Arabia	SAMA Foreign Holdings	n/a	598.4
	Public Investment Fund	2008	160
Saudi Arabia Total 758.4			
Kuwait	Kuwait Investment Authority	1953	592
Qatar	Qatar Investment Authority	2005	256
Oman	State General Reserve Fund	1980	34
	Oman Investment Fund	2006	6
Oman Total 40			
Bahrain	Mumtalakat Holding Company	2006	11.1

Source: SWFI (2016).

translate current resource wealth into the foundation for a more sustainable economic model. This is not only about economic prosperity for the few, or, in the small Gulf States, the "many"; rather, it is about the long-term stability of current political ruling bargains. More specifically, it is about the legacy of the modern state model in the Gulf that rests on the states' continuous ability to ensure high living standards and guarantee a share in their nation's original natural resource wealth for all citizens.

The Gulf States remain among the world's least diversified economies, with a high degree of economic dependence on the hydrocarbon sector for economic output, exports, and government revenues. Economic output remains heavily dependent on oil and gas export revenues, while public sector activity continues to drive economic growth and investment in a variety of economic sectors, financed mainly by oil and gas revenues. An overwhelming share of the GCC national population is employed by the state, tying the state's ability to provide adequate wage and benefit packages directly to oil and gas revenues (cf. Table 6.1). This includes public sub-sectors that are not directly linked to the export industry, such as government services, education, and health, the expansion of which has formed a critical part of the GCC economies' rapidly rising living standards over the past four decades.[3] Indeed, around 80 percent of Qatari nationals and over 90 percent of UAE nationals are employed in public service.[4]

Table 6.6 Alternative measures of fiscal space in the GCC oil exporters, 2015

	Fiscal buffers		*Financial needs*		*Borrowing capacity*	
	Years to exhaust fiscal buffers	*Hydrocarbon reserves in percent of 2014 GDP*	*Fiscal balance in percent of GDP, 2015*	*Government debt-to-GDP ratio, 2015*	*Government debt-to-bank-assets ratio, 2014*	*Moody's rating as of mid-2015*
Bahrain	Small	Small	Small	Limited	Medium	Medium
Kuwait	Large	Large	Large	Large	Large	Large
Oman	Limited	Limited	Small	Large	Large	Medium
Qatar	Large	Large	Large	Medium	Medium	Large
Saudi Arabia	Limited	Large	Small	Large	Large	Medium
UAE	Large	Medium	Limited	Large	Large	Large

Source: IMF (2015b, p. 73). Includes data from Moody's.

The perceived abundance of oil and natural gas reserves and low domestic energy prices has also influenced the composition of GCC economies' domestic energy mix. For countries with large remaining reserves such as Kuwait, the UAE, and, in the case of natural gas, Qatar, the most immediate question to consider is not a lack of domestic energy resources as a starting point. Rather, the question is whether these producers can, and want, to continue consuming rising shares of their own finite energy resources to the detriment of exports – and thus export revenues. From a fiscal point of view, what is at stake for these countries is their long-term ability to continue collecting these export revenues – revenues which provide the fiscal basis for their ability to distribute resource rents and welfare among their national populations and the foundation for their unwritten social contract.

The GCC economies are only beginning to exploit the economic potential of alternative energy sources, such as renewable energy and nuclear power. The pricing of conventional energy sources, specifically petroleum liquids and natural gas, in the GCC domestic markets is far below international levels, leaving alternative energy resources uncompetitive with traditional fuels when it comes to cost. However, this is changing slowly, due to GCC governments' increasing awareness of the opportunity cost of continued reliance on oil for power generation and the shortage of adequate volumes of domestically produced gas in an increasing number of GCC states;[5] as well as the parallel sharp fall in prices for renewable energy technologies, particularly solar power.[6]

Falling oil prices do not affect the observation that alternative sources of energy, primarily renewables and in the cases of the UAE and Saudi Arabia nuclear power, can offer the region a structural solution to rising domestic energy demand and reliance on fossil fuels. This case becomes even stronger as the cost of solar power in the region keeps falling rapidly, as the case of Dubai's Al Maktoum Solar Park has impressively demonstrated – Dubai's cost profile for solar PV is below four US cents/kWh, the lowest in the world.[7]

There have been tentative steps toward including renewable energy on GCC governments' agendas. However, progress remains constrained by the combination of an incomplete regulatory framework, missing financial incentives, and limited private sector involvement in the energy sector, and sporadic – albeit numerically increasing – "green" projects such as 100 MW solar parks.[8] Nuclear power is also likely to form a part of the region's energy portfolio within the next ten years. However, the role of nuclear power may remain marginal in the short term, as the UAE is currently the only GCC state with an advanced civilian nuclear program likely to deliver electricity before the end of the decade.[9]

Domestic energy subsidy reform

The difficulties arising from past energy pricing policies in the GCC that have decoupled domestic markets from international ones have become increasingly apparent since the collapse in oil prices in June 2014. Conventional wisdom holds that as international prices fall, the urge for subsidy reforms declines as a result of reduced fiscal pressure in many subsidized markets. At the same time, the political sensitivity of subsidy reform will prevent governments from attempting to change domestic energy market pricing. For example, Coates-Ulrichsen from James Baker III argues,

> Another policy option that likely will be resisted for as long as possible will be cuts to current spending on politically sensitive issues such as wages and subsidies. Here, the dilemma for officials in Saudi Arabia (and other Gulf States) is that, while increases in government spending largely kept pace with rises in oil prices, they are far harder to bring down when revenues fall.[10]

Of course, a considerable element in the state's political legitimacy in the region rests on the state's role as an allocator of citizens' welfare,[11] a benevolent economic guardian of economic welfare and growth.[12] This has arguably contributed significantly to the GCC states' comparable resilience to popular demands for political change in the aftermath of the outbreak of the Arab Spring in December 2010/January 2011, a resilience which is frequently linked to these states' continued ability to spend.[13]

This chapter would argue, however, that large oil exporters such as the GCC economies have actually been experiencing the reverse case: dependent on oil export revenues for the majority of their public budgets, the rapid fall in international oil prices has significantly reduced the scope for fiscal spending unless savings or debt markets are tapped to compensate for the shortfall in revenues. While high oil prices and revenues reduced pressure and political rationale for structural reform efforts like domestic energy subsidy reform, lower oil prices have offered GCC governments a window of opportunity – and significant economic pressure based on the prospect of worse to come if current spending is not rationalized – to tackle otherwise unpopular structural reforms.

One of the most important areas in which further progress is expected is the ongoing energy subsidy reform trend in the region. Since the fall of oil prices in June 2014, and amid the prospect of a sustained period of oil prices far below the $100/bl range as occurred during the early 2010s, the GCC states are faced now more than ever with the choice of cutting welfare spending, increasing debt, and drawing upon reserves, or reforming the one sector that keeps draining vast amounts of revenue from the state: domestic energy markets. Logic would dictate that the longer the current oil price crisis lasts, the higher the pressure will be for GCC governments to reform areas of large fiscal outlays and reduce forgone revenue losses. This is also an opportunity to promote and push for initiatives to gradually reduce these economies' dependency on oil – in some parts of the GCC more than in others. Energy subsidies are a considerable fiscal burden across the Gulf and the wider Middle East, and are also partly to blame for the region's rapidly growing energy consumption, per-capita energy consumption, and considerable waste of energy and water in the absence of efficiency measures.[14]

One of the most recent cases illustrating the opportunity for regional energy price reform is the UAE's July 2015 announcement that end-user gasoline and diesel prices would be linked to international prices starting in August 2015.[15] This measure was hailed in national and international media as a painful but necessary reform step taken by a government determined to rationalize fuel demand while building a stable economy that functions without government subsidies.[16] Prices for gasoline in August increased by an average of 24 percent, while diesel prices fell by around 29 percent, with monthly adjustments thereafter. The IMF has estimated that the UAE will save some $500 million from the gasoline and diesel price reform alone by the end of the year.[17]

While the reform was undoubtedly partial, applicable only to end-user prices and particular fuels, and occurred in a country with very high average income rates among nationals, it nevertheless illustrates that government decisiveness, coupled with adequate preparation and effective communication, can render price reforms politically and economically viable. Indeed, there was no popular protest in the UAE, and the population has largely been understanding of the government's reform efforts. Oman, Qatar, and Bahrain have subsequently introduced similar fuel price reforms,[18] as has Saudi Arabia (discussed in Chapter 9, this volume). Thoroughly reforming wider energy market frameworks across utility sectors, industries and final consumer sectors will undoubtedly be a challenge for all of the GCC economies, particularly given the political unpopularity of such reforms. However, the current low oil price environment may eventually prove an opportunity for structural change, putting fiscal pressure on governments to reform the way energy resources are priced and allocated within their economies.

Conclusions

Every oil price cycle has its own special features, and this cycle is no different: the advent of the "US shale revolution" and the associated shifts in crude oil and product trade flows, the entry of a new set of players with a new business model, and the changing nature of the geopolitical risks, just to mention a few. However, there are some fundamental features that run across all previous cycles: the problem of excess supplies (*ex-ante*) caused by supply–demand imbalances, the rising levels of inventories, OPEC cohesiveness and its relation with non-OPEC producers, OPEC's fundamental trade-off between maximizing revenues and maintaining market share, and the role of market sentiment. In view of these dynamics, there is reason to expect a prolonged period of lower oil prices, or, as former OPEC Secretary General Abdallah El-Badri put it in 2015,

> Now the cycle is down, we have to live with it. [...] We have to adjust to the new reality. The market does not recognize $100 anymore.[19]

For the small Gulf States, maintaining current levels of spending in the face of substantially lower oil prices will require a trade-off between maintaining current spending and drawing increasingly upon fiscal reserves, between adjusting spending structurally now or potentially being forced to cut spending more drastically in the future when fiscal reserves are eventually depleted and foreign borrowing becomes a main tool of fiscal survival.

Translating lower oil prices into long-term growth is no easy task and will involve difficult decisions, including structural revisions in the way the state uses oil revenues to the benefit of their citizens. While larger neighboring economies, in particular Saudi Arabia, may have the largest available financial resources in absolute terms, it is actually the small, per-capita-rich GCC members – Kuwait, the UAE, and Qatar – which will likely find the current period less painful at the outset. This is not only because of their larger reserves relative to their much smaller populations, but is also due to their demonstrated room for economic policy maneuver beyond what has been ascribed to them in the past.

The domestic debates which several GCC economies currently face about the reform of domestic energy pricing systems and energy subsidies illustrates the enormous potential of the current low oil price environment, both in challenging governments and providing opportunities for reform. It is clear now more than ever that under low oil prices GCC governments will be unable to continue to afford the practice of subsidizing domestic energy prices.

The remarkable lesson to be learned from these developments is that progressive policymaking and bold economic reforms, including the much-dreaded reform of domestic energy prices in previous decades, do not necessarily unleash the political storm long assumed to be the case in the Arab world. The UAE's highly visible fuel and utility price reforms of 2015, followed by similarly bold measures in Riyadh, Doha, Manama, and Muscat, have notably triggered none of the long-feared popular discontent over rising living costs that has prevented similar policy reforms across the Arab world for a decade.

This kind of "quiet" revolution in the region's energy sphere is no less than encouraging, as it offers tentative hope that under the right combination of regional policy instruments, the Middle East, and the Gulf economies in particular, could stand for much more than fossil fuels. These reforms are also a reminder that some changes happen quietly, in the background, and that reforms can occur during the perceived "good times" rather than solely being associated with riots and economic troubles. This would clearly be a very positive signal sent from within the Middle East, at a time when such positive news is rare indeed.

Notes

1 El-Katiri, 2013, 2014a.
2 EIA, 2016.
3 IMF, 2013.
4 Ibid., p. 7.
5 Al-Zeyoudi, 2015.
6 IRENA, 2016; El-Katiri/Hussain, 2014; Mills, 2015.
7 IRENA, 2016.
8 El-Katiri, 2014b, 2014c.
9 El-Katiri, 2012; The National, 2015b.

10 Coates-Ulrichsen, 2015.
11 Luciani, 1987.
12 El-Katiri, 2014a.
13 El-Katiri, 2013; Gause III, 2013.
14 El-Katiri/Fattouh, 2012.
15 Boersma/Griffiths, 2016.
16 See, e.g., *Wall Street Journal*, 2015; The Himalayan Times, 2015; The National, 2015a; Gulf News, 2015; Arabian Gazette, 2015.
17 Reuters, 2015.
18 MEES, 2016.
19 Platts, 2015.

Bibliography

Al-Zeyoudi, Thani (2015): *Diversifying the Energy Mix in the Heart of the Oil World.* Oxford Energy Forum, No. 102. Oxford: Oxford Institute for Energy Studies. Available at: www.oxfordenergy.org/wpcms/wp-content/uploads/2016/02/OEF-102.pdf.

Arabian Gazette (2015): UAE Fuel Subsidy Reform Gets a Thumbs Up from Moody's. July 27. Available at: www.arabiangazette.com/uae-fuel-subsidy-reform-moodys-20150727/.

Boersma, Tim/Steve Griffiths (2016): *Reforming Energy Subsidies: Initial Lessons from the United Arab Emirates.* Energy Security and Climate Initiative (ESCI). Washington, DC: Brookings Security and Climate Initiative/Masdar Institute. Available at: www.brookings.edu/wp-content/uploads/2016/07/brookings_masdar_reforming_energy_subsidies_uae_final.pdf.

Coates-Ulrichsen, Kristian (2015): How Resilient is Saudi Arabia to a Prolonged Oil Price Slump? Baker Institute Blog, Houston Chronicle, August 28. Available at: http://blog.chron.com/bakerblog/2015/08/how-resilient-is-saudi-arabia-to-a-prolonged-oil-price-slump/.

EIA (2016): *OPEC Revenues Fact Sheet.* Washington, DC: U.S. Energy Information Administration.

El-Katiri, Laura (2012): *The GCC and the Nuclear Question.* Oxford Energy Comment. Oxford: Oxford Institute for Energy Studies. Available at: www.oxfordenergy.org/wpcms/wp-content/uploads/2012/12/The-GCC-and-the-Nuclear-Question.pdf.

El-Katiri, Laura (2014a): The Guardian State and its Economic Development Model. *Journal of Development Studies* 50(1), 22–34.

El-Katiri, Laura (2014b): *A Roadmap for Renewable Energy in the Middle East and North Africa.* OIES Paper, MEP 6. Oxford: Oxford Institute for Energy Studies. Available at: www.oxfordenergy.org/wpcms/wp-content/uploads/2014/01/MEP-6.pdf.

El-Katiri, Laura (2014c): Why Renewable Energy Could Be a Chance for the GCC Economies. *Oxford Energy Forum* (96), 13–15.

El-Katiri, Laura/Bassam Fattouh (2012): *Energy Subsidies in the Arab World.* Arab Human Development Report, Research Paper Series, United Nations Development Programme. Available at: www.undp.org/content/dam/undp/library/Environment%20and%20Energy/UNDP-EE-AHDR-Energy-Subsidies-2012-Final.pdf.

El-Katiri, Laura/Muna Hussain (2014): *Prospects for Renewable Energy in GCC States: Opportunities and the Need for Reform.* OIES Paper, MEP 10. Oxford: Oxford Energy Forum. Available at: www.oxfordenergy.org/wpcms/wp-content/uploads/2014/09/MEP-10.pdf.

El-Katiri, Mohammed (2013): *The Future of the Arab Gulf Monarchies in the Age of Uncertainties.* Carlisle, PA: Strategic Studies Institute, U.S. Army War College Press.

Gause III, F. Gregory (2013): *Kings for All Seasons: How the Middle East's Monarchs Survived the Arab Spring*. Brookings Doha Center Analysis Paper Number 8. Washington, DC/Doha: The Brookings Institution. Available at: www.brookings.edu/wp-content/uploads/2016/06/Resilience-Arab-Monarchies_English.pdf.

Gulf News (2015): UAE Energy Subsidy Reforms to Boost Public Finances. August 2. Available at: http://gulfnews.com/business/sectors/banking/uae-energy-subsidy-reforms-to-boost-public-finances-1.1559972.

IMF (2013): *Labour Market Reforms to Boost Employment and Productivity in the GCC*. Annual Meeting of Ministers of Finance and Central Bank Governors. Ryadh: IMF. Available at: www.imf.org/external/np/pp/eng/2013/100513.pdf.

IMF (2015a): *Regional Economic Outlook Update, Middle East and Central Asia*. Washington, DC: International Monetary Fund.

IMF (2015b): *Regional Economic Outlook, Middle East and Central Asia*. Washington, DC: International Monetary Fund.

IMF (2016): *Economic Diversification in Oil-exporting Arab Countries*. Annual Meeting of Arab Ministers of Finance. Manama: International Monetary Fund. Available at: www.imf.org/external/np/pp/eng/2016/042916.pdf.

IRENA (2016): *Renewable Energy Market Analysis: The GCC Region*. Abu Dhabi: International Renewable Energy Agency.

Luciani, Giacomo (1987): Allocation vs. Production States: A Theoretical Framework. In Luciani, Giacomo/Hazem Beblawi (Ed.): *The Rentier State*. London: Croom Helm.

MEES (2014): *GCC Economies "Hooked" on Bumper Oil and Gas Revenues – S&P*. Middle East Economic Survey.

MEES (2016): *Oman, Bahrain, Qatar Follow Saudi n Hiking Fuel Prices*. Middle East Economic Survey.

Mills, Robin (2015): The New Viability of Solar Power in the Middle East. *Oxford Energy Forum* (102), 13–16.

Platts (2015): OPEC Faces Up to New Oil Price Reality; Badri Says Era of $100/b is Gone. June 8. Available at: www.platts.com/news-feature/2015/oil/opec-guide/opec-oil-price-reality-0608.

Reuters (2015): UAE Savings from Fuel Price Reform to Swell in Coming Years – IMF. August 4. Available at: www.reuters.com/article/emirates-budget-oil-idUSL5N10F3SR20150804.

SWFI (2016): *Sovereign Wealth Fund Rankings*. Sovereign Wealth Fund Institute.

The Himalayan Times (2015): UAE to Scrap Subsidized Price Controls on Fuel. July 22. Available at: http://thehimalayantimes.com/business/uae-to-scrap-subsidised-price-controls-on-fuel/.

The National (2015a): UAE Business Chiefs Praise Landmark Plan to Scrap Fuel Subsidies. July 22. Available at: www.thenational.ae/business/energy/uae-business-chiefs-praise-landmark-plan-to-scrap-fuel-subsidies.

The National (2015b): UAE Nuclear Project Enters Critical Phase. July 7. Available at: www.thenational.ae/business/energy/uae-nuclear-project-enters-critical-phase.

Wall Street Journal (2015): U.A.E. Moves to Tie Domestic Fuel Prices to Global Market. July 22. Available at: www.wsj.com/articles/u-a-e-moves-to-tie-domestic-fuel-prices-to-global-market-1437556977.

7 Iranian energy between nuclear deal, oil price decline, and the new US administration

David Ramin Jalilvand

Iran's position in the Middle East and North Africa is distinct in several ways. Not only is Iran a predominantly Shia country in a mostly Arab-Sunni region, but the 1979 revolution also led to the establishment of a political system *sui generis*, an Islamic Republic. The country's complicated international relations, especially with the West, have resulted in the adoption of sanctions against Iran. These hampered the development of the economy in general and the energy sector in particular. Sanctions notwithstanding, oil income on a per-capita basis has always been comparably low in Iran as the country boasts a large population of about 80 million.

Against this backdrop, Iranian energy is affected not only by global energy developments but also by international politics. Two trends have unfolded in parallel. Changes in international energy, epitomized by the oil price decline, coincided with the negotiation, adoption, and implementation of the Iran nuclear deal, the Joint Comprehensive Plan of Action (JCPOA). As a result, Iran was able to re-enter the international energy scene at a time when worldwide supply was ample.

This chapter argues that the effects of both the JCPOA and the oil price decline have been relatively modest for Iran. In the energy sector, following the implementation of the JCPOA, Iran was able to more or less restore oil production and exports to its pre-sanctions levels. However, further progress can only be expected in the more long term – not the least due to a number of remaining political uncertainties. With regard to the broader political economy, the effect of falling oil prices was softened by a series of policies, which Iran had previously adopted in response to sanctions. Moreover, during the past decades Iran's dependency on oil revenue has remained substantially lower than other countries in the region, especially arch rival Saudi Arabia. The stance of the new US president toward Iran has also dramatically increased uncertainty surrounding the future of Iranian energy.

The chapter begins with a brief analysis of the status quo in Iranian energy. This is followed by a discussion of the impact of the nuclear deal upon Iranian energy, followed by an examination of how international energy developments are affecting Iran's political economy. The political implications of these developments are then assessed, followed by a discussion of the outlook for Iranian energy.

The status quo: a restrained energy giant

Iran holds vast energy riches which amount to the world's fourth-largest oil and largest natural gas reserves. No other country in the world possesses more oil and natural gas combined than Iran. Without a doubt, Iran is an important energy country – not the least because its vast reserves are hard to ignore in any analysis of international energy. The country is moreover situated at the crossroads of several producing and importing regions (Caspian Region/ Middle East and Europe/Asia, respectively). Within OPEC, Iran is also certainly among the more prominent members. Nevertheless, by and large, on the international stage Iran has – so far – not realized the full potential of its resource base.

Despite its vast wealth, Iranian production and exports fall significantly short of potential. While Iran holds 9.3 percent of the world's oil reserves, Iranian production accounts for only 4.5 percent of the global total. The gap is even wider for natural gas, as Iran's share in global production is a meager 5.7 percent as compared to its 18.2 percent share in global reserves.[1] In absolute terms, total Iranian oil production (crude and condensate) was 3.9 mbpd in 2015. This was an increase over previous years, as international sanctions had reduced Iranian crude oil production from 3.7 to 2.7 mbpd between 2011 and 2013.[2] Despite the setbacks for oil, Iran was able to gradually expand natural gas production over time, and in the past ten years it has almost doubled, from 102.3 bcm/y in 2005 to 192.5 in 2015.

Compared to its vast reserve base and thus potential, Iran's oil and gas exports have also been limited in recent years. Sanctions halved oil exports, from 2.6 mbpd in 2011 to around 1.3 in 2013.[3] Meanwhile, natural gas exports have been marginal since the revolution and have never amounted to more than 10 bcm/y.[4] The development of Iran's upstream industry has been complicated not only by international sanctions but also by unfavorable fiscal terms for international companies. As a result, Iran's position in international energy is arguably restrained.

In stark contrast to the supply side, demand-side developments have been very dynamic. Since 2005, total primary energy consumption has grown by more than 50 percent, reaching 267 mtoe in 2015. Oil consumption has increased by 15 percent to 1.9 mbpd and natural gas by 86 percent to 191.1 bcm/y over the same period. Since 2002, natural gas has overtaken oil as the dominant domestic source of energy. Natural gas accounts for 64.4 percent of Iran's energy mix, oil for 33.3 percent, renewables (including hydro) for 1.5 percent, coal for 0.4 percent, and nuclear for 0.3 percent.

The rapid increase in domestic energy consumption may be explained by a combination of factors. First, population growth: Iran's population has more than doubled during the past decades, from 29 million in 1970 to 79 million in 2015. Second, economic growth: between the end of the Iran–Iraq War in 1988 and 2014, Iran's real GDP increased by some 2.7 times.[5] Finally, domestic energy consumption also increased substantially due to massive overconsumption largely driven by subsidies.[6] Iran's energy needs to produce the same unit of GDP are 1.5 times higher than the Middle Eastern and even 2.7 times higher than the world average.[7]

The huge imbalance between supply- and demand-side developments has led to a structural transformation of the energy sector's role in the political economy. In the 1970s, prior to the revolution, Iran exported more than 90 percent of its combined oil and natural gas production while less than 10 percent was consumed domestically. Since 2015, this picture has changed fundamentally. Iran is currently consuming more than 75 percent of its combined production inside the country while exporting less than a quarter of its production.

As a result of these developments, the energy sector has been integrated into the political economy. While few links existed between the energy sector and the rest of the economy in previous times, the current situation is fundamentally different. The energy sector, both upstream and downstream, is now integrated into the broader economy. This highlights an ongoing diversification of the Iranian economy away from mere crude oil exports, reflected by the declining importance of crude oil exports both in absolute and relative terms.[8]

Huge potential and huge obstacles: Iran's energy sector following the nuclear deal

Iran's role as a restrained energy giant was caused in large part by sanctions adopted against the country during the dispute over its nuclear program. As a result, Iran was sanctioned by the USA (following the 1979 revolution and enhanced in 1996 and afterwards), the United Nations (enacted in 2006 to target Iran's nuclear program), and the EU (enacted in 2007 and enhanced after 2010). As a result of the sanctions, Iran has faced numerous limitations in areas including but not limited to investment, trade, finance, and insurance.

Sanctions have effectively reduced Iran's profile in international energy. Among others, they have caused a decline in oil production and exports, slowed the growth of natural gas production, banned Iranian exports to Europe, prevented Iranian LNG projects, and led to the withdrawal of Western companies from the Iranian energy sector. Given the impact of sanctions upon the energy sector, the nuclear deal received great attention from the energy industry both inside and outside Iran. In 2015, Iran and the E3+3 (France, Germany, and the UK plus China, Russia, and the US) agreed on a settlement of the nuclear dispute, adopting the JCPOA. Under the JCPOA, several sanctions are lifted in exchange for a reduction of Iran's nuclear program and greater international inspections.[9]

The implementation of the JCPOA in January 2016 has raised the question of an Iranian comeback to international energy. Vast reserves and cheap production costs suggest a huge potential for Iran to assume a greater profile, even in a low price environment.

In fact, the JCPOA did provide a boost to Iranian energy – albeit only a modest one. Following JPCOA implementation, Iran has by and large re-established its pre-sanctions position in terms of oil production and exports. Oil output reached 3.7 mbpd by the end of 2016, on a par with levels prior to the EU's 2012 oil ban.[10] Similarly, Iran's oil exports peaked in September 2016 at 2.6 mbpd (some sources are putting the figure at 2.8 mbpd).[11]

In order for Iran to move beyond its pre-sanctions position (i.e., to expand its oil and natural gas production and export capacity), the country needs international investment and technology. In this context, officials have stated that Iran's energy sector requires foreign capital of $100 billion.[12] However, a number of important obstacles will need to be overcome before Iran can significantly expand cooperation at the international level. The issues outlined below continue to complicate Iranian efforts to expand cooperation and energy sector expansion.

The first issue is the nature of sanctions relief. Iran was subject to a very complex set of sanctions, characterized as a "spider web"[13] adopted by the EU, the UN, and the USA. It is thus important to note that JCPOA implementation did not bring about a complete and definite termination of all sanctions adopted against Iran. Rather, two key issues continue to complicate the nature of sanctions relief.

It must first be understood that the JCPOA has not and does not end all sanctions adopted against Iran. While all nuclear-related sanctions were terminated or lifted from January 16, 2016 onward,[14] the USA has also imposed a significant number of sanctions against Iran related to human rights violations and terrorism. These sanctions are not affected by the JCPOA and remain in force, and prohibit US individuals and businesses from engaging in the Iranian energy sector. Moreover, there is substantial risk from the potential application of secondary US sanctions[15] against Europeans and others with business interests in Iran.[16] This risk substantially increased following the inauguration of the Trump Administration in the USA.

The JCPOA also entails a "snapback" provision. If a member of the JCPOA were to accuse Iran of violating its commitments under the deal, the UN Security Council would need to adopt a resolution rejecting this claim. Thus, any permanent member of the Security Council is holding the keys via veto power to reimpose sanctions. As the JCPOA does not protect investments in the event of a sanctions snapback, this is a huge risk for any long-term engagement in the Iranian energy sector.

The second issue is the details of the new Iranian oil contracts. Iran is reforming the fiscal terms under which international companies are allowed into the country's energy sector. Iran's previous contract framework, the "buyback scheme", only allowed international companies into Iran's energy sector as service providers without any rights to reserves and/or a share in production. Recognizing Iran's tremendous investment needs, the Iran Petroleum Contract (IPC), the framework of a new fiscal scheme, was announced. The IPC is designed to allow international partners to book reserves, receive remuneration in oil, and to commit to the Iranian energy sector for a longer period of time.

This is intended to be attractive for companies, as their value rises when they own physical oil. At the same time, international companies are required to partner with a local company in an attempt to enhance domestic capacity building and to give domestic stakeholders a share in the development of the country's energy reserves.

The IPC framework legislation reflects the Rohani government's attempt to strike a balance to accommodate the more conservative elements in the Islamic Republic. These conservative forces wield considerable economic and political power and have substantially expanded their profile during the sanctions years.[17]

Despite these changes, at the outset of 2017 Iran had not yet concluded contracts with international companies, although numerous memoranda of understanding were signed throughout 2016. In January 2017, Iran's Petroleum Ministry released a list of 29 international companies entitled to bid for oil and natural gas projects in Iran. However, final and binding contracts have yet to be signed and thus it remains uncertain what the details of the IPC will eventually look like.[18]

The third issue is the domestic power struggle over the energy sector. Following the promotion by former President Mahmoud Ahmadinejad (in power from 2005 to 2013), businesses connected to the Islamic Republic Revolutionary Guards have expanded their profile in the Iranian energy sector, especially at the giant South Pars natural gas field. While the government-controlled Ministry of Petroleum and its National Iranian Oil Company continue to remain in charge of Iran's energy sector, there is a heavy degree of interest and involvement by the Guards (which are closer to the more conservative factions and controlled by the Supreme Leader, not the government). Given the economic and political power of the more conservative elements in the Islamic Republic's complex political system, the Rohani Administration seems to be attempting to strike a balance and to accommodate the Guards' interests, as reflected by the IPC framework legislation. The requirement that IOCs partner with a local firm ensures that Iranian businesses and their stakeholders also benefit from the development of Iranian oil and natural gas. The first (and thus far only) IPC contract was awarded to a holding overseen by Supreme Leader Ali Khamenei, underscoring the government's outreach to the conservatives.[19] The debate about the extent to which businesses of the conservatives will be involved in energy sector development is likely to continue behind the scenes. Moreover, as remaining sanctions prevent European firms (and other actors with business relationships with Europe and the USA) from engaging with the Revolutionary Guards and similar entities in Iran, the involvement of these entities must be clearly separated from the National Iranian Oil Company's engagement with IOCs. Until this is the case, uncertainty will continue to loom.

The fourth issue is Iran's energy policy and the conflicting goals announced by Iranian officials. Following the conclusion of the JCPOA, officials in Tehran announced that Iran would become the "number one energy player in the Middle East".[20] However, the route to achieving this remains unclear. On the one hand, aggressive export targets have been articulated. Iran hopes to double oil exports to 4 mb/d from current levels of around 2 mb/d, a target that exceeds Iran's current total output.[21] Iran also announced plans to export more than 150 bcm of natural gas.[22] However, these ambitions are contradicted by developments on the ground. Oil production has stagnated over the past two decades, and while natural gas production increased, Iran continued to be a net importer throughout most of this period, and domestic energy demand in Iran has risen rapidly. Until Tehran puts forward a realistic strategy outlining how production, domestic consumption, and export ambitions are to be reconciled, uncertainty over the course of Iran's future energy policy will remain.

A "resistance economy" in times of low oil prices

As is the case with other oil-exporting countries, Iran is challenged by the decline of international oil prices in recent years. However, Iran is somewhat better prepared to cope with the consequences of reduced oil export revenue, as its political economy is comparably less dependent on oil. Unlike other countries in the region, Iran has never been able to live off oil revenue alone, and oil revenue on a per-capita basis in Iran has always been relatively low due to a large population. In 2011, just before the introduction of EU sanctions banning Iranian oil exports to Europe, Iran's per-capita oil revenue amounted to only $3.7 per day.[23] As a result, it was always necessary for Iran to generate domestic economic activity outside the energy sector in order to advance the living standards of its population.

Several indicators reflect Iran's comparably lower dependence on oil revenue.

- *Oil rent share in GDP*. According to the Central Bank of Iran, oil rents comprise only about a 10 percent share in the country's economy. Even in the event that this official assessment is too optimistic, there is nevertheless substantial economic activity in Iran beyond the production and export of crude oil. Increasingly, an industrialization process is underway. As a result, the oil rent share in GDP has declined while the industry share rose.[24]
- *Oil rent share in the government budget*. In 2015/2016, less than one-third (29%) of Iran's government income came from oil exports.[25] While this remains a substantial contribution, it is much less than that in other countries (e.g., Saudi Arabia, where oil revenue accounts for 80 to 90 percent of the government budget[26]).
- *Non-oil exports* and *the non-oil trade balance*. Iran's non-oil exports are also on the rise, indicating the degree of increasing economic activity beyond exporting crude oil. While focused largely on energy-intensive products (electricity, petrochemicals, steel, etc.), there is increasing economic activity inside Iran. Parts of this activity (i.e., production of Iran's economy) are subsequently exported. As a result, after narrowing in recent years, Iran's non-oil trade balance became positive in the Iranian year 1394 (2015/2016).[27] Thus, from a macroeconomic point of view, Iran no longer requires income from crude oil exports to finance its import needs.

Taking a long-term perspective, the current state of the political economy is the result of what may be characterized as the integration of the energy sector into the political economy. In contrast to several decades ago, on the supply side Iranian labor and technology are currently engaged across the entire production chain. On the demand side, about three-quarters (73%) of the country's combined oil and natural gas production is consumed domestically, while more than 90 percent of production was exported in 1974. Due to the degree to which the energy sector is integrated and the economy diversified, the decline of oil revenue had only modest effects on Iran's political economy – at least in comparison to other major exporters.

Next to these more fundamental or long-term factors, short-term developments have also played into Iran's favor. The major shock to Iran's economy resulting from sanctions preceded the decline in international oil prices. Sanctions imposed by the EU and USA have reduced Iran's oil earnings since 2010/2011 by halving exports. As a result, Iran's economy experienced two consecutive years of negative growth in 2012/2013 and 2013/2014.[28]

In response to sanctions, Iran introduced a series of policies to soften the impact of reduced oil earnings under the umbrella of what was labeled the "resistance economy". Although several different policy proposals are discussed with reference to this term, the resistance economy generally seeks to reduce Iran's economic dependency on the global economy by strengthening domestic capacities. Imports are to be reduced in the hopes of expanding wealth creation inside the country.[29] Thus, when oil prices began to fall in mid-2014, Iran was already adapting to the impact of declining oil revenue. For the Iranian state, this included expanding the availability of alternative means of finance (largely taxation and asset sales).

The decline in oil prices also coincided with increasing sanctions relief as the negotiations over Iran's nuclear program advanced. In November 2013, Iran and the E3+3 agreed a roadmap toward a final deal, the Joint Plan of Action (JPOA), which granted temporary relief for several sanctions. The final nuclear deal – the JCPOA – was concluded in July 2015 and implemented in January 2016.

The impact of sanctions relief in the context of the nuclear negotiations and deal has outweighed the harm caused by the decline in oil revenue. As a result, Iran is currently the fastest-growing economy in the MENA region, with an estimated growth rate of 6.6 percent in 2016/2017, according to the IMF.[30] Iran has also attracted some $11 billion of foreign direct investment to its economy, while trade with Europe has increased by 42 percent.[31] However, this does not suggest that Iran's economy has overcome all challenges – quite to the contrary. A number of problems remain, including high (youth) unemployment, an insufficient legal system, widespread corruption, and the prospect of new or renewed sanctions (a threat which has risen considerably under the Trump Administration).

By and large, the country is on a path of economic growth despite the fact that oil prices have fallen dramatically. The impact of changes in international energy on Iran, therefore, is relatively modest and it does not appear that the country is fundamentally challenged by these developments.

Energy and Rohani's moderation project: a challenge

While the impacts of the nuclear deal – in the short term – as well as the oil price decline upon Iran's economy are rather modest, there are nevertheless important implications for the country. With respect to Iranian politics, these implications center around the question of whether or not post-nuclear deal economic recovery is meeting the (high) expectations of the Iranian people.

In the 2013 presidential elections, Hassan Rohani won a campaign in which he promised a nuclear deal and, as a tangible outcome of this deal, economic recovery. With the conclusion and implementation of the JCPOA, his administration has delivered on the former. In May 2017, Rohani secured re-election – despite the fact that economic progress was barely felt by ordinary citizens. Therefore, it remains to be seen if the extent and pace of economic recovery is enough to guarantee public support for the moderation project in the long run. Although hard evidence is difficult to come by, it appears that expectations are very – if not too – high.

As discussed, Iran is back on the path of growth and is currently the fastest-growing economy in the MENA region. However, most Iranians have yet to see a considerable improvement in their living conditions (which as a measure is obviously quite subjective). Under a best-case scenario, Tehran and the international community would jointly address all remaining challenges tied to the lifting of sanctions as quickly as possible. However, even under such a scenario – which in the meantime became basically impossible with the Trump Administration assuming power in the USA – it is reasonable to assume that it will be several years before sanctions are untangled, the institutions in Iranian politics and economy are reformed and updated to international standards, and the confidence of foreign businesses is fully established.

Whether or not voters will understand that economic recovery and growth require time is a difficult question and a political long-term challenge for the moderation project initiated by the Rohani government. As such, this question is relevant to the mid-term outlook for the entire moderate political camp in the Islamic Republic's political landscape (arliamentary elections will be held in 2020 and the next presidential elections in 2021). If the extent of economic recovery does not meet the expectations of Rohani's voters, these voters could abstain from the ballot or vote for other, potentially more radical candidates.

In this context, falling oil revenue is quite relevant. Despite the overall modest impact, lower oil income reduces the government's ability to spend on items that advance its legitimacy and/or improve economic prosperity. This is illustrated by the government budget proposed to the Iranian Parliament for the upcoming Iranian year 2017/2018, which outlines high oil rent income and higher expenditure following the modest recovery of international oil prices in 2016 and the increase in Iranian exports following implementation of the nuclear deal. Therefore, while both the nuclear deal and falling oil prices have not produced radical impacts upon Iran in the short term, they do impact the pace of economic recovery and thus indirectly influence the success or failure of President Rohani and his moderation project.

The way forward: Trump and uncertainty

As the Rohani government seeks to reap the benefits of the nuclear deal and navigate Iran through the ups and downs of oil price volatility, Iran is being confronted with a new situation. The change in the US presidency from Barack Obama to Donald Trump is calling into question the incremental improvement in relations with Washington as part of the JCPOA.

During his campaign, then-candidate Trump has expressed opposition to the JCPOA in the strongest terms and announced his "number-one priority is to dismantle the disastrous deal".[32] Since his inauguration, Trump and his administration have maintained their harsh rhetoric toward Iran. Although Trump did not repeat his campaign promise to dismantle the deal and in fact maintained JCPOA implementation, his administration has introduced new sanctions on Tehran in response to Iran's January 2017 ballistic missile test. While neither Iran's missile test nor the US sanctions constitute a violation of the nuclear deal, the prospect of worsening Iran–US relations and potentially new sanctions on international banks and companies engaged with Iran is dramatically increasing uncertainty for Iranian energy. Fears in this regard have dramatically increased following the visit of Trump to Riyadh in May 2017, after which both Saudi Arabia and the USA stepped up hostile rhetoric toward Iran.

US energy policy developments in recent years further exacerbate uncertainty for Iran's energy sector. The production of so-called unconventional oil and natural gas in the USA (and Canada) has dramatically increased global supply, and production has proved resilient even in the face of declining oil prices. The Trump Administration has also announced its intentions to ease regulations on US producers.[33] With ample supplies available around the globe, the relative appeal of Iranian oil and natural gas declines in light of complex domestic and international politics, at least in the short to mid-term, even despite relatively low production costs in Iran from a technical point of view.

Beyond energy, a more radical Iran policy by the Trump administration could prevent Iran from translating the nuclear deal into economic progress. Such an outcome could in turn strengthen hardliners in Tehran and possibly bring Rohani's moderation project to an end. The hardliners have already accused the Rohani government of engaging naively with Washington by negotiating the JCPOA. On the whole, the Trump Administration is causing uncertainty for Iranian energy as well as for the future course of the country. Until uncertainty is reduced, it is unlikely that international companies will engage in Iran's energy sector. At any rate, even if IOCs committed to Iran by concluding binding contracts, it would be years before new engagements would materialize. Therefore, similar to the impacts of the nuclear deal upon Iranian energy and falling oil prices upon the political economy, the outlook for Iranian energy is also relatively modest.

Notes

1 Unless stated otherwise, all data are from BP, 2016.
2 U.S. Energy Information Administration, 2015.
3 Ibid.
4 Jalilvand, 2013.
5 World Bank, 2016.
6 In 2010, Iran began cutting subsidies by increasing prices for gasoline, natural gas, and other products. However, due to rapid inflation and mismanagement of the reform, effects have been relatively modest.
7 IEA, 2016.
8 The integration of the energy sector into the political economy has led to a transformation of the Iranian political economy. See Jalilvand, 2017b.
9 Samore, 2015.
10 EIA, 2017.
11 Reuters, 2016a.
12 IRNA, 2016.
13 ICG, 2013.
14 The EU and UN have terminated all sanctions. Due to opposition in Congress, the US government of President Obama was unable to end sanctions but committed to waiving their application, using executive orders ("presidential waivers").
15 US primary sanctions target US individuals and entities. US secondary sanctions target non-US individuals and entities and are enforced also outside areas of US jurisdiction (i.e., outside the USA).
16 In the past, European banks have been subjected to fines of more than $13 billion for facilitating Iran-related finance.
17 Jalilvand, 2017a.
18 Ibid.
19 Setade Ejraye Farmane Emam. See Reuters, 2016b.
20 PressTV, 2015.
21 Bloomberg, 2016.
22 Jalilvand, 2013.
23 Jalilvand, 2017b.
24 Ibid.
25 IMF, 2015.
26 See Sons, Chapter 9, this volume.
27 Donya-e Eqtesad, 2016.
28 IMF, 2015.
29 Khajehpour, 2014.
30 IMF, 2016.
31 ICG, 2017.
32 Time, 2016.
33 The White House, 2017.

Bibliography

Bloomberg (2016): Iran Plans to Double Crude Exports to Regain Market Share. July 11. Available at: www.bloomberg.com/news/articles/2016-07-11/oil-price-seen-stable-even-as-iran-plans-to-boost-crude-exports.

BP (2016): *BP Statistical Review of World Energy June 2016*. London: BP.

Donya-e Eqtesad (2016): rāz-e možbat šodan-e tarāz-e teǧārī (The Secret of the Trade Balance Becoming Positive). April 10. Available at: http://donya-e-eqtesad.com/news/1040179/.

EIA (2017): *Short-term Energy Outlook (STEO)*. Washington, DC: U.S. Energy Information Administration. Available at: www.eia.gov/outlooks/steo/archives/jan17.pdf.

ICG (2013): *Spider Web: The Making and Unmaking of Iran Sanctions*. Middle East Report No. 138. Available at: https://d2071andvip0wj.cloudfront.net/138-spider-web-the-making-and-unmaking-of-iran-sanctions.pdf.

ICG (2017): *Implementing the Iran Nuclear Deal: A Status Report*. Brussels, and Washington, DC: International Crisis Group. Available at: https://d2071andvip0wj.cloudfront.net/173-implementing-the-iran-nuclear-deal-a-status-report.pdf.

IEA (2016): *Key World Energy Statistics 2016*. Paris: International Energy Agency.

IMF (2015): *Islamic Republic of Iran 2015 Article IV Consultation*. Washington, DC: International Monetary Fund. Available at: www.imf.org/external/pubs/ft/scr/2015/cr15349.pdf.

IMF (2016): *IMF Staff Completes 2016 Article IV Mission to Islamic Republic of Iran*. Washington, DC: International Monetary Fund. Available at: www.imf.org/en/News/Articles/2016/12/19/PR16569-Islamic-Republic-of-Iran-IMF-Staff-Completes-2016-Article-IV-Mission.

IRNA (2016): Zanganeh: $100bn Investment in Upstream Oil Industry Needed. October 4. Available at: www8.irna.ir/en/News/82256242/.

Jalilvand, David Ramin (2013): *Iran's Gas Exports: Can Past Failure Become Future Success?* NG 78. Oxford: Oxford Institute for Energy Studies. Available at: www.oxfordenergy.org/wpcms/wp-content/uploads/2013/06/NG-78.pdf.

Jalilvand, David Ramin (2017a): *Iranian Energy: A Comeback with Hurdles*. Oxford: Oxford Institute for Energy Studies. Available at: www.oxfordenergy.org/wpcms/wp-content/uploads/2017/01/Iranian-Energy-a-comeback-with-hurdles.pdf.

Jalilvand, David Ramin (2017b): *Transformation des Rentierstaats Iran: Zur Rolle des Energiesektors in der politischen Ökonomie*. Wiesbaden: Springer VS.

Khajehpour, Bijan (2014): *Decoding Iran's "Resistance Economy"*. Al-Monitor. Available at: www.al-monitor.com/pulse/originals/2014/02/decoding-resistance-economy-iran.html.

PressTV (2015): Nuclear Deal to Render Iran First Regional Energy Power. May 7. Available at: www.presstv.ir/Detail/2015/05/07/409837/Nuclear-deal-Iran-first-regional-energy-power.

Reuters (2016a): Iran Oil Exports Hold Near Five-year, Pre-sanctions Level High: Source. October 18. Available at: www.reuters.com/article/us-iran-oil-exports-idUSKCN12I0KQ.

Reuters (2016b): Iran Signs Key Oil Contract with Khamenei-linked Firm. October 4. Available at: www.reuters.com/article/us-iran-oil-contract-idUSKCN1242BM.

Samore, Gary (2015): *The Iran Nuclear Deal: A Definitive Guide*. Cambridge, MA: Belfer Center for Science and International Affairs, Harvard University. Available at: http://belfercenter.ksg.harvard.edu/files/IranDealDefinitiveGuide.pdf.

The White House (2017): *An America First Energy Plan*. Washington, DC: The White House. Available at: www.whitehouse.gov/america-first-energy.

Time (2016): Read Donald Trump's Speech to AIPAC. March 21. Available at: http://time.com/4267058/donald-trump-aipac-speech-transcript/.

U.S. Energy Information Administration (2015): *Iran Country Analysis Brief*. Washington, DC. Available at: www.eia.gov/beta/international/analysis_includes/countries_long/Iran/iran.pdf.

World Bank (2016): *Iran, Islamic Rep*. World Bank Open Data. Washington, DC: The World Bank. Available at: http://data.worldbank.org/country/iran-islamic-rep.

8 Struggling with low oil prices

From bad to worse in crisis-torn Iraq?

Luay Al-Khatteeb

Introduction

Since 2003, Iraq's transition to democracy has failed to undo many of the former regime's economic legacies. This legacy includes generous fuel subsidies, accounting for up to 10 percent of GDP, and the use of oil revenues to create mass public sector employment, with jobs often allocated based on personal connections or political affiliation rather than on qualifications.

Iraq has created a state that is both large and unwieldy and institutionally weak, and will struggle to remain stable in a low oil price environment. The International Monetary Fund (IMF) has ranked Iraq the most oil revenue-dependent nation in the MENA region.[1] Oil revenues constitute 43 percent of GDP, 99 percent of exports, and 90 percent of all federal revenues.[2]

Background: oil and Iraqi politics

Despite these challenges, Iraq managed to increase oil exports to an average of 3.2 million bpd by July 2016. However, sustaining this achievement faces a number of problems, which will be examined in this chapter. Iraq currently does not export natural gas, but the country has exported a number of shipments of condensate and liquefied petroleum gas in 2016 from the Basra Gas Company Joint Venture, established in 2010 to eliminate flaring in southern Iraq.[3] In Iraq's northern export corridor, the Kurdish Regional Government exported over 500,000 bpd of oil in July 2016 through the Turkish port of Ceyhan.[4] In 2015, Iraq imported around 100,000 bpd of petroleum products, burning approximately 168,000 bpd of fuel in power stations.[5]

These developments are threatened by chronic institutional weakness in both Arab Iraq and the Kurdish Region. Iraq remains a bloated and mismanaged state, held together politically by high oil revenues, which exceeded $100 billion in 2012. However, even with high oil prices, political conflict between the center and the provinces, especially the Kurdish Region of Iraq, has persisted, as well as within provinces and political groupings over oil revenue and the right to export and contract with IOCs. The logic follows therefore that successful reforms require some form of political consensus among the various parties and regions.

When discussing energy in Iraq, it is important to realize that a bifurcated system based on a contested idea of federalism has been constructed. Following regime change, representatives of the Kurdish Region of Iraq (KRI), a region which enjoyed quasi independence after receiving support from the American-led coalition following the 1991 Gulf War, went to Baghdad to argue for specific rights regarding oil and gas. They had already exercised autonomy after signing a 2002 deal with Genel Energy, which took the form of a Production Sharing Contract (PSC) for the Taq Taq oilfield, later amended in 2004.[6]

Later that year, international oil firm DNO signed a PSC for the Tawke oilfield, finalizing the agreement one day before the Coalition Provisional Authority's "Transfer of Sovereignty".[7] The decision by the Kurdish Regional Government (KRG) to enter into contracts without Baghdad drew condemnation from stakeholders in the Sunni and Shia communities. Then-Minister of Petroleum (as the Ministry was formerly called) Thamir Ghadhban accused the Kurds of "dealing through the window, rather than knocking on the front door".[8]

In 2001 and 2007 there was an attempt to rectify this situation by providing a constitutional legal framework that would federalize Iraq (a unique situation in the Middle East) and clarify the rights of producing provinces and autonomous regions. Under this arrangement, the KRI would be legally defined as a semi-autonomous region comprising the governorates of Dohuk, Sulaymaniyah, and Erbil. However, language relating to oil and gas exploitation rights that was included in the 2005 Iraqi constitution was open to interpretation and widely discussed. In the summer of 2016, Baghdad and Erbil were once again discussing yet another revenue-sharing and exports deal. However, based on the track record of other political agreements on oil exports from the Kurdish Region, discussions will likely collapse without either a supporting law passed in Parliament or a constitutional amendment.

It is worrisome that consensus on the management of Iraq's oil and gas could not be built during a time of high oil revenues. It can only be assumed that high oil revenues, which allowed parties in the KRI and Arab Iraq to provide jobs for supporters through control of ministries, muted the urgency for resolution. Furthermore, solutions to revenue sharing and export rights are not the only issues delayed by oil prices. High oil prices have also delayed urgently needed economic strategies and the creation of an attractive business market to enable private sector jobs, while the government has continued to rely on public hiring. As of 2015, Iraq's official unemployment rate was already 25 percent, setting the stage for an impending unemployment disaster should low oil prices persist.

Amid this difficult internal situation, Iraq faces a price collapse in the oil market. The influence of US shale and other unconventional fossil energy has contributed to a diversifying energy mix that has impacted the market fundamentals of oil supply and demand. This has led to low oil prices that could continue indefinitely, particularly as shale producers are becoming more efficient, aided by the policies of President Donald Trump. The expansion of production by major producers like Saudi Arabia prior to the November 30, 2016 OPEC deal offered little comfort to oil-dependent economies such as Iraq. Figure 8.1

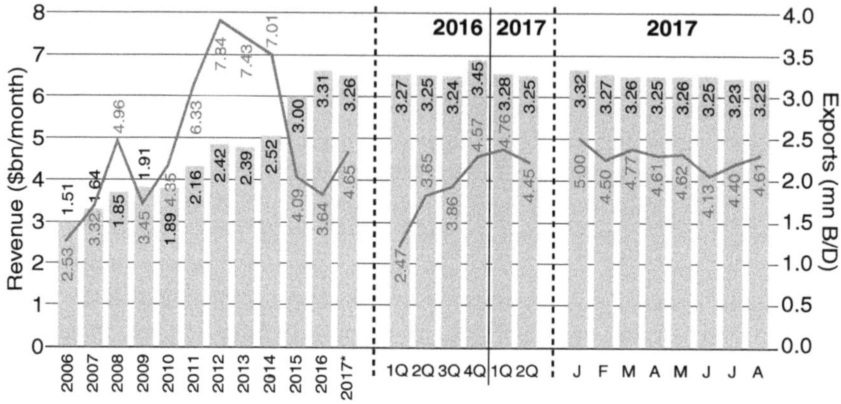

Figure 8.1 Iraq's federal oil revenue.

Source: Based on Iraq's Federal Ministry of Oil and MEES calculations.

Note

* Projection based on futures prices as of September 8, 2017. Federal exports only.

shows the sharp and sustained fall in oil revenues from Q4 2014, with a moderate respite in mid-2015 and the spring of 2016 as production increased and prices climbed moderately.

Fierce competition over market shares has been exacerbated by the lifting of sanctions on Iran, while Iraq earned the status of top oil supplier to India over Saudi Arabia in July 2016, albeit at the expense of a steep price discount.[9] Over the long term, even if Saudi Arabia decides to cut production or the market readjusts significantly as US shale and Canadian oil sands producers struggle under low prices, there is still the possibility of Libya coming back online. The unpredictability of President Trump's foreign policy in the region makes any of these scenarios even harder to forecast. With leadership seemingly driven by populist sentiment, it is unclear whether the USA will (for example) prioritize stability in Libya or overturn Iran sanctions relief. Iraq can take some relief from Trump's apparent favoring of the Abadi government, exemplified by a meeting between the two leaders in March 2017.

Against this backdrop of internal and external challenges, Prime Minister Haidar al Abadi warned that Iraq is too dependent on oil revenues when he addressed the World Economic Forum in January 2015. During the speech, al Abadi stressed that a major challenge for Iraq is to diversify the economy, which he noted was formerly one of the most diverse in the region (Figure 8.2).[10]

At present, the best-case scenario is that low prices will create the impetus for rapid reform; however, this will require a change in the working culture of ministries. A lack of auditing has fostered a culture of corruption. Formerly, Article 136 B of the Iraqi Criminal Code allowed ministers to terminate corruption investigations into their departments, a measure that the Integrity Commission

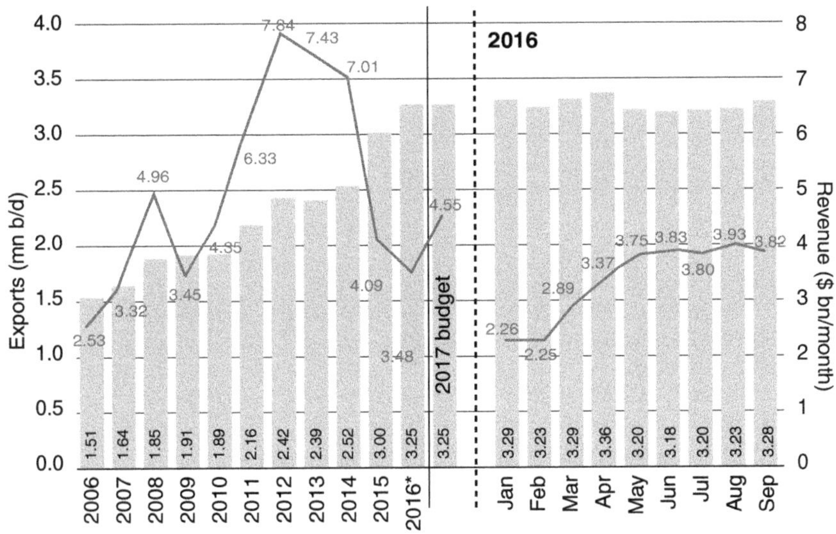

Figure 8.2 Federally controlled exports (million B/D) (US$ billion/month).

Source: Based on Iraq's Federal Ministry of Oil and MEES calculations.

Note

* MEES calculation based on January to September prices and export levels and average 2016 futures curve as of October 11, federally controlled exports only.

said was used over 200 times between 2005 and 2008 alone, the Ministry of Oil being the worst offender.[11] While Article 136 B was abolished in 2011, corruption has endured.[12]

Oil revenues and public spending

The Ministry of Oil's focus on highly optimistic and inflated production targets has occurred at the expense of other sectors. There are some signs that the current government recognizes the urgent need to reverse this and to attract foreign direct investment. Government spending on ministry salaries is typically 70 percent of the budget, while only 30 percent is allocated for investment and development.[13]

Rising public sector expenditure has endured despite the stated aim of successive Iraqi governments after 2003 to develop the private sector. Instead, positive resource shocks like the oil price spike of July 2008 have encouraged excess spending (see Figure 8.3), with ministries divided by political groups competing to capture oil revenues in a "redistributive struggle".[14] This struggle comes at the expense of any significant improvement in public services.

Furthermore, this follows on the heels of years of waste. In 2011, the Justice Ministry announced that the number of government employees with falsified

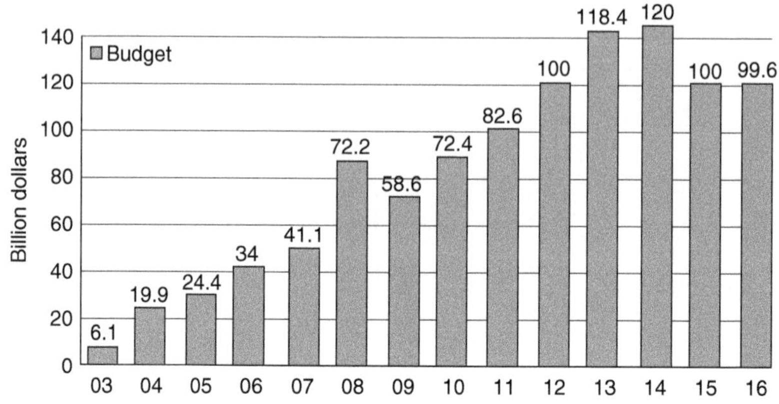

Figure 8.3 Iraq's budgets, 2003 to 2016 (US$ billion).

Source: Based on Iraq's Federal Ministry of Finance.

qualifications may have been as high as 50,000.[15] Likewise, a UN study the same year also found that a substantial percentage of ministry employees hired through political connections were not properly assessed based on their qualifications.[16] This caused a row in government over whether to punish ministers, or those with false degrees. Subsequent reform was minimal.

In 2014, new PM Haider al Abadi announced plans to tackle the persistence of "ghost employees" in the security services and in ministries. "Ghost employees" are employees who are on the payroll but not attending work, and whose salaries are a form of corruption. The persistence of this problem exposes the gap between demands for reform, as Maliki did in response to the false qualifications scandal, and actually implementing reform, the challenge which Abadi now faces.

The Iraqi political economy and backlog of reforms

The culture of waste supports the views of analysts who have noted that high oil revenues can lead to a loss of fiscal control in emerging economies at the expense of sustainable economic productivity.[17] Currently, the Iraqi population are mobilizing and calling for sweeping political reform in Baghdad, and indeed have been doing so for many years. In March 2016, radical cleric Moqtada al Sadr warned the government to enact change and issued an ominous deadline, threatening to storm the Iraqi Parliament with protesters if action was not taken. The cleric followed through with this threat, only to back down amid violent clashes with protesters inside the Iraqi Parliament complex and a renewed pledge by Abadi to push through reforms. Whatever the outcome of this embattled reform effort, the crisis is likely to worsen as, due to low oil prices, Iraq can no longer maintain public sector salaries or invest in critical infrastructure, such as the new Al Faw port. The same applies to the Kurdish Region of Iraq, which faces mass protests over the inability to pay government employees.

Reform efforts will be difficult, as the Iraqi workforce has grown accustomed to rising per-capita income since 2003. Any changes which lower living standards run the risk that discontent could spread from the unemployed to Iraq's middle class. Many already blame the government for the poor economic situation, as many of Iraq's long-term unemployed have missed out on the opportunities associated with rising oil revenues, a situation which is similar in the Kurdish Region.

Recent history may provide some insight into how this will impact political risk. In 2011, many Iraqis still had memories of the crippling poverty associated with the sanctions of the 1990s, which, according to UNICEF, caused per-capita income to fall to as low as $450 in 1996. Iraq's return to early 1980s levels of oil production, combined with record oil prices, has since created the illusion of an economic miracle, as per-capita income had grown to $4500 by 2011, despite extremely high unemployment.

As things stand, the majority of Iraq's labor force is used to either being in government employment, with wages that do not reflect the real economy, or being underemployed or supported by someone in state employment. As Iraq's budget becomes increasingly unsustainable and faces a $2.5 billion monthly shortfall, those who rely on income or assistance from the government will soon experience a significant decline in living standards. This includes four million public sector workers, in addition to one million Iraqi security forces and two million Iraqis receiving retirement and social income support for a total of seven million people,

Recent history in Iraq suggests that street protests, rather than widespread civil violence, are the likely outcome of economic collapse. Most of Iraq's ruling parties overlap ideologically, and no single movement is strong enough to launch a government takeover (e.g., a coup d'état). Furthermore, the ongoing threat of ISIL, although waning, will likely help maintain a general sense of national unity through 2017. This sentiment is reflected in the political statements of various opposition parties, who have condemned the Sadrists' threatening rhetoric as undermining the war against terrorism.

Nonetheless, more protests in Iraq are likely and will typically occur in response to any attempt at economic reform. For example, in February 2011 the government announced a new pricing system for electricity in response to public protests. The new payment system provided the first 1000 MW of usage per month for low-income families, an amount higher than the average US household.[18] Perhaps fearing further electricity protests, which previously turned fatal in the province, the Basra governorate has already rejected a proposed 2016 price increase.[19] However, these kinds of subsidies are no longer sustainable in the current oil price and supply environment. Iraq currently imports electricity to meet rising demand, and will struggle to maintain supply. If blackouts occur during the summer (a regular occurrence), higher prices and lack of service will no doubt lead to more protests.

Iraq is also struggling with the impact of poor national planning based on (perhaps unfounded) optimism. According to a 2011 Central Bank of Iraq (CBI) estimate, per-capita income was expected to reach $10,000 by 2015, a forecast that assumed a fantastic expansion of oil production and persistent high prices.[20] Driving the CBI's optimism was $70 billion in oil revenues in the first nine months of 2011, and a late 2010 Ministry of Oil (MoO) announcement that Iraqi production could reach 12 million BPD by 2017, a target dismissed at the time by many analysts.[21] Ironically, such an increase in exports would have placed high downward pressure on prices, as current increases in Iraqi exports have already caused price decreases on the global market. However, the CBI forecast was wrong. By 2014, GNI per capita was over $6000[22] and falling, and infrastructure problems had forced Iraq to revise production targets to nine million bpd by 2020,[23] a target that now stands at 6 mbpd.[24] Furthermore, by 2014 unemployment was soaring, as over 250,000 Iraqis entered a stagnant labor market each year with little prospect of employment.

It is clear that high oil prices have previously encouraged optimism that deferred important decisions, until now. In response, Prime Minister Abadi has shifted his rhetoric from optimism to expectation management. The PM now correctly notes that Iraq's oil revenues are 15 percent of what they once were, and began to warn the public at the end of 2015 that the oil price collapse was a serious threat.

Unfortunately, Iraq needs funds to alleviate the symptoms of its resource curse, but these funds were largely depleted under the profligate former government. Until 2015, the Iraqi government's record of chronic overspending continued, despite changes in the oil price, rising 30 percent even as oil revenues fell by the same level in 2009. A lack of political will to implement austerity pushed Iraq's fiscal breakeven price to $104 to $106 in 2014, while poor economic planning has consistently been based on misplaced assumptions about oil exports and prices.[25] It is this crisis that could pressure the Iraqi government to undertake necessary reforms and identify the weakest and strongest sectors of the non-oil economy (see Figure 8.4).

Despite falling oil prices through 2014 (reaching a low $59 in December 2014), Iraqi government expenditure increased by 26 percent from 2013.[26] Since then, the Government of Iraq (GOI) has remained consistently over-optimistic about the oil price, projecting $60 per barrel for the budget in 2015 and $45 a barrel in 2016, mitigating the urgency of critical reforms.[27]

Amid this crisis, the Iraqi government has implemented certain reforms, including abolishing some government ministries and more symbolically eliminating the vice-presidency positions. One of Abadi's early achievements, in addition to removing 50,000 "ghost employees" from payrolls, was establishing a new anti-corruption committee in an attempt to reduce money lost through graft. However, it remains to be seen whether PM Abadi has the political capital to overhaul Iraq's cumbersome bureaucracy. Notably, one of his initial moves to reduce mid-level civil servant salaries was met with widespread protest.[28]

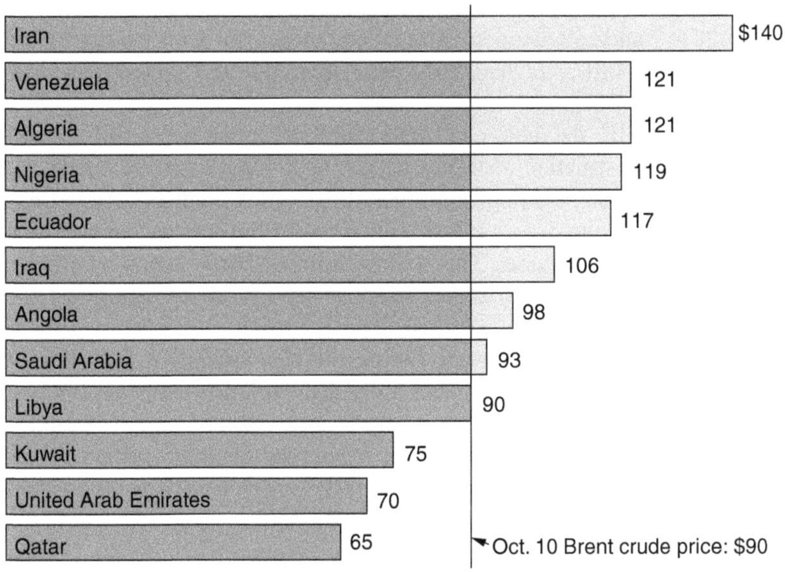

Figure 8.4 Estimated oil price needed to balance 2014 government budgets (US$).

Sources: Based on *Wall Street Journal* (2014), OPEC fiscal in 2014.

Reforms are only the beginning: more challenges ahead

Reform of government ministries is a huge political challenge, and indeed only one step in revitalizing an overwhelmingly public sector-driven economy. More unsettling than Iraq's high fiscal breakeven price is Iraq's "crisis price", namely the price at which critical government functions are threatened, which by one estimate was as high as $70 in 2015,[29] while Iraq's oil traded as low as $21 a barrel in early 2016.[30] Subsequently, the Central Bank of Iraq's foreign currency reserves fell from $78 billion at the end of 2013 to around $59 billion in mid-2015, dropping to $43 billion by spring 2016. By the end of 2015, Iraq's deficit was climbing to over 8 percent of GDP and was forecast to rise to 25 percent of GDP in 2016. By the spring of 2016, the deficit reached 20 percent of GDP, a situation which was beginning to stabilize in Q1 2017 as the oil market showed continued signs of rebalancing. In late spring 2017, Fitch predicted that the deficit for 2017 would be 5 percent of GDP, driven by rising oil prices.[31]

To stave off further crises, and to avoid going over the fiscal cliff, the government has increasingly looked to the IMF and the World Bank for loans. Iraq borrowed $1.7 billion from the World Bank in July 2015, while the IMF arranged a $1.25 billion emergency loan the same month, and approved a $5.4 billion standby arrangement in May 2016 after Iraq agreed to an IMF monitoring program.[32] The monitoring program, a precursor to further IMF funding, will be a challenge. The IMF will require concrete plans to reduce and phase out various subsidies, placing further political strain on Abadi's embattled government. Iraq has explored other funding options, borrowing over $566 million from Germany in February 2016[33] and calling upon allies to lend money for arms purchases and donate arms to fight ISIL.[34] In June 2016, Iraq secured a $2.7 billion loan from the USA to purchase weapons.[35]

With regard to ISIL, the main challenge which the group poses to Iraq's oil situation is not the destruction of infrastructure, as in most cases oil operations are located far from the fighting. However, ISIL poses another very serious threat to Iraq, namely the drain on Iraq's diminished finances as defense now absorbs 20 percent of the budget. This will undoubtedly have knock-on effects, including the potential to cause further social instability in Iraq and the KRI, where over three million internally displaced people reside in temporary accommodation. In particular, the contested Kirkuk oilfields straddle a fault line of Sunni tribes, Kurdish groups, Shias, and a divided Turkmen minority, who all lay claim to this area in northern Iraq where security has collapsed. ISIL also presents a longer term unknown: even in the event that the group suffers a catastrophic defeat in Mosul, the unpredictability of the ongoing Syria conflict could yet present new threats to Iraq's vulnerable western border.

Another "wild card" regionally has been the election of President Donald Trump, whose election campaigning was partly built on what some would deem Islamophobic rhetoric. This has led some to speculate that this rhetoric would catastrophically undermine America's standing in the region, leading to greater regional instability and pushback against the USA. This does not seem to have transpired during Trump's time in office, and much of his rhetoric now appears to have been electioneering. Nonetheless, Iraq remains caught between several competing and politically uncompromising states. This is a political challenge for PM Abadi, who must manage these regional tensions and mitigate political risk as far as possible if Iraq is to continue to attract investment. The Trump Administration's unpredictable policies in the region will not help matters, and will also complicate strategic planning for the Kurdish Democratic Party, whose main regional ally, Turkey, has also displayed increasing volatility.

Cleavages among the Kurds

The public sector in the KRI is similarly large as in Arab Iraq. Up to 70 percent of the population is on the public payroll, resulting in excessively large and inefficient institutions and an unsustainable financial situation.[36] The Kurdish Democratic Party has subsequently based a bid for independence on the hope that high oil prices for exports outside of the federal system will replace federal budget transfers from Baghdad. This appears increasingly unlikely, putting greater political pressure on the ruling Kurdistan Democratic Party (KDP) that has outlived its constitutional mandate to the KRI presidency.

This could force the KDP to abandon its independence bid, as rival parties argue for renegotiation with Baghdad. There are already signs of new Kurdish divisions, including the announced alliance between the Patriotic Union of

Kurdistan and the Change Movement (Gorran). They are contesting the ruling KDP, whose constitutional mandate to the presidency expired in 2013.[37] This tension, stemming in part from accusations that the KDP has pursued autocratic policies, has worsened amid heightened economic suffering, as central government transfers, accounting for 17 percent of the federal budget, were cut off by Baghdad in early 2014 following a nine-year dispute over independent exports. In mid-2017, the prospect for resolving political tension in the KRI, still burdened with debt, appeared to worsen when Nashirwan Mustafa, leader of Goran, passed away.[38] President Massoud Barzani now appears to be attempting to unite Kurdish groups behind a fresh independence referendum in late 2017.

Regardless of the direction of Kurdish politics, the 2014 budget cut off by Baghdad caused a KRI budget crisis even before the oil price collapse, while the massive downgrading of oil reserves at two key Kurdish oilfields, Taq Taq and Barda Rash, was another setback for KDP leader Massoud Barzani.[39] In a further severe blow to Kurdish hopes, Taq Taq was again downgraded in March 2017, causing Genel to issue a warning over profits, with the company's value falling to $215 million from a peak value of over $3 billion.[40] These downgrades led some to argue that the KRI's touted reserves of 70 billion barrels may be closer to 10 bbl.[41] Combined with public disputes with IOCs, including a dispute over alleged insider trading involving DNO and a dispute with Dana Gas overpayments, the downgrades further jeopardize continued IOC investment. The KRI was also forced to discount its oil due to the political risk of lawsuits from Baghdad (which deems the sales illegal), a situation that has resulted in the KRI operating on less than half of its budgetary requirement following the price collapse. In the absence of federal transfers, workers in the KRI have gone for months without pay, prompting protests and a series of reforms aimed at revising salaries and attracting investment.

Despite this, the KRI has prioritized paying IOCs their share of oil extracted under the PSAs favored in the region after the budgetary cut-off from Baghdad caused debts to accrue to IOCs. However, the KRI has struggled to make payments, as they further heighten the budget crisis, which reached a peak in early 2016 following sabotage of the Iraq–Turkey pipeline which took 600,000 bpd offline.[42] This act may have been the work of Kurdish separatist rebels in Turkey who strongly oppose KDP ties to Ankara, further indicating mounting political risk in the region. Operator Gulf Keystone, already struggling with late payments from the Kurdish Region's Ministry of Natural Resources, was taken to the brink of insolvency by the sabotage in another setback for the small IOCs willing to take the risk of operating in the KRI against the wishes of Baghdad.[43]

State-owned enterprises and subsidies

In southern Iraq, protests over wages were occurring before the oil price collapse. From mid-2014 on, protests over delayed wages were occurring near textile factories in Kut and Hillah.[44] The textile factories, along with cement plants, automobile assembly factories, and fertilizer plants, make up some of

Iraq's approximately 200 state-owned enterprises (SOEs), many of which were established under the Baath Party. These SOEs remain dominant employers, accounting for over half a million government jobs.

There are several issues plaguing SOEs and the broader Iraqi economy. The World Bank has ranked Iraq 161 out of 189 countries in its ease of Doing Business ranking, a distinction bestowed thanks to long and complicated procedures for starting a business and a weak legal environment for commercial arbitration (despite the ICSID convention).[45] This will need to improve dramatically if Iraq is to increase FDI in the wake of collapsing oil income.

The UNDP estimates that total state employment in Iraq currently exceeds four million, with the security sector making up a huge percentage.[46] High salary outlays are not the only threat to SOEs: they also rely on oil revenues for the subsidization of fuel and electricity. Furthermore, problems with the Iraqi government's approach to privatizing SOEs have diluted investor interest in Iraq's preferred joint venture (JV) investment model. One factor deterring business partnerships is local politicians' insistence on maintaining large payrolls when partnering with foreign companies.

Subsidies also make it difficult to determine the profitability of SOEs and create economic distortions. By 2011, fuel subsidies were estimated to account for as much as 14 percent of Iraqi GDP. A current estimate puts fuel subsidies at $15 billion a year; thus any amount Iraq is able to borrow will be a fraction of the amount lost to subsidies.[47] In late 2015, an Iraqi government official denied that fuel subsidy removal was a requirement of IMF loans.[48]

Thanks to subsidies, Iraq budgetary outlays for refined fuel imports are substantial, due in part to long-delayed refinery projects. This situation has become critical, as fighting with ISIL took the 300,000 bpd nameplate capacity Baiji refinery off line in 2014, causing fuel shortages across northern Iraq and the Kurdish Region.[49] Iraq is unlikely to have sufficient refining capacity before 2020 at the earliest, when new refineries at Maysan and Karbala are scheduled to come online provided there are no delays[50] At the same time, Iraq's use of fuel for generators to power through the summer when the national grid suffers outages further adds to the fuel import bill. In 2015, Iraq imported around 100,000 bpd of petroleum products, burning around 168,000 bpd of fuel for power stations.[51]

Natural gas: a master plan without implementation

Fuel subsidies are not the only energy sector inefficiency in Iraq. In 2010, Iraq announced a target to eliminate gas flaring by 2015. Flaring was costing the country $1.8 billion per year, wasting gas that could have been used in power stations or factories producing cement and fertilizers. This inefficiency had further knock-on effects, as power stations have in many cases remained reliant on costly liquid fuel and expensive gas feedstock imported from Iran, a wasteful strategy in a country with 126 tcf gas reserves.[52]

The need for gas imports is due in part to delays in implementing Iraq's Gas Master Plan, devised by Shell and the Ministry of Oil in 2005. As part of this plan, the Basra Gas Company (BGC), a joint venture between the South Gas Company (51%), Shell (44%), and Mitsubishi (5%), was formed in 2010, aimed at eliminating flared gas by 2015. Delays have been due in part to resistance to the project from Iraqi MPs who argued that Shell and MoO negotiated the deal in semi-secret circumstances. The terms of the contract also restricted the MoO from negotiating with other IOCs, which some criticized as a 25-year monopoly.[53]

The initial political disagreements over the project were followed by the oil price collapse, further delaying the estimated $17 billion in needed investment to complete the project. The target for eliminating flaring has been moved beyond 2020, years behind schedule. As of December 2015, Iraq was capturing only 728 mcfd of gas per day while burning 1901 mcfd (see Figure 8.5).[54]

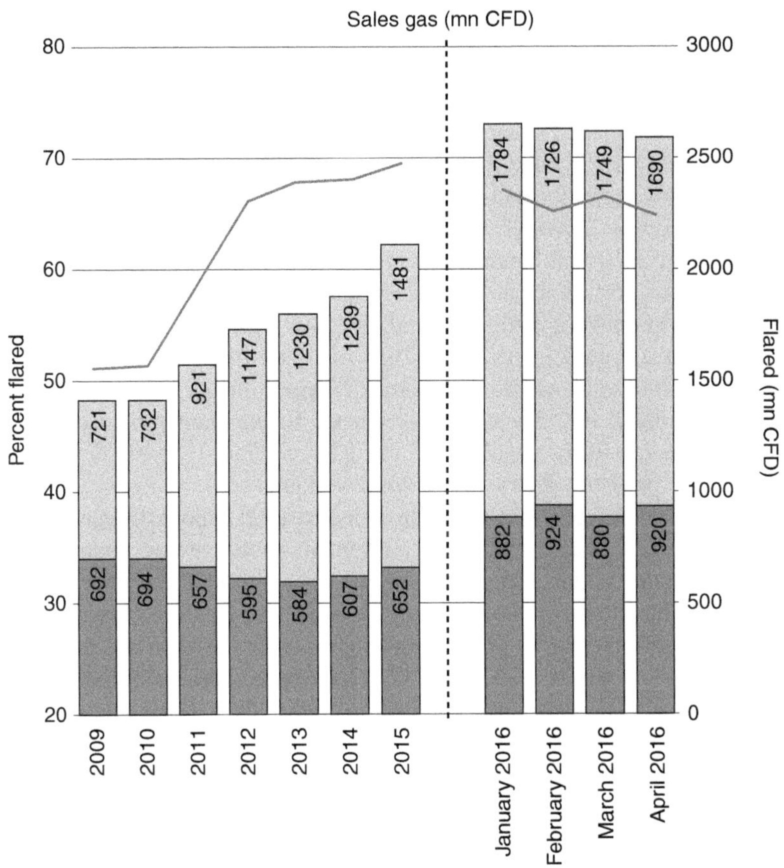

Figure 8.5 Gas sales vs. flared gas (%) (million CFD).

Source: Based on Iraq's Federal Ministry of Oil and MEES calculations.

Note

Iraq produced 2.63 bcf/d of associated gas in April 2016; sales hit a record 920 mcf/d but flaring was still two-thirds of gross output.

By early 2016, the BGC had seen some modest improvement as southern Iraq became self-sufficient in liquid petroleum gas (LPG) and began exporting the surplus in February 2016.[55] Exports of condensate also began in 2016.[56] However, as revenues from these shipments went to the BGC to pay for the investment, Iraq's government saw limited gains. The biggest improvement from the BCG has been the provision of gas to the national grid; however, this remains a small victory, as Iraq still imports nine billion kilowatt hours (kWh) of power from Iran and Turkey, out of a total of 69 kWh produced domestically.[57] According to BGC estimates, if all of Iraq's associated gas was captured and used for electricity generation, it could power up to 15 million homes.[58]

Ongoing risks for IOCs

Iraqi politics is defined by a complex interrelationship of political rivals, loosely allied through the division of oil revenues and shared historical grievances. Despite widespread public discontent, the only political movement that could mobilize Iraq's unemployed masses and turn on the government is in itself a part of the government, namely the Sadrist Movement. The main Iraqi opposition parties, the Badr Organization and the Islamic Supreme Council of Iraq, also hold government ministries. However, the failure to deliver public services despite a budget surplus in 2010 and hundreds of billions of dollars in oil revenues has reduced popular support for the political class as a whole to low levels.

These dynamics make it difficult to imagine how economic collapse would alter political risk calculations for IOCs. That said, inter-tribal violence and protests over jobs in the south of Iraq, where Iraq's major oilfields are located, have sporadically disrupted IOC logistics. Any change in the short term would be superficial, although likely problematic for IOC contracts, which may face tougher demands on issues such as hiring Iraqi workers.

Despite these challenges, Iraq was able to increase oil exports following the onset of the price collapse, with only minimal public sector contraction. However, while the initial impact of low oil prices upon Iraqi society was limited, the combination of falling revenues and depleting currency reserves is akin to a time bomb waiting to go off. In the short term, the main risk is to the durability of Abadi's government, but if it or subsequent administrations prove unable to produce significant improvements in Iraqis' daily lives the situation could become dangerous.

Aside from political risk, one of the casualties of the price collapse is payment to IOCs. These expenses compete with rising government expenditures to combat ISIL, while oil prices remain comparatively low. As a result, the Iraqi government has struggled to remunerate IOCs. By the end of 2014 Iraq owed IOCs $8 billion, and an additional $9 billion by the end of 2015.[59]

The fall in oil prices has impacted Iraq's Technical Service Contracts, which remunerate IOCs with a fixed per barrel fee which must be paid within a quarter. As Iraq struggled with falling oil revenues and the expansion of an already large security sector, payments to IOCs fell into arrears. Iraq faces the dilemma of either paying IOCs in oil or selling oil to maintain an operational budget. This has also created a shortage of investment in critical infrastructure. The situation also has a knock-on effect on Iraq's most strategically critical infrastructure project, the water injection Common Seawater Supply Project (CSSP). Without the project, dropping pressure at six southern oilfields, including relatively young fields, could lower potential output after 2016.

The price collapse has also resulted in a series of moves by the Iraqi government to renegotiate oil contracts to include greater risk sharing, prompting some in the industry to remark that the new contracts would move closer to the PSA model, which was politically controversial and rejected by Iraq in the first-bid rounds in 2009.[60] At the end of 2014, the Iraqi government recognized the threat from "the rapid drastic decrease in crude oil prices".[61] In letters to IOCs, the Iraqi government asked the IOCS both to reduce costs by a certain percentage and to pressure subcontractors to reduce costs in a way that reflected the new price environment. By 2017, it is likely that the effects of cost cutting will be felt on the global market, as Iraq was the world's fastest-growing oil exporter in 2015 before falling to the second-fastest in 2016.

By the summer of 2016, this difficult situation appeared to be easing for the Iraqi government thanks to an IMF loan approval and the prospect of billions in lending through 2016/2017. Iraq would use some of the initial funds to pay the $4.6 billion in arrears to IOCs by September 2016.[62]

An important factor that could influence the next stage of Iraq's oil industry is the effect of competition from neighboring Iran. When Iraq was in negotiations with IOCs over contract amendments, Iran was finalizing its own Petroleum Contract to replace the "Buy-back" model. If the Iranian model proves more attractive to IOCs than some of the terms Iraq is offering for new fields, Iraq could face more challenges from its neighbor beyond market share competition.

One potential strategy for Iraq is to aggressively revise commercial terms of contracts and aim to double production by 2025, maximizing revenue for both state and investor. As noted above, Iraq's contracts are now widely seen as having failed to balance the interests of both the government and the IOCs. However, with record low oil discoveries and new projects worldwide in 2016 (according to the IEA), the strategic importance of Iraq's reserves is not in question. This could leave the playing field open for more inventive contract types.[63]

Outlook

Like all oil producers, Iraq faces the prospect of long-term low oil prices. However, there is only a short period where the government will have the political capital to implement reforms and prepare Iraq for a new era. In the short term, more street protests over jobs and services are likely before the 2018 elections. In the medium term, we can expect a serious challenge to PM Abadi's chances of winning a second term. In this case, the new government would be unlikely to follow a radically different path for the energy sector.

More immediate questions surround contract negotiations and investment decisions critical in preventing a decline in oil output. Internationally, Iraq's challenge is to maintain its market share, especially against Saudi, Iranian, and Russian competition in Asia. Whether Iraq can maintain this market share against tough competition may ultimately be of little relevance to the country's long-term prospects for economic recovery. That is because, as argued here, Iraq has no option but to diversify its economy. In times of high oil prices, plans to implement change could easily be deferred; now PM Abadi has been forced into action, publishing a 104-page plan to reform ministries in April 2016. If this plan is closely coordinated with the IMF, Iraq's borrowing options will improve – an option not available for the KRI if the latter opt to seek independently from the federal government, which lacks international financing options, as it is not a sovereign state but part of a sovereign one. Regardless of the outcome, Iraq is entering a new era, and time is running out to implement difficult reforms.

Notes

1 Gunter, 2013.
2 Al-Khatteeb, 2015b.
3 Gulf News, 2016c.
4 AMEinfo, 2016.
5 Eurasia Review, 2016.
6 Mills, 2016.
7 Visser, 2009.
8 *Financial Times*, 2005.
9 Oil Price, 2016.
10 Al-Abadi, 2015.
11 ICG, 2011.
12 Savage, 2013, p. 201.
13 Al-Khatteeb, 2015b.
14 Lane/Tornell, 1998.
15 Al-Tamimi, 2011.
16 UNODC, 2013.
17 Karl, 2007; Rosser, 2006.
18 See Gunter, 2013.
19 Iraq Oil Report, 2016.
20 Iraq-Business News, 2011.
21 Reuters, 2010.
22 World Bank, 2016.
23 USA Today, 2013.
24 Platts, 2015.
25 Al-Khatteeb, 2015a.
26 EIA, 2015.
27 Al-Khatteeb, 2015b.
28 Sowell, 2015.
29 Gunter, 2015.
30 AFP, 2016.
31 CPI Financial, 2017.
32 *Wall Street Journal*, 2016.
33 Deutsche Welle, 2016.
34 Reuters, 2015b.

35 Business Insider, 2016.
36 Iraq-Business News, 2015b.
37 Reuters, 2015c.
38 Rudaw, 2017.
39 Iraq-Business News, 2015a.
40 *Financial Times*, 2017.
41 Mills, 2016.
42 Reuters, 2016.
43 *Telegraph*, 2016.
44 Al-Monitor, 2015.
45 Doing Business, 2016.
46 UNDP, 2016.
47 Bloomberg, 2014.
48 ZAWYA, 2015.
49 *New York Times*, 2015.
50 Brelsford, 2015.
51 EIA, 2016.
52 Natural Gas World, 2015.
53 UPI, 2008.
54 Gulf News, 2016b.
55 Platts, 2016.
56 Gulf News, 2016a.
57 Eurasia Review, 2016.
58 Basrah Gas Company, 2015.
59 EIA, 2016.
60 Basra Gas Company, 2016.
61 Reuters, 2015a.
62 IMF, 2016.
63 IEA, 2017.

Bibliography

AFP (2016): Iraq Faces "Harsh Year" Due to Oil Price Fall: Minister. January 21. Available at: www.yahoo.com/news/iraq-faces-harsh-due-oil-price-fall-minister-151904526.html?ref=gs.

Al-Abadi, Haider (2015): A Vision for Iraq Prime Minister Haider Al-Abadi World Economic Forum. *Davos*, January 23.

Al-Khatteeb, Luay (2015a): Gulf Oil Economies Must Wake Up or Face Decades of Decline. Op-Ed, Brookings Institution, August 14. Available at: www.brookings.edu/research/opinions/2015/08/14-gulf-oil-economies-alkhatteeb.

Al-Khatteeb, Luay (2015b): Iraq's Economic Reform for 2016. Op-Ed, Brookings Institution, December 13. Available at: www.brookings.edu/research/opinions/2015/12/13-raq-economic-reform-for-2016-alkhatteeb.

Al-Monitor (2015): Iraqi Workers Protest for Wage Payment. June 10. Available at: www.al-monitor.com/pulse/originals/2015/06/iraq-industrial-sector-financial-collapse.html.

Al-Tamimi, Aymenn Jawad (2011): Iraq in Crisis. *MERIA Journal* 15(2). Available at: www.aymennjawad.org/10196/iraq-in-crisis.

AMEinfo (2016): Iraq's Oil Exports from South Rose to 3.2 Million bpd in July. August 1. Available at: http://ameinfo.com/energy/oil-gas/iraqs-oil-exports-from-south-rose-to-3-2-million-bpd-in-july/.

Basrah Gas Company (2015): A Wasted Resource Today. Available at: www.basrahgas.com/a-wasted-resource-today.

Bloomberg (2014): Why Fuel Subsidies in Developing Nations Are an Economic Addiction. March 14. Available at: www.bloomberg.com/bw/articles/2014-03-13/why-fuel-subsidies-in-developing-nations-are-an-economic-addiction.

Brelsford, Robert (2015): Iraq Lets Contract for Karbala Refinery. *Oil and Gas Journal*. Available at: www.ogj.com/articles/2015/03/iraq-lets-contract-for-karbala-refinery.html.

Business Insider (2016): The US is Giving Iraq a $2.7 Billion Loan for Military Equipment. June 29. Available at: http://uk.businessinsider.com/r-iraq-secures-27-billion-us-loan-from-for-military-equipment-2016-6.

CPI Financial (2017): Iraq: Hanging On. May 2. Available at: www.cpifinancial.net/features/post/40871/iraq-hanging-on.

Deutsche Welle (2016): Germany Offers Iraq Loan for Reconstruction. February 12. Available at: www.dw.com/en/germany-offers-iraq-loan-for-reconstruction/av-19044041.

Doing Business (2016): *Ease of Doing Business in: Iraq*. Washington, DC: The World Bank Group.

EIA (2015): *Crude Oil Prices Down Sharply in Fourth Quarter of 2014*. Washington, DC: U.S. Energy Information Administration.

EIA (2016): *Country Analysis Brief: Iraq*. Washington, DC: U.S. Energy Information Administration.

Eurasia Review (2016): Iraq Energy Profile: OPEC's Second-largest Crude Oil Producer – Analysis. April 28. Available at: www.eurasiareview.com/28042016-iraq-energy-profile-opecs-second-largest-crude-oil-producer-analysis/.

Financial Times (2005): Alarm as Kurds Drill for Oil. December 2. Available at: www.ft.com/content/69b2f3b2-6317-11da-be11-0000779e2340.

Financial Times (2017): Tony Hayward to leave Genel Energy. April 24. Available at: www.ft.com/content/57efae0b-f463-3392-b972-50b9591456f6.

Gulf News (2016a): Iraq Exports Third Gas Condensates Cargo. May 22. Available at: http://gulfnews.com/business/sectors/markets/iraq-exports-third-gas-condensates-cargo-1.1832685.

Gulf News (2016b): Iraq's Oil Industry Must Stop its Self Destruction. March 27. Available at: http://gulfnews.com/business/analysis/iraq-s-oil-industry-must-stop-its-self-destruction-1.1698572.

Gulf News (2016c): *Iraqi Claims that Have No Basis in Facts*. April 17. Available at: http://gulfnews.com/business/analysis/iraqi-claims-that-have-no-basis-in-facts-1.1714115.

Gunter, Frank R. (2013): *The Political Economy of Iraq: Restoring Balance in a Post-conflict Society*. Cheltenham: Edward Elgar.

Gunter, Frank R. (2015): Isis and Oil: Iraq's Perfect Storm. *Foreign Policy Research Institute*, January. Available at: www.fpri.org/article/2015/01/isis-and-oil-iraqs-perfect-storm/www.fpri.org/article/2015/01/isis-and-oil-iraqs-perfect-storm/.

ICG (2011): *Failing Oversight: Iraq's Unchecked Government*. Middle East Report No. 113. Baghdad/Brussels: International Crisis Group. Available at: https://d2071andvip0wj.cloudfront.net/113-failing-oversight-iraq-s-unchecked-government.pdf.

IEA (2017): *Global Oil Discoveries and New Projects Fell to Record Lows in 2016*. Paris: International Energy Agency. Available at: www.iea.org/newsroom/news/2017/april/global-oil-discoveries-and-new-projects-fell-to-historic-lows-in-2016.html.

IMF (2016): *IMF Executive Board Approves US$5.34 Billion Stand-by Arrangement for Iraq*. Washington, DC: International Monetary Fund (IMF).

Iraq-Business News (2011): Iraq's Per Capita Income to Double by 2015. March 14. Available at: www.iraq-businessnews.com/2011/03/14/iraqs-per-capita-income-to-double-by-2015/.

Iraq-Business News (2015a): Afren Slumps on Barda Rash Downgrade. January 12. Available at: www.iraq-businessnews.com/2015/01/12/afren-slumps-on-barda-rash-downgrade/.

Iraq-Business News (2015b): Kurdish Regional Government Fights Reform Battle. December 24. Available at: www.iraq-businessnews.com/2015/12/24/kurdish-regional-government-fights-reform-battle/.

Iraq Oil Report (2016): Basra Pushes toward Financial Autonomy. March 23. Available at: www.iraqoilreport.com/news/basra-pushes-toward-financial-autonomy-18400/.

Karl, Terry L. (2007): *Oil-led Development: Social, Political, and Economic Consequences*. CDDRL Working Papers: No. 80. Stanford, CA: Center on Democracy, Development, and The Rule of Law (CDDRL). Available at: http://cddrl.fsi.stanford.edu/sites/default/files/No_80_Terry_Karl_-_Effects_of_Oil_Development.pdf.

Lane, Philip R./Aaron Tornell (1998): *Voracity and Growth*. Development Discussion Papers No. 654. Cambridge, MA: Harvard Institute for International Development. Available at: www.cid.harvard.edu/hiid/654.pdf.

Mills, Robin (2016): *Under the Mountains: Kurdish Oil and Regional Politics*. OIES Paper: WPM 63. Oxford: Oxford Institute for Energy Studies (OIES). Available at: www.oxfordenergy.org/wpcms/wp-content/uploads/2016/02/Kurdish-Oil-and-Regional-Politics-WPM-63.pdf.

Natural Gas World (2015): Iran, Iraq Sign 6-year Gas Deal. November 11. Available at: www.naturalgaseurope.com/iran-iraq-sign-natural-gas-deal-26320.

New York Times (2015): Iraqi Forces and Shiite Militias Retake Oil Refinery from ISIS. October 16. Available at: www.nytimes.com/2015/10/17/world/middleeast/iraqi-forces-and-shiite-militias-retake-oil-refinery-from-isis.html?_r=2.

Oil Price (2016): Saudi Arabia Loses No. 1 Spot to Iraq in Crude Exports to India. May 13. Available at: http://oilprice.com/Latest-Energy-News/World-News/Saudi-Arabia-Loses-No-1-Spot-to-Iraq-in-Crude-Exports-to-India.html.

Platts (2015): Iraq Capable of Crude Production of at Least 6 Million b/d by 2020: Minister. June 5. Available at: www.platts.com/latest-news/oil/vienna/iraq-capable-of-crude-production-of-at-least-27482474.

Platts (2016): Iraq Makes First LPG Shipment of 10,000 cu m: Oil Ministry. March 21. Available at: www.platts.com/latest-news/shipping/dubai/iraq-makes-first-lpg-shipment-of-10000-cu-m-oil-26401588.

Reuters (2010): Iraqi Oil Output Plans Overambitious – Executives. October 13. Available at: www.reuters.com/article/iraq-oil-plans-idUSLDE69C1IE20101013.

Reuters (2015a): EXCLUSIVE – Oil Companies Offer to Cut 2015 Spending in Iraq. March 12. Available at: http://uk.reuters.com/article/iraq-oil-contracts-idUKL5N0WE4OJ20150312.

Reuters (2015b): U.S. to Deliver 2,000 Anti-tank Weapons to Iraq, Pentagon Says. May 21. Available at: www.reuters.com/article/us-mideast-crisis-iraq-arms-idUSKBN0O62BH20150521.

Reuters (2015c): Uncertainty Reigns in Iraqi Kurdistan as President's Mandate Expires. August 20. Available at: www.reuters.com/article/us-iraq-kurds-presidency-idUSKCN0QP1V620150820.

Reuters (2016): Kurdish Oil Flows Shut as Pipeline Sabotaged in Turkey. February 23. Available at: www.reuters.com/article/us-iraq-oil-pipeline-turkey-idUSKCN0VW24U.

Rosser, Andrew (2006): *The Political Economy of the Resource Curse: A Literature Survey*. IDS Working Paper No. 268. Brighton: Institute of Development Studies. Available at: www2.ids.ac.uk/futurestate/pdfs/wp268.pdf.

Rudaw (2017): Nashirwan Mustafa, Gorran Leader, Laid to Rest in Sulaymaniyah. May 20. Available at: www.rudaw.net/english/kurdistan/20052017.

Savage, James D. (2013): *Reconstructing Iraq's Budgetary Institutions: Coalition State Building after Saddam*. New York: Cambridge University Press.

Sowell, Kirk H. (2015): Abadi's Failed Reforms. SADA, Carnegie Endowment for International Peace, November 17. Available at: http://carnegieendowment.org/sada/?fa=62004.

Telegraph (2016): Gulf Keystone Shares Rocked by Debt Default. July 4. Available at: www.telegraph.co.uk/business/2016/07/04/gulf-keystone-shares-rocked-by-debt-default/.

UNDP (2016): *UNDP in: Iraq*. UNDP.

UNODC (2013): Corruption and Integrity Challenges in the Public Sector of Iraq: An Evidence-based Study. United Nations Office on Drugs and Crime (UNODC). Available at: www.unodc.org/documents/publications/2013_Report_on_Corruption_and_Integrity_Iraq.pdf.

UPI (2008): Shell-Iraq Gas Company is a Monopoly, Secret Agreement Shows. November 4. Available at: www.upi.com/Business_News/Energy-Industry/2008/11/04/Shell-Iraq-gas-company-is-a-monopoly-secret-agreement-shows/13121225814147/.

USA Today (2013): Iraq Eyes 29% Boost in Oil Production in 2014. June 12. Available at: www.usatoday.com/story/money/business/2013/06/12/iraq-targets-45-million-barrels-2014/2415427/.

Visser, Reidar (2009): *Bremer Speaks on DNO and Galbraith*. Iraq and Gulf Analysis, November 25. Available at: https://gulfanalysis.wordpress.com/2009/11/25/bremer-speaks-on-dno-and-galbraith/.

Wall Street Journal (2014): Oil-price Slump Strains Budgets of Some OPEC Members. October 10. Available at: www.wsj.com/articles/oil-price-slump-strains-budgets-of-some-opec-members-1412952367.

Wall Street Journal (2016): Prime Minister Haider al-Abadi Says Iraq Hopes to Secure IMF Loans. January 22. Available at: www.wsj.com/articles/prime-minister-haider-al-abadi-says-iraq-plans-to-seek-imf-loans-1453506033?mg=id-wsj.

World Bank (2016): *Country Data: Iraq*. Washington, DC: The World Bank Group.

ZAWYA (2015): Iraq Has No Plans to Lift Fuel Subsidies – Govt Adviser. December 14. Available at: www.zawya.com/story/Iraq_has_no_plans_to_lift_fuel_subsidiesgovt_adviser-ZAWYA20151214052212/.

9 In dire need of a new social contract

Saudi Arabia's socioeconomic and political challenges

Sebastian Sons

Introduction

Since 2014, Saudi Arabia's economy along with its political decision-makers have come under severe pressure due to the decreasing oil price, the second shock for the Saudi royal family following the 2011 Arab Uprisings that led to turmoil in Egypt and Tunisia, and military conflicts in Yemen and Syria.[1]

Following the rise of shale production in the United States and in order to keep its share in the international oil market, in November 2014 Saudi Arabia flooded the international oil market with cheap oil in the hopes of weakening competitors producing at higher costs. As the impacts of this strategy began to be felt by other OPEC producers who rely on oil revenue, the Kingdom widely ignored pleas to reduce oil production in order to stabilize falling oil prices.[2] Today, it seems that this energy policy has backfired and Saudi Arabia's decision to maintain production levels and market share at the expense of price has opened Pandora's Box: The rapid fall in international oil prices, from over $100 per barrel in the summer of 2014 to less than $30 per barrel in March 2016, has resulted in a historic high budget deficit in the Kingdom, although oil prices have slightly recovered to around $50.[3] In combination with other political and socioeconomic obstacles in the aftermath of the Arab Uprisings and rising domestic energy demand, the traditional rentier system,[4] based on high oil revenues to provide widespread welfare allocation to several strata of the society, is in question.

These economic and financial obstacles are only the tip of the iceberg. Long-lasting structural problems in the inefficient non-oil economy, the educational system, the bloated public administration, costly client networks, growing youth unemployment, and social frustration have also intensified over recent years.[5] Almost 85 percent of total exports still stem from oil exports.[6] These chronic structural problems in the economy, combined with the drop in oil prices, create an explosive mélange that could lead to a more destabilized social and political situation within the Kingdom.

Saudi Arabia's foreign policy is also directly affected by low oil prices. The Kingdom relies heavily on oil revenues to stabilize external allies such as Egypt and Pakistan. As oil income decreases, the capacity for such financial support diminishes. This could result in less Saudi leverage in these countries and hamper the political influence of Saudi Arabia within the region. Furthermore, Saudi Arabia is facing several external challenges, including its explosive rivalry with Iran, the military campaign in Yemen, and security threats within the country posed by Da'ish, accelerated by limited state resources due to lower oil incomes.[7]

If the Saudi leadership is unable to provide future prospects in terms of job opportunities, welfare, and security for its own population, both its legitimacy and domestic stability may be damaged. In this regard, the traditional social contract between the Sa'ud family and influential stakeholders in politics, religion, and administration must be redefined and extended to those formerly outside the classical patronage networks. This means that the current economic and political crisis could also offer a chance to reform the traditional structure of the Saudi political economy toward liberalization and diversification.

This chapter attempts to shed light on the impacts of the low oil price upon Saudi Arabia's energy and economic situation, as well as the implications for the country's fragile external and internal security situation, and the leadership's reform agenda.

Saudi Arabia's traditional social contract on the brink: the end of the rentier state?

Oil is an intrinsic part of Saudi Arabia's history. Saudi Arabia is the world's largest oil exporter and holds some 16 percent of global reserves.[8] Between 1990 and 2016, oil production increased from 6.4 mbpd to 10.2 mbpd. Saudi Arabia also has the fifth-largest proven gas resources in the world. However, gas is only used on a domestic level and is not exported.

Saudi Arabian society has changed dramatically since the commercial exploitation of its oil resources, ranked second in the world, first began in 1938.[9] Oil became the driving force of urbanization and industrialization processes that created a Saudi middle class without strong tribal and genealogical links,[10] along with new political and economic elites and the implementation of a national welfare system based on free healthcare and education, non-taxation, and a cradle-to-the-grave system of social alimentation. Following the huge influx of oil revenues during and after the 1973 oil crisis,[11] the 1980 nationalization of the former US oil company Aramco and its renaming as Saudi Aramco in 1988,[12] the Kingdom was thereafter defined as the prototype of the classical "rentier state".[13]

Traditionally, the royal family has been the most important "distributor of wealth rather than an extractor and arguably this remains the central pillar of monarchial revival".[14] With the assistance of oil rents, the royal family established an opaque system of client networks among influential merchant families, and members of its own family, including princes and princesses, and co-opted former opposition movement players.[15] In addition, the Wahhabi clergy was transformed into a state apparatus and a subcontractor of the Sa'ud family ("junior partner").[16]

The rise in oil exports, coupled with high international oil prices, significantly improved the living conditions of the Saudi population in the 2000s. The gross domestic product per capita doubled, from $12,000[17] to $24,000, between 1990 and 2014. Between 2003 and 2013, household income rose by 75 percent, from $2100 to $3600 per month, and 1.7 million jobs were created for Saudis, including a growing number of jobs for Saudi women. By 2014, Saudi Arabia had become the nineteenth largest economy in the world, an achievement enabled in part by joining the World Trade Organization (WTO) in 2005, which resulted in better market access for foreign investors.[18] In addition, public spending quadrupled during the decade, and about $450 billion of public capital investment was spent on programs to improve education, health, social welfare, infrastructure, and transport.[19]

However, socioeconomic development remains heavily reliant on high oil incomes and is therefore vulnerable to oil price fluctuations. Thus, times of low energy prices present a challenge to further economic progress as reduced financial capacities affect the welfare system of the Saudi state. In addition, structural deficits within the Saudi economy remained unaddressed despite high oil prices over the past decade.

In this regard, demographic growth is the main challenge for the Saudi economy. The Kingdom must contend with a huge youth bulge. Every year, 200,000 to 300,000 male and female Saudi nationals are entering the job market, and by 2030, approximately 4.5 million new Saudi employees will need to be integrated into the job market. However, demographic growth of 2.2 percent per annum (2014)[20] and the over-representation of migrant workers in the private sector cause severe problems in absorbing the young generation of university graduates. More than half of the population is under the age of 25, and by 2030 the number of Saudis aged 15 years and over will likely increase by about six million to 19 million, comprising more than 70 percent of the total population.[21] As domestic energy demand increases, demographic growth is pushing the traditional welfare system of high energy and water subsidies to the brink. Today, 2.8 mbpd of total oil production are consumed domestically, almost double the consumption levels in 2000. In addition, the entirety of Saudi gas production is consumed domestically.[22] In times of low oil prices, the Saudi leaders have to deal simultaneously with higher energy demand and reduced funds for an energy system transition. This will further challenge the spending mentality of the Saudi rentier state.

Accustomed to the Kingdom's long-standing social welfare system based on oil rents, the majority of the Saudi workforce continues to rely on the state as caretaker and energy provider, looking to the state for public sector jobs and demanding high salaries and short working hours. This so-called *mudir* (Arabic: "boss", "director") mentality[23] is one factor to blame for the inefficiency of the Saudi economy. Another is that most young Saudis are not prepared to meet the requirements of the private job market, or are seeking "fake" jobs in which they do not really have to work. As a result, youth unemployment (15–24 years) reached 41 percent in 2013, while youth labor participation was just 14 percent in 2014.[24]

For decades, the Saudi government wants to attract more Saudi workers to the private sector and to "nationalize" the domestic job market in order to create jobs and overcome the dependence on foreign workers. However, all political measures to this end have thus far failed. Job opportunities for women in particular remain limited due to the country's traditional gender segregation. However, the number of working Saudi women has been rising and reached 1.2 million, or 18 percent of the female working-age population, in 2014, and an increasing number of Saudi women are finding opportunities to enhance their business activities, often through informal channels.[25] While the state seeks to better integrate women into the job market in order to utilize their human capital, hurdles to workforce participation still exist. The traditional ban on driving for women hampers female mobility, and 48 percent of the Saudi society employs a private driver,[26] as public transport remains lacking.[27] In times of low oil prices, subsidy cuts, and rising socioeconomic tensions, not every middle-class family can afford drivers for their wives or daughters. As more women become breadwinners and an increasing number of families become dependent on two incomes, inflexible and costly drivers' services, which can cost one-third of monthly wages, will continue to hinder women from working.

Saudi Arabia's current oil price policy: turning a blind eye to the risks?

The drop in oil prices from more than $100 per barrel in June 2014 to around $40 per barrel in May 2016 likely marks the beginning of a sustained period of moderate oil prices.[28] Given that oil revenues account for around 90 percent of central government fiscal revenues and 85 percent of export revenues[29] and the oil sector comprises over 40 percent of overall GDP (see Table 9.1),[30] this low oil price environment will have significant impacts upon the Saudi fiscal budget and the socioeconomic situation.

It is indeed already possible to see the effects, as the Kingdom's budget went from a surplus of 6.5 percent of GDP in 2013 to a deficit of –2.3 percent in 2014 as revenue from oil exports dropped[31] and foreign exchange assets and savings declined, from $746 to $669 billion between mid-2014 and mid-2015.[32] The IMF has projected a continued fiscal deficit in Saudi Arabia for the foreseeable future, amounting to $38.7 billion in 2015 (15% of GDP) and an expected increase to

Table 9.1 Dependence on oil, 2005 to 2015 (in %)

	2005–2007	*2010–2014*	*2015*
Oil GDP/GDP	50.0	46.0	30.4
Oil exports/GDP	49.5	42.5	28.5
Oil exports/exports G&S	83.3	82.6	73.8
Oil revenue/revenue	88.5	89.6	81.0

Source: IMF (2015a).

$86.9 billion (17.8% of GDP) in 2016 (see Table 9.2). In addition, GDP growth slowed to 1.4 percent in 2016, down from 4.1 percent in 2015, and is expected to decrease to 0.4 percent in 2017.[33]

In the short and medium term, financing this deficit may be covered by drawing down the stock of foreign assets accumulated in recent years and the financial capacity to issue debt.[34] Moreover, for the first time since 2002, the government announced a cut in budget spending in December 2015. Under the reduced budget, total government spending will be equivalent to 48.4 percent of 2016 non-oil GDP, lower than the 64.7 percent average over the past five years.[35]

There has been much debate as to whether the Saudi oil policy will weather this test, and critical voices have chastised the new Saudi government for its reluctance to decrease its oil production in order to stabilize global oil prices. For a long time, Saudi Arabia's new leadership has avoided decreasing oil production and has instead focused on securing its global market share amid rising competition from Iran, Russia, and the USA. In May 2017, OPEC, including Saudi Arabia and Russia, agreed to cut oil production by almost 1.8 million barrels a day during the first half of the year in order to lift oil prices.[36] Since then, daily crude oil production continued at a high level of around 10.2 mbpd.[37] Although the domestic challenges posed by further shrinking oil revenue are significant, Saudi Arabia's leadership is focusing more on its competition with other oil producers, who are themselves unwilling to reduce production.[38]

The Saudi decision is driven by the calculation that it can better withstand sustained low oil prices than its rivals thanks to its substantial foreign currency reserves.[39] Increased US oil production from shale enabled by new technology resulted in a significant transformation of US energy production, to the detriment of Saudi Arabia, historically one of the USA's most important energy suppliers.[40] As U.S. shale production increased in recent years from around 1 mbpd in 2010 to 3.5 mbpd in 2013, Saudi Arabia share in the US market declined.[41] In order to weaken US oil production by increasing its own domestic production capacity, Saudi Arabia expanded its rig count, from 114 in 2013 to 155 in 2015, the third-largest rig expansion in Saudi history.[42] The subsequent drop in oil prices put pressure on a large number of US oil companies, and in 2015 some 40 went bankrupt.[43]

Table 9.2 Budgetary indicators (in SR billion)

	2009	*2010*	*2011*	*2012*	*2013*	*2014*	*2015*	*2016F*	*2017F*
Government revenue	510	742	1118	1247	1156	1040	608	488	568
Government expenditure	596	654	827	873	976	1111	975	890	901
Budget balance	−87	88	291	374	180	−71	−367	−402	−333
(% GDP)	−5.4	4.4	11.6	13.6	6.5	−2.5	−15.0	−17.8	−13.3

Source: Jadwa (2016).

Saudi Arabia also views the international comeback of Iran, its geostrategic rival in the Gulf region, with great concern. Following the lifting of international sanctions against Iran in January 2016 as part of the nuclear deal, Saudi Arabia fears Iran as a future oil market competitor. Thus, Saudi Arabia's market share strategy must also be seen in the framework of this bilateral struggle for regional hegemony.

The Kingdom in political crisis: surrounded by political and ideological enemies?

The low oil price further affects the Kingdom's foreign policy. Historically, Saudi Arabia used its oil-derived financial resources to support and co-opt external allies and partners, providing financial incentives such as free energy provision to allies, including Egypt and Pakistan. However, it remains to be seen whether this policy will be sustained amid decreasing oil export revenues. Furthermore, a shift in the traditional Saudi foreign policy approach may be observed in several policy areas under the new King Salman.[44]

The conflict with Iran: Saudi Arabia's foreign policy shift

The geopolitical rivalry between Iran and Saudi Arabia has dramatically escalated in recent years. After the Shiite-driven popular uprising in Bahrain and the outbreak of the Syrian civil war in 2011, Saudi Arabia's fear of being surrounded by pro-Iranian enemies has increased.[45] The beginning of the military campaign in Yemen in March 2015 further illustrates a clear reconfiguration of Saudi foreign policy, formerly non-assertive and diplomatic, to a more aggressive and confrontational policy of direct intervention. The military campaign also raised the financial burden on the Saudi budget amid low oil prices. The costs of Saudi participation are estimated at around $200 million a day, amounting to approximately $150 billion since the war began.[46] Thus, the rivalry with Iran in Syria, Yemen, Bahrain, Lebanon, and Iraq not only causes further destabilization of the region as a whole, but also challenges the financial capacities of the kingdom. As oil income diminishes and the costs of military campaigns increase, the socioeconomic domestic situation will become increasingly fragile.

Neglecting Da'ish: Saudi Arabia's halfhearted fight against militant jihadism

As Saudi Arabia's regional policy is primarily concerned with Iran, Da'ish ('Islamic State', IS) has benefitted and become a formidable challenge for the Kingdom. Since 2015, combatants affiliated with Da'ish committed several terror attacks in various parts of Saudi Arabia, including in the capital Riyadh and the Medina.[47] It is estimated that more than 2200 Saudi jihadists are fighting in Da'ish's ranks – the largest national group after Tunisia.[48] The potential destabilizing impact of Da'ish in Saudi Arabia could also mean significant threats to

Saudi energy infrastructure, located largely in the Eastern Province targeted by Da'ish. While no jihadist attacks on Saudi oil or gas pipelines or processing facilities have occurred thus far, the energy industry could become a target in the future.

If the state is no longer able to deliver economic welfare for a great proportion of its people, a potential consequence of low oil prices, the level of domestic frustration and disillusionment may increase. Such a situation could play into the hands of Da'ish and undermine the legitimacy of Saudi leaders, particularly as Da'ish presents itself as the pure Sunni antipode to the "Westernized" and "decadent" Saudi royal family. While Saudi Wahhabism and the Jihadi ideology of Da'ish share certain ideological similarities in terms of their anti-Shiite stance[49] and denouncement of entertainment, the growing radicalization of mostly young Saudi men is also a result of the Saudi self-perception as the role model for Wahhabism and anti-Shiism in the Islamic world. Domestic socioeconomic obstacles also fuel this radicalization process as joining the jihad became an alternative for young Saudis to the blurred social values and the increasing lack of prospects. Falling oil prices could intensify this development.

Modifying the US–Saudi partnership: Saudi euphoria on Trump

In terms of energy cooperation, the United States and Saudi Arabia closely cooperated in the 1970s in order to maintain free flows of oil from the Kingdom in exchange for a US security umbrella.[50] This cooperation has largely endured through subsequent decades and remains one of the main pillars of the bilateral partnership.[51]

However, the energy partnership has deteriorated in recent years due to rising US shale oil production. Political relations have also cooled since 2011, as US President Barack Obama's decision to withdraw support for the long-standing US and Saudi ally Hosni Mubarak in Egypt[52] and the reluctance to foster the fall of Syria's President Bashar al-Assad have eroded the trust of former King Abdullah, while US efforts to broker the nuclear deal was perceived by new Saudi leaders as completely pro-Iranian. In addition to feeling betrayed, the Saudis have become increasingly aware of the fact that not only has US shale oil production widened the gap between both states, but political perspectives on ongoing developments in the Near and Middle East regarding Iran, Syria, and Yemen have diverged.

Given the circumstances, it remains to be seen whether the US–Saudi relationship will normalize. The new US President Donald Trump symbolically showed his willingness to improve the relationship with Saudi Arabia when his first foreign trip led him to Riyadh. After the difficult Saudi–US period under Obama, the Saudi leadership now shows optimism and even euphoria to re-improve its relationship with the US under Trump. His harsh anti-Iranian propaganda has been praised by the Saudi leaders because he is considered a good friend of Saudi Arabia and an enemy of Iran. Nonetheless, it remains to be seen whether Trump is really willing to meet these high expectations. In addition to that, a massive bilateral weapon deal with a volume of $110 billion which was concluded in May 2017 has to be seen as another indicator in order to strengthen the common front against Iran.[53] As well as the relationship with the USA, other coalitions and ad hoc partnerships with China or Russia will become more important for Saudi Arabia.[54]

The reform agenda: overcoming oil dependency?

In the short term, Saudi Arabia aims to keep the oil price low in order to sell it cheaply before the global energy transition and related diversification process gains more momentum, a transition that could reduce Saudi Arabia's role as a significant fossil resource exporter. Saudi Arabia's new leadership is aware of the necessity to overcome its oil revenue dependence and to establish a diversified private economy based on non-oil incomes. In combination with the external and internal obstacles, the need to realize these reforms is more urgent than ever before. Crown Prince Muhammad bin Salman, the young son of King Salman who was appointed Minister of Defense and Head of the newly established Council of Economic and Development Affairs (CEDA, *Majlis ash-Shu'un al-Iqtisadiyya wa-l-Tanmiyya as-Sa'udi*),[55] is in charge of initiating full-fledged economic reforms that promote privatization, diversification, and liberalization.[56]

To outline the future reform initiatives of the Kingdom, Muhammad bin Salman announced the so-called "Vision 2030" in April 2016. The main goal of "Vision 2030" is a full-fledged diversification of the Saudi economy away from oil dependency. Muhammad bin Salman asserted that "within 20 years, we will be an economy or state that doesn't depend mainly on oil".[57] Under the plan, the share of oil and gas in overall GDP should be decreased from 47 percent to 11 percent by 2030.[58] With respect to the energy sector, the following main pillars of the reform program are either under intensive discussion or in the process of implementation.

Personnel and institutional reshuffling in energy administration

Various political reshuffling has taken place since King Salman came to power. The political leadership has shifted positions traditionally held by influential members of the royal family to technocrats to improve the professional performance of governmental institutions. The King also promoted members of his own family to secure the future influence of his clan in political affairs, including his sons Muhammad and Abdulaziz, appointed Deputy Minister of Petroleum and Mineral Resources, and Chairman of the Executive Committee of the Saudi Centre for Energy Efficiency respectively.[59] Furthermore, long-serving Oil Minister Ali al-Naimi was replaced by Aramco CEO Khaled Al-Falih, now in charge of the newly created Ministry of Energy, Industry and Natural Resources. These personnel shuffles could breed frustration among the marginalized members of the royal family and spark criticism of the King's decisions. Indeed, "the visibility of this new line-up of technocrats is being interpreted as the first signs of a shift in power away from the practices of the 'old-style' Al-Saud policy formulation".[60]

Privatization of Saudi Aramco

Included in "Vision 2030" is a planned 5 percent initial public offering (IPO) of the national oil company Saudi Aramco. This privatization is intended to generate new assets of around $2 trillion,[61] but it appears that only non-sensitive and less important business sectors of the company will likely be included in the IPO. Saudi Aramco also has to improve the transparency of its currently opaque business reports, a change that may be met with resistance by the company's inner decision-making circle and raise public criticism about business strategies and financial assets.

Energy efficiency policy reforms

The critical combination of decreasing oil income and rising domestic energy demand is negatively impacting the reform measures. Despite the fact that Saudi Arabia is one of the largest oil exporters in the world, 2.8 mbpd are used to meet rapidly increasing domestic energy consumption. In addition, all gas production is utilized for domestic household and industrial consumption and reinjection.[62] Saudi Arabia has the world's highest energy consumption per capita, three times higher than the global average. Since 2000, energy consumption has more than doubled and the annual electricity consumption growth rate is 6 to 8 percent. Indeed, if current energy consumption patterns do not change significantly, Saudi Arabia could become an energy importer by 2038. To avoid such an outcome, there are plans to invest heavily in domestic energy infrastructure, including $133 billion that must be spent on energy infrastructure by 2023 in order to increase the electricity production, from 58 GW in 2013 to 120 GW in 2032. However, it is not enough to only improve the energy infrastructure. In order to avoid persistent blackouts and a severe domestic energy crisis, two challenges have to be tackled. First, the government has to support and even subsidize energy-efficient industrial and residential solutions, and second, the mentality of the energy consumers has to be changed. Over the past decades, ubiquitous air-conditioning and flagrant energy spending have become an integral part of Saudi daily life. Absent efforts to raise awareness for energy efficiency and incentives and education, the energy consumption behavior of most Saudi consumers will change only marginally. However, neither of these issues is addressed in the "Vision 2030".

Cut in energy subsidies

At the beginning of 2016, the Saudi government decided to cut energy subsidies, and, as result, tariffs for gasoline, diesel, crude oil, natural gas, fuel oil, and electricity were all increased. Since then, the average domestic crude oil price has risen to $0.16 per barrel from $0.10 in 2015,[63] while the gasoline price has increased by 50 to 67 percent.[64] These subsidy cuts will cost the average household an extra $140 a month and could thus decrease domestic energy consumption. It is estimated that the price reform will enable the government to increase its domestic oil revenues by an additional $18 billion per year for the period 2016 to 2035, rising from $7 billion in 2016 to $36 billion in 2035.[65] In the past, energy was highly subsidized, costing nearly $80 billion, or 10 percent of GDP.[66] Oil has been sold for 50 US cents per gallon. Gas stations are provided with oil for $4 a barrel, which translates to a real loss of state income of $26 at an oil price of $30 per barrel. Muhammad bin Salman has argued that subsidies should be channeled to those in need rather than to the wealthy elites, saying, "We do not deserve subsidies. [...] The people who deserve and need subsidies are those who are on average incomes and less."[67] However, cutting subsidies could result in increased public frustration. Given this sensitivity, reform should be accompanied by a widespread awareness campaign in order to avoid public unrest.

Expansion of renewable energy

The expansion of renewable energy in Saudi Arabia has already been promoted in recent years and is an important pillar of the new "Vision 2030".[68] In particular, renewable energy may be utilized to meet rising domestic energy demand, and, according to the "Vision", renewable energy capacity should have increased to 9.5 GW by 2023. However, as of today, the share of renewable energy capacity in Saudi Arabia is less than 1 percent.

There have been attempts to foster renewable energy projects, but success has thus far been elusive. The King Abdullah City for Atomic and Renewable Energy (K.A.CARE), established in 2010, did not succeed in implementing the first phases of previous governmental plans.[69] Saudi Aramco and the Saudi Electricity Company are also engaged in the renewable energy business, involvement that has thus far resulted in unclear hierarchies and delayed decision-making processes.[70] Future prospects for renewable energy in the Kingdom are limited by a lack of know-how and expertise, technological difficulties, and the mentality of energy users accustomed to subsidized fossil resources rather than alternative energy.[71] In addition, new administrative and legal frameworks have to be approved in order to enable SMEs to invest in the Independent Power Producer sector (IPP) and thus foster the privatization of the state-controlled energy sector.[72]

Diversification of the petrochemical industry

Saudi Arabia plans to further diversify its petrochemical industry away from petroleum and petrochemical commodities to more downstream activities due to an increased number of SMEs in the Kingdom. Saudi Arabia's vision to create a world-class downstream sector is based on maximizing the value of Saudi

Arabia's crude oil production. This includes vertical and horizontal integration across the hydrocarbon chain, enabling the creation of conversion industries that produce semi-finished and finished goods to diversify the economy, and developing advanced technologies and innovation. In the past, Saudi Arabia has gone to great lengths to improve its petrochemical industry by enhancing production facilities and transport capacities, investing in joint ventures with companies in China, and implementing new technologies and production processes.[73] The Saudi Basic Industries Corporation (SABIC), which is 70 percent owned by the Saudi state, has played a leading role in this diversification process and has become a global driving force of the petrochemical manufacturing sector in recent years.

Presentation as a reliable partner in UNFCCC

For Saudi Arabia, climate change is a double-edged sword. Due to its oil production, the Kingdom is a large contributor to CO_2 emissions. However, Saudi Arabia is highly vulnerable to the adverse effects of global warming thanks to its arid and dry climate.[74] In order to cope with these challenges, decision-makers have promoted policy initiatives such as the 2008 National Energy Efficiency Programme (NEEP) and the Saudi Energy Efficiency Centre (SEEC) in 2010 to reduce energy consumption. Saudi Arabia also submitted its Intended Nationally Determined Contribution (INDC) to the United Nations Framework Convention on Climate Change (UNFCCC) Secretariat in November 2015 to contribute to international climate policy.[75]

However, it remains to be seen whether those political statements will translate into concrete actions. Similar to Saudi Arabia's participation in other UN organizations, the UNFCCC's commitment may be seen more as part of an overall Saudi strategy to be accepted as an integral part of the multilateral community and a reliable, responsible, and constructive player, rather than as a commitment to undertake real measures to implement a sustainable climate policy.

To conclude, it remains uncertain whether these actions can substantially reform Saudi energy policy in the long run. "Vision 2030" is not the first reform effort of the Saudi leadership in recent decades, and thus far sustainable diversification of the energy sector has not been achieved. Therefore, while "Vision 2030" may appear to be an ambitious strategy, it is (thus far) lacking in details and can at present be characterized as old wine in new bottles rather than as a new and innovative reform agenda.

Outlook: in need of a new social contract in Saudi Arabia

In combination with external and internal political and security challenges, the low oil price environment exerts significant pressure on the traditional Saudi rentier state system. Lower oil income means fewer financial resources to sustain the past welfare spending policy and may also reduce financial assistance for allied partner countries such as Egypt or Pakistan as financial resources decrease.[76] Moreover,

Saudi Arabia's oil price policy, intended to weaken international competitors, has backfired and destabilized Saudi Arabia's economic position.[77] Long-term administrative inefficiency, rapidly rising domestic energy consumption, and an oil-reliant mono-economy have resulted in chronic socioeconomic problems characterized by rising youth unemployment and social frustration.

Thus, Saudi Arabia is in dire need of a sustainable and full-fledged economic diversification to overcome oil dependency by strengthening the non-oil sector, creating job opportunities, and modifying domestic energy consumption. The combination of rising domestic demand, external challenges such as shale oil production and the negative global business climate has influenced Saudi Arabia's energy policy and pressured the Kingdom to quickly implement sustainable reforms. However, financial resources are limited due to the low oil price, which negatively affects the implementation of needed reforms.

In addition, diversification policy should foster investments in cultural and religious tourism, health, education, financing, the construction sector, the labor market, administrative efficiency and transparency such as advanced e-government services,[78] the retail and wholesale trade sector, manufacturing, and mining and mineral exploitation. Furthermore, the efficiency and productivity of oil production needs to be improved to deepen the value chain. The Saudi government must also facilitate the market access of foreign investors. This includes improvements in visa approvals, legal frameworks, and trade conditions, as well as promoting local investment by improving R&D and incentivizing companies to adopt more investment-intensive business models.[79] Although the announced "Vision 2030" is a step in the right direction, the private sector needs more support to transform Saudi Arabia into a non-fossil fuel, industrial-based economy that attracts foreign investors.

> Consequently, political reform, and in particular greater accountability, will be key to creating a more predictable and business-friendly environment for investors. However, neither the energetic deputy crown prince nor his colleagues in government have shown any great interest in this area.[80]

King Salman and his son not only have to work on a long-term solution to political and economic obstacles, they must also redefine the historical social contract with Saudi society,[81] a contract still based on the political *leitmotiv* "no representation without taxation". The combination of the current low oil price cycle amid a completely changed energy environment has put severe pressure on the Saudi leadership to reconfigure this traditional social contract, and indeed for the first time in modern Saudi history there is a discussion about the introduction of VAT by 2018.[82] A new agreement between rulers and people should be based on an expanded concept of the elite, which includes former outsiders, such as private businessmen and youth, and brings them into the state elite. A new contract should also include a moderate rethinking of the traditional alliance with the Wahhabi *ulama,* address the youth bulge by fostering private entrepreneurship, integrate women into the job market, and close the gap between what the education system delivers and what the job market requires. While the new government addressed most of these issues in its "Vision 2030", it is not yet clear whether it will prove willing to realize these ambitions, which will require painful reforms and working against the influence of the strong oil lobby, the *mudir* mentality, and the clientelism networks.

Of course, even in an almost absolute monarchy such as Saudi Arabia, state-sponsored reforms have to be supported by the people. Thus far, the chances for public support seem good. The majority of the young generation understand that the golden age of their parents is over, and that young Saudi men and women must compete with other Saudi and foreign job seekers in the job market. To do so, Saudi youth must demonstrate more engagement and commitment to meet the high working standards of the private business sector, as public sector opportunities will diminish further.

The royal family still remains the undisputed leader, trusted by the majority of the Saudi population in tumultuous times. For much of the Saudi population, security is perceived as the highest priority, while political reform or democratization have lost relevance due to the destabilizing effects of the Arab Spring on neighboring countries. This widespread popular trust buys the royal leaders time to implement reforms. However, they need to deliver in order to satisfy the expectations of the people and avoid further frustration and destabilization.

Notes

1 Soubrier, 2014.
2 Foreign Policy, 2016.
3 Dollas, 2015.
4 Beblawi, 1987, pp. 46–62.
5 Yamani, 2000.
6 Al-Darwish et al., 2015, p. 65.
7 Sons, 2016b, pp. 76–81.
8 OPEC, 2015.
9 Vassiliev, 2000, pp. 288–290.
10 Al-Rasheed, 2002, p. 113.
11 Between 1972 and 1973, the Saudi GDP increased from 40.5 billion Saudi Riyal to 99.3 billion Saudi Riyal. See ibid., p. 138.
12 Davidson, 2012, p. 40.
13 On rentier states, see Beblawi, 1987, pp. 49–62. On Saudi Arabia as a rentier state, see Niblock/Malik, 2007, p. 14.
14 Davidson, 2012, p. 49.
15 Lacroix, 2011.
16 Steinberg, 2007, pp. 175–196; Steinberg, 2010, pp. 121–154.
17 Bloomberg, 2016b.
18 WTO, 2012.
19 McKinsey Global Institute, 2015.
20 World Bank, 2016.
21 McKinsey Global Institute, 2015.
22 EIA, 2014b.
23 Champion, 1999, pp. 49–73.
24 McKinsey Global Institute, 2015.

25 Sons, 2013, pp. 197–236.
26 Dickinson, 2016.
27 In Riyadh, a public metro system with a network length of 176km and 85 stations in total is planned to be in operation by 2019. Similar projects are under construction in Jeddah, Medina (operation is planned to start in 2020), and Mecca (operation is planned to start in 2019).
28 Bloomberg, 2016c.
29 Saudi Arabian Monetary Agency, 2015a.
30 IMF, 2015.
31 Saudi Arabian Monetary Agency, 2015b.
32 As-Safir, 2016.
33 IMF, 2017, p. 203.
34 Arabian Business, 2015.
35 However, in similar times of decreasing oil prices such as during the financial crisis period from 1998 until 2000, budget spending also dropped significantly. See Jadwa, 2016.
36 Reuters, 2017.
37 Ibid.
38 *Wall Street Journal*, 2014.
39 Gause III, 2015.
40 Westphal et al., 2014, p. 6.
41 EIA, 2014a.
42 Oil Price, 2016.
43 Deutsche Welle, 2016.
44 Al-Quds Al-Arabi, 2016.
45 On Bahrain, see *New York Times*, 2011. On Syria, see The National, 2012; *Guardian*, 2013. However, the replacement of the head of intelligence Prince Bandar bin Sultan with Mohamed bin Naif bin Abdulaziz Al Saud in April 2014 was also interpreted as a signal of the reformulation of the policy toward militant Islamists. See *Guardian*, 2014.
46 Al-Monitor, 2015. More conservative calculations estimate monthly costs of about $175 million. See Sons, 2015, pp. 34–35.
47 *Independent*, 2016; *Guardian*, 2016.
48 See Homeland Security Committee, 2015, p. 11. By November 2015, 690 Saudi jihadists who had joined the ranks of jihadi groups since 2011 had returned to the Kingdom.
49 See, on Wahhabiyya, Steinberg, 2011, pp. 163–182.
50 Cooper, 2012.
51 Abukhalil, 2004.
52 For more information on Saudi Arabia's economic and political relationship with Egypt see Sons, 2016a, pp. 37–39.
53 Aljazeera, 2017.
54 Sons/Wiese, 2015.
55 Kéchichian, 2015.
56 In order to establish CEDA, the Supreme Council for Petroleum and Minerals, the Supreme Economic Council, and the Supreme Council of the King Abdullah City for Atomic and Renewable Energy were abolished in January 2015.
57 Bloomberg, 2016a.
58 Frankfurter Allgemeine Zeitung, 2016.
59 Jones Day Publications, 2015.
60 Thompson, 2016, pp. 22–23.
61 Handelsblatt, 2016.
62 Saudi Arabia holds the sixth-largest natural gas reserves in the world, with 294 trillion cubic feet in 2015. See EIA, 2015.

63 Jadwa, 2016.
64 MEED, 2016.
65 Jadwa, 2016.
66 This has contributed to improved living conditions in recent years. In this regard, the proportion of families living in extreme poverty was 1.63 percent in 2004 and decreased to 0.8 percent in 2008. See UNDP, n.d.
67 Al-Arabiya, 2016.
68 Saudi Gazette, 2016.
69 Reuters, 2015.
70 Espey, 2014.
71 Interviews in Riyadh in December 2014.
72 Al Sulayman, 2016, pp. 9–11.
73 Arabian Industry, 2016; Lenkeit, 2013.
74 Nachmany et al., 2015.
75 UNFCCC, 2015.
76 On Saudi Arabia's development assistance on Egypt, see Sons/Wiese, 2015.
77 Foreign Policy, 2016.
78 Ministry of Finance, 2015.
79 McKinsey Global Institute, 2015.
80 Economist Intelligence Unit, 2016.
81 "The traditional Gulf social contract has never been more fragile, and attempts to drastically rewrite it by GCC governments no doubt comes with its risks" (Al Qassemi, 2016).
82 Arab News, 2016.

Bibliography

Abukhalil, As'ad (2004): *The Battle for Saudi Arabia: Royalty, Fundamentalism, and Global Power*. New York: Seven Stories Press.

Al-Arabiya (2016): Full Transcript of Prince Mohammed bin Salman's Al Arabiya Interview. April 25. Available at: http://english.alarabiya.net/en/media/inside-the-newsroom/2016/04/25/Full-Transcript-of-Prince-Mohammed-bin-Salman-s-Al-Arabiya-interview.html.

Al-Darwish, Ahmed et al. (2015): *Saudi Arabia: Tackling Emerging Economic Challenges to Sustain Growth*. Washington, DC: International Monetary Fund.

Al-Monitor (2015, 28): Saudi Arabia's Mounting Security Challenges. December 28. Available at: www.al-monitor.com/pulse/originals/2015/12/saudi-yemen-security-salman-houthi-gulf.html.

Al-Quds Al-Arabi (2016, 17 January): One Year into King Salman's Term on the Arab and Regional Levels (in Arabic). Available at: www.alquds.co.uk/?p=466787.

Al-Rasheed, Madawi (2002): *A History of Saudi Arabia*. Cambridge: The Press Syndicate of the University of Cambridge.

Al Qassemi, Sultan (2016): *The Gulf's New Social Contract*. Middle East Institute. Available at: www.mei.edu/content/article/gulfs-new-social-contract.

Al Sulayman, Faris (2016): *The Obstacles Facing Renewables in the Gulf. Energy and the State: The Impact of Low Oil Prices*. Oxford: The Oxford Gulf and Arabian Peninsula Studies Forum (OxGAPS).

Aljazeera (2017): US and Saudi Arabia Sign Arms Deals Worth almost $110bn. May 20. Available at: www.aljazeera.com/news/2017/05/saudi-arabia-sign-arms-deals-worth-110bn-170520141943494.html.

Arab News (2016): No Income Tax, but VAT Starts in 2018. May 5. Available at: www.arabnews.com/news/no-income-tax-vat-starts-2018.

Arabian Business (2015): Saudi Facing "A Crisis in the Next 3–5 Years" if Oil Price Remains Low. November 18. Available at: www.arabianbusiness.com/saudi-facing-a-crisis-in-next-3-5-years-if-oil-price-remains-low-612626.html#.VuvhKuZws6x.

Arabian Industry (2016): Saudi's SABIC to Build China Petrochemical Project. May 31. Available at: www.arabianindustry.com/construction/news/2016/may/31/saudis-sabic-to-build-china-petrochemical-project-5389280/.

As-Safir (2016): Saudi Arabia and the Major Transformation (in Arabic). October 7. Available at: http://assafir.com/Article/20/449112.

Beblawi, Hazem (1987): The Rentier State in the Arab World. In Beblawi, Hazem/ Giacomo Luciani (Ed.): *The Rentier State*. London: Croom Helm.

Bloomberg (2016a): Saudi Arabia's Deputy Crown Prince Outlines Plans: Transcript. April 4. Available at: www.bloomberg.com/news/articles/2016-04-04/saudi-arabia-s-deputy-crown-prince-outlines-plans-transcript.

Bloomberg (2016b): Saudi Life with $30 Oil. January 14. Available at: www.bloomberg.com/news/articles/2016-01-14/saudi-life-with-30-oil-shock-spending-cuts-and-even-smiles.

Bloomberg (2016c): World's Largest Energy Trader Sees a Decade of Low Oil Prices. February 8. Available at: www.bloomberg.com/news/articles/2016-02-08/world-s-largest-energy-trader-sees-a-decade-of-low-oil-prices.

Champion, Daryl (1999): The Kingdom of Saudi Arabia: Elements of Instability Within Stability. *Middle East Review of International Affairs* 3(4), 49–73.

Cooper, Andrew Scott (2012): *The Oil Kings: How the U.S., Iran, and Saudi Arabia Changed the Balance of Power in the Middle East*. New York: Simon & Schuster.

Davidson, Christopher M. (2012): *After the Sheikhs. The Coming Collapse of the Gulf Monarchies*. London: Hurst.

Deutsche Welle (2016): Riad und Moskau begrenzen Ölförderung. February 16. Available at: www.dw.com/de/riad-und-moskau-begrenzen-%C3%B6lf%C3%B6rderung/a-19051186.

Dollas, Leo (2015): How Long Can Saudi Arabia Sustain Low Oil Prices? Energy Insights, July. Available at: www.mckinseyenergyinsights.com/insights/saudi-arabia-and-low-oil-prices.

Economist Intelligence Unit (2016): Deputy Crown Prince Launches "Vision 2030". April 26. Available at: http://country.eiu.com/article.aspx?articleid=1664164750&Country=Saudi%20Arabia&topic=Economy.

EIA (2014a): *Annual Energy Outlook*. Washington, DC: U.S. Energy Information Administration. Available at: www.eia.gov/outlooks/archive/aeo14/pdf/0383(2014).pdf.

EIA (2014b): *Country Analysis Brief: Saudi Arabia*. Washington, DC: U.S. Energy Information Administration.

EIA (2015): *International Energy Statistics*. Washington, DC: U.S. Energy Information Administration.

Espey, Robert (2014): *Saudi-Arabien ohne Konzept für erneuerbare Energien*. Germany Trade and Invest.

Foreign Policy (2016): Saudi Arabia's Destructive Oil Freeze. March 14. Available at: http://foreignpolicy.com/2016/03/14/saudi-arabia-oil-opec/.

Frankfurter Allgemeine Zeitung (2016): Saudi-Arabien will bis 2030 vom Erdöl unabhängig sein. April 25, p. 16.

Gause III, F. Gregory (2015): *Sultans of Swing? The Geopolitics of Falling Oil Prices*. Policy Briefing. Doha: Brookings Doha Center/Brookings Institution. Available at: www.brookings.edu/wp-content/uploads/2015/03/En-Gause-PDF.pdf.

Guardian (2013): Saudi Arabia: Syrian Rebels Must Be Armed. June 25. Available at: www.theguardian.com/world/2013/jun/25/saudi-arabia-syria-rebels-armed?CMP=twt_gu.

Guardian (2014): End of an Era as Prince Bandar Departs Saudi Intelligence Post. April 16. Available at: www.theguardian.com/world/2014/apr/16/prince-bandar-saudi-intelligence-syria.

Guardian (2016): Suicide Bombers Attack Sites in Saudi Arabia Including Mosque in Medina. July 4. Available at: www.theguardian.com/world/2016/jul/04/saudi-arabia-bombings-jeddah-medina-prophets-mosque-qatif.

Handelsblatt (2016): Wenn Reformen das Öl ersetzen. April 25. Available at: www.handelsblatt.com/politik/international/grosser-umbau-in-saudi-arabien-wenn-reformen-das-oel-ersetzen/13500418.html.

Homeland Security Committee (2015): *Final Report of the Task Force on Combating Terrorist and Foreign Fighter Travel*.

IMF (2015): *Saudi Arabia. Selected Issues*. IMF Country Report No. 15/286. Washington, DC: International Monetary Fund. Available at: www.imf.org/external/pubs/ft/scr/2015/cr15286.pdf.

IMF (2017): *World Economic Outlook: Gaining Momentum?* Washington, DC: International Monetary Fund.

Independent (2016): Saudi Arabia Mosque Suicide Bombing: At Least Two Dead and Seven Hurt after Shia Muslims Attacked. January 29. Available at: www.independent.co.uk/news/world/middle-east/saudi-arabia-mosque-suicide-bombing-at-least-two-dead-and-seven-hurt-after-shia-muslims-attacked-a6841476.html.

Jadwa (2016): *The Saudi Economy in 2016*. Jadwa.

Jones Day Publications (2015): Saudi Arabia's Oil and Gas Sector – An Update: Part 1. Available at: www.jonesday.com/saudi-arabias-oil-and-gas-sectoran-update-part-1-08-12-2015/.

Kéchichian, Joseph A. (2015): Saudi Arabia's Succession Shakeup and the Rise of Mohammed bin Salman. Middle East Institute (MEI), May 20. Available at: www.mei.edu/content/article/saudi-arabia's-succession-shakeup-and-rise-mohammed-bin-salman.

Lacroix, Stéphhane (2011): *Awakening Islam*. London: Harvard University Press.

Lenkeit, Daniel (2013): *Saudi-Arabiens Petrochemie investiert in die Zukunft*. Germany Trade and Invest.

McKinsey Global Institute (2015): Saudi Arabia beyond Oil. The Investment and Productivity Transformation. McKinsey Global Institute. Available at: www.mckinsey.com/global-themes/employment-and-growth/moving-saudi-arabias-economy-beyond-oil.

MEED (2016): Saudi Arabia: Riyadh Willing to Make Unpopular Decisions. April 25. Available at: www.meed.com/sectors/government/saudi-arabia-riyadh-willing-to-make-unpopular-decisions/5001380.article.

Ministry of Finance (2015): *Recent Economic Developments and Highlights of Fiscal Years 1436/1437 (2015) & 1437/1438 (2016)*. Kingdom of Saudi Arabia: Ministry of Finance.

Nachmany, Michal et al. (2015): *Climate Change Legislation in Saudi Arabia*. The 2015 Global Climate Legislation Study, London School of Economics. Available at: www.lse.ac.uk/GranthamInstitute/wp-content/uploads/2015/05/SAUDI_ARABIA.pdf.

New York Times (2011): Saudi Troops Enter Bahrain to Help Put Down Unrest. March 14. Available at: www.nytimes.com/2011/03/15/world/middleeast/15bahrain.html?pagewanted=all&_r=0.

Niblock, Tim/Monica Malik (2007): *The Political Economy of Saudi Arabia*. London: Routledge.

Oil Price (2016): Why Saudi Arabia Has No Intention To End The Oil Glut. March 9. Available at: http://oilprice.com/Energy/Energy-General/Why-Saudi-Arabia-Has-No-Intention-To-End-The-Oil-Glut.html.

OPEC (2015): *Annual Statistical Bulletin*. Vienna: Organization of the Petroleum Exporting Countries.

Reuters (2015): Disagreements over Scope and Ownership Delay Saudi Solar Projects. September 8. Available at: www.reuters.com/article/saudi-solar-idUSL5N10Y0OU20150908.

Reuters (2017): Saudi Arabia, Russia Push to Extend Oil Output Cut until March 2018. May 15. Available at: www.reuters.com/article/us-opec-saudi-russia-idUSKCN18B06K.

Saudi Arabian Monetary Agency (2015a): *Appendix of Statistical Tables of the Forty-sixth Annual Report*. Riyadh: Saudi Arabian Monetary Agency.

Saudi Arabian Monetary Agency (2015b): *Fifty First Annual Report 1436H (2015)*. Ryadh: Saudi Arabian Monetary Agency.

Saudi Gazette (2016): Full text of Saudi Arabia's Vision 2030. April 26. Available at: http://saudigazette.com.sa/saudi-arabia/full-text-saudi-arabias-vision-2030/.

Sons, Sebastian (2013): Eine egalitäre Geschlechterordnung in Saudi-Arabien? Frauen als Akteure des Wandels. In Schröter, Susanne (Ed.): *Geschlechtergerechtigkeit durch Demokratisierung?* Bielefeld: Transcript.

Sons, Sebastian (2015): Der Junge schafft das nicht. *Zenith* (4), 34–35.

Sons, Sebastian (2016a): End of Generosity. *D+C* (3). Available at: www.dandc.eu/en/article/saudi-arabia-has-supported-egypts-economy-decades-those-days-now-seem-be-over.

Sons, Sebastian (2016b): König Salman und die Krisen. *Internationale Politik* (2), 76–82.

Sons, Sebastian/Inken Wiese (2015): The Engagement of Arab Gulf States in Egypt and Tunisia since 2011. Rationale and Impact. *DGAPanalyse* 9. Available at: https://dgap.org/en/article/getFullPDF/27232.

Soubrier, Emma (2014): *Regional Disorder and New Geo-economic Order: Saudi Security Strategies in a Reshaped Middle East*. Cambridge: Gulf Research Center.

Steinberg, Guido (2007): Saudi-arabische Religionspolitik nach 2001: Instrument zur Fortsetzung eines Zweckbündnisses. In Faath, Sigrid (Ed.): *Staatliche Religionspolitik in Nordafrika/Nahost: Ein Instrument für modernisierende Reformen?* Hamburg: German Institute of Global and Area Studies.

Steinberg, Guido (2010): Saudi-Arabien, die Schiiten und die saudische Regionalpolitik. In Faath, Sigrid (Ed.): *Rivalitäten und Konflikt zwischen Sunniten und Schiiten in Nahost*. Berlin: Deutsche Gesellschaft für Auswärtige Politik.

Steinberg, Guido (2011): The Wahhabiya and Shi'ism, from 1744/45 to 2008. In Litvak, Meir/Ofra Bengio (Ed.): *The Sunna and Shi'a in History: Division and Ecumenism in History*. New York: Palgrave Macmillan.

The National (2012): Syria Rebels "Buy Arms with Gulf and US Help". May 17. Available at: www.thenational.ae/news/world/middle-east/syria-rebels-buy-arms-with-gulf-and-us-help.

Thompson, Mark (2016): *Opening up the Decision-making Process in Saudi Arabia*. Gulf Affairs. Oxford: The Oxford Gulf and Arabian Peninsula Studies Forum.

UNDP (n.d.): *Eradicate Extreme Hunger and Poverty*. UN Development Program.

UNFCCC (2015): *The Intended Nationally Determined Contribution of the Kingdom of Saudi Arabia under the UNFCCC*. Riyadh: UNFCCC.

Vassiliev, Alexei (2000): *The History of Saudi Arabia*. London: New York University Press.

Wall Street Journal (2014): Why Saudis Decided Not to Prop Up Oil. December 21. Available at: www.wsj.com/articles/why-saudis-decided-not-to-prop-up-oil-1419219182.

Westphal, Kirsten/Marco Overhaus/Guido Steinberg (2014): *The US Shale Revolution and the Arab Gulf States: The Economic and Political Impact of Changing Energy Markets*. SWP Research Paper. Berlin: SWP. Available at: www.swp-berlin.org/file admin/contents/products/research_papers/2014_RP11_wep_ovs_sbg.pdf.

World Bank (2016): *Data: Population Growth (Annual %): Saudi Arabia*. Washington, DC: The World Bank.

WTO (2012): *The Kingdom of Saudi Arabia: Executive Summary*. World Trade Organization.

Yamani, Mai (2000): *Changed Identities: Challenge of the New Generation in Saudi Arabia*. London: The Royal Institute of International Affairs.

10 The Eastern Mediterranean

An energy region in the making

Charles Ellinas

Introduction

In recent years, the Eastern Mediterranean has experienced some major gas discoveries, with potentially more to come. At the same time, the region is also going through major geopolitical challenges. All of this is happening amid fundamental changes in global energy markets, including changes in the way oil and gas are produced and traded as a result of very low prices and the impact of renewables, dynamics which are anticipated to last over the long term.

The prospects for significant increases in oil prices, which would allow more expensive reserves to be produced, are being dashed by the combination of global oversupply and weak demand, coupled with climate change mitigation. The advent of new technology, shale oil/gas and renewables, also means that the world is entering an era of "plenty". This will entail long-term structural changes in the oil and gas industry, as prices are likely to remain low for a long time to come.

The form of energy most relevant for developments around the Eastern Mediterranean is natural gas, which will be the focus of this chapter. The major gas discoveries shaping views about the Eastern Mediterranean are summarized in Table 10.1 and Figure 10.1.

The discovery of substantial natural gas fields in the Eastern Mediterranean starting in 2009 raised huge expectations in the region and to some extent in the EU. The emergence of the Eastern Mediterranean as a gas-rich region is a new development in international energy. In terms of developing, marketing, and

Table 10.1 Major natural gas discoveries in the Eastern Mediterranean

Gas field	*Probable reserves (bcm)*	*Discovery date*	*Status*
Tamar – Israel	280	2009	Producing
Leviathan – Israel	620	2010	Pursuing gas sales
Aphrodite – Cyprus	127	2011	Pursuing gas sales
Zohr – Egypt	845	2015	Being developed

Source: Authors' compilation.

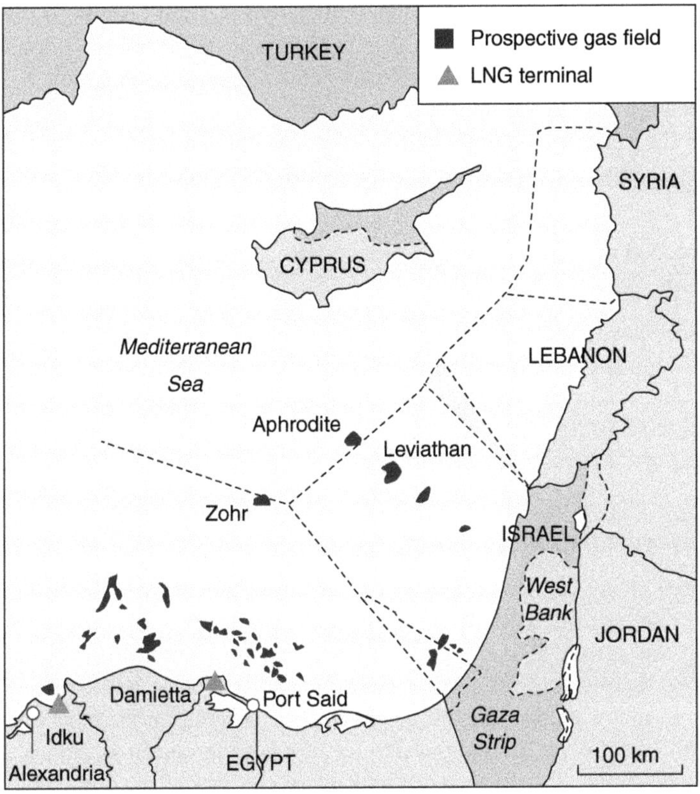

Figure 10.1 Major natural gas discoveries in the Eastern Mediterranean.
Source: Based on *The Economist* (2015).

exporting the gas, key options under consideration include regional markets, pipeline exports, and LNG, all of which contribute to the formation of a "region".

However, the region is volatile and experience shows that regional geopolitics and instabilities undergo frequent upheavals. In addition, the economics and geopolitics of gas and energy are transforming the wider region. The commercial development of Eastern Mediterranean gas can attract the necessary investments from companies and banks only if profitable markets are secured and risks are satisfactorily addressed and managed.

Contrary to local perceptions in the Eastern Mediterranean, political will alone will not make projects happen. Over the medium term, the development of the Egyptian gas field Zohr will have the biggest influence on the gas situation in the Eastern Mediterranean. Looking forward, the discovery of more gas and the development of the Leviathan field could add to this complex picture. Resource development in Cyprus will be dominated by and revolve around potential progress on and solution to the long-standing division of the island. The development of the Aphrodite field, future resource development, and exports in the wider Eastern Mediterranean region depend on this, and while recent efforts have increased expectations of progress, the outcome still remains to be seen.

This chapter will discuss the impact of gas discoveries in the Eastern Mediterranean upon the countries of the region, and assess options for development and export of these resources and the implications for the region's future.

Changes in global energy and impact upon the Eastern Mediterranean

This section examines fundamental developments in energy that shaped a global era of "plenty", and the impact of this new era upon global and European gas and LNG markets. Following an assessment of what these developments mean for Europe and the Eastern Mediterranean, this section draws consequences for the development of Eastern Mediterranean gas.

The global framework: an era of "plenty"

The current era of plenty was enabled by a number of fundamental developments since the 2008/2009 price downturn. These encompass breakthroughs in technology, including the advent of hydraulic fracturing and horizontal drilling, and improvements in supply-side efficiency. However, while these developments have yielded vast new supplies, the era of plenty they ushered in has made the commercial viability of expensive-to-develop Eastern Mediterranean gas fields a challenge. It is becoming increasingly difficult to secure gas sales contracts in the current environment and, even when possible, the prices are generally low, increasing the risk that some of these resources could become stranded.

However, before concentrating on gas, it is important to consider oil prices, as LNG/gas prices are often linked to the price of oil in long-term sales contracts. The period 2014 to 2016 was difficult for the oil industry. In 2016, the industry experienced further cost cutting, restructuring, refinancing where possible, and in some cases bankruptcy when it was not, making it a tough year for companies with weak balance sheets and focused exclusively on production. This situation is unlikely to end soon, as no sudden changes are expected in the oil price, even after the September 2016 OPEC agreement to curb production.[1] While producers will not continue to produce and invest in oil at a loss, as excess supplies dry up, prices are likely to stabilize and inch upward. However, recent developments like the lifting of the US oil crude oil export ban and the recovery of Iranian oil production following the lifting of sanctions will keep any price recovery low, while the US shale industry will act as a cap on any price rally.

The shale revolution and accompanying new technologies have transformed oil market dynamics. Not only did US shale trigger the oil price collapse, it also distinguishes the current situation and future recovery from previous market cycles. Shale is also shaping the course of the recovery, and will eventually define the features of the new energy landscape that emerges. In short, US shale has entirely changed the balance of power in the global oil market, along with gas markets (as a result of US LNG exports), and there is little OPEC can do about it.

Renewables are also profiting from technological improvements and falling costs. Renewables are and will continue to be the fastest-growing form of energy, expected to contribute 18 percent of the increment in energy production to 2035.[2] Investment in renewables and market penetration are also increasing. Renewables were further given a boost by the Paris Climate Agreement, which entered into force in November 2016 after being agreed upon at the 2015 COP 21 meeting.

These changes are occurring as the growth of global energy demand and consumption is decelerating due to increasing efficiency, China's move away from heavy industry, and declining European natural gas demand. With respect to demand, natural gas is under particular pressure. Due to slow growth in the European economy, cheap coal (about half the price of gas), and the subsidization of renewables, the International Energy Agency predicts a difficult environment for natural gas in its 2016 Medium-term Gas Market Report.[3] There is no prospect of these factors being reversed anytime soon, nor does there appear to be a prospect of realistic carbon pricing.

Global natural gas and LNG markets

The state of global and European natural gas and LNG markets is of relevance to the potential development and export of Eastern Mediterranean gas.[4] The current global gas situation, characterized by oversupply and relatively low gas prices, presents a challenge for the development of Eastern Mediterranean resources.[5]

Due to the glut of LNG supply entering the market and slow increases in demand, the global LNG market is going through difficult times, a situation reflected by low prices. Beginning in 2014, global LNG supplies outstripped demand, a situation that is anticipated to persist well into the next decade thanks in part to sluggish demand growth.[6] The next six years will likely see relatively low gas prices across the globe, with huge quantities of LNG coming into what is already an oversupplied market. While LNG demand growth will continue to outpace gas demand growth, it is not strong enough to absorb the glut of LNG coming into the market, and will not be until well into the 2020s.[7] All of this makes life for the LNG industry difficult. While global LNG trade[8] reached 335 bcm per year in 2015, this only accounts for around 10 percent of global gas trade.[9] Based on committed projects, global liquefaction capacity is set to grow by over 175 bcm per year by 2020 in comparison to 2015, with more increases expected thereafter.[10]

LNG projects are capital intensive, and usually require long-term sales contracts, often oil-indexed, to be secured before FIDs can be taken. However, changes in market conditions and the LNG glut are making the sanctioning of new LNG projects difficult, as oil-indexation is losing ground amid a shift to gas-on-gas pricing and spot-LNG trading.[11] The tension in the market between increasingly expensive projects and more price-sensitive buyers is apparent, creating a conflict for sellers. This has led to a major growth in spot- and short-term LNG trading, which accounted for 29 percent of global LNG trade and over 60 percent of gas trading in Europe in 2015. This is expected to further increase in the future[12] as long-term contracts are renegotiated on more buyer-friendly terms in the low price environment, but this is not guaranteed.

Provided that no new LNG projects are built, the future of LNG in the longer term (i.e., after the mid-2020s) is expected to be brighter, as demand is eventually expected to outstrip supply.[13]

In the meantime, the LNG industry is facing a bleak period due to the aforementioned oversupply and slack demand. As a result, project developers will be less willing to commit to capital-intensive liquefaction projects, and it will be increasingly difficult to convince financial institutions to loan large sums of money to projects to increase capacity. In this environment, smaller and more flexible LNG options are increasingly attractive, as evidenced by a rise in floating LNG (FLNG) capacity. At the end of 2015, four FLNG projects were under construction totaling 12 bcm per year capacity, and 24 more are proposed totaling 235 bcm per year capacity.[14]

While Europe is the world's largest natural gas importer, Europe imported just over 50 bcm of LNG in 2015, satisfying 12 percent of EU gas demand.[15] Although the European Commission put in place a LNG strategy in 2016 to improve access for all member states to LNG, pricing remains a problem. In the EU, piped gas is cheaper than LNG imports,[16] limiting LNG market penetration, and Gazprom is well positioned to counter competition from LNG thanks to low production costs and export overcapacity.[17] Most LNG providers, even US-based Cheniere LNG, which has a low cost base, are finding it difficult to make inroads into the EU gas trading hubs. As a result, LNG may provide more of a strategic and supportive role in cases of spikes in demand.

Furthermore, while many LNG providers anticipated high costs in European markets, this dynamic is slowly changing. When many of the projects currently coming online were sanctioned, gas prices in Japan exceeded $16/MMBtu, while in Europe prices were above $13/MMBtu. However, in 2016 spot prices in Europe dropped as low as $4/MMBtu. This drop in prices has profound implications for both the global and the European gas trade, as well as for plans to develop and export gas from the Eastern Mediterranean.[18] These factors may eventually mean that gas fields sitting at the high end of the cost curve, and dependent on exports to Europe, may remain stranded.[19]

The impact upon Eastern Mediterranean gas: in search of a market

Eastern Mediterranean gas is comparatively expensive to develop, due to water depths of about 1500 to 2000 m, reservoir depths of over 4000 m below seabed level, and a lack of infrastructure in the region. The gas cost base of Eastern

Mediterranean fields is about $4 to $5 per MMBtu, making it difficult for Eastern Mediterranean LNG to enter the European market even when setting aside additional costs and challenges related to pipeline transport, liquefaction, transportation, and regasification. Thus, while Israel and Cyprus made gas exports to Egypt for liquefaction and onward export to Europe central to the development of Leviathan and Aphrodite, the cost of producing and transporting the gas to Egypt via pipeline, liquefying it, transporting to Europe, and re-gasification makes this option commercially challenging. In addition, Eastern Mediterranean gas is also challenged by the arrival of US LNG as well as meeting its tough time schedules and low gas cost base. Moreover, as Asian LNG markets become saturated, more LNG is being diverted to Europe and competing with piped gas, putting downward pressure on prices.

The options for pipeline exports are also bleak in light of the factors described above: competition of lower cost Russian gas, limited market shares due to flattening demand, and geopolitical obstacles in the Eastern Mediterranean. These conditions create a context where the emphasis is on production projects with quick paybacks, such as Zohr, while limiting exploration and longer term developments. In other words, gas producers in captive domestic markets, such as Egypt and Israel, will fare better as prices are less dependent on global factors. Turkey is also completely reliant on gas imports, and is thus also a viable export market for Eastern Mediterranean gas.[20] However, to take advantage of this opportunity, the issue of the long-standing division of Cyprus must be resolved.

If regional politics thwart pipeline options, FLNG could potentially unlock Eastern Mediterranean gas exports, and should be seriously considered by Israel and Cyprus, along with FCNG.[21] Looking ahead ten years, LNG may become a viable export option if additional gas is discovered in the Eastern Mediterranean.

Geopolitics of energy in the Eastern Mediterranean

This section analyzes recent geopolitical developments in the Eastern Mediterranean and the Middle East, and discusses their impact upon energy,[22] the countries of the Eastern Mediterranean, and future prospects for developing and exporting the gas.

Current regional dynamics and future prospects

The Eastern Mediterranean region is fraught with risk, meaning that energy solutions which seem justifiable today may no longer be appropriate tomorrow.[23] The key problem is instability. However, the economics and geopolitics of gas and energy are transforming the wider region, providing opportunities for economic development that should be implemented and managed in the context of wider regional cooperation.

Moreover, the situation in the Eastern Mediterranean is very volatile, resulting in constantly changing prospects for energy cooperation.[24] Quite recently, and to a certain extent currently, a pipeline link between Israel and Cyprus to

Egypt was considered high priority, partly driven by the USA's efforts to strengthen cooperation in the region. However, this possibility now faces real commercial challenges. Other shifting geopolitical situations include the ups and downs of the Cyprus peace process, and glimmers of hope for a resolution, while Israel and Turkey recently repaired their relationship following an estrangement dating back to the 2010 Mavi Mara incident.

While gas pipelines to Turkey or Egypt may appear to be positive options, they must be considered in light of these constantly shifting dynamics and in the context of the fate of projects like the Egypt–Israel gas pipeline. In order to minimize risks, multiple export routes may need to be considered, while it should be remembered that pipelines require the active support of governments. On this front, *rapprochement* between Israel and Turkey, Turkey and Russia, Israel and Egypt, and possibly Egypt and Turkey, may shape regional politics for the better, while a resolution to the Cyprus problem would be a major contributor to regional stability. Indeed, when it comes to energy, it is possible that key players are realizing that cooperation is better than confrontation.

Developing natural gas fields and export projects may also transform the Eastern Mediterranean into a more integrated region. Over the next decade, gas trading is expected to evolve and increasingly take place in markets and trading places ("hubs"), and the Eastern Mediterranean is a good candidate for such a hub. A hub could foster cooperation and minimize conflict by establishing a platform for common commercial and energy interests.

However, there is neither a market mechanism to buy or sell gas in an efficient manner, nor a pricing mechanism to determine spot prices in the Eastern Mediterranean at this point, and gas sales remain based on traditional long-term, oil-indexed bilateral agreements. Of the countries in the Eastern Mediterranean region, only Cyprus and Egypt could be candidates for the establishment of a gas trading hub and, even so, major market reforms would be required to achieve this.

A glimpse at national developments in the Eastern Mediterranean

Israel

Israel's views on the Eastern Mediterranean are evolving. Gas has changed Israel's foreign policy perceptions, and the country is now looking outward to the future. Within Israel, a new and important Eastern Mediterranean policy is evolving, both in terms of political alignments and security, driven by energy considerations.

Alignment with Cyprus and Greece is important to Israel, particularly when it comes to security and support within the EU. However, alignments are not necessarily alliances, and Israel does not see this alignment as a substitute to Turkey. Thus, relations with Cyprus/Greece, including in the energy sector, will not be developed at the expense of relations with Turkey, but rather in parallel. In addition to politics, Israeli cooperation with Turkey is also driven by commerce and gas, which may have played a role in the recent *rapprochement* and restoration of diplomatic relations, also driven in large part by Turkey's increasing isolation and security challenges. Future cooperation between Israel and Turkey can only be good for the region and potentially for energy flows. Egypt and Jordan are also politically important for Israel and the wider region, but they are economically weak. In particular, the benefits of political stability in Egypt are enormous, a situation Israel appears determined to support.

Egypt

Egypt is experiencing a rapid energy transformation, and is expected to go from being a LNG importer to a net exporter by 2021/2022. This change is driven by three key factors. First, President Al-Sisi has made energy self-sufficiency a cornerstone of his presidency. Second, the Egyptian domestic energy market is hungry for gas and ready to absorb whatever its gas fields can produce – and, as a result, sellers do not have to go far to find a customer. Third, gas prices recently negotiated between the government and the gas companies are high, with assured high profits, encouraging investment and field development.

Based on the new discoveries and developments in progress, Egypt may more than double current gas production by 2019/2020, bringing online another 50 to 60 bcm of gas.[25] Egypt is well placed to continue expansion of its gas production well into the next decade, and while challenges related to the security and fiscal environment (and ability to pay its debts) remain, improvements would enable huge growth potential in oil and gas development. In a dramatic reversal of fortunes, these increases should not only help Egypt achieve self-sufficiency and do away with expensive LNG imports, but excess gas should also be available for export. However, this would also dampen the hopes of Israel and Cyprus to export gas to Egypt, as in addition to commercial challenges the markets for it would no longer be available.

Turkey

For Turkey, the Eastern Mediterranean region is an unstable neighborhood of unresolved disputes, including the unresolved dispute with Cyprus[26] and complicated relations with Israel. Turkey's gas demand is around 50 bcm per year, 55 percent of which is provided by Russia, with whom it also has a complicated relationship. However, the recent *rapprochement* between the two countries and perceptions that Russia is a reliable partner have enabled renewed cooperation, including on the Turkish Stream project.

While Turkey's future demand growth rates may be slowing from more recent rates of 4 to 5 percent, the country is investigating different energy scenarios to meet demand that go beyond just diversification of gas supply. Even though low oil prices have taken some of the pressure off,[27] Turkey is limiting its gas dependency by increasing use of coal, indigenous lignite, hydro, and renewables. If successful, the pressure to secure alternative gas supplies may be lessened. Turkey also wants to limit gas supply dependence on any one country to less than 50 percent,[28] and is investigating LNG import options, for example, from Qatar and the USA, and new pipelines, such as Kurdistan, Eastern Mediterranean, Iran, etc.

Turkey realizes that achieving its energy goals requires cooperation with its neighbors and potential partners, and playing an active role in promoting stability in its neighborhood. To achieve this, Turkey has engaged in and supported talks with Israel and Egypt, and between Greek and Turkish Cypriots. However, this is only the beginning, as Turkey's decision-making model is being revised.[29] Depending on how this develops and with no threats to existing Russian gas supplies, its need for Eastern Mediterranean gas may no longer be a high priority.

Cyprus

Future energy developments in Cyprus will depend on the progress in resolving the Cyprus issue, regarding which there are hopeful signs. However, given the centrality of the island's division to energy developments, both the possibility of achieving a resolution and failing to do so should be considered.[30] *In the absence of a solution to the Cyprus issue, prospects of natural gas production are low.* This outcome would prevent export to Turkey, and as the Egyptian domestic market is increasingly met with domestic production, FCNG or FLNG would likely be the only other options left for Cyprus, neither of which has been seriously considered thus far. Thus, 2016 may see the development of Aphrodite going back on the planning table, pushing the prospects for gas exports well into the 2020s. New substantial discoveries could revive the LNG export option.

However, even *with a solution*, a number of challenges remain. First, Cyprus would need to set up a federal political system, including a governance solution for hydrocarbons. Given that no preparation has been made for hydrocarbons, considerable effort and time may be required to develop a workable system. Meanwhile, Israel and Turkey could proceed more seriously with subsea pipeline gas export negotiations given that a deal with Cyprus may be possible.[31] Even if gas exports to Turkey become possible, Turkey's demand for gas from the region is finite. With more discoveries expected, Israel and Cyprus will still need to find other, and most likely international, markets to sell their gas.[32] Moreover, while many hope that new drilling in 2017 will lead to new discoveries and create new opportunities, much depends on global gas prices.

A new player in the Eastern Mediterranean: Russia

Russia's regional involvement has changed the Eastern Mediterranean's regional reality. Russia's involvement and influence in Syria, along with potential interest in securing a foothold in Eastern Mediterranean hydrocarbon production, has the potential to influence regional politics as well as energy production, with implications for each country in the region.

Russian action in Syria is of particular relevance to Turkey, whose geographic position makes it a strong option for transporting gas supplies from the Middle East, Russia, and Asia to Europe. Indeed, Turkey aspires to be a regional gas hub, a goal reflected in the Turkish Stream and the desire to access Eastern Mediterranean (particularly Israeli) gas.[33]

Russian interest in Eastern Mediterranean hydrocarbons may be wider than just Syria. Russia has expressed interest in participating in future gas development projects in Cyprus, and, in another twist to an already complex plot, there are rumors of potential Russian involvement in the development of Israel's Leviathan field,[34] rumors that were reinforced by high-level Israel–Russia contacts in 2016. While controversial, the article states that it could enhance Israel's security and strengthen its broader geopolitical position. Interestingly, the Israeli Energy Minister recently invited Russian oil and gas companies to participate in offshore exploration in Israel's EEZ. However, at a time when the USA and the EU seek to lessen Gazprom's influence on European gas, Israel can expect intense pressure from the Americans not to work with Gazprom. However, if Israel's options to export Leviathan gas to Turkey do not materialize, engagement with Gazprom may still receive domestic support.

Conclusions

Gas discoveries in the Eastern Mediterranean have major consequences for the region, even if these are often overstated. However, low gas prices globally are challenging their development and calling their commercial viability and export options into question. While looking to regional markets may seem to be a feasible option, there are challenges to be faced here as well. Egypt is fast becoming self-sufficient and may resume LNG exports by 2021/2022, while access to the Turkish gas market will be easier if the Cyprus problem is settled.

In an age of plenty, there are no easy markets for Eastern Mediterranean gas. While Israel and Cyprus made gas exports to Egypt for liquefaction and onward export to Europe central to the development of Leviathan and Aphrodite, the cost of producing and taking the gas to Egypt by pipeline, liquefying it, transporting to Europe, and re-gasifying it makes this option commercially challenging. In addition, Eastern Mediterranean LNG will have to compete with US LNG, which has a much lower cost base and is already available in Europe.

Moreover, future energy developments in Cyprus will depend on settlement of the Cyprus problem, which would open up the export of Cypriot and Israeli gas to Turkey. Without a solution, FLNG and FCNG may need to be considered, with prospects for exports being pushed back well into the 2020s. Meanwhile, Egypt is undergoing an energy transformation, bringing with it a dramatic reversal of fortunes for Egypt from gas shortages to self-sufficiency and exports.

These energy changes and challenges occur against the backdrop of a volatile region, illustrating that regional politics and upheavals can have implications for energy developments. However, as often happens, this sense of crisis can and should generate an opportunity for retooling regional strategies and prioritizing energy cooperation. However, political will, while necessary, is not sufficient to make energy projects happen. Indeed, the commercial development of Eastern Mediterranean gas can only attract the necessary investments if risks are satisfactorily addressed and managed. In the end, when it comes to gas sales commercial realities prevail, not politics.

Ultimately, Eastern Mediterranean gas dynamics are changing rapidly, and the era of plenty, along with peaking global energy demand, means that low prices are here to stay. In accounting for this new reality, the Eastern Mediterranean region needs to plan with realism and pragmatism if it is to succeed in developing its gas profitably.

Notes

1 Bloomberg, 2016.
2 BP, 2015.
3 IEA, 2016; InCyprus, 2016f; BP, 2015; InCyprus, 2016d.
4 InCyprus, 2016g.
5 IEA, 2016; InCyprus, 2016l, 2016h.
6 InCyprus, 2016g.
7 InCyprus, 2016j; IEA, 2016.
8 IGU, 2016.
9 Ibid.; InCyprus, 2016g.
10 IGU, 2016.
11 IEA, 2016.
12 IGU, 2016.
13 InCyprus, 2016g.
14 IGU, 2016.
15 Ibid.
16 InCyprus, 2016d.
17 InCyprus, 2016g.
18 Ibid.
19 InCyprus, 2016f.
20 Natural Gas World, 2016.
21 InCyprus, 2016c.
22 InCyprus, 2016e.
23 InCyprus, 2016a.
24 InCyprus, 2016e.
25 InCyprus, 2016b.
26 Natural Gas World, 2016.
27 Ibid.
28 Ibid.
29 Ibid.; Ellinas, 2016.
30 InCyprus, 2016e.
31 InCyprus, 2016i; Ellinas, 2015.
32 InCyprus, 2016c.
33 InCyprus, 2016k.
34 Reuters, 2016.

Bibliography

Bloomberg (2016): OPEC Agrees to First Oil Output Cut in Eight Years. September 28. Available at: www.bloomberg.com/news/articles/2016-09-28/opec-said-to-agree-on-first-oil-output-cut-in-eight-years.

BP (2015): *Energy Outlook 2035*. BP.

Ellinas, Charles (2015): Turkey–Israel–Cyprus: Could This Be the Next Gas Triangle? Charles Ellinas, SigmaLive, December 23. Available at: www.sigmalive.com/en/blog/charles.ellinas/2015/12/993/turkeyisraelcyprus-could-this-be-the-next-gas-triangle.

Ellinas, Charles (2016): *Global Oil and Gas Market and Prices and their Impact on the Development of Med Projects*. Rome: IRN.

IEA (2016): *IEA Medium Term Gas Market Report 2016*. International Energy Agency.

IGU (2016): *World Gas LNG Report – 2016 Edition*. Fornebu: International Gas Union.

InCyprus (2016a): *East Med Gas Export Risk*. January 6. Available at: www.iene.eu/east-med-gas-export-risks-p2362.html.

InCyprus (2016b): Egypt Gas Impact: Cyprus and Israel. February 5. Available at: http://in-cyprus.com/egypt-gas-impact-cyprus-and-israel/.

InCyprus (2016c): FLNG for the East Med. September 17. Available at: http://in-cyprus.com/flng-for-the-east-med/.

InCyprus (2016d): Gas Competitiveness in Europe. August 14. Available at: http://in-cyprus.com/gas-competitiveness-in-europe/.

InCyprus (2016e): Gas Dynamics and Prospects in East Med. February 16. Available at: http://in-cyprus.com/gas-dynamics-and-prospects-in-the-east-med/.

InCyprus (2016f): Global Gas Demand Growth Down. June 18. Available at: www.ecoiko.eu/global-gas-demand-growth-down/.

InCyprus (2016g): Global LNG Market and Europe. March 13. Available at: http://tekmormonitor.blogspot.de/2016/03/global-lng-market-and-europe-in-cyprus.html.

InCyprus (2016h): Impact of World Energy Investment Cuts on Gas. October 1. Available at: http://in-cyprus.com/impact-of-world-energy-investment-cuts-on-gas/.

InCyprus (2016i): Israel–Turkey *Rapprochement*. February 28. Available at: http://tekmormonitor.blogspot.de/2016/02/israel-turkey-rapprochement-in-cyprus.html.

InCyprus (2016j): Low Energy Prices Here to Stay. August 28. Available at: http://in-cyprus.com/low-energy-prices-here-to-stay/.

InCyprus (2016k): Russian Interest in East Med and Cyprus Gas. March 20. Available at: http://tekmormonitor.blogspot.de/2016/03/russian-interest-in-east-med-and-cyprus.html.

InCyprus (2016l): Unsettling Outlook for Gas. September 25. Available at: http://in-cyprus.com/unsettling-outlook-for-gas/.

Natural Gas World (2016): Turkey Changes Tack for the 2020s: Energy Specialist. February 24. Available at: www.naturalgasworld.com/interview-turkeys-energy-strategy-towards-2020s-28302.

Reuters (2016): Why Russia May Be a Smart Business Partner for Israel. February 23. Available at: http://af.reuters.com/article/commoditiesNews/idAFL2N1622F0.

The Economist (2015): ENI in Egypt: Euregas! The Italian Energy Giant's Strategy Seems to Be Paying Off. September 5. Available at: www.economist.com/news/business/21663249-italian-energy-giants-strategy-seems-be-paying-euregas.

11 Cyprus

Energy hopes and political troubles

Harry Tzimitras and Ayla Gürel Moran

Introduction

Until recently, the island of Cyprus had nothing to do with the hydrocarbons industry, except as an importer of petroleum products. This changed in 2011 with the discovery of the Aphrodite field in the island's southern offshore. The Aphrodite reservoir is geographically close to Israel's Tamar and Leviathan fields, and together they have an estimated capacity of about 990 billion cubic meters (bcm). This is a fairly modest amount in global terms but represents a huge opportunity for the region. If developed wisely and optimally, these resources could transform the energy landscape in the Eastern Mediterranean and even redefine regional political relations.

Moreover, the finds at Aphrodite as well as at Tamar and Leviathan seem to support the US Geological Survey's (USGS) assessment of the Levant Basin's resource potential. According to a March 2010 USGS report, the Levant Basin, which overlaps offshore areas of Cyprus, Israel, Lebanon, and Syria, holds an estimated average of 3453 bcm of recoverable gas and 1.7 billion barrels of oil.[1]

Given this assessment, it is reasonable to assume that additional gas and even oil could be discovered in the offshore areas of Cyprus. This explains the interest shown by numerous large international oil and gas companies in the last two tenders for offshore exploration licenses held by the Republic of Cyprus in 2012 and 2016. While the first round in 2007 attracted just three bidders for the 11 blocks on offer, there were 15 bids for the 12 blocks up for lease in 2012, including from big energy firms such as Total, Eni, Kogas, Woodside, Gazprombank, and Petronas of Malaysia.[2] In the third round only three blocks were available and submissions were made for all of them, and a number of major oil and gas companies, including Eni, Total, ExxonMobil, and Statoil, were involved.[3] In December 2016 the Government of Cyprus awarded blocks 6, 8, and 10 to the consortium Eni-Total, Eni, and the consortium ExxonMobil-Qatar Petroleum, respectively. A major reason for the high interest in 2016, despite challenging market conditions, was the discovery in August 2015 of the field in Egypt's offshore, the largest-ever Mediterranean gas find estimated at 850 bcm and located only 6 km away from the Egypt–Cyprus maritime border.[4] Given these dynamics, the island clearly appears set to become an important part of the unfolding story of natural gas in the Eastern Mediterranean.

The Republic of Cyprus is determined to pursue its goal of becoming a significant gas producer and exporter. However, there are several challenges to achieving this goal, as demonstrated by the complete lack of progress in developing the Aphrodite field almost five years after its discovery, with no definite production and export plans or sales agreements in place by the second half of 2016. These challenges include technical issues, as the fields are located many miles offshore, in ultra-deep waters, and many hundreds of meters below the seabed,[5] but more important considerations include commercial uncertainties caused by the drop in gas prices globally and, last but not least, the risks associated with the political situation in and around Cyprus. The latter is particularly important, as the more advantageous solution for the development and export of current and potential future resources requires regional cooperation, both in terms of infrastructure and markets, which in turn requires less conflict and more political stability.

Politically, there are several causes for concern, including an unresolved maritime boundary dispute (involving mainly Cyprus and Turkey, but also Greece and Egypt to an extent[6]), as well as the unresolved division of the island itself and its two communities, the internationally recognized Republic of Cyprus and the Turkish Republic of Northern Cyprus, recognized only by Turkey, referred to more generally as the Cyprus problem. The absence of a political settlement in Cyprus severely limits the possibilities for monetizating the island's offshore energy resources. Therefore, the development of offshore natural gas resources could be an incentive for each side to make the necessary compromises for a settlement. Since the Aphrodite discovery there has been much talk both within and outside the island about the potential for natural gas to be a catalyst in solving the age-old Cyprus problem.

However, subsequent developments have not necessarily supported the idea that resources could help catalyze compromise. Due to the sides' diametrically opposed views on the current political status quo on the island and the related issue of "sovereignty", offshore hydrocarbons became the subject matter of a new dispute with a serious potential to wreck the ongoing negotiations. The crisis of October 2014 to May 2015, during which talks broke down, demonstrated the degree to which hydrocarbons became a source of tension rather than a catalyst for compromise.[7] One potential snag in the catalyst theory is that, in linking gas with the Cyprus problem, each side perceives that the other side's need associated with gas is greater than its own, and hence presumes that the other side has a greater desire to solve the Cyprus problem, i.e., to compromise at the negotiating table.[8]

The sovereignty issue and offshore energy resources

The aforementioned disruption in the negotiation process between October 2014 and May 2015 was the latest episode of the ongoing dispute over the right to natural resources within Cyprus's offshore involving the Greek Cypriots, the Turkish Cypriots, and Turkey. This controversy had been brewing since at least the mid-2000s, but it attracted little attention until the first real escalation of tensions in the run-up to the Republic of Cyprus' initial exploratory drilling at the Aphrodite field in September 2011.[9] While tensions subsided within a few months without disrupting talks, the issue was left festering until a full-blown crisis erupted three years later, when the Republic of Cyprus permitted exploratory drilling by Eni in September 2014. Fortunately there was no military confrontation, but the crisis raised the stakes and firmly underscored the role of parties' positions on offshore drilling in the diplomatic battle over "sovereignty".

When Eni began drilling, the Turkish Cypriot side protested and warned of reciprocal action (in cooperation with Turkey). Turkey issued a navigational warning (NAVTEX), designating areas in the island's southern offshore for seismic surveys to be carried out by the Turkish state-owned petroleum company (TPAO) in accordance with licenses granted by the TRNC in 2011.[10] The Greek Cypriot side reacted by suspending participation in the broader negotiations.[11] The crisis abated only after Eni, having found no "exploitable hydrocarbons", removed its drillship from the area, and Turkey's second NAVTEX simultaneously expired and TPAO's survey vessel left Cyprus' waters.[12]

Turkey's position

Turkey has thus far made a point of using its navy to monitor the Republic of Cyprus' exploration activities without intervening. For instance, this has been the case with Noble's first drilling in Aphrodite in 2011, and again with Eni's drillings during September 2014 and March 2015. As part of its support for the Turkish Cypriots, Turkey has also been, in its own words, providing the "necessary assistance for the completion of seismic researches and proceeding with drilling [...] within the license areas granted to [...] TPAO by the TRNC in the south of the Island".[13]

In addition to and separate from its support of the Turkish Cypriots' rights and interests, Turkey has another complaint regarding the RoC's offshore prospecting activities. Turkey's continental shelf claims in the Eastern Mediterranean overlap with almost all of the EEZ areas proclaimed by the Republic of Cyprus in the island's west, i.e., overlapping with several Republic of Cyprus exploration blocks. Turkey has repeatedly stated that it "will not allow any activity" in these areas.[14] Due to the Cyprus problem, resolution of these overlapping claims is virtually impossible. So long as the Greek Cypriot-run government is not recognized by Turkey as the legitimate Republic of Cyprus government, it is difficult to see the claimants coming together to negotiate a compromise or resorting to an international adjudicative mechanism or tribunal.

Positions of the two Cypriot sides[15]

The Government of the Republic of Cyprus maintains that it alone has the sovereign right to explore and exploit the natural resources in its EEZ, and that the exercise of this right is "inalienable", "non-negotiable", and not conditional on a settlement. As such, from the Greek Cypriot perspective it is not a bi-communal matter for discussion at, or alongside, the settlement negotiations. The Greek Cypriot side accepts – as does the international community – that the island's offshore energy resources belong to both communities and that their management will be a federal competence under a settlement that will reunite Cyprus. Yet, pending reunification, the government's position is that the Republic will not suspend exercising its sovereign rights because of these negotiations, and revenues from offshore resources will be shared with the Turkish Cypriots only within the framework of a united Cyprus.

The Turkish Cypriots (and Turkey) contend that the Greek Cypriots alone cannot legitimately represent the RoC, as this is contrary to the Cyprus Constitution and to relevant international treaties. In their view, no single constitutionally competent authority to represent Cyprus as a whole (i.e., Greek Cypriots and Turkish Cypriots together) has existed since 1963. Consequently, Turkish Cypriots object to any Greek Cypriot action related to the EEZ and offshore energy resources, as this involves the exercise of sovereign rights – rights that Turkish Cypriots maintain are possessed jointly by the two communities by virtue of their position as equal co-founders of the Republic. According to this view, any action by Greek Cypriots in this regard is seen as unilateral, and any Greek Cypriot action of this kind in the absence of a settlement ignores the legitimate rights and interests of the Turkish Cypriots, and creates *faits accomplis* prejudicing the terms of a prospective settlement with regard to sovereignty to the disadvantage of the Turkish Cypriots.

With the Republic of Cyprus determined to proceed with its offshore exploration activities, the Turkish Cypriots and Turkey have moved to restore the political balance, as they see it. Since September 2011 they have adopted a policy of responding to the Republic of Cyprus' actions by "reciprocal steps of equal significance". Such steps have included the signing of the TRNC–Turkey Continental Shelf Delimitation Agreement; TRNC's awarding of licences to TPAO for seven offshore blocks, two of which overlap with approximately 40 percent of the RoC exploration area to the island's southeast; and, with the help of Turkey, launching seismic research operations in these blocks whenever the RoC authorizes drilling. The purpose of these "reciprocal steps" is to register the Turkish Cypriots' claim to their equal share with the Greek Cypriots in sovereign rights regarding offshore exploration and exploitation, the lack of a negotiated settlement notwithstanding.

These attitudes clearly indicate that the dispute over the right to offshore resources is actually linked to the fundamental disagreement between the two sides regarding sovereignty in divided Cyprus, along with the related question of how "a new state of affairs would come into being" with a settlement.

The two sides' approaches to sovereignty, which have remained consistent over the years, were once summarized in a 2003 UN report on Cyprus as follows. In the Greek Cypriot view, a new state of affairs in Cyprus will come about through the writing of a new constitution that transforms the existing, internationally recognized RoC into a bi-communal, bi-zonal federation, essentially reintegrating the Turkish Cypriot community into that state. The Turkish Cypriot understanding, on the other hand, is that a new state of affairs in Cyprus will be established through the founding of a new state based on partnership between the two sovereign states/administrations/separate polities that currently exist on the island. These entities would devolve some of their sovereignty to the new state, but would otherwise retain sovereignty in their hands.

The arguments employed by each side to defend their entrenched positions are essentially the same arguments that inform their stances vis-à-vis the hydrocarbons issue. This is the reason that past Turkish Cypriot proposals – calling for cooperation between the two sides on hydrocarbons, pending a Cyprus settlement – were seen by the Greek Cypriot side as aimed at boosting the Turkish Cypriots' status and strengthening their negotiating position. This is perceived by the Greek Cypriots as an attempt to challenge "the sovereignty of the existing RoC" and to put "on an equal par the unrecognized TRNC with the legitimate state, the RoC, which is internationally recognized".

Conversely, the Greek Cypriots' determination to continue unilaterally with offshore exploration is perceived by the Turkish Cypriot side as connected with the RoC government's quest for further confirmation that the present sovereign independent state status is unproblematic (as the EU, which allowed the RoC to join in 2004, seems to believe), and their position that the existing RoC should essentially be preserved under any settlement.

Given the connection between attitudes about hydrocarbons and broader positions on sovereignty, contrary to expectations that natural gas would help bring about a settlement, the issue has thus far served to increase tensions and undermine mutual confidence, resulting in a hardening of stances.

It is also clear that a settlement of the broader Cyprus issue would significantly improve the political and economic environment for oil and gas development, making it more attractive to investors and allowing Cyprus to negotiate more favorable terms with international energy companies, which would translate to higher revenues. Moreover, some of the more attractive options for exporting the gas that are currently not possible for Cyprus (e.g., export via pipeline to Turkey and onward to European markets) would become feasible. On the face of it, this should be an attractive proposition for all parties. Given the struggling economies on both sides of the island, Cyprus (both Greek Cypriots and Turkish Cypriots) needs cash. With a Cyprus–Turkey pipeline, gas revenues could start flowing before the end of the decade, providing much needed revenue. Turkey also needs more gas from alternative sources, and it would enhance its potential as a gas transit company by tapping into gas from Cyprus.

However, the promised economic benefits are far outweighed by the parties' deep-seated political differences and their strategic interests as they see them – especially given that the amount of gas discovered thus far is not vast. Thus, for the moment, the prospect of Cyprus setting a precedent of energy incentivizing peace between states in conflict[16] appears rather remote.

The current state of play in offshore exploration and development

The Republic of Cyprus initiated its search for offshore hydrocarbons in 2006. It has since concluded two international tenders for exploration licenses, while a third tender, launched in May 2016, remains in progress at the time of writing.

Energy companies involved

At present, the Republic of Cyprus has engagements with several international oil and gas companies. Rights to develop the Aphrodite gas field are owned by Noble Energy in partnership with British Gas (which was acquired in 2016 by Royal Dutch Shell) and Israel's Delek Drilling and Avner Oil. Italy's Eni together with South Korean partner Kogas have exploration licenses for blocks 2, 3, and 9, with all three licenses extended for two years from early 2016. France's Total gave up its exploration rights in block 10 without drilling any wells, but still has a lease for block 11, extended for two years from early 2016.

Exploration and development plans

So far, only two drillings have been conducted on behalf of the RoC, both by Noble and Delek in the Aphrodite field. Initially thought to be 198 bcm (seven trillion cubic feet), the estimate for the Aphrodite gas reservoir was later reduced to 128 bcm (4.5 trillion cubic feet) of gas.[17] This is a significant volume of gas for Cyprus. Given the country's small-size potential domestic market, most of the gas could be exported, provided other conditions are right for the field's development (e.g., availability of markets, and sufficiently high gas prices to ensure commercial viability of development projects).[18] Following Eni's failure to detect any exploitable gas in two drilling operations in block 9 in 2014/2015,[19] and TOTAL's finding no tangible evidence of deposits worth drilling for in blocks 10 and 11,[20] for now Aphrodite remains the only Cypriot gas discovery.

In the early stages of the gas discoveries, the Republic of Cyprus hoped to construct a land-based liquefied natural gas (LNG) plant, as this would offer the greatest flexibility in exporting the surplus gas, including to distant lucrative markets. This option was also seen by the Republic of Cyprus as a way to turn the island into an "energy hub" capable of attracting natural gas from neighboring countries (Israel, Lebanon) for processing and shipping.[21] However, the appraisal drilling made clear that Aphrodite lacked sufficient gas to make a LNG terminal commercially viable.[22] The idea was effectively abandoned in early 2015, when it became clear that the chances of finding the required additional volumes of gas in the future were relatively slim.

Since then, and especially given the plunge in petrol prices that affected gas prices and the oil and gas investment climate, there has been a shift toward a seemingly more feasible option of exporting to regional markets, such as Egypt. In June 2015, Aphrodite partners Nobel and Delek submitted a development plan to the Republic of Cyprus that includes the construction of an independent floating production platform and a gas pipeline to Egypt.[23] As discussed elsewhere in this volume, however, the cost identified thus far for getting the gas to Egypt, let alone exporting it, is too high to make such plans feasible.[24]

Another problem holding up development of Aphrodite, located partially in Israeli waters, is the lack of a unitization agreement between the Republic of Cyprus and Israel. The two sides' differing views on the field's overlap with the Israeli EEZ appear to have become an obstacle in the ongoing intergovernmental negotiations to reach such an agreement. Israel asserts that the gas reservoir extends into its EEZ in commercial quantities, while Cyprus claims that only 1 percent of the field is on the Israeli side.[25] In the absence of a unitization agreement, in theory each side could proceed in separately developing their part of the Aphrodite field, although experts believe that neither side wants to go down that road.

The announcement on November 23, 2015 that British Gas (BG) (a Shell subsidiary since February 2016) would acquire half of Noble's interests (amounting to 35 percent) in RoC block 12, which includes Aphrodite, created some excitement. The Republic of Cyprus government hopes this will facilitate the field's development and enable Cypriot gas exports to Europe via BG's LNG plant at Idku, Egypt, and the Cypriot Energy Minister has since said that production could start in 2020. However, energy analysts are more cautious, pointing out that BG's involvement does not solve the problem of low gas prices discouraging investment, a situation generally expected to prevail into the early part of the next decade.[26]

The broader energy scene and implications for Cyprus[27]

The issue of exploration and exploitation of Cyprus' hydrocarbons is inextricably linked to a number of international, regional, and local factors. The issue also has political, strategic, financial, and technical parameters that need to be evaluated independently as well as linked to a realistic appraisal of future prospects.

The global energy landscape was characterized in part by a LNG glut in 2016, triggered by new supplies from Australia, coupled with weakening Asian (mainly Japan and South Korea) consumption. This situation is projected to continue, with additional supplies coming from the USA (see Chapter 10, this volume). The International Energy Agency (IEA) has predicted that the oversupply in the gas markets will continue until at least 2021, with slowing growth in global demand for gas.

This has created a "buyers' market, giving buyers the leverage to renegotiate unfavorable long-term contracts and dictate supply terms".[28] Under these circumstances, oil and gas companies are more likely to focus on production projects that promise quick and reasonable returns, rather than on expensive exploration and longer term development plans.

This shift in the energy markets has been affecting gas development in Cyprus since about 2014. These changing dynamics have undoubtedly been a major reason behind Noble's lack of interest in further drilling in block 12, Total's decision not to drill during its three-year tenure of blocks 10 and 11, and Eni's preference to defer further drilling for at least two years after 2015 in blocks 2, 3, and 9.

The regional and European landscapes

The gas finds in offshore Cyprus are closely linked to other regional discoveries, and to relations between the regional states and the interests of third states. In addition, the viability of exploration and exploitation is part of a wider scheme, including strategic, economic, political, technical, and market parameters. Thus, the gas findings need to be understood within the framework of gas findings of other neighboring states, both in competitive and complementary terms. The development prospects of Cypriot hydrocarbons should be understood with reference to the other East Med littoral states: as potential markets; as possible collaborators for joint ventures targeting third markets; and as parties to a larger arrangement regarding (primarily European) energy security as well as security more broadly construed.

The bilateral and trilateral relationships developed between Cyprus and other states in the region (Egypt, Greece, Israel, and Jordan) are important developments in partly tackling this issue through cooperation. Although frequently blown out of proportion and presented as alliances, relationships cultivated among states that are more closely akin to alignments are also important, as they provide the political framework to enable businesses to consider engagement in the exploration and exploitation of natural resources. However, at the end of the day it is the companies that will commercially venture if they engage in a country. Political agreements facilitate business operations, but do not themselves amount to extractive and marketing processes, a point governments would do well to bear in mind.

On the other hand, the needs and interests of other states, like Israel and Turkey, both play a significant role in shaping prospects for Cypriot gas, and are linked to Cyprus more broadly. Israel is very eager to export gas, while from a market point of view Turkey may be the best chance for exports given supply and price realities. Turkey has growing energy needs and is keen to diversify its import sources. In light of the recent Israeli–Turkish *rapprochement*, energy cooperation between the two states is conceivable. Although, strictly speaking, direct arrangements (e.g., a pipeline) between Turkey and Israel could be possible without Cypriot participation or indeed agreement, the likelihood of this occurring is low given the consequences from a political point of view. This does, however, offer a useful impetus for Cyprus to urgently evaluate its options and priorities. In this respect, a solution to the Cyprus issue would of course be a win-win scenario for all involved, as it would unlock the possibility for East Med, including Cypriot gas, to reach Turkey, both a profitable end market and a transit route to Europe.

This would in turn further European energy security and diversification, lessening dependency on Russian gas. However, at the moment this option faces various challenges, including oversupply of gas in Europe and low prices, and disagreements between various European countries on the issue. Within the EU, certain states favor the option of gas from the south through Turkey, while others prioritize Russia as a trusted gas supplier and have no interest in endangering this relationship. These states are thus more reserved in offering any real support for East Med gas plans. Yet another obstacle is Russia, which is not keen on losing any of its European market share or its Turkish customer. Indeed, the current Russian–Turkish understanding and upgrading of bilateral relations, combined with Turkey's cultivation of other energy diversification relations, could severely affect East Med and Cypriot gas prospects. A final challenge pertains to EU–Turkey relations, which are going through their most difficult phase in decades. Energy relations between the two are also expected to suffer, as they form part of the broader equation.

Finally, forced by circumstances to drop initial plans for a land-based LNG plant, the Republic of Cyprus has been mulling over the option of gas sales to Egypt since 2014. However, the government now accepts that this option is also not commercially viable due to low gas prices globally and in Europe (in addition to the fact that Egypt is projected to have more gas than it needs by 2020). As discussed above, a remaining commercially serious option is exporting via pipeline to Turkey, which is heavily dependent on energy imports and accordingly paying comparatively high prices. This makes Turkey an attractive market for Cypriot, as well as Israeli, gas, but this option does not seem possible without a solution to the Cyprus problem.[29]

The local landscape

Cyprus seems to be locked in a vicious circle: the hydrocarbons conflict is yet another episode in the saga in the fundamental conflict of principle, as each side's energy stance is informed by their respective position on the Cyprus issue. Instead of advancing cooperation, the hydrocarbons issue has exacerbated the existing conflict between the island's two communities as well as between Cyprus and Turkey, which has in turn precluded timely solutions to natural resources development for the broader region.

The main reason for this in Cyprus – as has been the case with other regional states – is that politics have nearly exclusively informed the debate and/or dictated decisions. It is not an exaggeration to say that energy in the Eastern Mediterranean has fallen victim to and been hijacked by local domestic and regional politics. Of course, politics are important for securing the framework within which hydrocarbons development can take place. However, at the end of the day, if development choices and decisions are to be viable, they need to make business sense. For private companies that develop oil and gas, any operation must be commercially feasible and meaningful. Especially in states that wish to engage IOCs and are unwilling or unable to invest by themselves, exploration plans need primarily to be financially sensible and sustainable. In Cyprus, the prioritization of options with fundamental challenges (like an LNG plant at the time and given quantities) and the adoption of seemingly inflexible positions resulted in an inability to adapt to changing circumstances and the loss of valuable time and opportunities.

Finally, the creation and maintenance of expectations at the public level is a local issue that has introduced a further set of challenges. Public dialogue on the gas development and export options has largely been fragmented, problematic, and outdated. This has led to the formation of specific views and expectations regarding quantities, modes of extraction, markets, timing, and revenues that became static. This had two unfortunate outcomes. First, it became exceedingly difficult to introduce alternative plans and rhetoric when changing international realities rendered previously advocated plans untenable. Second, cementing the belief on the exclusivity of rights with the expectation of quick and sizable revenues led to a complete absence of willingness to discuss with the other side or consider sharing potential incomes.

Concluding remarks

Constructively addressing the Cyprus issue, as well as Cypriot and Eastern Mediterranean gas more broadly, requires pragmatism, an understanding of the sense of urgency, detachment from past entanglements and obsolete mindsets, and out-of-the-box thinking. Confirmed Cypriot gas quantities remain too small to support any mode of extraction, and thus the best – and perhaps the only – chance for Cyprus' gas is linkage with other regional states' gas. At the same time, marketing opportunities even for regional states with sufficient quantities seem to have diminished dramatically. Price challenges, gas oversupply, and the LNG glut have significantly affected the global gas terrain. In addition, renewables, the US gas supply, technological developments like FLNG and CNG, as well as new actors in play, have made the European gas landscape particularly challenging and Europe as a market for East Med and Cypriot gas unlikely under current conditions.

There is considerable discussion regarding new potential discoveries and opportunities, but gas in the ground does not amount to anything. A pragmatic appraisal of prospects that takes into account current and expected realities should be the guiding principle. Often, the problem is that standpoints, understandings, and debates in the East Med region are overly local in nature, and regional at best. However, broader global parameters such as prices, markets, and supply shape conditions that impact the viability of gas development. Thus, regional viewpoints would benefit from taking a bird's eye view of the region situated within the wider European and global perspectives. Such a perspective would provide a rational account of prospects, opportunities, and obstacles.

At the same time, an appreciation of the sense of urgency associated with planning in a rapidly changing and challenging international environment is essential to avoid missing opportunities, as has happened in the past. For instance, in 2005 it was forecast that European consumption would increase by 50 percent, informing planning expectations accordingly. However, European gas consumption actually decreased by 20 percent, rendering previous hopes and plans obsolete. Needs change, as do the quantity and diversity of supplies. Finally, supply- and demand-side needs and interests prompt states to reconsider relationships. In international relations friends are not forever – but then again, neither are enemies.

The prospect of mutual gains on the basis of energy could offer excellent incentives for cooperation, reconciliation, and ending conflict. Cyprus would greatly benefit from facilitating, rather than obstructing, potential cooperative arrangements between regional states. This would (1) allow Cyprus to assume a catalytic role and potentially influence developments; (2) provide a market for the limited Cypriot gas quantities by joining in larger volume transportation and trading; and (3) prevent potential adverse effects for Cyprus from becoming an objector (e.g., to a possible Israeli–Turkish pipeline project). Even during this period of challenging realities for hydrocarbons, the Eastern Mediterranean region still has the chance to follow a path that will ensure its relevance and the realization of its potential. Moreover, regional parties could use this period of commercial difficulties and delays to develop plans and forge strong ties among themselves that would enable the quick facilitation of practical arrangements when market conditions become conducive. Through forward, realistic, innovative thinking that goes beyond outmoded stances, Cyprus should ensure that it is not left behind and instead should seize the opportunity to lead developments and export options through its unique position and characteristics.

Notes

1 USGS, 2010.
2 Energy-Pedia News, 2012.
3 InCyprus, 2016c.
4 In 2016, the interest was also due to the August 2015 Zohr discovery offshore Egypt, the largest-ever Mediterranean gas find which is estimated at 850 bcm and is only 6 km away from the Egypt–Cyprus maritime border.
5 For instance, Aphrodite lies at a water depth of about 1600 m of seawater and a total depth of about 7200 m. See Cyprus Mail, 2013b.
6 See: Gürel et al., 2013, pp. 26–28.
7 Daily Sabah, 2015.
8 See Gürel/Le Cornu, 2014, pp. 11–33.
9 See Gürel et al., 2013, ch. 5.
10 *Cyprus Mail*, 2014c.
11 *Cyprus Mail*, 2014b.
12 Reuters, 2015a.
13 MFA, 2013, 2014.
14 See, e.g., MFA, 2012.

15 For a comprehensive discussion of the positions of all interested parties and references see Gürel et al., 2013, pp. 41–60.
16 Shaffer, 2014.
17 Reuters, 2014.
18 MIT, 2013.
19 Reuters, 2015b.
20 *Cyprus Mail*, 2015.
21 Natural Gas World, 2014.
22 Cyprus Mail, 2013a.
23 Globes, 2015c.
24 See also InCyprus, 2015.
25 Globes, 2015a, 2015b.
26 InCyprus, 2016b.
27 Oil Price, 2015; IEA, 2016.
28 InCyprus, 2016d.
29 InCyprus, 2016a.

Bibliography

Cyprus Mail (2013a): Experts Debate the Viability of a LNG Plant. November 25. Available at: http://cyprus-mail.com/2013/11/25/experts-debate-the-viability-of-a-lng-plant/.

Cyprus Mail (2013b): Explanations for Downsizing of Aphrodite Gas Field. October 13. Available at: http://cyprus-mail.com/2013/10/13/explanations-for-downsizing-of-aphrodite-gas-field/.

Cyprus Mail (2014a): Joint Declaration: Final Version as Agreed between the Two Leaders. February 11. Available at: http://cyprus-mail.com/2014/02/11/joint-declaration-final-version-as-agreed-between-the-two-leaders/.

Cyprus Mail (2014b): President Says: I Had No Other Choice. October 7. Available at: http://cyprus-mail.com/2014/10/07/president-says-i-had-no-other-choice/.

Cyprus Mail (2014c): Turkey Trespasses for Fourth Time since Hydrocarbons Discovered. October 21. Available at: http://cyprus-mail.com/2014/10/21/turkey-trespasses-for-fourth-time-since-hydrocarbons-discovered/.

Cyprus Mail (2015): Total Likely to Ditch Cyprus Offshore Gas Search. January 21. Available at: http://cyprus-mail.com/2015/01/21/total-likely-to-ditch-cyprus-offshore-gas-search-updated/.

Daily Sabah (2015): UN Adviser to Cyprus: Strong Ties between Ankara and Cypriot Turks Favor Us. January 16. Available at: www.dailysabah.com/politics/2015/01/16/un-adviser-to-cyprus-strong-ties-between-ankara-and-cypriot-turks-favor-us.

Energy-Pedia News (2012): Cyprus Says Response to Second Licensing Round "Beyond Expectations". May 13. Available at: www.energy-pedia.com/news/cyprus/new-150283.

Globes (2015a,): *Cypriot President to Visit Israel for Gas Talks*. November 10. Available at: www.globes.co.il/en/article-cypriot-president-to-visit-israel-for-gas-talks-1001080015.

Globes (2015b,): Cyprus Unhappy with Israel's Ishai Discovery Declaration. November 22. Available at: www.globes.co.il/en/article-cyprus-unhappy-with-israels-yishai-discovery-declaration-1001083018.

Globes (2015c): Delek and Noble Present Aphrodite Development Plan. June 11. Available at: www.globes.co.il/en/article-delek-and-noble-present-aphrodite-development-plan-1001043737.

Gürel, Ayla M./Laura Le Cornu (2014): Can Gas Catalyse Peace in the Eastern Mediterranean? *The International Spectator* 49(2).

Gürel, Ayla M. et al. (2013): *The Cyprus Hydrocarbons Issue: Context, Positions and Future Scenarios*. PRIO Report. Nicosia: PRIO Cyprus Center. Available at: http://file.prio.no/publication_files/Cyprus/Report%202013 1%20Hydrocarbons.pdf.

IEA (2016): *IEA Medium Term Gas Market Report 2016*. International Energy Agency.

InCyprus (2015): *Energy Turbulence*. December 26. Available at: http://in-cyprus.com/energy-turbulence/.

InCyprus (2016a): Cyprus Gas – Time to Take Stock. July 11. Available at: http://in-cyprus.com/cyprus-gas-time-to-take-stock/.

InCyprus (2016b): East Med Gas Export Risk. January 6. Available at: www.iene.eu/east-med-gas-export-risks-p2362.html.

InCyprus (2016c): Energy Search Gets Lift-off. July 31. Available at: http://in-cyprus.com/energy-search-gets-lift-off/.

InCyprus (2016d): Global Oil and East-Med Natural Gas. February 6. Available at: http://in-cyprus.com/global-oil-and-east-med-natural-gas/.

MFA (2012): Press Release Regarding the International Tender for Off-shore Hydrocarbon Exploration and Exploitation Opened by the Greek Cypriot Administration, No. 140. May 18.

MFA (2013): Press Release Regarding the Second Drilling Activity of the Greek Cypriots, No: 170. June 14.

MFA (2014): Press Release Regarding Drilling Activity of the Greek Cypriots, No: 311. October 4.

MIT (2013): *Natural Gas Monetization Pathways for Cyprus: Economics of Project Development Options*. Interim Report for the Study. Cambridge, MA: MIT Energy Initiative. Available at: https://energy.mit.edu/wp-content/uploads/2013/10/MITEI-RP-2013-001.pdf.

Natural Gas World (2014): Cyprus and ENI-KOGAS Sign MoU. June 30. Available at: www.naturalgasworld.com/eni-kogas-cyprus-gas-mou.

Oil Price (2015): LNG Glut Set To Worsen Considerably Over Next 3 Years. November 11. Available at: http://oilprice.com/Energy/Gas-Prices/LNG-Glut-Set-To-Worsen-Considerably-Over-Next-3-Years.html.

Reuters (2014): Firms Developing Cyprus Gas Field Raise Reserve Estimate 12 pct. November 18. Available at: www.reuters.com/article/delek-group-noble-energy-cyprus-idUSL6N0T83UJ20141118.

Reuters (2015a): U.N. Cyprus Envoy Says Sees no Obstacle to New Peace Talks. April 7. Available at: www.reuters.com/article/us-cyprus-un-talks-idUSKBN0MY12J20150407.

Reuters (2015b): *UPDATE 2-Eni, KOGAS Find No Exploitable Hydrocarbons off Cyprus*. March 26. Available at: http://in.reuters.com/article/cyprus-natgas-eni-idINL6N0WS3M420150326.

Shaffer, Brenda (2014): *Can New Energy Supplies Bring Peace?* GMF Policy Brief, GMF. Available at: www.gmfus.org/publications/can-new-energy-supplies-bring-peace.

USGS (2010): *Assessment of Undiscovered Oil and Gas Resources of the Levant Basin Province, Eastern Mediterranean*. U.S. Geological Survey Fact Sheet 2010–3014. Denver: World Petroleum Resources Project. Available at: https://pubs.usgs.gov/fs/2010/3014/pdf/FS10-3014.pdf.

12 The impact of natural gas discoveries upon Israeli politics, geopolitics, and socioeconomic discourse

Elai Rettig

Introduction

Since its inception, Israel had struggled to ensure reliable and affordable supplies of energy resources to its domestic economy. Virtually devoid of natural resources, Israel has existed as an "energy island", engaged in continuous conflict with its neighbors and completely dependent on imports by sea. Numerous political constraints, including an Arab oil embargo dating back to 1948, made procuring energy resources a difficult challenge for Israeli policymakers.[1] Over the years, Israel has constantly sought to wean itself off of its energy import dependency as a top strategic necessity. This has included largely unsuccessful attempts at domestic oil exploration, the promotion of renewable energy technologies, and occasional suggestions to introduce nuclear energy.[2] Despite these efforts, reaching energy independence became a "holy grail" for Israeli leaders, and one that would likely never be found.

This picture changed dramatically with the discovery of two large offshore natural gas fields in Israel's Exclusive Economic Zone (EEZ) in 2009 and 2010. The two fields, "Tamar" and "Leviathan", were seen as both an important economic blessing and a major geopolitical asset that could bring high levels of energy independence to the State of Israel. Moreover, the fields gave Israel an unprecedented opportunity to export gas to its neighbors, signaling a complete reversal of its long-standing "siege mentality" in the region. Israel's Prime Minister Benjamin Netanyahu went so far as to describe the discoveries as a divine gift, stating, "God gave us gas that will turn Israel into an energy power".[3] Although a number of changes in global energy markets have since decreased the potential economic impact of Israel's newfound gas, this appears not to have altered Israel's high geopolitical expectations in the least.

Despite the initial sense of euphoria over the discoveries, the seven years that followed were characterized by a series of highly contentious regulatory and political feuds in Israel that left the development of the "Leviathan" field and the export of gas unrealized. On the surface, these feuds involved important economic concerns related to the proper utilization of the gas findings; yet their timing and impact touched upon deep-rooted social and political divides within Israeli society which extend far beyond resource issues. The heated public debate that developed exposed some of the problematic processes through which economic decisions are reached in the Israeli political system while also tapping into pre-existing social grievances that simmered for years among large parts of the Israeli public. The high and at times unrealistic expectations which gas development created in the minds of the Israeli public created a socioeconomic discourse that grew emotional and uncompromising over time, making the task of developing the gas fields and transforming the East-Mediterranean into a "gas region" an increasingly difficult one. The discoveries thus created two parallel yet very different stories of Israel as a "gas-rich nation", revealing the contrasting ways in which energy developments can transform a country and its surroundings.

This chapter will first provide a brief background on Israel's energy sector before and after the discovery of gas, and then outline the profound impact which the gas findings have had upon Israel's regional perception and opportunities. It will then attempt to explain the origins of the highly emotional public and political backlash the gas created within Israel, followed by an analysis of the predicted economic benefits of the gas. Finally, a number of conclusions will be presented that are relevant to the region as a whole.

Background

Up until the 1980s, Israel was completely dependent on oil in its electricity and transportation sectors, consuming around 150,000 barrels per day mostly imported from Iran.[4] The 1973 OPEC oil embargo and the fall of the Iranian Shah in 1979 led Israel to switch to coal for its electricity needs.[5] Natural gas was introduced to the Israeli electricity sector only in 2004, following the 1999 and 2000 discoveries of "Noa" and "Meri", two small offshore gas fields close to the city of Ashkelon which together contained 33.5 bcm.[6] Israel supplemented these findings with Egyptian gas imports through a pipeline from Sinai which came online in 2008, providing for 40 percent of Israel's gas needs. By 2010, Israel was consuming 5.3 bcm per year of natural gas, of which 90 percent went to the state-owned Israel Electric Corporation (IEC) for electricity generation.[7] Natural gas began to rapidly replace coal as a cheaper and cleaner source of fuel, and by the end of 2010 comprised 40 percent of the IEC's fuel mix. That same year, Israel's total primary energy consumption stood at 24.08 mtoe, of which oil made up 46 percent, coal 37 percent, and gas 17 percent.[8] However, Israel soon realized that its small offshore gas fields were rapidly depleting and would completely cease production by 2012. In addition, repeated sabotage of the gas pipeline from Egypt coupled with dwindling Egyptian reserves caused the flow of gas to come to a complete halt by early 2012.[9] This led to an emergency situation in Israel's electricity sector in 2012, as additional coal and expensive oil were purchased to compensate for the sudden loss of natural gas, resulting in a 24 percent spike in electricity bills within a single year.[10]

Against the backdrop of this precarious situation, the discovery of two major offshore gas fields in 2009 and 2010 was enthusiastically welcomed throughout Israel. The "Tamar" field, announced in January 2009, is estimated to hold reserves of 282 bcm, while the "Leviathan" field, announced in December 2010, is believed to hold approximately 500 bcm.[11] The two major fields were later supplemented by the discovery of two smaller fields, "Tanin" (discovered in 2012) and "Karish" (discovered in 2013), which together hold approximately 55 bcm. All fields were discovered by a private Israeli–American partnership consisting primarily of two companies: the Israeli Delek Group and its subsidiaries, and Texas-based Noble Energy. The discoveries theoretically ensured that Israel will have enough gas for the next half-century and beyond, and in 2014 the "Tamar" field already provided for all of the domestic market's needs of that year (7.5 bcm). The electricity sector remained the main customer, with 85 percent going to the IEC and accounting for 40 percent of its fuel mix. In 2014, Israel's total primary energy consumption continued to consist mainly of oil (250,000 b/d), but its share had decreased in the overall energy mix (42%) while the share of natural gas had increased substantially (28%), mainly at the expense of coal (29%).[12] Renewables have continued to play a marginal role in Israel's total energy consumption (1%), seemingly a consequence of the domestic gas discoveries. The Ministry of Energy projected that the role of gas in Israel's energy sector would continue to grow, reaching 60 percent of the electricity generation mix by 2020, with annual consumption rates expected to climb to 12 bcm by that year and to 18 bcm by 2030.[13]

Impact

The impact upon Israeli geopolitics

The relatively large amount of gas found in Israel's EEZ as compared to its small domestic gas market provided Israel with an opportunity to export to other countries. Israeli policymakers began to see this as a rare chance to fundamentally alter Israel's historic role in the region. Plans to construct pipelines and export gas to neighboring countries like Jordan and Egypt slowly began to break the traditional concept of Israel as an "energy island", a country completely disconnected from its region and lacking a common infrastructure. Moreover, the possibility that Israel could export gas to more distant countries like Cyprus, Greece, and Turkey meant that it no longer had to remain a "black sheep" in a region called the Middle East, but instead could become an integral part of a new region called the "East Mediterranean". This realization seemed to open up a new frontier for Israeli foreign relations.

Despite its prominent place in Israel's geography and trade, the sea was considered secondary in Israel's strategic perception prior to the gas findings. Although 99 percent of Israel's foreign trade is carried by sea, 70 percent of its population lives near the sea, and most of its critical infrastructure is located on the shoreline, Israel has never developed a maritime strategy policy and its navy has traditionally been the least funded of all military branches.[14] This was mainly due to the lack of substantial security threats emanating from the sea, as the naval forces of Israel's neighbors were traditionally marginal. The tendency among Israeli leadership to view Israel's borders as "frontlines" to be defended left its peaceful western border largely unattended, and contributed to the country's sense of regional isolation.

Following the gas discoveries, this perception changed dramatically. Israeli decision-makers became eager to define Israel's EEZ and to utilize the gas deposits in a new area that was twice the size of Israel itself. The discoveries also brought new maritime border disputes with Lebanon, as well as threats by Hamas and Hezbollah to attack offshore drilling rigs. As a result, the budget for Israel's navy was substantially increased and new procurement boosted the Israeli naval presence in the EEZ.[15] More importantly, this created an understanding that Israel has a western border with a new region, and more specifically with Cyprus, a country that could become an important trade and diplomatic partner. The government saw an opportunity to strengthen economic and political alliances with the countries of the East Mediterranean through "pipeline diplomacy". A number of consecutive visits in 2016 from leading Greek and Cypriot figures helped strengthen this perception of a nascent new alliance, and an official treaty to mend ties between Israel and Turkey in June 2016 was attributed in large part to a potential gas deal between the two countries.[16] PM Netanyahu fervently advocated the idea of gas exports as an effective geopolitical tool to cement Israel's position in the region, stating, "a country that exports things that are crucial for the surroundings or for other countries has far more power. Alliances and peace are made with the strong and not with the weak."[17]

These high geopolitical expectations led some hardline members of the "Likud" ruling party to claim that Israel can even use its gas as a weapon. Tourism Minister Yariv Levin went so far as to argue that Israel would be able to "shut the lights" on Europe should the EU decide to boycott Israeli products or impose economic sanctions.[18] Such statements grossly overestimate the actual influence Israel will have over countries that receive its gas (or the legal capacity to deny contractual obligations made by private companies). However, they illustrate the high expectations and excitement of the perceived geopolitical benefits of gas held by the Israeli leadership. This overexcitement became especially apparent when substantial developments in regional and global energy markets since 2014 had little impact upon Israel's strategic assessments. Events and trends such as the steep fall in global oil prices, the growing glut of LNG supplies, increased competition over gas supplies in Europe, Jordanian intentions to import LNG, and the discovery of a major offshore gas field in Egypt ("Zohr") did not win attention in Israel's official security forums; nor did they lead to a revision of policy reports submitted by the Ministry of Foreign Affairs or the Council of National Security regarding the "power" of Israeli gas.[19]

It would appear that Israeli leadership is so transfixed by the idea of becoming a regional gas exporter that this goal will be politically pursued regardless of regional and global changes in energy markets. Yet even amid these changes, Israel still provides convincing economic justifications to promote exports to its neighbors. With regard to Jordan, the export of dry gas through a fixed pipeline from Israel remains a far more reliable and less volatile solution to Jordan's energy needs than LNG imports, even during periods where the price difference is not substantial. And indeed, in September 2016 the "Leviathan" partnership signed a contract to supply 45 BCM of natural gas to Jordan's National Electric Power Company (NEPCO) over the next 15 years at a cost of $10 billion, despite the vocal opposition of the Jordanian streets. With regard to Egypt, Israel estimates that the newfound "Zohr" field will likely be used primarily for domestic consumption, leaving Egypt's dormant gas liquefaction facilities still open for "Leviathan" gas which could then be exported to Europe as LNG. Turkey is another viable destination for Israeli gas exports, bilateral political relationship permitting, as the issue of price (which will likely be more favorable from other sources than from Israel) takes a back seat in Turkey to concerns of diversification and growing domestic consumption. In contrast, a more ambitious plan to construct an underwater pipeline from Israel to Greece and Italy does not seem to be economically viable, despite being politically desirable to both sides.

In addition to enhancing Israel's strategic ties with these countries, increased regional gas usage comes with numerous environmental and economic benefits, especially once global oil prices rise again.[20] More importantly, Israel views increasing regional gas consumption as a rare opportunity to advance Israeli interests, as the growing need for Israeli gas will help the country send roots into its neighbors' grounds (both metaphorically and physically in the form of pipelines) and become a permanent and necessary fixture in an environment that traditionally rejected its very existence. Given its geopolitical history, this is not an opportunity Israel will easily abandon, and explains the seemingly inattentive attitude of Israeli policymakers to changing global market dynamics. The election of Donald Trump to the presidency of the United States in late 2016 further encouraged this sense of optimism, as Trump's seemingly positive stance toward the current right-wing Israeli government, along with his choice of former ExxonMobil CEO Rex Tillerson as Secretary of State, was seen as conducive to advancing energy deals in the region.

The impact upon domestic politics

To realize the regional potential of its newfound gas fields, the Israeli government first had to reach a development agreement with the private gas companies which discovered them, a task that proved much more difficult than initially anticipated. The political struggle that evolved over the gas fields severely delayed their development, as domestic policies ran in parallel and at times contrary to the government's ambition of utilizing the gas for regional benefits. Three major issues have defined the politics of natural gas development in Israel since 2009: (1) the amount of revenue the government should take from the fields; (2) the amount of gas that should be exported, and (3) the conditions under which competition can form in the Israeli domestic gas market.

Although not without conflict, the first two issues were settled following the establishment of two committees: the "Sheshinski committee" in 2010, which substantially raised taxes on natural resource extraction, and the "Zemach committee" in 2011, which allowed for 40 percent of the gas reserves to be exported. The smaller "Tamar" field was thus quickly developed and gas started flowing onto Israel's shoreline in March 2013. In addition, initial understandings with Jordan and Egypt to export gas were underway at the time, the centerpiece of which was a deal with BG International to export gas to the Idku LNG terminal in Egypt and on to Europe. Additional plans to export gas to Cyprus, Turkey, and Greece through various methods began to develop, though none were confirmed.

Despite this progress, the issue of domestic competition turned out to be the most politically contentious. In November 2012, Israel's Antitrust Authority announced that the private partnership which had discovered and developed the gas fields constituted a monopoly.[21] Although the Antitrust Authority had previously permitted the partnership to jointly develop the fields, it became concerned that following the end of Egyptian pipeline gas exports in early 2012, Israel had become wholly dependent on a single supplier that controlled supply and price. The Antitrust Authority thus demanded that some of the discovered fields be sold to an outside developer which could compete with the partnership in the domestic gas market. These demands presented substantial difficulties for the Israeli government, as it had to force the gas companies to sell shares of their fields while simultaneously providing them with enough incentives to proceed with development.

Following a series of undisclosed deliberations, in July 2015 a framework was reached between the government and the gas companies. Under the agreement, the partnership will have to sell its two smaller fields, "Karish" and "Tanin", to a new developer and dilute its holdings in "Tamar". In return, the partnership will receive more favorable conditions that will expedite the development and export of "Leviathan" gas. These conditions also included a "stability clause", which guaranteed that the government would not change the established regulatory conditions for the next ten years, regardless of future shifts in the global energy markets.

The proposed framework immediately met with strong public and political opposition, namely claims that it was much too favorable toward the gas companies. The fields, "Karish" and "Tanin", were said be too small to present any serious competition for the larger fields, in which the partnership retained a dominant presence. In addition, a number of basic preconditions proposed by the Zemach Committee to ensure Israel's energy security were missing from the framework, such as a demand to build another pipeline from the fields to Israel's shoreline before exports were allowed. The proposed price mechanism for domestic gas sales was also contested, as it essentially made the partnership immune to the predicted fall in global gas prices. As a result, large and highly publicized public protests began to occur on a weekly basis, creating pressure on government officials not to "back down" from the demands of the gas companies.

Riding a wave of public and media support, the Antitrust Commissioner announced his resignation in May 2015 in an act of protest against the government's proposed framework, forcing the government to either reopen negotiations or somehow bypass the Antitrust Authority altogether. The latter option was chosen, but was only possible by invoking Article 52 of the Antitrust Law, a provision that allowed the government to completely circumvent the Antitrust Authority based on national security reasons.

In order to justify the unprecedented use of Article 52, the government turned to the geopolitical dimensions of the gas findings to substantiate supposed national security reasons to expedite gas development. The government provided three main arguments to this end. The first was that Israel had to quickly deliver gas to its neighboring states to prevent them from destabilizing. The government argued that a lack of sufficient gas supplies to Egypt and Jordan would create severe electricity and water shortages that would lead to mass protests,[22] while the resulting instability could spill over to Israel's borders and jeopardize its security. The second argument was that if Israel failed to provide Jordan and Egypt with gas, Iran would in the hopes of gaining influence in those countries, thus threatening Israel's security. The third argument was that exporting gas to EU members such as Cyprus and Greece would help prevent the European Parliament from passing resolutions or sanctions against Israel, as this would require the consensus of all member states.[23]

These arguments to justify the use of Article 52 were met with a number of factual hurdles. First, the August 2015 discovery of the "Zohr" field in Egypt substantially weakened the argument that Egypt (and consequently Jordan) would soon face severe gas shortages. Second, Iran is believed to be years away from exporting gas to Israel's neighbors due to a lack of infrastructure and issues of competitive pricing compared with Israeli and Egyptian gas. Third, there is no precedent to support the claim that Israeli gas exports would prevent the EU from issuing sanctions against it, a lesson Russia quickly learned following its invasion of Ukraine. With these facts in mind, a special parliamentary committee advised against the use of Article 52, but was ignored by the government.

Despite these inconsistencies, in December 2015 the Israeli government invoked Article 52 and approved the framework. Shortly thereafter, civil NGOS backed by opposition parties submitted petitions to the High Court of Justice. The Court essentially approved the majority of the framework but ruled that the ten-year "stability clause" damaged Israeli governance and should be changed. Within months, a softened stability clause was introduced and the framework was once again approved.

In hindsight, the long and protracted political battle over the gas findings exposed some unseemly processes through which economic decisions are made in the Israeli political system. This was prominently exposed by the Israeli media and served to further damage the government's credibility with large parts of the public. Transparency and due process were questioned, the noticeable involvement of lobbying and interest groups on behalf of the gas companies was exposed, and the blatant use of misleading security justifications to expedite economic policies was heavily criticized. Most importantly, the political debate further widened a growing rift not only between the government and its Parliament, but also between the government and its own regulatory authorities.

Insinuations of corruption, malpractice, and incompetence between various offices surfaced as a result of the gas debate, damaging the political process in Israel.

The impact upon public discourse

Although politics often took center stage, perhaps the most profound domestic impact of the gas discovery was upon the Israeli public itself. The announcement of the discoveries created high expectations that only increased with time. The widespread belief that the newfound gas would bring relief to Israel's notoriously high cost of living encouraged public involvement in every step of the political process. However, the highly emotional reaction many Israelis expressed in this process is reflective of deeper social and economic grievances extending far beyond the simple question of gas. Weekly protests against the government's proposed framework grew violent at times, signifying a growing frustration not only with the gas companies or the current political leadership, but with the very structure of the Israeli economy. As these grievances permeated the gas debate, attempts to reach a political compromise became increasingly difficult and fraught with personal feuds and bad blood. Thus, the politics of the gas cannot be understood without also appreciating the deeper social issues they stirred up, and the transition in Israeli discourse which this symbolized.

Although initially unrelated to the gas findings, the public struggle over Israel's economy began in the summer of 2011, as hundreds of thousands of Israelis marched in the streets in what became one of the largest rallies in Israel's history.[24] The demonstrators, mostly young, Jewish, and urban members of the middle class, protested against the high cost of living in Israel, the cost of housing and food products being most emblematic. For many of the protestors, the highly centralized market in Israel was the main culprit, seen as dominated by a few "monopolies" and "tycoons". The monopolies and their owners were accused of deliberately preventing competition from forming in order to maintain high profits. These beliefs became particularly common following a widely successful reform of the cellular market in 2010, as a series of legal struggles between the Ministry of Communications and the three major network providers that controlled the Israeli market led to an 80 percent decrease in consumers' average monthly bills.[25] The "cellular revolution", as it was called in the media, marked a turning point among consumers, and the deep sense of frustration for the years of unwarranted high bills created anger at the very term "monopoly". The remedy of introducing competition to "break the monopolies" thus gained the overwhelming support of the public on both the left and right, to the point that creating competition became an end in and of itself.

Amid these developments, the Antitrust Authority's November 2012 announcement that the gas companies formed a monopoly over Israel's gas supply was primed for a highly emotional backlash. The idea of "breaking the gas monopoly" and forcing competition in the gas market struck an immediate chord among many in the public. Mass demonstrations called for the gas companies to concede to the Antitrust Authority's full demands, carrying signs with the slogan "The gas belongs to all of us". Rapidly, the "struggle over the gas" became a core issue for young activists and NGOs disappointed by the limited results of the 2011 social protests. They were quickly joined by leaders of opposition parties in Parliament, and over time became increasingly politically oriented and uncompromising. The private owners of the gas companies were portrayed as enemies of the public and thieves trying to steal the people's gas, while banners depicting the Prime Minister and the owner of Delek Group as pirates were disseminated by leftist opposition groups. Weekly protests to "stop the gas theft" conveyed a deeper sense of political frustration among left-leaning protestors following the 2015 re-election of Prime Minister Netanyahu and his right-wing Likud party. The rapid fall in global oil prices further exacerbated this frustration, as Israeli gas prices kept increasing due to a flawed pricing formula. The perception that the gas was being stolen from the people grew increasingly more popular and populist. This sentiment was so prevalent in Israeli popular culture that a clothing company ran television ads in August 2015 showing male and female models defiantly shutting down an offshore drilling rig while touting the slogan "claim what's yours".[26]

Ultimately, the public struggle over the gas symbolized a deeper transition in Israeli discourse, from a security-dominated to an economy-dominated debate. As the concept of an immediate existential threat to the State of Israel lost traction among large parts of Israeli society over the years, so did the traditional acceptance of the costs and sacrifices that this situation demanded of the economy and the public. The results of the 2013 general elections, in which a newly formed economy-focused party ("Yesh Atid") became the second largest in Parliament, signaled that many Israelis were willing to vote according to their economic grievances rather than their approach to security and peace. Political leaders quickly reflected this change, as the slogan of social justice began to be used across the political spectrum, while the gas debate became a potent source to galvanize popular support either for or against the government.

The impact upon the economy

Although the public's involvement in the gas debate signified an important change in social discourse, it was also mired in misconceptions and influenced by unrealistic economic expectations. The gas findings were initially presented as a solution to Israel's most pressing economic concerns, with the potential to not only lower the price of utility bills and food products, but also to lower taxes in general, fund sweeping education and health reforms, support large infrastructure projects, and finance Israel's high defense expenditures. These high expectations were encouraged by government and opposition members, the media, and the gas companies themselves, as each side exaggerated the economic meaning of the gas findings to promote its own cause. The resulting atmosphere was one in which protestors were less willing to compromise, since anything short of delivering on these promises was seen as the result of government incompetence and corruption.

The actual impact gas revenues will have upon the Israeli economy is indeed significant, although more modest than public sentiments often convey. Following the dramatic drop in global oil and gas prices in mid-2014, in December 2015 the Bank of Israel assessed that the state's total revenues from the "Tamar" and "Leviathan" fields would amount to approximately $69 billion (~265 billion NIS) over the entire period of the fields' predicted 30 years in operation.[27] This amounts to approximately $2.3 billion per year, equivalent to just over 2.7 percent of Israel's 2015 annual state budget.[28] However, the full amount of revenues will only begin flowing into the state once the gas companies achieve a certain level of profit, which will only occur after the "Leviathan" field is developed. Furthermore, it is unlikely that these revenues would contribute directly to the state's annual budget, as this would create a sharp appreciation of the local currency (a process known as the "Dutch Disease"). Revenues would instead accrue to a sovereign wealth fund and incur interest that would ideally fund specific projects that generate jobs and income independent of additional gas revenues. Global experience has shown that the use of oil and gas revenues to directly fund state welfare services (education, health) creates substantial long-term fiscal difficulties due to the extreme price volatility of energy commodities.[29] The prospect of substituting unreliable gas revenue in place of stable tax income has repeatedly proven economically and socially irresponsible. Therefore, Israeli citizens should not expect generally lower taxes as a result of the gas findings.

Beyond revenues, the much more important economic benefit of gas is the domestic use of a cheaper and less polluting source of energy. In the near term, natural gas would replace more expensive coal imports for electricity generation, and displace a portion of oil imports for transportation over the long term. Natural gas may also be used for water desalination in Israel, as 60% percent of the water supply comes from four major water desalination plants that demand significant amounts of energy and are especially amenable to natural gas.[30] The gas discoveries would make desalinated water cheaper and more reliable, helping alleviate an issue once prophesied to become the main source of conflict in the Middle East. In any scenario, the main market for the discovered gas will be domestic, and efforts are being made to further utilize this source of energy and adapt different sectors to use it, such as agriculture. In general, the more directly connected natural gas is to Israel's industrial, commercial, and residential sectors, the more it will benefit Israel's economy and environment. This also gives Israel the opportunity to become a global front runner in developing gas-related technologies, similar to its current role in the clean-tech and high-tech industries.

Conclusions

The discovery of major offshore gas deposits in Israel's EEZ affected not only the economy and the geopolitics of the country, but also its political and social system. The gas brought with it important economic benefits and the potential to strengthen Israel's geopolitical position by profoundly changing its isolationist role in the region. However, the gas finds also unearthed and amplified deep social, political, and economic grievances among the Israeli public, further widening existing cleavages. In this sense, the gas findings created two parallel stories that affect and contradict one another, revealing differing aspects of the impact energy developments may have upon a region, a country, and its people.

Although Israel tells a different story than that of other energy-rich countries in the region, the conclusions we can draw are broadly relevant. First, the Israeli case demonstrates the difficulty of detaching energy resources from their domestic context to focus solely on their regional role or geopolitical impact, as the two directly complement (or contradict) one another. Second, it demonstrates how quickly the public can be convinced that energy resources are a solution to social and economic grievances. Even without a history of oil-funded subsidies and sweeping social benefits, Israel is now grappling with the same public expectations as other energy-rich states in the region. The deeply entrenched idea that energy resources "belong to the people", and thus the people should directly benefit from them, also implies the inverse – that if the people do not receive the benefits they expect, the government is to be blamed and should be replaced. It is thus extremely difficult for a country to balance the responsible use of its energy resources with the need to constantly convey to the public the ways in which they too are prospering. In Israel, rather than offer sweeping economic reforms and subsidies, the government chose to focus on and at times overstate the regional and geopolitical advantages the gas will provide Israel. While this solution may work in the short term, as Israel starts to export gas in large volumes it will quickly find itself under pressure to utilize revenues in a fiscally irresponsible way, and its resolve to withstand these demands will be tested.

Notes

1 Bialer, 1998.
2 Bahgat, 2014, pp. 1–18.
3 The Jerusalem Post, 2015.
4 Up until 1979 Iran provided up to 85 percent of Israel's oil needs and even took part in a joint pipeline project (Bialer, 2007, pp. 29–67).
5 Coal became a more politically favorable source of fuel, since it originated from friendlier countries to Israel, such as South Africa, Poland, Australia, and Colombia.
6 Delek Energy, 2016.
7 Ministry of National Infrastructure, 2016.
8 EIA, 2016.
9 Shaffer, 2013.
10 Reuters, 2012.

11 Assessments on the volume of gas vary between sources. Data in this chapter reliy on estimates by the Ministry of Energy, as published on August 2, 2016, in their Hebrew website (http://energy.gov.il/Subjects/OilSearch/Pages/GxmsMniOilSearchAbout.aspx).
12 EIA, 2016.
13 Ministry of National Infrastructure, 2016.
14 Rubin/Eiran, 2015.
15 Brom/Landau, 2016.
16 Reuters, 2016.
17 Bar-Eli, 2015.
18 Comments given before audience at the Jewish Statesmanship Center, March 17, 2016.
19 Ministry of Foreign Affairs, 2016; National Security Council of Israel, 2015.
20 On such benefits see Shaffer, 2011.
21 Antitrust Authority, 2012.
22 See reports by the Ministry of Foreign Affairs and the National Security Council, n. 19.
23 When speaking before a special parliamentary committee in December 2015, Prime Minister Netanyahu stated that "The ability to export gas makes us more immune to international pressure. We don't want to be vulnerable to boycotts" (Haaretz, 2015). This argument took special hold following the EU's decision in November 2015 to label products originating from Israeli settlements.
24 Haaretz, 2011.
25 Personal communication with Eden Bar Tal, former Director-General, Ministry of Communications, May 26, 2016.
26 Shahar, 2015.
27 This assessment was given by the Governor of the Bank of Israel, Dr. Karnit Flug, Bank of Israel, 2015.
28 Israel's budget for FY2015 stood at 328 billion NIS (~$88 billion on date of approval) (Haaretz, 2014).
29 See the introduction in Humphreys et al., 2007.
30 Tenne, 2010, p. 10.

Bibliography

Antitrust Authority (2012): *The General Director of Restrictive Trade Practices Declares the Partners in the Natural-Gas Reservoir "Tamar" to have a Monopoly on Israel's Natural-Gas Supply.*

Bahgat, Gawdat (2014): Alternative Energy in Israel: Opportunities and Risks. *Israel Affairs* 20(1), 1–18.

Bank of Israel (2015): *Remarks by the Governor of the Bank of Israel to the Knesset Economics Committee Regarding the Natural Gas Outline Plan.*

Bar-Eli, Avi/Zvi Zrahiya (2015): Netanyahu Defends Contentious Natural Gas Deal as "National Security" Interest. *Haaretz*, December 8. Available at: www.haaretz.com/israel-news/business/.premium-1.690654.

Bialer, Uri (1998): *Oil and the Arab–Israeli Conflict, 1948–1963*. Basingstoke: Palgrave Macmillan.

Bialer, Uri (2007): Fuel Bridge across the Middle East – Israel, Iran, and the Eilat-Ashkelon Oil Pipeline. *Israel Studies* 12(3), 29–67.

Brom, Shlomo/Emily B. Landau (2016): Confidence Building at Sea: Advancing Maritime Security in the Mediterranean in a Regional Framework. *INSS Insight* 821. Available at: www.inss.org.il/publication/confidence-building-at-sea-advancing-maritime-security-in-the-mediterranean-in-a-regional-framework/.

Delek Energy (2016): *Yam-Tethys*. Available at: www.delekdrilling.co.il/en/project/yam-tethys.
EIA (2016): *International Energy Statistics – Israel*. U.S. Energy Information Administration.
Haaretz (2011): Some 450,000 Israelis March at Massive "March of the Million" Rallies across Country. September 3. Available at: www.haaretz.com/israel-news/some-450-000-israelis-march-at-massive-march-of-the-million-rallies-across-country-1.382366.
Haaretz (2014): Cabinet Approves $88 Billion Budget for 2015. October 8. Available at: www.haaretz.com/israel-news/business/.premium-1.619851.
Haaretz (2015): Netanyahu Defends Contentious Natural-gas Deal as "National Security" Interest. December 8. Available at: www.haaretz.com/israel-news/business/.premium-1.690654.
Humphreys, Macartan/D. Jeffrey Sachs/Joseph E. Stiglitz (2007): *Escaping the Resource Curse*. New York: Columbia University Press.
Ministry of Foreign Affairs (2016): *National and Strategic Aspects to the Development of the Gas Fields*.
Ministry of National Infrastructure, Energy and Water Resources (2016): *The Natural-sector in Israel*.
National Security Council of Israel (2015): *Natural-gas Sector in Israel – National Security Aspects and Repercussions from Delays in the Expansion and Export of Natural-gas*.
Reuters (2012): Israel Electric to Sell More Bonds as Cash Crisis Deepens. November 7.
Reuters (2016): Israel, Turkey Restore Ties in Deal Spurred by Energy Prospects. June 27. Available at: www.reuters.com/article/us-israel-turkey-erdogan-idUSKCN0ZD0DS.
Rubin, Aviad/Ehud Eiran (2015): *Dwelling at the Haven of the Sea: Maritime Strategic Report for Israel 2015*. Haifa: Haifa Research Center for Maritime Policy and Strategy.
Shaffer, Brenda (2011): Israel – New Natural-gas Producer in the Mediterranean. *Energy Policy* 39(9), 5379–5387.
Shaffer, Brenda (2013): Natural-gas Supply Stability and Foreign Policy. *Energy Policy* 56(C), 114–125.
Shahar, Shiri (2015): *Dark Jeans by Renuar – Claim What's Yours*. Tel-Aviv: Avraham ADV. Available at: www.youtube.com/watch?v=4KhQD7T70Ag.
Tenne, Abraham (2010): *Sea Water Desalination in Israel: Planning, Coping with Difficulties, and Economic Aspects of Long-term Risks, State of Israel Water Authority*. Ministry of Infrastructure Publication. Tel-Aviv: State of Israel Water Authority. Available at: www.water.gov.il/hebrew/planning-and-development/desalination/documents/desalination-in-israel.pdf.
The Jerusalem Post (2015): Netanyahu Signs Off on Controversial Natural-gas Deal. December 17. Available at: www.jpost.com/Israel-News/Politics-And-Diplomacy/Netanyahu-signs-off-on-natural-gas-deal-437620.

13 Jordan

Overcoming energy insecurity

Ayoub Abu-Dayyeh

Introduction

In several respects, Jordan's position in the Middle East is unique. While neighboring countries are experiencing political crises (Egypt, Lebanon) and violent conflicts (Iraq, Syria), the Hashemite Kingdom enjoys relative stability. Meanwhile, in energy, Jordan has been and continues to be dependent on imports – in stark contrast to its energy-rich neighbors Iraq and Saudi Arabia. Guaranteeing energy security, therefore, is of crucial importance, not only for economic growth but also for overall political stability in the Kingdom.

It is against this backdrop that changes in international energy affect Jordan. This chapter argues that these changes have – in multiple ways – a profound impact upon politics and the economy. In order to illustrate and explain this, the chapter will discuss the most important developments in Jordanian energy since the 2003 Iraq War, their impact upon Jordan's energy policy, and will then assess the impact of these developments upon the country's political economy.

Trends in Jordanian energy

Jordan's energy situation

Jordan's energy mix is dominated by fossil fuels, which accounted for 98 percent of the country's primary energy supply in 2014. Among the fossil fuels, there is an extreme concentration on oil, which accounts for 90 percent of the total supply (see Figure 13.1). Due to a lack of indigenous production, Jordan is extremely dependent on imports, and all of the country's fossil fuel needs – 98 percent of the country's energy mix – have to be imported.

Jordan's reliance on fossil fuel imports comes with two severe risks, both of which have a direct impact upon the Jordanian political economy. First, there is the danger of the physical interruption of supplies, which has proven to be a particular problem afflicting natural gas. When imports from Egypt collapsed in 2011/2012, the share of natural gas in Jordanian electricity production plummeted from 80 percent to 20 percent, causing shortages in power generation.

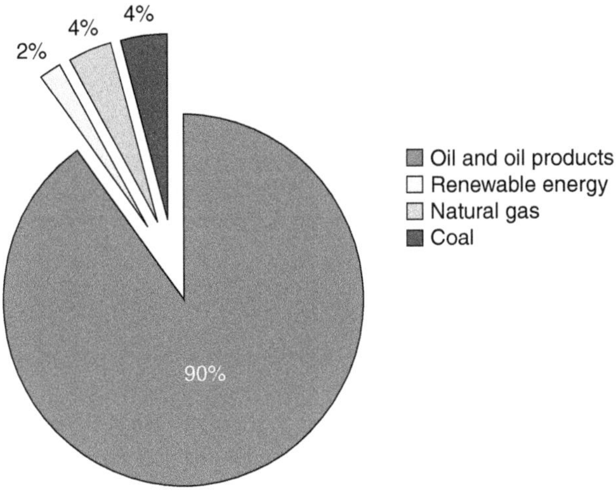

Figure 13.1 Jordan's primary energy mix.

Source: IEA (2016).

Second, Jordan is highly exposed to energy price fluctuations, making it vulnerable to developments in international energy markets.

The costs of energy insecurity

As a comparatively small country, the Kingdom has practically no influence on global price developments. Jordan is therefore forced to purchase oil internationally, regardless of the market price. Over the years, this has led to an increasing import bill, and until the recent oil price slump the costs of energy imports had grown from 7.5 percent of GDP in 2000 to 16.2 percent in 2013.[1] The financial resources used to procure these energy imports had of necessity to be diverted from other – potentially more productive – sectors of the economy.

Exposure to oil price volatility is severely complicating current and long-term planning efforts in the Jordanian economy. Uncertain energy costs and an undiversified portfolio heavily reliant on oil pose difficulties for decision-making in the energy sector and industry. In considering potentially available conventional energy sources, IMF estimates highlight the high responsiveness to changes in international energy prices (see Table 13.1). This is especially important with respect to LNG, the only fossil fuel alternative to oil imports Jordan is currently pursuing.

Therefore, restructuring the Jordanian energy system to move away from oil would bring great uncertainty as to whether alternative sources could be cost-competitive. Amid other challenges, this suggests that diversification of the Jordanian energy system can only succeed with sufficient government support both for diversification as a goal as well as for alternative energy sources.

Table 13.1 Costs of various fossil fuels

	$45/bbl	*$70/bbl*	*$99/bbl*	*$115/bbl*
Egyptian gas*	6	6	6	6
Diesel+	9	14	19	22
Heavy Fuel Oil+	8	11	16	18
LNG±	9–13	10–14	11–15	12–16
Gas from the Eastern Mediterranean±	6–7	6–7	8–10	8–10

Source: Gamba (2015).

Notes
* Based on negotiated contract.
+ Indicative.
± Range reflects lack of spot market; gas has not followed the recent decline in price of oil; final price to be negotiated.

Factors influencing Jordanian energy

In a period of about two decades, Jordan has experienced several drastic changes that have fundamentally affected its energy landscape. The following brief background discusses the most important features relevant to the understanding of Jordanian energy.

Relations with Iraq: During the Saddam Hussein era, Jordan's energy needs were satisfied largely by oil imports from neighboring Iraq. Iraq was the exclusive oil supplier to Jordan, exporting some 40 million barrels per year – half of which came free of charge and the other half at heavily subsidized prices. The 2003 US-led invasion of Iraq, which ended Saddam Hussein's rule, thus had a drastic impact upon Jordan's energy security. Oil imports from Iraq dwindled, forcing the country to search for alternative (and more expensive) supplies with basically no time for preparation.

Moreover, following the onset of the Iraq War in 2003, Jordan has taken in an increasing number of refugees from its neighbor, amounting for several years to hundreds of thousands (see below). Apart from sociopolitical consequences, the growing numbers of refugees also contributed to a rise in Jordanian energy demand, which increased on average some 3.5 percent per year between 2000and 2014.[2] Jordanian energy demand has further increased following the influx of Syrian refugees from 2011 onward, as has demand for water and liquefied petroleum fuel for cooking.

The increase of international energy prices after the world economic crisis: As mentioned above, Jordan relies almost entirely on energy imports to meet demand.[3] As international oil prices have risen, the country's import bill has grown, creating a huge burden for the Kingdom. For this reason, Jordan has begun to show interest in both nuclear and renewable energy (see below). Furthermore, as domestic prices were set based on a fixed tariff which failed to increase along with international levels, much of the burden of increasing energy costs was born by the Jordanian National Electric Power Company (NEPCO), a key contributor to the substantial rise of Jordanian debt levels since 2011.

Imports of natural gas from Egypt: In order to diversify both the energy mix and the import portfolio, Jordan began importing natural gas from Egypt in 2008 via the Arab Gas Pipeline, which runs through the Sinai Peninsula and Aqaba, with a capacity of 10 bcm per year. However, during the 2011 Egyptian revolution, the pipeline was frequently sabotaged and services ultimately ceased in 2012. The loss of Egyptian supply constituted a major setback for Jordan's attempts at diversifying its energy mix, increasing the importance of oil (imports).

The discovery of natural gas in the Eastern Mediterranean: Jordan does not have a maritime border with the Eastern Mediterranean, and consequently the country has no claim to the natural gas resources which have been discovered in the Levant Basin since 2009. Nevertheless, the discoveries in close proximity to Jordan have sparked a debate about whether natural gas could be imported from Egypt and/or Israel. The prospects for this, however, are slim, as Egypt is confronted with rapidly growing domestic needs, making export projects unlikely in the foreseeable future, while imports from Israel, regardless of whether or not sufficient gas is available, are politically unfeasible. Public sentiment is against the "normalization" of relations and as such against deepened economic cooperation, including natural gas trade. Considering the tense political situation in Jordan, it appears unlikely that the government could launch and sustain a project to import natural gas from Israel for over 15 years, despite having signed a contract to this end.[4] For the time being, it appears that Jordan is unlikely to benefit from any natural gas production in the Eastern Mediterranean – at least in the upcoming years.

The oil price decline: As unconventional production in North America has entered the markets in recent years, fierce competition among producers has caused a worldwide oversupply of oil. As a result, oil prices plummeted between 2014 and 2016. For Jordan, this constitutes a mixed blessing. On the one hand, the country's import bill is shrinking, and the savings, if used wisely, could be invested in Jordan's economy, including diversification of the country's energy mix. On the other hand, a significantly smaller import bill has reduced pressure on the government to do exactly that. Thus, low oil prices could negatively affect the search for alternatives (particularly oil shale). However, they do not appear to substantially affect the currently existing momentum to expand the use of renewables, particularly solar PV which has reached very low competitive prices.

The Aqaba LNG terminal: In July 2015, a LNG terminal was opened in Aqaba, allowing for imports through the Red Sea and the Gulf of Aqaba. The terminal supplies Jordan with 4.2 million cubic meters per day (some 1.5 bcm per year), equal to 16.5 percent of the country's 2014 primary energy supply. Natural gas from the Aqaba terminal is used for power generation. Until the Jordanian power sector adapts to accommodate increasing natural gas supply, the country will not utilize the terminal's full capacity, and thus has entered into a memorandum of understanding with Egypt to re-export excess imports. The inauguration of the Aqaba terminal in May 2015 coincided with a slump in international LNG prices, a development that has benefitted the Kingdom by facilitating a cost-competitive diversification of the energy supply.

Impact upon Jordan's energy policy

Dealing with energy insecurity

In order to address over-reliance on oil, Jordan has launched several initiatives aiming both at the diversification of supplies as well as the energy mix. As discussed, the country began using LNG in 2015, and previously imported via a pipeline from Egypt between 2008 and 2012. In 2013, Jordan and Iraq agreed on the construction of an oil and natural gas pipeline from Basra to Aqaba. However, in light of Iraq's chronic security problems, the execution of a project of this magnitude seems highly unlikely anytime soon.

Looking beyond imports, the Kingdom is also seeking to use indigenous sources. There is no a priori discrimination favoring a particular source of energy, as the Kingdom is examining all options available. Jordan holds large unconventional oil reserves (oil shale), which have given rise to hopes among decision-makers and the public to replace imports with domestic production. However, for the time being, Jordan's unconventional reserves were deemed non-commercial by international companies – due in part to the oil price decline.

Looking into alternatives

As indigenous fossil fuels are not an option in the foreseeable future, Jordan is left with two further options: nuclear and renewable energy. In 2007, King Abdullah II announced Jordan's intention to use nuclear energy for power generation, and the Jordanian Atomic Energy Commission (JAEC) was established a year later, in 2008. Soaring oil prices at the time, coupled with the belief that uranium is abundantly available in Jordan, gave rise to public support for this initiative. In 2015, Jordan signed a $10 billion preliminary deal with Russia whereby the Russian firm Rosatom would develop the country's first nuclear power plant, consisting of two 1000 MW reactors, by 2020.[5]

However, the future of nuclear power in Jordan is not without its problems. Jordan's electricity demand is relatively small – at least in comparison to more populous and industrial countries. Therefore, nuclear power would produce more electricity than base-load demand, resulting in surplus production of electricity. Due to conflicts in neighboring countries, it appears unlikely that additional production could be exported. Moreover, Jordan would need to keep additional electricity generation capacity readily available in the event of a shutdown of nuclear power (for maintenance or irregularities), incurring substantial further costs.

Moreover, there are pressing environmental questions. The disposal of nuclear waste is likely to add substantial environmental (and also financial) costs, while risks associated with nuclear accidents are tremendous. In addition to human mistakes and natural hazards (especially earthquakes and climate change effects), nuclear power plants in Jordan could become targets of domestic or international terrorists as well as regional conflict parties. Moreover, as elsewhere in the world, the consequences of a nuclear accident would be horrific. The catastrophes at Fukushima (2011) and Chernobyl (1986) provide tragic examples in this regard. Last but not least, the operation of nuclear power plants requires substantial amounts of water for cooling, and indeed nuclear power has the highest water usage among all thermoelectric technologies. In Jordan, one of the most water-poor countries in the world and prone to frequent drought, this constitutes a serious problem.

Parallel to nuclear energy, Jordan is also seeking to advance the use of renewable energy. The combination of Jordan's lack of domestic energy resources and limited water supply makes renewable resources an attractive option, while Jordan's domestic profile boasts great renewable potential. Located in the "sun-belt zone", solar radiation in Jordan is among the highest worldwide, with more than 300 days of sunshine on average per year. From a technological point of view, Jordan's entire electricity demand could be supplied with solar energy, though sufficient storage and/or backup capacity would be needed. There is also potential for wind energy in the country's north and west, where average wind speeds exceed 7 m/s.[6]

Jordan's Parliament adopted a renewable energy law in 2012, in the hopes of capitalizing on the country's endowments and reducing import dependency. A feed-in tariff was implemented in 2012 to attract private investors. The renewable energy law also included ambitious targets, mandating that some 10 percent of Jordan's energy consumption is to be supplied by renewable energy by 2020. Based on current estimations, this would equate to an installed capacity of 680 MW by 2020.[7] A new strategy was announced in late 2015, aiming to increase the share of renewables in electricity generation to 20 percent by 2020. The renewable energy law has provided the framework for the increased use of solar and wind energy, and has benefitted from cost reductions, particularly for photovoltaic modules. Jordan's installed renewable capacity was 180 MW as of January 2016, amounting to 6 percent of peak demand (3.1 GW). Projects with an accumulated capacity of 914 to 1039 MW are currently under development, equal to about 30 to 34 percent of current peak demand, or 13 to 15 percent of the projected peak demand in 2020 (6.8 GW).[8]

However, overall renewable energy continues to account for only a small proportion of Jordan's energy mix, some 2 percent in 2014 (however, it should be noted that during this time energy consumption was also growing).[9] In this context, it is important to note that Jordan is a developing country with a per-capita GDP of 1670 Jordanian Dinar (some €2100) in 2014,[10] and households generally face difficulties in affording installations like photovoltaic panels. Therefore, it will require time and, crucially, government support (i.e., financial support or incentives) before households and industry will embrace renewable energy on a large scale.

From the Jordanian state's point of view, there are also severe financial risks to the deployment of renewable energy. The feed-in law, adopted in 2012, reflects the costs and prices of that time and established a fixed tariff whose design did not foresee the adaptation to developments in cost/price. As a result, drastic increases or decreases of international oil prices could have harsh consequences, as was the case following the 2011 cut-off of Egyptian gas and the need to substitute with more expensive imports. The national power company was forced to cover the difference between the domestic market price and the international one, taking on substantial debt in the process. On the one hand, if oil prices increase beyond the level at which renewable energy requires subsidization in Jordan, the state would pay an additional premium (i.e., a subsidy) without any economic necessity. On the other hand, if oil prices fall below a certain level, the Jordanian state will be forced to purchase renewable energy from private producers at the same 2012 fixed rate. The state, in other words, has committed to purchasing renewable energy regardless of the difference in market prices, bearing the full price risk. This risk is a real one amid the current low price environment, since, according to the IMF, oil price levels starting at $50 per barrel and below would make renewables more expensive than oil.[11]

Impact upon Jordan's political economy

Energy and domestic political stability

Jordan's exposure to oil price volatility is set against the backdrop of a tense political atmosphere. During past years, several demonstrations occurred in Amman, the capital city. People have expressed their anger and dissatisfaction at the government's inability to deal with the country's economic problems, which include unemployment, soaring inflation, and increasing tax burdens. People expressed also their opposition to the government's plans to reduce subsidies.

To some extent, these demonstrations have been inspired by protests in other Arab countries as part of the Arab Spring in the years following 2010/2011. Indeed, during the Arab Spring, the Jordanian government reversed its policy of reducing subsidies on many consumer goods, including energy, and instead increased them in the hopes of alleviating social and political pressure. However, these subsidies have been lifted completely on fuel, and the government now only subsidizes electricity bills up to a level of 600 kWh per month for low-income families.

Jordan's problems have been intensified by the influx of large numbers of refugees. Conflicts in neighboring countries, in Iraq since 2003 and in Syria since 2011, have resulted in several hundred thousand people migrating to Jordan. Currently, in 2016, Jordan is host to some 656,000 refugees from Syria, amounting to around 7 percent of the Jordanian population, in addition to 58,000 Iraqi refugees still in the Kingdom.[12] While it is certainly true that Jordanian resources were constrained pre-crisis, the influx of Syrian refugees is exacerbating an already tight electricity supply environment. The 2015 Jordanian Response Plan states that total residential energy consumption in Jordan increased from 4926 GWh in 2009 to 6265 GWh in 2013,[13] indicating that population increases have exacerbated "long-standing structural challenges in the energy sector".[14]

This situation is also relevant to the energy–water nexus in Jordan, as the consumption of water has also dramatically increased, particularly in the most hydro-insecure governorates. Jordan has one of the world's lowest levels of water resources per capita, and falls well below the UNDP water-scarcity threshold, and issues related to water provision are relevant both for energy production and social stability. Currently, Jordan relies on thermoelectric sources of energy which are highly water intensive, while the production, transportation, and treatment of water in Jordan is likewise highly energy intensive.

Compared to its regional neighbors, Jordan enjoys relative political stability. However, the role of parties in Jordanian politics has traditionally been weak, and politics are riven with identity issues. In recent years, political stability has been challenged to a certain degree by Islamists, and the Jordanian branch of the Muslim Brotherhood, capitalizing on the momentum of the Brotherhood's victory in Egypt, has been particularly active. However, the spectrum of political Islamic actors is now fragmented, preventing them from playing a greater role in the political process.

In the Jordanian political system there is a Parliament, but real political power is more with the royal court. The role of parties has been traditionally weak. Effectively, tribal-based networks, rather than formal parties, are more decisive. A modification of the electoral law ahead of the September 2016 parliamentary election aimed at an increased role for political parties. However, considering that parties were forced to take a back seat for decades, this did not have a major effect in the short term. Hence, parties are generally not fulfilling the task of articulating the people's demands in the political arena.[15] However, the regional security environment has to some degree softened agitation for reform among the general public.

These conditions, namely a quasi-permanent economic crisis coupled with what many perceive as an exclusion from the political process, have led to a relatively high level of frustration among the Jordanian population. Against this backdrop, energy developments could profoundly shock Jordan's political system. The energy bill accounts for a large proportion of the average Jordanian household's costs already today, which is possibly providing grounds for future social tensions. Moreover, Jordan's efforts to accommodate refugees came with high costs, which have only partly been covered by international aid. Should the government continue to support people coming to the Kingdom from abroad while the Jordanian population is suffering economically, this could have consequences for political stability. Possibly more than in the past, therefore, should energy prices increase (because of subsidy cuts, a rise in international oil prices, or a combination of both), this may lead to further protests and demonstrations.

Energy and the economy: the government as buffer

Changes in the international price of oil had little effect on Jordanian energy demand. Neither the increase of prices in the late 2000s nor the decline since 2014 has had any major impact, and indeed domestic demand continued to increase dramatically. Between 1990 and 2014, Jordanian energy consumption more than doubled, reaching a level of 5275 kgoe.[16] As is the case throughout the MENA region, rising domestic demand has been driven by a combination of economic and population growth. Between 2000 and 2014, the country's GDP increased from 8.46 to 35.83 billion US dollars,[17] similar to growth levels in other MENA countries. However, Jordan's population growth has been extraordinary, as its stature as a relatively stable country in a turbulent region made it the destination of choice for migrants seeking shelter from conflicts in the region.

Amid the contribution of these factors to increasing domestic energy demand, oil price fluctuations, especially rising oil prices, have had basically no moderating effect. While this is surprising from a purely economic point of view, as at least some correlation between price signals and demand may be expected, there is no such correlation in Jordan (see Figure 13.2).

The reason for the development of energy consumption independent from international oil prices is the role of the Jordanian state. Domestic energy prices are regulated by the government and heavily subsidized. This ensures affordability but also encourages consumption/discourages improvements in efficiency.

Moreover, Jordan's government has undertaken tremendous efforts to provide energy (including electricity) to refugees. Although average energy consumption of a refugee is about three-quarters that of a Jordanian, the vast number of refugees has contributed to a significant increase in energy consumption in Jordan. In some governorates, the population has increased by some 30 percent in only three years. This has resulted in sharply rising needs of energy and water.[18]

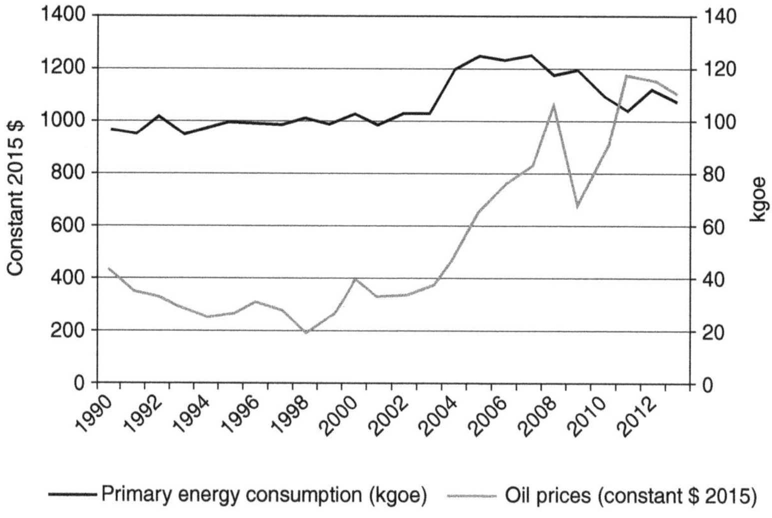

Figure 13.2 Oil prices and energy consumption.

Sources: BP (2016); World Bank (2016).

Ensuring access to energy while regulating and subsidizing domestic prices, the government acts as a buffer between domestic consumers and international markets. As a result, the Jordanian state must cope with fluctuations in international energy prices, the effects of which are felt by the government, and particularly born by NEPCO. Although the energy bill for private households (large consumers) is high, it is not the economy at large bearing the brunt of costs. Increasing energy prices, together with rising costs for hosting growing numbers of refugees, have contributed to a huge increase in government debt (see Figure 13.3). Indeed, in its 2015 end-of-year report on Jordan, the IMF said that continued reduction of Jordan's public debt is imperative to its economic health – and reliant on steadfast implementation of energy reforms.[19] In 2016, public debt reached a level of 93 percent of GDP.[20]

In 2012, Jordan's government began cutting energy subsidies. At the time, all gasoline, diesel, and kerosene subsidies were removed. Moreover, subsidies on LGP were cut. Low-income households, whose earnings were less than JD 10,000 (around €13,200) per year, some two-thirds of households in Jordan, were provided with cash handouts to compensate for the increased costs. Electricity subsidies, however, are still in place, causing the government debt to grow.[21]

Conclusion

Jordan remains extremely dependent on energy imports and thus is vulnerable to international energy developments. Energy security, both with regard to physical availability of supplies, sustainability, and affordability, is therefore of central importance. The inability to access energy imports would bring the country to

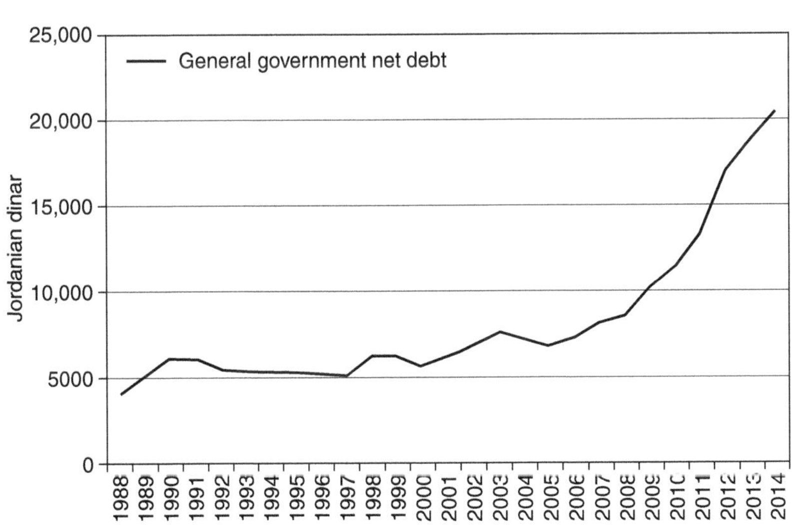

Figure 13.3 Government debt.

Source: IMF (2015).

the brink of economic collapse and, as such, has the potential to trigger a profound political crisis, while rising energy prices could result in social unrest and dissatisfaction, with implications for political stability.

However, in the current context, low oil prices improve the government's financial position, at least in relative terms, and create an opening for reform and progress. This opportunity should be used in order to advance the diversification of the Jordanian energy supply, particularly toward clean and renewable sources of energy. If successful, this would also constitute a major step forward in ensuring economic and political stability. If Jordan wishes to free itself from the vagaries of international energy markets, it must reduce imports. To reduce the government debt as well as import dependency, which are in part related, Jordan will need to develop domestic energy sources on a large scale. However, even in the best-case scenario, this is only possible over the long term. Nuclear energy is an unsuitable domestic option, for economic, political, and environmental reasons.

The way forward, therefore, is the expansion of renewable energy, combined with improvements in energy efficiency.

Notes

1 Gamba, 2015.
2 IEA, 2016.
3 Ibid.
4 Al-Monitor, 2016.
5 Meanwhile, there is talk about postponing the deadline to the mid-2020s.
6 Friedrich-Ebert-Stiftung, 2016.
7 Davies et al., 2016.
8 Ibid.
9 IEA, 2016.
10 IMF, 2016.
11 Gamba, 2015 (with the drastic drop of the costs of wind and PV in 2016–2017, this needs to be revised, though).
12 UNHCR, 2016.
13 Hashemite Kingdom of Jordan, 2014, p. 19.
14 Ibid., p. 88.
15 Wehler-Schoeck, 2016.
16 IEA, 2016.
17 IMF, 2016.
18 Lahn et al., 2016.
19 IMF, 2015.
20 World Bank, 2016.
21 Atamanov et al., 2015.

Bibliography

Al-Monitor (2016): Jordanians Fuming over Gas Deal with Israel. October 5. Available at: www.al-monitor.com/pulse/en/originals/2016/10/jordan-israel-gas-deal-popular-protest.html.

Atamanov, Aziz/Jon Robbert Jellema/Umar Serajuddin (2015): *Energy Subsidies Reform in Jordan: Welfare Implications of Different Scenarios.* Policy Research Working

Paper No. 7313. Washington DC: The World Bank Group. Available at: http://documents.worldbank.org/curated/en/595761467998814982/pdf/WPS7313.pdf.

BP (2016): *Statistical Review of World Energy*. London: BP.

Davies, Michelle/Shakeeb Ahmad/Yanxiang Wang (2016): *Developing Renewable Energy Projects – A Guide to Achieving Success in the Middle East*. Available at: www.pwc.com/m1/en/publications/documents/eversheds-pwc-developing-renewable-energy-projects-4th-edition.pdf.

Friedrich-Ebert-Stiftung (2016): *A Guide to Renewable Energy in Egypt and Jordan: Current Situation and Future Potentials*. Amman: Friedrich-Ebert-Stiftung.

Gamba, Andrea (2015): *New Energy Sources for Jordan: Macroeconomic Impact and Policy Considerations*. Working Paper No. 15/115. IMF. Available at: www.imf.org/external/pubs/ft/wp/2015/wp15115.pdf.

Hashemite Kingdom of Jordan (2014): *Jordan Response Plan for the Syria Crisis 2015*. Jordan Response Platform for the Syria Crisis, Ministry of Planning and International Cooperation. Available at: https://static1.squarespace.com/static/522c2552e4b0d3c39ccd1e00/t/57724779c534a592318575db/1467107258056/Annual+Report+-+Final+-+June+28.pdf.

IEA (2016): *Statistics Search Report–Jordan Balances for 2014*. London: BP.

IMF (2015): *Jordan: Seventh and Final Review under the Stand-by Arrangement*. IMF Country Report No. 15/225. Washington, DC: International Monetary Fund. Available at: www.imf.org/external/pubs/ft/scr/2015/cr15225.pdf.

IMF (2016): *World Economic Outlook Database*. Washington, DC: International Monetary Fund.

Lahn, Glada/Owen Grafham/Adel Essayed Sparr (2016): *Refugees and Energy Resilience in Jordan*. Moving Energy Initiative. Amman: The Royal Institute of International Affairs. Available at: www.chathamhouse.org/sites/files/chathamhouse/publications/research/2016-08-03-refugees-energy-jordan-lahn-grafham-sparr.pdf.

UNHCR (2016): *Jordan: UNHCR Operational Update*.

Wehler-Schoeck, Anja (2016): Parliamentary Elections in Jordan – A Competition of Mixed Messages. *International Policy Analysis*. Available at: http://library.fes.de/pdf-files/iez/12783.pdf.

World Bank (2016): *Jordan's Economic Outlook – Spring 2016*. Washington, DC: The World Bank Group.

14 Turkey

In between global trends and regional politics

Ellen Scholl

Introduction

Low global energy prices, a historic climate agreement, an increasingly global natural gas market, and energy trade across and between regions profoundly impact Turkey's domestic politics, economic situation, and position in regional politics. Situated amid European consumers and Middle Eastern and Central Asian producers and the liberalized markets of the former and the state-controlled economies of the latter, Turkey has long sought to leverage its strategic location for political gain. However, it is worth asking whether Turkey is capitalizing on its position in the middle, or is caught in between. As an energy importer and emerging market economy with rapidly growing energy demand, Turkey is vulnerable to external energy trends, particularly prices, which, compounded with internal political developments, including the centralization of power by the executive, could further destabilize the domestic economy and undermine the business climate in Turkey.

Energy in Turkey is both a commercial good, with partially liberalized markets and a market-based energy sector, and a strategic good, connected to foreign policy and a "proxy for larger geopolitical constellations".[1] The larger geopolitical constellations are numerous and difficult to disentangle from Turkey's energy prerogatives. From energy partnerships with the Kurdistan Regional Government (KRG) and Iran, to the relationship with and between Russia and the EU, from the Southern Gas Corridor (SGC) to the Eastern Mediterranean, energy partnerships and projects are commercial and strategic.

This chapter first situates Turkey geographically between regions and politically and economically as an energy importer and transit country vulnerable to energy trends. It then explains how Turkey's strategic position and role as an importer and taker of energy trends impacts upon and is impacted by domestic and regional politics, focusing on the liability and opportunity of natural gas as a strategic challenge. The chapter concludes that Turkey's desire for regional energy leadership and emphasis on growth is vulnerable to external energy developments even as domestic politics complicate these goals.

Locating Turkey amid competitive regions[2]

As Turkish author Elif Shafak writes, "identity is an insoluble dilemma in Turkey".[3] Straddling Europe, the Middle East, and Central Asia, Turkey is often called a crossroads or bridge, part of, yet distinct from, these regions. Rather than emphasize belonging, Turkish officials champion Turkey's role "in between" and its aspirations to play a regional energy and global political leadership role.[4] To make up for in strategic location what it lacks in resource endowment, Turkey leverages location for political gain. Although positioning itself as a key transit state, Turkey remains at the mercy of regional developments and geopolitical struggles. Regardless of any political leverage its position may afford, Turkey remains an energy price taker, reliant on imports and vulnerable to global energy prices.

As a non-Arab country in the Middle East, Turkey vacillates between looking to and beyond the neighborhood for partnership. Despite then Foreign Minister Davutoglu's "zero problems with neighbors" strategy, Turkey and its neighbors are mired in the complicated set of allegiances and proxies in the Syria conflict and in Iraq. The conflict has reignited Turkey's fear of an ethnic Kurdish state on its southern border and its domestic battle with the Kurdistan Workers Party (PKK), even as it seeks to deepen energy and economic ties with the KRG in northern Iraq.

Turkey's continued commitment as a Western partner is also in question. As changes in global energy markets shift traditional supply, demand, and trade patterns, it is unclear whether Turkey will continue to identify with the West and remain committed to liberalization and free markets, or align with different blocs and utilize energy as a strategic resource. The coalescence of executive power by President Erdogan and rifts over the Syrian conflict are driving a wedge between Turkey and its Western partners. EU membership prospects have grown "more distant and less desirable" on both sides,[5] even as Turkey's strategic importance remains clear. A shadow has also been cast over Turkey's relationship with the United States, as Ankara expresses vocal and public displeasure at US support for the People's Protection Unit (YPG), a Syrian Kurdish militia which Turkey regards as a branch of the PKK, and calls for the USA to extradite cleric Fethullah Gulen, blamed by Ankara for the abortive coup attempt in 2016. Expectations that the Trump Administration may usher in an era of renewed partnership were found wanting when the Trump Administration announced that it would expand support for the YPG in advance of President Erdogan's May 2017 visit. While this goes beyond energy, particularly given Turkey's role in NATO, the answer has implications for domestic and regional energy politics, development, and trade.

Like the EU, Turkey is an energy importer and shares energy dependency concerns, which has led to cooperation on energy.[6] As a crux of the Southern Gas Corridor, Turkey is crucial to the EU's diversification strategy, while Gazprom's proposed Turkish Stream project connects Turkey to Russian plans to diversify away from Ukrainian transit. Turkey is an Energy Community observer (resistant to full membership, saying it is not a substitute for EU accession)[7] and has pursued moderate energy sector liberalization under the auspices of its EU candidacy, even as the energy chapter remains closed due to the Cyprus issue. Turkey's electricity sector has moved from a state-owned monopoly to a competitive market,[8] and the Energy Community Secretariat said that Turkey "can be considered a pioneer of liberalization and a benchmark for a region still struggling to overcome its unfortunate fragmentation", referring to the state of many contracting parties.[9] TEIAS, the Turkish transmission system operator, became the first observer to ENTSO-E in 2016 following a long-term synchronization agreement connecting Turkey to the European system.

Gas market liberalization has been slower. Key components of the 2001 Natural Gas Market Law, aimed at reducing the state's role in the gas sector, have not been implemented and reforms remain pending. State-owned BOTAS has not been fully unbundled, and it dominates imports, trade, and wholesale while just 20 percent of imports have been allotted to private firms, compared to the 80 percent envisioned under the 2001 reforms.[10]

Amid shifting political and energy dynamics, Erdogan has insinuated that Turkey could look elsewhere for partnership, expressing interest in a customs union with the Eurasian Economic Union and Shanghai Cooperation Organization (SCO) membership. As a Dialogue Partner, Turkey is the first non-member country to hold the SCO Energy Club Presidency in 2017. Efforts to promote East–West connectivity and to create common spaces for (energy) trade and investment across Asia, like China's One Belt, One Road initiative, may become increasingly attractive as Turkey's EU prospects fade and its relationship with the USA remains fraught.[11] While serious overtures have not been made, Eurasian cooperation on issues from energy to counter-terrorism could appear increasingly appealing.[12]

Turkey shares some ethnic and linguistic ties with the Central Asian Republics and interest in energy transit routes connecting these energy-rich states to European customers via Turkey. However, the Caspian's unresolved legal status, China's role in the region, and Turkey's often-volatile relationship with Russia loom large. Turkey, Gazprom's second largest gas customer after Germany, relies on Russia for over half of its gas imports, while Russia is using the Syria conflict to expand its influence in the region, particularly amid new energy discoveries in the Eastern Mediterranean. Despite the Turkish downing of a Russian jet, the assassination of the Russian ambassador in Ankara, and the accidental death of Turkish soldiers in Russian airstrikes, Ankara recognizes that it must work with Russia in Syria to secure its national security interests. The two collaborated to broker a ceasefire in late 2016 and have conducted joint airstrikes.

Turkey as a taker of energy trends

As a growing importer in an unpredictable region and an energy price taker in a volatile global market, Turkey is impacted by global energy trends, namely energy prices, rising demand growth, and potential regional energy trade. Like its Middle Eastern neighbors, Turkey has experienced rapid energy demand growth over the last decade, second only to China (a fact often touted proudly by Turkish politicians), as well as rising energy imports, energy intensity,[13] and energy-related CO_2 emissions.

Meeting rising current and future domestic energy consumption needs is a major challenge, as Turkey is reliant on imports for around 80 percent of total energy needs and nearly all of its oil and gas.[14] Imports have risen as domestic energy demand has increased dramatically. Total primary energy consumption increased 52 percent, from 86.4 to 131.3 MTOE between 2005 and 2015.[15] Natural gas is the largest source of energy, accounting for 30.2 percent in 2015, followed by oil (30.1%) and coal (27.3%),[16] while electricity demand, along with installed electric generation capacity, has nearly doubled between 2004 and 2014.[17,18] Nearly 70 percent of electric generation comes from fossil fuels, with natural gas accounting for nearly 40 percent.[19] Energy-related CO_2 emissions have increased steadily from 1990 to 2014, and consumption has not yet decoupled from growth.[20] Energy intensity continues to increase despite the official goal of a 20 percent reduction by 2023.

Growing demand and import dependency leaves the Turkish economy vulnerable to external energy developments. The increasing current account deficit through the 2000s, which reached a record \$75 billion in 2011 due in part to high energy (primarily oil) prices illustrates the vulnerability to global prices.[21] While the post-November 2014 oil price drop has helped lower import bills and bring the deficit down to \$32.2 billion in 2015, a decrease of \$13.6 billion over 2014,[22] lower global prices have not translated into lower prices for household consumers due in part to the instability of the lira. Absent domestic economic reforms, including changes in interest rate policy, and meaningful efforts to curb energy demand or improve energy efficiency, Turkey will remain vulnerable to energy prices and a rising current account deficit should global oil prices rise.

The intersection of energy trends and geopolitical dynamics contributes to and is exacerbated by domestic political instability and deteriorating domestic security. Following polarized elections in 2015, the collapse of the armistice between the Turkish government and the PKK, a resurgence of terrorist attacks, and the influx of nearly three million Syrian refugees fleeing conflict on Turkey's southern border, instability has become the new normal. Add the summer 2016 failed coup attempt and subsequent purge of civil servants, a rash of arrests, and a seemingly perpetual state of emergency, and Turkey has all the hallmarks of instability and uncertainty. Moreover, while President Erdogan has touted the economic advantages of changes to the Turkish constitution centralizing power in the executive, approved by a narrow 51.4 percent margin in the April 2017 referendum, it remains to be seen whether investors will return to a country not only deeply divided, but also where the potential for political interference in the economy is high.

The combination of energy price volatility and political instability could be detrimental, particularly for the ruling Justice and Development Party, or AKP, whose electoral success is based partly on rapid growth and improving the living conditions of its 80 million citizens. While President Erdogan built his reputation on consumption-driven growth, including in energy, the AKP has failed to address structural weaknesses in the Turkish economy, leading to a high current account deficit and external debt. Erdogan's attempts to consolidate executive power have contributed further to a decline in foreign investment and a "meltdown" of the lira.[23] This is exacerbating growing foreign currency-denominated external debt, driven partially by energy imports and sensitive to rising energy prices. The 2016 appointment of Erdogan's son-in-law as Energy Minister illustrates Erdogan's tightening personal control over executive branch functions to fortify and expand his power over Turkey's energy future.

The deterioration of domestic political stability and the overall security climate are eroding investor confidence and Turkey's credit rating, as lending institutions downgraded Turkey to non-investment grade in early 2017.[24] The centralization of power and targeting of businesses (including the Anatolian Tigers, previously supportive of and supported by Erdogan) in the ongoing post-coup attempt purges have sparked fears that Turkey, having transitioned from a state-controlled to a liberal economy over the past decade, may be regressing. A resurgence of attacks on energy infrastructure, including the February 2016 attack on the pipeline transporting KRG oil to Turkey, undermines Turkey's perceived attractiveness and reliability as an energy corridor, while Erdogan's willingness to use the deteriorating security challenges as a rationale for increasing executive authority further exacerbates uncertainty.

Meeting domestic demand: a defining challenge

Exposure to international energy trends and vulnerability to price changes not only impact Turkey's domestic economy, but also drive energy policy, including the emphasis on the diversification and utilization of domestic resources. Turkey's energy policy goals, as outlined in the AKP's 2023 Vision (intended to make Turkey a top ten global economy by 2023) and the Ministry of Energy and Natural Resources' (MENR) Strategic Plan, include "resource diversity" of resource type and import country and optimization of domestic resources to reduce "risks associated from import dependency".[25] The Turkish government hopes to diversify imports while increasing the consumption of coal, nuclear, and renewables (overwhelmingly, though not exclusively, hydro) in the hopes of reducing reliance on "external"[26] sources, i.e., natural gas. Energy Minister Albayrak elaborated on this effort, announcing a new energy and mining strategy in 2017 focused on domestic resources, primarily through mining for domestic coal, potentially problematic in the absence of efforts to improve workplace safety standards following the 2014 Soma mine disaster, and expanding LNG and oil and gas storage capacity.

The focus on energy security, driven by a prioritization of economic growth undergirded by a preference for coal consumption, could pit energy security against sustainability. Despite G20 commitments to reduce fossil fuel subsidies and promises to reduce greenhouse gas emissions under the Paris Agreement, the Turkish government has recommitted to domestic coal production and consumption even as coal's future is increasingly in question. Coal, Turkey's most abundant domestic fossil resource, is valued by the government as a source of diversification, a buffer against foreign dependence, and integral in delivering on promises of economic growth and meeting growing energy demand.

The Turkish government aims for domestic coal consumption to exceed 60 billion kWh annually by the end of the decade, essentially doubling over the 2014 to 2019 strategic planning period.[27] According to the International Energy Agency, over 30 GW of potential new coal projects are in the pipeline: 7 GW under construction, 13 GW under evaluation, 3 GW proposed, and the rest announced with little progress,[28] placing Turkey fourth after China, India, and Russia in planned new coal-fired generation.[29] This could lock in coal as a substantial part of Turkey's energy future, potentially exposing the country to the risk of stranded resources and assets under a more stringent global climate regime and the environmental harm and air pollution from increased coal utilization.

Although touted as indigenous, the bulk of Turkey's domestic coal consumption is imported hard coal, while domestic coal reserves are almost entirely low-quality lignite. Nearly all (95%) of Turkey's hard coal, over half of total consumption, comes from imports, mostly from Colombia, Russia, South Africa, and Australia.[30] Despite the aim to reduce imports, prioritization of coal consumption also implies reliance on external suppliers and prices, even if the market is more liberal and prices have been lower in recent years (although prices were on the upswing in late 2016 due to curtailed Chinese production). To limit the effects of import dependency, Turkey enacted an import duty on coal used in power generation from non-EU/European Free Trade Association countries.[31]

Nuclear power also plays a theoretical, if yet unrealized, role in Turkey's diversification plans, even as long-unfulfilled nuclear aspirations have implications for security debates over nuclear developments across the Middle East and raise questions about spent fuel storage and disposal, seismic activity, and regional and domestic security. The Turkish government has signed Intergovernmental Agreements with Russia and Japan for the construction of facilities at Akkuyu on the Eastern Mediterranean coast and Sinop on the Black Sea coast, respectively. The Akkuyu plant, to be built by Rosatom, will total four 1200 MW units, with construction anticipated to begin in 2018 and the first unit online by 2023, the same year that the first of Sinop's four 1150 MW units is expected to come online.[32] Turkey has plans for a third project with China following an agreement between the two countries on the peaceful use of nuclear power. While viewed as a means to alleviate dependency, Turkey's nuclear aspirations are not free from political influence, as progress on Akkuyu stalled during the diplomatic row between Turkey and Russia. Nor is domestic nuclear development immune to external energy trends: as Russia comes increasingly under pressure from low oil prices and international sanctions, its ability to meet its financial obligations under the Build Own Operate model could be hampered.

While renewables are part of the diversification strategy on paper, they remain insignificant in political attention and proliferation with the exception of hydropower, the bulk of current and historical renewable generation. Turkey is also vulnerable to climate variability, which could make Turkish hydropower far less reliable. For example, during the 2014 dry season, hydropower accounted for around 16 percent of electricity production, compared to an average of 23 percent over the past ten years.[33] Turkey implemented a domestic Renewable Energy Law in 2010, and installed wind and solar capacity increased over 70 percent and nearly 100 percent, respectively, between its passage and 2015.[34] Installed solar capacity rose from 6 to 249 MW. While still far behind countries like Germany (nearly 40,000 MW) or Italy (nearly 19,000 MW), Turkey has the highest capacity among Central Asian and Middle Eastern countries with the exception of Israel[35] and could take advantage of falling solar PV costs.

Natural gas: domestic challenge or strategic opportunity?

Gas, with its fixed infrastructure, contracts, and systems, offers Turkey the (real or perceived) opportunity to use location to its benefit, while the burden of meeting rising domestic gas demand and enabling continued growth plays heavily into domestic political expectations. Natural gas is both a facilitator and an indicator of rising domestic consumption and a component of Turkey's energy leadership. However, it is also considered a "strategic liability"[36] and key risk to be mitigated by decreasing its share in the electricity portfolio and diversifying imports.[37]

Meeting rapid and steep natural gas growth is a major challenge, complicated by internal infrastructure constraints, global energy prices, regional energy trade, and geopolitical dynamics. Natural gas consumption in Turkey has more than doubled, from approximately 20 bcm in 2003 to nearly 48 bcm in 2014,[38] nearly all of which is satisfied by imports (99 percent in 2015),[39] which have grown to almost 80 percent since 2005.[40] Demand is currently reaching the limits of the country's transmission infrastructure and import capacity, and limited storage means that any import disruption could impact domestic supply, with potentially negative political implications for faith in the AKP to deliver on its economic growth promises. However, gas demand growth appeared more sluggish in late 2016 and early 2017, potentially indicating that the Turkish government's emphasis on domestic resources may be having an impact or that the overall economic slowdown is dampening demand.

Turkey's natural gas consumption has increased steadily and steeply since the 1986 signing of the first gas sales contract between BOTAS and the USSR's Soyuzgaz and commencement of gas flow in 1988, with the exception of a decline and subsequent surge in 2009.[41] Gas represents an increasingly large share of power production, while industry consumption is the fastest-growing sector.[42] In 2015, imports totaled 48.2 bcm, coming from Russia (55.1%), Iran (16.2%), Azerbaijan (12.3%), Algeria (8.1%), and Nigeria (2.9%).[43] Russian gas is delivered via the Trans-Balkan Pipeline and Blue Stream Pipeline, while gas from Iran comes via the Tabriz–Ankara pipeline and from Azerbaijan through the South Caucuses Pipeline. LNG imports accounted for 7.5 bcm in 2015[44] making Turkey the world's eighth largest LNG consumer.[45]

While LNG has played a marginal role in ensuring gas supply security, the increasingly liquid global LNG market provides potential options for diversification, like supplies from Qatar or spot purchases, including from the USA in 2016. In addition to the BOTAS-owned Marmara Eregesli (5.9 MTPA) and Egegaz-owned Aliaga LNG, (4.4 MTPA), in December 2016 Turkey commissioned the Neptune, its first floating storage and regasification unit (FSRU).[46] The additional 20 mcm per day capacity will provide needed storage capacity and address fluctuating seasonal demand, which often spikes and exceeds total capacity in winter. At the facility's opening ceremony, Erdogan said Turkey should "prioritize LNG investments in order to establish a more healthy balance of our natural gas business",[47] emphasizing that global gas market dynamics may influence Turkey's strategic calculations.

While the establishment of a FSRU and the potential to increase LNG imports are in line with trends in global markets, the stalled liberalization of the domestic gas market prevents changes occurring elsewhere from being felt in the Turkish domestic market. For instance, while long-term contracts (LTCs) and indexing the price of LNG to oil is slowly changing in European markets, LTCs are still dominant in Turkey, where BOTAS remains the dominant player in import contracts, impeding the development of gas trading and gas-on-gas competition.

Many of Turkey's natural gas purchase agreements expire in the mid-2020s, potentially making meeting natural gas demand over the medium term a significant challenge: 40 bcm per year in supply contracts are set to expire by 2026, while 15 bcm per year is set to expire in the next five years.[48] This is particularly difficult given limitations on BOTAS' ability to sign or renew contracts and private companies' lack of ability to buy gas from BOTAS partners under the Natural Gas Market Law.[49] Amid uncertainty in meeting future demand, the Turkish government aims to reduce imports from a single country to less than 50 percent, a goal potentially at odds with security of supply.[50] This disproportionately targets Russian supply, even as Gazprom has been a reliable supplier, and fails to address the challenges of other, less reliable suppliers, namely Iran. The gas relationship, cemented by the Iran–Turkey pipeline and the 1996 gas supply agreement, has been fraught with disputes over volume and price, and mired in broader geopolitical issues related to Iranian sanctions.[51] Supply is often expensive and unreliable, particularly in winter when Iran prioritizes domestic needs, while investment in Iranian infrastructure and capacity is sorely needed. In 2016, the International Arbitration Court ruled in favor of Turkey in a suit over prices (though not on issues of volume and specifications), finding that Iran overcharged for gas exports from 2011 to 2015.

Given the challenge of meeting domestic gas demand, particularly as existing contracts expire, and the goal of becoming a critical energy corridor, regional gas developments are critical for Turkey and vice versa. Turkey hopes that these projects will diversify and secure future supply and cement its role as an energy hub (although corridor is more accurate). Future pipeline plans are intertwined with broader geopolitical issues among Turkey, the EU, Russia, and its regional neighbors and are impacted by changing energy trends. The following projects are particularly important for Turkey's energy future and regional energy dynamics.

Southern Gas Corridor (SGC): The SGC is the most recent iteration of aspirations to bring gas from the Central Asian Republics via Turkey to Europe. Comprised of multiple pipelines, the Project of Common Interest is a key component of EU–Turkey energy cooperation and the EU's overall diversification strategy. The project aims to deliver 6 bcm annually to Turkey from the Shah Deniz II field beginning in 2018/2019, and 10 bcm annually to Europe by 2020, with the potential to scale up total capacity to 32 bcm.

The proposed 1850 km Trans-Anatolian Pipeline (TANAP) will connect to the expanded South Caucasus pipeline to bring Azeri gas from Georgia to the Turkish–Greek border, and connect to the Trans-Adriatic pipeline (TAP), which will bring gas from Greece across Albania and the Adriatic Sea before terminating in Italy. Construction on TANAP's eastern Turkish segment commenced in 2015 and on TAP in 2016. The EU continues to express hopes that the Trans-Caspian pipeline will be constructed and Turkmen gas added to the system, but opposition from Iran and Russia, the two major Caspian states, and the still unresolved (sea or lake) legal status make this unlikely.

The project is the newest evolution of previous (unsuccessful) efforts to bring Azeri (and Central Asia and Middle Eastern) gas to Europe via Turkey. TANAP, driven by producer-backed bilateral agreements between Azerbaijan and Turkey, put an end to the ill-fated Nabucco, a multilateral, multi-supplier project with US and EU political backing but plagued by financial obstacles. While Nabucco would have come under EU law, TANAP will be managed under Turkish law,[52] and does not provide for Third Party Access. The potential strength of TANAP's producer-driven approach lies in the financing through Azeri state-owned SOCAR, the senior partner (58%) to Turkey's BOTAS (30%), through oil revenues. However, in a lower oil price environment, SOCAR has received loans from the AIIB ($600 million)[53] and the World Bank ($400 million).[54] The high cost of the project also means that viability relies in part on future expansion, which is not guaranteed in the current price environment and given Gazprom's pursuit of Turkish Stream.

Turkish Stream: While crucial to EU plans to diversify away from Russian gas imports, Turkey is part of Russian efforts to diversify away from Ukrainian transit, and is seen as an attractive growing market. Following Russia's December 2014 cancellation of South Stream, Turkish Stream arose seemingly in its place, originally proposed with the same capacity as South Stream (63 bcm) in four strings. One string was to deliver 14 bcm per year to Turkey while the other three would end at the Turkish–Greek border, requiring either a renegotiation of delivery points stipulated in LTCs with European customers or the construction of additional pipelines in order for the gas to make it to its intended European customers.[55]

The project was suspended during the November 2015 to June 2016 spat between Turkey and Russia, and later revived (along with cooperation on the Akkuyu nuclear plant) following Erdogan's apology, at half the capacity. The proposed project is potentially two strings, one supplying the Turkish domestic market (15.75 bcm[56]) with another line ending at the Greek border to supply (in theory) the EU while avoiding compliance with the Third Energy Package and Third Party Access rules. The project is part of intentions to dramatically reduce transit through Ukraine following the 2019 expiration of the transit contract with Naftogaz.

Russian exports via Ukraine to Europe (including Turkey) were approximately 80 bcm per year[57] in 2013 and 62 bcm in 2014, and two-thirds of Turkey's Russian gas imports transit Ukraine (27.3 bcm in 2014).[58] While Russian gas exports to Europe via Ukraine will not be replaced by a single (and unlikely) 15.75 bcm line, Gazprom, along with European partner companies, proposed the 55 bcm Nord Stream II project, potentially running from Russia under the Baltic Sea to Germany.

In October 2016 the governments signed (and later ratified) an Intergovernmental Agreement, laying the legal foundations for the construction of the two strings.[59] However, while Russia has an interest in building offshore strings to reach the Turkish domestic market and Europe, progress in obtaining permits and construction contracts is limited to the string intended for the Turkish domestic market. Continuing low energy prices, the existence of a 25-year supply contract between the Shah Deniz consortium and European companies, and EU regulatory requirements make construction of the second string to Europe unlikely; however, Gazprom could request Third Party Access to TAP following the initial 25-year exemption.

Eastern Mediterranean: As discussed in this volume, the discoveries of the Aphrodite, Tamar, and Leviathan fields off the coast of Cyprus and Israel, and Zohr in Egypt's offshore, are shaking up regional gas dynamics. These developments could undergird a new regional "Eastern Mediterranean" identity, provide an impetus for parties to come to the table to address long-standing issues, and to underwrite a potential shared economic future. The Turkish market is a potentially attractive and viable export market and route for these resources, providing Turkey with new sources of gas supply and producing countries with an export market.

However, this is far from guaranteed. Low global commodity prices impact the future of these projects, as the gas is comparatively expensive to develop and finding export markets is challenging. However, export markets must be secured to make these projects economically viable. The size, growth, and proximity of the Turkish market make it an attractive option, particularly as the discovery of the Zohr field and major investment announced by BP and Eni has changed long-term export prospects to Egypt, while re-export to the EU through Egypt could be cost prohibitive.

In Cyprus, Turkey's role in the ongoing dispute over the divided island could stymie gas development, even amid hopes that gas could serve as a catalyst to address long-standing issues. Turkey does not recognize the Republic of Cyprus' EEZ and claims that Cyprus does not have the right to exploit its natural resources until the island's political situation and competing territorial water claims have been resolved. Turkey has attempted to intimidate exploration vessels of multinational corporations granted offshore drilling licenses by the Republic of Cyprus.[60] Potential gas production has also raised questions of revenue sharing among the island's Greek and Turkish Cypriot communities and broader sovereignty issues.

Potential gas development likely played a role in the July 2016 restoration of diplomatic ties between Turkey and Israel, ending the estrangement since the Mavi Marmara raid. The countries' energy ministers met in October 2016, the first ministerial meeting since the *rapprochement*, and established a dialogue to discuss a potential pipeline to bring Israeli gas from the Leviathan field to Turkey.[61] However, this cooperation could also become embroiled in larger questions related to Cyprus.

Conclusion: an uncertain energy outlook

Turkey is and finds itself at a global energy crossroads. Turkey's energy future is contingent on the interplay between domestic, regional, and international factors. Meeting rising energy demand is both a key challenge for the Turkish government and an opportunity for Turkey to capitalize on and leverage its strategic location. While Turkey's centrality to numerous cross-border projects is crucial for meeting future domestic needs and may help Turkey become an increasingly important energy corridor, this does not necessarily mean that Ankara will achieve its broader energy hub goal.

Turkey's domestic and external energy policies reflect a geostrategic and security-focused approach potentially at odds with sustainability. Domestically, the AKP's focus on growth, absent efforts to reduce energy intensity and improve efficiency, will continue to drive energy demand. Demand will drive imports and thus contribute to Turkey's current account deficit and precarious economic situation even as Erdogan seeks to use his expanded executive authority to stave off economic instability before Turkey's next election. As domestic politics become increasingly fragmented and power is centralized in the executive, questions about Turkey's commitment to liberal markets and concerns about the vulnerability of private sector firms and investment to volatile politics and potential targeting could undermine Turkey's ability to attract investment in domestic energy infrastructure.

In particular, developing the energy sector to meet domestic needs and capitalizing on its position as an energy crossroads will require the confidence of investors and partners. Following a winter of record demand curtailments and looking toward the mid-2020s, the need for such investment is clear. Turkey's energy future depends on whether it inspires confidence as a reliable energy partner and transit state or elicits concern as an unstable country that politicizes energy relations. Thus, Turkey's energy future is dependent not only on international energy developments, but also contingent on perceptions of stability and reliability, which remain far from guaranteed amid the complex web of domestic and regional political, economic, and security issues.

Notes

1 Richert, 2016b, p. 101.
2 This term appears in Scholl/Westphal, 2017.
3 *Financial Times*, 2017a.
4 Richert, 2016a.
5 Yabanci, 2016, p. 4.
6 Ibid., p. 9.
7 Kopac/Ekinci, 2015.
8 This was achieved largely through the passage of the 2001 Electricity Market Law n. 4628, which unbundled the state electricity provider and established the independent Energy Market Regulatory Authority (EMRA) and amended energy market legislation n. 6446 in 2015.
9 Energy Community Secretariat, 2015, p. 7.
10 IEA, 2016a, p. 116.
11 Koru/Kaymaz, 2016.
12 Kuzmina, 2015.
13 According to a presentation by IEA Director Fatih Birol, IEA Europe average energy intensity has decreased by 16 percent on average since 2005 while Turkey's energy intensity increased by 7 percent over the same period (IEA, 2016b).
14 IEA, 2016a, p. 30.
15 BP, 2016, p. 40.
16 IEA, 2016a, p. 71.
17 Ibid., p. 9.
18 IEEFA, 2016, p. 15.
19 IEA, 2016a, p. 131.
20 Ibid., p. 33.
21 Al-Monitor, 2014.
22 *Hurriyet Daily News*, 2016.
23 *Financial Times*, 2017b.
24 Reuters, 2017.
25 Republic of Turkey Ministry of Energy and Natural Resources (MENR), 2014, p. 32.
26 This is in quotation marks, as most of Turkey's coal consumption is imported hard coal. However, given the difference in the international coal market versus more domestic and regional gas markets and less liberalized trade, this is seen as qualitatively different.
27 Republic of Turkey Ministry of Energy and Natural Resources (MENR), 2014, p. 33.
28 IEA, 2016a, p. 92.
29 Sahin, 2016, p. 7.
30 IEA, 2016a, p. 89.
31 Platts, 2016.
32 World Nuclear Association, 2016.
33 Energy Community Secretariat, 2015, p. 38.
34 Author's own calculations based on data from IRENA, 2016.
35 Ibid., p. 30.
36 Cagaptay/Evans, 2013, p. 6.
37 Republic of Turkey Ministry of Energy and Natural Resources (MENR), 2014, p. 23.
38 IEA, 2016a, pp. 103–105.

39 EIA, 2017.
40 IEA, 2016a, p. 103.
41 Rzayeva, 2014, p. 5.
42 IEA, 2016a, p. 192.
43 Ibid., p. 104.
44 BP, 2016, p. 29, Table, Gas trade in 2014 and 2015 in billion cubic meters (bcm).
45 IGU, 2016, p. 10.
46 Ibid., p. 5.
47 Daily Sabah, 2016.
48 Austvik/Rzayeva, 2016, pp. 7–8.
49 Ibid., p. 15.
50 Republic of Turkey MENR, 2014, p. 39.
51 Kinnander, 2010.
52 Rzayeva, 2014, p. 60.
53 AIIB, 2016.
54 World Bank, 2016.
55 Pirani/Yafimava, 2016, p. 11.
56 Gazprom, 2016b.
57 CIEP, 2013.
58 Pirani/Yafimava, 2016, p. 60, Table A3.
59 Gazprom, 2016a.
60 Holland, 2015.
61 Al-Monitor, 2016.

Bibliography

AIIB (2016): AIIB Approves $600 Million to Support Energy Project of Azerbaijan. December 21. Available at: http://euweb.aiib.org/html/2016/NEWS_1222/199.html.

Al-Monitor (2014): Can Turkey Work Miracle on Current Account Deficit? April 14. Available at: www.al-monitor.com/pulse/originals/2014/04/turkey-deficit-energy-current-account-economy.html.

Al-Monitor (2016): Turkey, Israel to Examine Building Gas Pipeline. October 13. Available at: www.al-monitor.com/pulse/sites/almonitor/contents/afp/2016/10/turkey-israel-energy-gas-politics.html.

Austvik, Ole Gunnar/Gulmira Rzayeva (2016): *Turkey in the Geopolitics of Natural Gas*. Working Paper Series No. 66, Harvard Kennedy School M-RCBG. Available at: www.diplomatieglobal.de/archiv/2016/RzayevaTurkeyinGeopoliticsofNaturalGas092016.pdf.

BP (2016): *Statistical Review of World Energy 2016*. London: BP.

Cagaptay, Soner/Tyler Evans (2013): *The Geopolitics of Natural Gas: Turkey's Energy Policy and the Future of Natural Gas*. University's Baker Institute Center for Energy Studies and the Harvard Kennedy School Belfer Center for Science and International Affairs. Available at: www.bakerinstitute.org/media/files/Research/f1cb2090/CES-Pub-Geogas-Turkey5.pdf.

CIEP (2013): *Russian Gas Imports to Europe and Security of Supply – Fact Sheet*. Clingendael International Energy Programme

Daily Sabah (2016): Turkey's First FSRU Opened, Ready to Boost Energy Supply Security by 20M cbm Daily. December 23. Available at: www.dailysabah.com/energy/2016/12/24/turkeys-first-fsru-opened-ready-to-boost-energy-supply-security-by-20m-cbm-daily.

EIA (2017): *Country Analysis Brief: Turkey*. Washington, DC: U.S. Energy Information Administration.

Energy Community Secretariat (2015): *Energy Governance in Turkey. Report on Compliance with the Energy Community Acquis*. Vienna: Energy Community. Available at: www.energy-community.org/portal/page/portal/ENC_HOME/DOCS/3894261/25824B882CF017E0E053C92FA8C0EE59.PDF.

Financial Times (2017a): Chess Is a Troubling Metaphor as Turkey Turns to the East. January 8. Available at: www.ft.com/content/cefc19ee-ccea-11e6-b8ce-b9c03770f8b1.

Financial Times (2017b): Lira Fall Imperils Erdogan's Grand Designs in Turkey. January 12. Available at: www.ft.com/content/107ed46c-d8ba-11e6--944b-e7eb37a6aa8e.

Gazprom (2016a): *Alexey Miller: Legal Framework for Turk Stream Established*.

Gazprom (2016b): *Construction Contract Signed for First String of TurkStream's Offshore Section*.

Holland, Andrew (2015): *Energy and Geopolitics in the Eastern Mediterranean*. Perspective, American Security Project. Available at: www.americansecurityproject.org/wp-content/uploads/2015/07/Ref-0194-Energy-and-Geopolitics-in-the-Eastern-Mediterannean.pdf.

Hurriyet Daily News (2016): Turkey's Current Account Deficit Narrows by $13.6 Billion. February 11. Available at: www.hurriyetdailynews.com/turkeys-current-account-deficit-narrows-by-136-billion.aspx?pageID=238&nID=95058&NewsCatID=344.

IEA (2016a): *Turkey 2016 Review*. Energy Policies of IEA Countries. Paris: IEA. Available at: www.iea.org/publications/freepublications/publication/EnergyPoliciesofIEACountriesTurkey.pdf.

IEA (2016b): *Turkey's Energy Policies in a Global Perspective*. Energy Policy Review. Istanbul: IEA. Available at: www.iea.org/newsroom/speeches/160930TurkeyEnergyPolicyReviewDrBirol.pdf.

IEEFA (2016): *Turkey at a Crossroads: Invest in the Old Energy Economy or the New*. IEEFA. Available at: http://ieefa.org/wp-content/uploads/2016/09/Turkey-Crossroads-Invest-in-the-Old-Energy-Economy-or-the-New_June-2016-v2.pdf.

IGU (2016): *World Gas LNG Report – 2016 Edition*. Fornebu: International Gas Union.

IRENA (2016): *Renewable Energy Capacity Statistics*. Abu Dhabi: The International Renewable Energy Agency.

Kinnander, Elin (2010): *The Turkish–Iranian Gas Relationship: Politically Successful, Commercially Problematic*. NG 38. Oxford: Oxford Institute for Energy Studies. Available at: www.oxfordenergy.org/wpcms/wp-content/uploads/2010/11/NG38-TheTurkishIranianGasRelationship-ElinKinnander-2010.pdf.

Kopac, Janez/Mehmet Ekinci (2015): *Turkey as a Member of the Energy Community*. Daily Sabah.

Koru, Selim/Timur Kaymaz (2016): *Turkey: Perspectives on Eurasian Integration*. European Council on Foreign Relations. Available at: www.ecfr.eu/article/essay_turkey_perspectives_on_eurasian_integration.

Kuzmina, Elena (2015): Expansion in Free Trade. In Hett, Felix/Susanne Szkola (Ed.): *The Eurasian Economic Union: Analyses and Perspectives from Belarus, Kazakhstan, and Russia*. Berlin: Friedrich Ebert Stiftung.

Pirani, Simon/Katja Yafimava (2016): *Russian Gas Transit across Ukraine Post 2019: Pipeline Scenarios, Gas Flow Consequences, and Regulatory Constraints*. OIES Paper NG 105. Oxford: Oxford Institute for Energy Studies. Available at: www.oxfordenergy.org/wpcms/wp-content/uploads/2016/02/Russian-Gas-Transit-Across-Ukraine-Post-2019-NG-105.pdf.

Platts (2016): Turkey Imposes Selected Import Duty on Coal for Power Generation. August 2. Available at: www.platts.com/latest-news/coal/istanbul/turkey-imposes-selected-import-duty-on-coal-for-26509546.

Republic of Turkey MENR (2014): *MENR Strategic Plan 2015–2019 Presentation*. Ankara: Ministry of Energy and Natural Resources. Available at: www.enerji.gov.tr/File/?path=ROOT%2F1%2FDocuments%2FStrategic%20Plan%2FStrategicPlan2015-2019.pdf.

Reuters (2017): In Double Whammy for Turkey, Fitch Cuts to Junk after S&P Slashes Outlook. January 27. Available at: www.reuters.com/article/us-turkey-ratings-s-p-idUSKBN15B1Z5.

Richert, Jörn (2016a): Turkey's Energy Leadership Ambitions and Their Implications for Energy Governance in the Eastern Mediterranean. *Energy Cooperation and Security in the Eastern Mediterranean: A Seismic Shift towards Peace or Conflict?* 8, 47–63.

Richert, Jörn (2016b): *Turkey: Great Potential, Missing Will. Sustainable Energy in the G20*. Potsdam: Institute for Advanced Sustainability Studies (IASS). Available at: www.iass-potsdam.de/sites/default/files/files/iass_study_dec2016_en_sustainableenergyg20_0.pdf#page=99.

Rzayeva, Gulmira (2014): *Natural Gas in the Turkish Domestic Energy Market*. OIES Paper: NG 82. Oxford: Oxford Institute for Energy Studies. Available at: www.oxfordenergy.org/wpcms/wp-content/uploads/2014/02/NG-82.pdf.

Sahin, Ümit (Ed.) (2016): *Coal Report: Turkey's Coal Policies Related to Climate Change, Economy, and Health*. Istanbul: Istanbul Policy Center. Available at: http://ipc.sabanciuniv.edu/wp-content/uploads/2016/01/IPM_eng_KomurRapor_13.04.16_WEB1.pdf.

Scholl, Ellen/Kirsten Westphal (2017): *European Energy Security Reimagined: Mapping the Risks, Challenges and Opportunities of Changing Energy Geographies*. Berlin: Stiftung Wissenschaft und Politik. Available at: www.swp-berlin.org/fileadmin/contents/products/research_papers/2017RP04_Scholl_wep.pdf.

World Bank (2016): *World Bank Group Supports Diversification of Azerbaijan's Gas Export Markets and Security of Energy Supply for Turkey and Europe*. The World Bank Group.

World Nuclear Association (2016): *Country Profile: Turkey*.

Yabanci, Bilge (2016): *The Future of EU–Turkey Relations: Between Mutual Distrust and Interdependency*. Online Paper No. 1. FEUTURE. Available at: www.feuture.uni-koeln.de/sites/feuture/user_upload/Yabanci_Online_Paper_No1_final_upload.pdf.

15 Energy politics in Egypt

A quick fix for economic problems?

Stephan Roll in cooperation with Mahmoud Ibrahim

Introduction

In Egypt, energy-related developments and political stability go hand in hand. Income from hydrocarbon exports and revenues from the Suez Canal, an important transit route for oil shipments from Arab Gulf countries, have been an important contributor to the Egyptian state budget for decades. Energy subsidies have also been part of the informal social contract between political leadership and the population since the 1950s. However, the nexus between energy and politics has never been clearer than in summer 2013, when a national gasoline shortage and frequent electrical blackouts triggered public unrest. Many Egyptians blamed President Mohamed Morsi for the energy crisis, which developed alongside a worsening budget crisis.[1] The public frustration laid the final groundwork for a military takeover that ended the one-year period of Muslim brotherhood rule.[2]

While the 2013 incident prompted Morsi's successor, President Abdel Fatah el-Sisi, to prioritize development of the energy sector, it was not the only reason. Following the August 2015 discovery of the "supergiant" Zohr gas field, the Sisi Administration began to recognize energy sector development as an opportunity to rid Egypt of its enormous economic public budget problems, which have increasingly limited room for political maneuver and thus negatively affected political stability. The September 2015 appointment of Sherif Ismail, the former minister of petroleum, as the new prime minister underscores the centrality of energy sector development to the current political agenda.

Given these developments, the leading question of this analysis is: "To what extend will current energy-related developments contribute to the economic recovery in Egypt, particularly public budget consolidation?" Following an overview of the general economic and public finance situation, the various measures taken by the Egyptian government to reduce energy-related spending and increase energy-related revenues will be discussed in order to answer this question. This will be supplemented by analysis of the extent to which external energy price developments either support or obstruct the respective government measures.

Point of departure: energy trends and the economic situation

The urgency of prioritizing energy policy for the Sisi Administration became clear in the face of two highly interrelated developments. The first is the dramatic increase in energy demand over the past decade, which has surpassed energy production. The emergence of electricity shortages during peak demand times, especially in 2013 and 2014, clearly illustrated this development. While the country needed 30 gigawatts of electricity at its 2013 peak to satisfy its consumption needs, it had access to only 26 gigawatts.[3] Given a high population growth rate of 2.1 percent per year (2015), the electricity demand in a country of currently nearly 95 million people could reach up to 96 gigawatts by 2035.[4] Thus, this situation could become more acute.

However, electricity cuts were a result not only of insufficient electricity generation capacity but also of an increasing shortage of fossil fuels. Due to increasing energy demand and stagnating production, Egypt – the biggest oil and gas consumer on the African continent – has transformed from a net energy exporter to a net energy importer. Egypt's own petroleum and other liquid production, an average 708,000 barrels per day, was not enough to satisfy consumption levels of 775,000 barrels per day[5] in 2014. Therefore, the country has been forced to import oil products to close this gap since 2006. This has also been the case with natural gas since 2014, which is of much greater importance in Egypt's energy mix: natural gas accounted for more than 50 percent of total primary energy consumption in recent years and more than 70 percent of total electricity production.[6] Despite a remarkable increase in Egypt's proven gas reserves, from 22.8 trillion cubic feet in 1995 to 77 trillion cubic feet at the beginning of 2015,[7] the country was forced to start importing gas for its own consumption. In 2016, the deficit between production and consumption was approximately 0.7 billion cubic feet per day.[8] The dramatic shift from being a gas-importing to a gas-exporting country has had a huge impact on Egypt's state budget. In the fiscal year 2007/2008, the country's peak as a gas exporter, Egypt earned more than US$3 billion from gas exports to Israel and Syria. For the fiscal year 2015/2016, Egyptian officials estimated that the country could spend up to US$3.5 billion on imported LNG.[9]

Increasing energy expenditures in the state budget have contributed to the second development which explains the rationale behind prioritizing energy sector development: Egypt's economic and fiscal crisis. Since 2011, Egypt has undergone a dramatic economic decline that has, among other things, negatively impacted public finances. This decline resulted in part from structural problems in the Egyptian economy that have developed over the past decades. The situation has grown even worse since 2011,[10] as economic growth more or less ceased during the political upheaval and has barely recovered since. After 2011, GDP growth slumped to under 2 percent per capita, while unemployment jumped to more than 12 percent according to official statistics. Moreover, public revenues and expenditures became completely unbalanced.[11] When the military took over in 2013, the Egyptian state was literally bankrupt. In that year, only 60 percent of public expenditures were covered by public revenue, creating a fiscal deficit of more than 13 percent of gross domestic product.[12] The currency reserves, which were sufficient to cover more than seven months of import expenditures in 2010, sharply declined by more than 50 percent. In 2013, the Egyptian central bank's foreign currency reserves amounted to only US$13.4 billion – not enough to cover even three months of imports. Consequently, after the military coup, Egypt's solvency was only secured following transfer payments from Saudi Arabia, Kuwait, and the United Arab Emirates.[13] Immediately after the coup, the three countries pledged an aid package worth about US$12 billion for Egypt.[14]

Against this backdrop, the Sisi Administration's energy policy has focused on measures to secure energy supplies by increasing energy imports and investing in increased electric generation capacity to mitigate public unrest over supply shortages. However, the new leadership's main goal became to reduce energy costs in the budget and, at the same time, to increase Egypt's energy production. As such, the following three objectives received the highest priority: reforming the energy subsidy system, increasing gas production, and developing a nuclear power program.

Energy subsidy reforms

The origins of the current subsidy system date to the early 1950s, when the Free Officers Movement established the Republic of Egypt. Planned as an instrument to improve social justice, the subsidy system expanded rapidly, sending budget costs out of control. Even as criticism from the international donor community – first and foremost the World Bank and the IMF – in the 1970s focused on subsidizing basic foodstuffs, the respective budget costs were only half that for energy subsidies.[15] The cost of energy subsidies became increasingly obvious in the 1990s and 2000s. Due to rising global energy prices and domestic energy consumption until the final year of Hosni Mubarak's presidency, the fiscal burden of petroleum subsidies in the state budget had grown to 5.5 percent of GDP, dwarfing spending for food subsidies (1.4 percent of GDP).[16] If economic distortions and inefficiency were taken into consideration, the subsidy bill could have been twice as high.[17]

Under Mubarak, while reforming the system was always on the stated political agenda, concrete efforts to do so remained limited. Minor increases in administrative prices in the early 2000s failed to close the fundamental gap between domestic and world gasoline, diesel and LPG prices. For example, in 2010, the pump price for diesel fuel was 0.25 cents per liter, less than 24 percent of the international average of US$1.07 per liter. The official Egyptian argument against subsidy reform held that cuts would have a dramatic negative impact upon the low-income population. However, in the case of energy subsidies, many studies refute this argument. In 2012, the bottom income quintile of the Egyptian population received only 13 percent of the subsidies, while the highest income quintile consumed more than one-third of total energy subsidies.[18] While the lower class consumed mainly subsidized food, the middle and upper class benefited from cheap energy. In fact the subsidy system had another objective: it constituted the informal social contract through which the Mubarak regime bought political acquiescence.

Given these dynamics, it appeared all the more remarkable that after taking office in 2014, President Sisi immediately took major steps to reduce subsidies by more than US$5 billion. Spending for energy subsidies alone was reduced by more than 40 percent, causing prices of diesel and gasoline to skyrocket by as much as 78 percent. However, a closer look suggests that Sisi's move was less remarkable than it seemed at the time, as he had no alternative. In 2012/2013, Egypt spent approximately 26 percent of government funds on its system of generalized price subsidies, which was "among the most extensive and generous in the world",[19] making cuts inevitable. Two-thirds of this spending –over US$20 billion in 2013 – was on energy subsidies.[20] Despite the aid package from the Gulf monarchies, Egypt could no longer shoulder this financial burden.

One important aspect of the 2014 subsidy cuts was that the reforms did not alter the fixed basis on which prices of various energy products were set in local currency.[21] There was still no automatic link to international energy prices, and thus any rise in US dollar-nominated oil and gas prices or the weakening of the Egyptian pound against the US dollar could have foreseeable negative effects on the Egyptian state budget. Egypt, as a net-energy importer, has benefited from lower oil prices since 2014. However, the country experienced a counter effect over the same period with the dramatic devaluation of the pound against the US dollar on the informal exchange market.[22] At the beginning of November 2016, the government was forced to allow the pound to trade freely, inducing a depreciation of more than 40 percent. Overall, the pound has lost nearly 100 percent of its value since 2014. To counter the negative cost effects on energy expenditures in the budget, the government once again raised energy prices immediately after the pound was floated. Nevertheless, compared to the international average, pump prices for diesel and gasoline converted in US dollars declined. Therefore, it remains an open question whether this second subsidy cut will be sufficient to preserve the initial positive effect of less public spending on energy. It appears unlikely that the Egyptian government will fulfill its promises to reduce fuel subsidies in the fiscal year 2016/2017, given that over 90 percent of the annual budget allocation for fuel had been consumed during the first six months.[23]

Gas sector development

Given the supply and budgetary pressures of meeting growing demand, gas exploration has climbed to the top of the political agenda as a way to increase state revenue. The government's stated aim is to transform Egypt again into an important gas-exporting country. However, two developments, which also caused Egypt to become a net gas importer in 2014, have become obstacles to achieving this aim.

The first development is the enormous rise in domestic natural gas demand, particularly in the power sector, resulting in part (though not exclusively) from dramatic population growth. Beginning in the 1990s, the Mubarak government encouraged households, businesses, and the industrial sector to consider natural gas as an alternative to petroleum products. This led to an average annual consumption increase of 7 percent, and Egypt began to import liquefied natural gas to satisfy this increase in consumption.[24]

The second development is the decline in domestic gas exploration and production. From its 2009 peak to 2014, Egypt's natural gas production fell by over 20 percent[25] due to falling field output and investment to maintain and increase production capacity. These declines were a result of outstanding debts to international energy companies working in Egypt, as the Egyptian government was unable to pay international oil and gas companies what it owed them as a result of dwindling foreign currency reserves. Despite expectations that the situation would ease in 2015, debt continued to increase until September 2016, reaching more than US$3.5 billion.[26]

Given the poor state of Egyptian production, many in the Egyptian Administration saw the discovery of the Zohr gas field by the Italian energy company Eni as a game changer. With its potential 30 trillion cubic feet of gas, Zohr is the largest gas field ever discovered in the Mediterranean.[27] Together with other new fields, its development could increase Egyptian gas production by more than 50 percent over the next three years, from 3.9 billion cubic feet per day in 2016 to between 5.5 and 6.0 billion cubic feet per day by 2019,[28] which could help Egypt to achieve energy self-sufficiency by 2022. However, while the Zohr field seems to be very promising for the Egyptian economy, questions also remain. Whether the Zohr gas field, as well as other newly discovered fields, will come online as quickly as the Egyptian government predicts is far from certain. Not only could technical problems or disputes over commercial terms delay production, but so could political problems. The case of Guilio Regeni, an Italian student who was brutally killed, most likely by state security officers, in Cairo in January 2016, could also cause delays. This incident damaged bilateral relations between Egypt and Italy and could impact the already ambiguous schedule of Eni, the company originally awarded the contract to develop the Zohr field.

Setting aside questions over the pace of development, the potential impact of exploiting the gas field on Egypt's budget is far from clear, and past experiences are cause for concern. While Egypt's position as a net gas-exporting country until 2015 had undeniable beneficial effects on state finances,[29] income from gas exports to Israel, Jordan, and Spain fell short of potential. As reported by the renowned Egyptian Initiative for Personal Rights,[30] the country most likely lost up to US$10 billion through corrupt export contracts between 2005 and 2011.[31] Even now, the dubious export deals of the Mubarak era are not completely transparent. To the contrary, the former minister of petroleum was finally acquitted over squandering public money in a questionable trial. Moreover, the current political leadership and judiciary's handling of past corruption indicates that in the case of the lucrative Zohr field, there is potential for revenue flows to be captured during the development process. In addition to export deals, the opaque nature of production-sharing agreements between multinational companies and the Egyptian government regulating the exploration and production of oil and gas could enable opportunities for mismanagement and waste.

Thus, the extent to which Zohr gas production could become a source of foreign exchange earnings is highly questionable. It remains to be seen not only how the regional gas market will develop, but also to whom and at what price Egypt could sell its gas. Consideration of the domestic market is also crucial, as Egypt will likely need most of this gas for its own energy consumption. Expansion of gas-fired electricity production through the construction of new natural gas power plants, including by the German company Siemens, will contribute to already rapidly growing gas demand.[32] Therefore, the question of whether and when Egypt can transform itself to a net gas-exporting country depends on how successful the Sisi Administration is in diversifying the country's energy sources.

Diversification strategy

Remarkably, when it comes to diversification, the Sisi Administration has not considered renewables, such as wind and solar power, as a first choice. Contrary to its official declaration in 2014 to develop wind and solar projects totaling 4.3 GW over three years,[33] the government de facto blocked foreign investors from its domestic market. The main dispute focused on the arbitration mechanisms in legal cases between Egyptian state institutions and foreign companies. The Egyptian government's insistence on domestic arbitration made project conditions very unattractive for foreign investors, and even the World Bank's International Finance Cooperation, an important back lender, decided against financing certain solar photovoltaic projects in 2016.[34] The Egyptian media reported that canceled renewable energy deals translate into a loss of up to 2.0 GW budgeted in Egypt's future energy plan.[35] While the Sisi Administration accepted international arbitration in contracts for the next phase of the solar power feed-in tariff scheme, it remains to be seen whether foreign investors can be brought back.[36]

Rather than focusing on developing Egypt's renewable energy potential, the Sisi Administration has turned to nuclear power. The country's nuclear ambitions are not new, as Egypt began a program for the civil use of nuclear power decades earlier. This program was interrupted several times due to financial difficulties and security concerns, especially following the 1986 Chernobyl explosion.[37] The new political alliance with Russia could pave the way for building Egypt's first nuclear power plant. In May 2016 President Sisi approved a US$25 billion loan from Moscow, intended to cover 85 percent of the project costs. The estimated cost of the entire project, to be implemented by the Rosatom State Atomic Energy Corporation through 2022, exceeds US$29 billion.[38]

Civil society organizations have expressed several doubts regarding the utility of nuclear power for the Egyptian energy system.[39] While a nuclear power plant could increase electricity production in the long run, it appears to be an inadequate step for resolving Egypt's current energy needs. In addition to concerns about potential safety issues and technical challenges like the lack of nuclear waste management capabilities, the main criticism from Egyptian civil society is focused on the agreement's financial dimensions. The US$25 billion loan from Russia creates a huge burden on Egyptian state finances, representing one-half of the current Egyptian government's external debt. Although the first installment will not be due until 2029, this is hardly a relief, as it only extends the debt burden to the next generation. There are also significant differences between the agreement's conditions and those of a similar agreement between Russia and Turkey, suggesting that the Egyptian agreement is overpriced. Despite similar plant capacities (both 4.8 GW), civil society representatives have pointed to huge differences in costs and payment methods. According to their calculations Egypt must pay US$9.4 billion more than Turkey,[40] an amount that is greater than the entire 2016 Egyptian education budget.[41] This reinforces suspicion that the nuclear agreement with Russia is purely politically motivated and intended to strengthen relations between Egypt and Russia. For the Sisi Administration, this new partnership could be an important "chip" in negotiations with Western countries and Gulf monarchies to secure urgently needed financial assistance.[42]

Negative budget effects related to low oil prices

In addition to the obvious importance of energy sector development, the question of whether the Sisi Administration will be successful in stabilizing state finances also hinges on external factors. International energy trends and changes in international oil prices in particular are important factors. At first glance, as a net energy importer, Egypt has benefited from the sharp drop in international oil prices since June 2014. However, the decline in oil prices also had a negative indirect impact upon state finances through three different avenues: Suez Canal income; worker remittances; and, most important, foreign financial aid from Gulf countries.[43]

Lower oil prices have pushed cargo ships to take the longer route around the Cape of Good Hope to avoid paying for use of the Suez Canal, which generates 8 percent of Egyptian public revenues.[44] Despite the enlargement of the canal in 2014 and 2015, a prestige project for President Sisi that cost the state more than US$8 billion, canal revenues have been stagnant at best.[45] Worker remittances are also highly dependent on the development of oil prices, as lower oil prices impact the economic climate in Gulf countries, which host around two million Egyptian guest workers.[46] As economic growth sputters, companies in the Gulf are laying off employees, and consequently, total remittances into Egypt have declined by more than 12 percent in the first nine months of the financial year 2015/2016, according to government figures.[47]

In the short term, the most important factor is the impact of oil prices upon foreign aid inflows from Gulf countries. Following the military coup, transfer payments from Saudi Arabia, the United Arab Emirates, and Kuwait have been

Egypt's lifelines. Following the 2013 military coup and Sisi's June 2014 take-over of the presidency, the three Gulf monarchies have been very generous, transferring an estimated US$25 to US$41.5 billion[48] in the form of grants, soft loans, and oil and gas products to support the new regime. However, since the beginning of 2016, Saudi Arabia in particular has become far less willing to continue to pay for Egypt's budget deficit, forcing the Egyptian government to ask the International Monetary Fund for support in August 2016. In a surprising move, the Kingdom even canceled oil shipments to Egypt that had been promised some months before in October 2016, forcing Egypt to procure oil from more expensive sources.[49] Saudi Arabia's reluctance could stem from political differences between the countries over regional foreign policy issues, such as the Syrian conflict, as well as from Egypt's unwillingness to enact economic reforms. Nevertheless, falling oil prices, which declined by 65 percent between July 2014 and December 2015, could also be an important reason why the Kingdom began to calculate its own costs and benefits in a much stronger way.

Conclusion

The Sisi Administration sees energy sector development as a panacea for economic problems in the Arab world's most populous country. Despite this seemingly optimistic outlook, a more realistic assessment of the situation raises doubts. By investing in power-generation infrastructure, the Egyptian government could successfully meet increasing electricity demand and avoid future power blackouts. By expanding gas exploration and production, it could also narrow, if not close, the gap between supply and demand in the domestic gas market, a gap that would otherwise widen dramatically due to demographic pressure. However, the effectiveness of these measures depends ultimately on additional reform of the subsidy system, as well as on how the development of new gas fields, the Zohr gas field in particular, will be conducted. Both issues require good governance, which the Egyptian government has lacked for decades.

In fact, and in particular, the current development of Egypt's nuclear program points in a different direction, as the economically irrational plan for building the country's first nuclear power plant will place a burden on state finances. Combined with the identified negative impacts of low international oil and gas prices, this project could dramatically increase Egypt's public debt. The Egyptian state currently spends more than 30 percent of its revenue on interest payments, an amount that will likely increase. While the energy supply situation could ease in the short run, questionable energy policy decisions could raise public debt to unsustainable heights in the middle and long run, with unpredictable consequences for political stability. Therefore, while energy sector development could mollify or reverse Egypt's ongoing economic and fiscal downturn in a best-case scenario, it is definitely not a quick fix for the country's economic and political woes.

Notes

1 Brookings, 2015.
2 *Guardian*, 2015.
3 Bottoms, 2016, p. 14.
4 Ibid., p. 47.
5 EIA, 2015, p. 3.
6 Ibid., pp. 2, 10.
7 Tsafos, 2015, p. 2; EIA, 2015, p. 5.
8 Sada, 2016.
9 Tsafos, 2015, p. 1.
10 Khan, 2014.
11 Zaazou/Abdou, 2013.
12 Ministry of Finance, 2013.
13 *Guardian*, 2013.
14 Reuters, 2013.
15 Harik, 1992, p. 487.
16 Vagliasindi, 2012, p. 205.
17 Ibid., p. 200.
18 ENID, 2013, p. 5.
19 IMF, 2014, p. 93.
20 James, 2015, p. 6.
21 Ibid., p. 9.
22 Bloomberg, 2016.
23 *Daily News Egypt*, 2017.
24 Hegazy, 2015, p. 8.
25 Sada, 2016.
26 Reuters, 2016a.
27 Enipedia, 2015.
28 Reuters, 2015.
29 BPN Paribas, 2013, p. 20.
30 EIPR, 2013.
31 Ibid.
32 Reuters, 2016d.
33 Reuters, 2016c.
34 Reuters, 2016b.
35 Youm7, 2016.
36 Reuters, 2016c.
37 BBC Arabic, 2010.
38 Reuters, 2016f.
39 Greenpeace, 2010.
40 Masralarabia, 2016.
41 Own calculations, data basis: Ministry of Finance, 2016.
42 Roll, 2016, pp. 17ff.
43 Carnegie Endowment for International Peace, 2016.
44 Loewe, 2015.
45 Mada Masr, 2016.
46 Reuters, 2016e.
47 Ahram Online, 2016.
48 Sailer, 2016, p. 7.
49 Reuters, 2016g.

Bibliography

Ahram Online (2016): Egypt's BoP Deficit Jumps 260pct in July–March on Falling Tourism Revenues, Transfers. July 3. Available at: http://english.ahram.org.eg/NewsContent/3/12/232432/Business/Economy/Egypts-BoP-deficit-jumps-pct-in-JulMar-on-falling-.aspx.

BBC Arabic (2010): The Egyptian President Mubarak Approves Dabaa To Establish A Nuclear Plant. August 8. Available at: www.bbc.com/arabic/middleeast/2010/08/100825_egypt_nuke.shtml.

Bloomberg (2016): Egypt Pound Hits Record Low as Bets Mount for Second Devaluation. July 19. Available at: www.bloomberg.com/news/articles/2016-07-19/egypt-pound-hits-record-low-as-bets-mount-for-second-devaluation.

Bottoms, Isabel (2016): 80 Gigawatts of Change: Egypt's Future Electricity Pathways. Heinrich Böll Stiftung. Available at: http://tn.boell.org/sites/default/files/80_gigawatts_of_change_-_en_-_pages.pdf.

BPN Paribas (2013): *Egypt: Crisis in the Energy Sector*. Eco Emerging, BNP Paribas. Available at: http://economic-research.bnpparibas.com/Views/DisplayPublication.aspx?type=document&IdPdf=23025.

Brookings (2015): Egypt's New Gas Discovery: Opportunities and Challenges. September 10. Available at: www.brookings.edu/opinions/egypts-new-gas-discovery-opportunities-and-challenges/.

Carnegie Endowment for International Peace (2016): Cairo's Crude Crisis. March 30. Available at: http://carnegieendowment.org/sada/63178.

Daily News Egypt (2017): Brent Hike and Flotation Eats 91% of Fuel Subsidies Allocation in H1 of FY 2016/2017. January 3. Available at: www.dailynewsegypt.com/2017/01/03/brent-hike-flotation-eats-91-fuel-subsidies-allocation-h1-fy-20162017/.

EIPR (2013): Corruption in Gas Contracts in the Mubarak Era. Egyptian Initiative for Personal Rights. Egyptian Initiative for Personal Rights. Available at: http://eipr.org/sites/default/files/pressreleases/pdf/fsd_tqdt_lgz_fy_sr_mbrk.pdf.

ENID (2013): Subsidies and the Social Safety Net in Egypt. Policy Brief 012. Egyptian Network for Integrated Development. Available at: http://enid.org.eg/Uploads/PDF/PB12_subsidies_social_protection.pdf.

EIA (2015): Egypt – International Energy Data and Development. Energy Information Administration. Available at: www.eia.gov/beta/international/analysis_includes/countries_long/Egypt/egypt.pdf.

Enipedia (2015): *Eni's Activities in Egypt*. Cairo: Eni.

Greenpeace (2010): Some Questions and Answers about Nuclear Power in Egypt. Nuclear Reaction, Greenpeace, September 2. Available at: www.greenpeace.org/international/en/news/Blogs/nuclear-reaction/some-questions-and-answers-about-nuclear-powe/blog/26444/.

Guardian (2013): Egypt "Suffering Worst Economic Crisis since 1930s". May 16. Available at: www.theguardian.com/world/2013/may/16/egypt-worst-economic-crisis-1930s.

Guardian (2015): How Mohamed Morsi, Egypt's First Elected President, Ended Up on Death Row. June 1. Available at: www.theguardian.com/world/2015/jun/01/mohamed-morsi-execution-death-sentence-egypt.

Harik, Iliya (1992): Subsidization Policies in Egypt: Neither Economic Growth Nor Distribution. *International Journal of Middle East Studies* 24(3), 481–499.

Hegazy, Karim (2015): *Egypt's Energy Sector: Regional Cooperation Outlook and Prospects of Furthering Engagement with the Energy Charter*. Occasional Papers. Brussels:

Energy Charter Secretariat Knowledge Centre. Available at: www.energycharter.org/fileadmin/DocumentsMedia/Occasional/Egypt_and_the_Charter.pdf.

IMF (2014): *Subsidy Reform in the Middle East and North Africa: Recent Progress and Challenges Ahead.* Middle East and Central Asia Departmental Paper 14/3. Washington, DC: International Monetary Fund. Available at: www.imf.org/external/pubs/ft/dp/2014/1403mcd.pdf.

James, Laura M. (2015): *Recent Developments in Egypt's Fuel Subsidy Reform Process.* Research Report, April. Winnipeg: The International Institute for Sustainable Development. Available at: www.iisd.org/gsi/sites/default/files/ffs_egypt_lessonslearned.pdf.

Khan, Moshin (2014): *The Economic Consequences of the Arab Spring.* Issue Brief. Washington, DC: Atlantic Council.

Loewe, Markus (2015): *Suez Canal Expansion: What's in it for Egypt?* The Current Column. Bonn: Deutsches Institut für Entwicklungspolitik. Available at: www.die-gdi.de/uploads/media/German_Development_Institute_Loewe_24.08.2015.pdf.

Mada Masr (2016): *Sisi Claims Suez Canal Revenue is Increasing, but it Depends on How You Count it.* May 7. Available at: www.madamasr.com/en/2016/05/07/feature/economy/sisi-claims-suez-canal-revenue-is-increasing-but-it-depends-on-how-you-count-it/.

Masralarabia (2016): Significant Differences between the Egyptian and Turkish Nuclear Plants. June 13. Available at: www.masralarabia.com/%D8%B3%D9%88%D8%B4%D9%8A%D8%A7%D9%84-%D9%85%D9%8A%D8%AF%D9%8A%D8%A7/1106079-%D8%A7%D9%84%D9%85%D9%88%D9%82%D9%81-%D8%A7%D9%84%D9%85%D8%B5%D8%B1%D9%8A-%D8%A7%D8%AE%D8%AA%D9%84%D8%A7%D9%81%D8%A7%D8%AA-%D8%AC%D9%88%D9%87%D8%B1%D9%8A%D8%A9-%D8%A8%D9%8A%D9%86-%D9%85%D8%AD%D8%B7%D8%AA%D9%8A-%D9%85%D8%B5%D8%B1-%D9%88%D8%AA%D8%B1%D9%83%D9%8A%D8%A7-%D9%84%D9%84%D8%B7%D8%A7%D9%82%D8%A9-%D8%A7%D9%84%D9%86%D9%88%D9%88%D9%8A%D8%A9.

Ministry of Finance (2013): *Financial Statement on State Budget for Fiscal Year 2012–2013* (1st edn).

Ministry of Finance (2016): *Egyptian National Budget – Public Expenditure.*

Reuters (2013): Egypt Received $7 Billion of Promised $12 Billion in Gulf Aid – Central Bank. September 29. Available at: http://uk.reuters.com/article/uk-egypt-finances-idUKBRE98S05N20130929.

Reuters (2015): Egypt's Giant Zohr Gas Field Aims to Start Output in 2017: Minister. November 2. Available at: www.reuters.com/article/us-mideast-investment-egypt-gas-idUSKCN0SR1VJ20151102.

Reuters (2016a): Egypt's Debts to International Oil Companies Rise to $3.58 Bln at End-Sept: Minister. October 12. Available at: http://af.reuters.com/article/investingNews/idAFKCN12C0MN.

Reuters (2016b): Egypt's Solar Power Upset Clouds Outlook for Foreign Investors. August 4. Available at: www.reuters.com/article/egypt-economy-solar-idUSL8N1AL593.

Reuters (2016c): Egypt Agrees to International Arbitration in Next Phase of Solar Scheme. September 6. Available at: http://af.reuters.com/article/energyOilNews/idAFL8N1BI3LB.

Reuters (2016d): Egypt Chases Own Energy Sources as Government Struggle to Meet Demand. October 23. Available at: www.reuters.com/article/us-egypt-oil-idUSKCN12N0M2.

Reuters (2016e): Gulf Migrant Workers Will Be Biggest Victims of Oil Shock: Kemp. March 26. Available at: www.reuters.com/article/us-gulf-economy-migrants-kemp-idUSKCN0WS06Y.

Reuters (2016f): Russia to Lend Egypt $25 Billion to Build Nuclear Power Plant. May 19. Available at: www.reuters.com/article/us-egypt-russia-nuclear-idUSKCN0YA1G5.

Reuters (2016g): Without Saudi Oil Aid, Egypt Rushes Out Big Buy Tenders. October 7. Available at: www.reuters.com/article/egypt-saudi-energy-idUSL3N1CC2IY.

Roll, Stephan (2016): *Ägyptens Außenpolitik nach dem Putsch: Strategiewechsel zur Herrschaftssicherung*. SWP-Studie. Berlin: Stiftung Wissenschaft und Politik. Available at: www.swp-berlin.org/fileadmin/contents/products/studien/2016S16_rll.pdf.

Sada (2016): Egypt's Natural Gas Crisis. January 21. Available at: http://carnegieendowment.org/sada/62534.

Sailer, Matthias (2016): *Changed Priorities in the Gulf: Saudi Arabia and the Emirates Rethink Their Relationship with Egypt*. SWP Comments. Berlin: Stiftung Wissenschaft und Politik. Available at: www.swp-berlin.org/fileadmin/contents/products/comments/2016C08_sil.pdf.

Tsafos, Nikos (2015): *Egypt: A Market for Natural Gas from Cyprus and Israel?* Foreign and Security Policy Paper, the German Marshall Fund of the United States. Available at: www.gmfus.org/publications/egypt-market-natural-gas-cyprus-and-israel.

Vagliasindi, Maria (2012): *Implementing Energy Subsidy Reforms: Evidence from Developing Countries. Directions in Development; Energy and Mining*. Washington, DC: World Bank. Available at: http://documents.worldbank.org/curated/en/566201468177234043/Implementing-energy-subsidy-reforms-evidence-from-developing-countries.

Youm7 (2016): Crisis in Egyptian Electricity Plans Happens after the Withdrawal of 25 Investors from the Foreign Funded Renewable Energy Projects due to the Rejection of the Egyptian Government to the International Judiciary. The Ongoing Conflict Will Make Egypt Lose Investments that Sum Up to 3 Billion USD. June 24. Available at: www.youm7.com/story/2016/6/24/%D8%A3%D8%B2%D9%85%D8%A9-%D9%81%D9%89-%D8%A7%D9%84%D9%83%D9%87%D8%B1%D8%A8%D8%A7%D8%A1-%D8%A8%D8%B9%D8%AF-%D8%A7%D9%86%D8%B3%D8%AD%D8%A7%D8%A8-25-%D9%85%D8%B3%D8%AA%D8%AB%D9%85%D8%B1%D8%A7-%D9%85%D9%86-%D9%85%D8%B4%D8%B1%D9%88%D8%B9%D8%A7%D8%AA-%D8%A7%D9%84%D8%B7%D8%A7%D9%82%D8%A9/2774034.

Zaazou, Zeinab/Doaa S. Abdou (2013): The Egyptian Revolution and Post Socio-economic Impact. *Topics in Middle Eastern and African Economies* 15(1), 92–115.

16 Algeria

Global challenges, regional threats, and missed opportunities

Gonzalo Escribano

Introduction

Algeria has been severely affected by the global and regional energy trends analyzed in this volume: the collapse of oil prices, the reconfiguration of gas markets due to US shale, and booming domestic demand. These dramatic changes in Algerian economic fundamentals have caught the country between a difficult internal political situation and deteriorating regional security conditions. However, perhaps most worrying is that these developments have unfolded while both Algeria and the EU have demonstrated their inability to profit from the window of opportunity created by the shift toward a more diversified European natural gas supply and a seemingly more pro-reform stance from the Algerian government.

The chapter begins with a brief introduction to the Algerian energy sector, followed by an overview of the main global and regional drivers of change for Algeria. The third section explores how such drivers may alter Algeria's political economy, while the final section assesses the potential impact of these drivers upon the country's political stability in three different scenarios. The chapter argues that in spite of current economic difficulties (or perhaps because of them), there are signs from the Algerian government that indicate an increasing propensity for energy reform. Moves by Algeria to reform should be taken into account and met by an attractive European energy narrative that includes Algeria and its demand security preferences. However, if there is a lack of progress in Algerian domestic reform and in EU–Algeria energy relations, Algeria could go from being part of the solution to EU's energy challenges to a new problem, not only for energy security but also in broader security terms.

The chapter concurs with recent arguments for a EU–Algerian *rapprochement.*[1] However, it departs from these arguments by focusing on the kinds of incentives that could deliver genuine energy sector reform, namely improved access to European gas markets.[2]

The Algerian energy sector

The Algerian energy sector is dominated by oil and gas (Figure 16.1), with renewables and coal contributing only marginally to the energy mix. The country's economy relies heavily on hydrocarbon revenues, which represent around 40 percent of the country's gross domestic product, over 95 percent of export earnings, and over 50 percent of government revenues. Natural gas dominates the Algerian power sector, representing more than 90 percent of electricity generation. This reliance has pushed the government to try to diversify the generation mix by integrating renewables and eventually nuclear energy.[3]

Algeria has ambitious renewable targets. However, despite measures like the adoption of a feed-in tariff, deployment has been limited due to the dominance of the national utility Sonelgaz and its interests in the gas sector. In North Africa, Algeria is the poorest performing country with regard to meeting renewable energy targets.[4] Current financial difficulties may further hamper the development of Algerian renewable potential.

In 2009, Algeria announced plans to build its first nuclear power plant by 2020 and a further unit every five years thereafter; however, in 2013 the plans for the first plant were delayed until 2025. In 2014, Algeria and Russia signed an agreement to cooperate in the peaceful uses of nuclear energy, and in early 2016, a joint coordinating committee convened in Algiers to implement it. The country already operates two research reactors built by China and Argentina in the late 1980s. While Observatoire Méditerranéen de l'Énergie projects nuclear will enter the Southern Mediterranean regional generation mix in the late 2020s, it also warns that delays may be significant.[5] As happens with renewables, in cash-strapped Algeria severe difficulties with finance for nuclear projects are likely to occur.

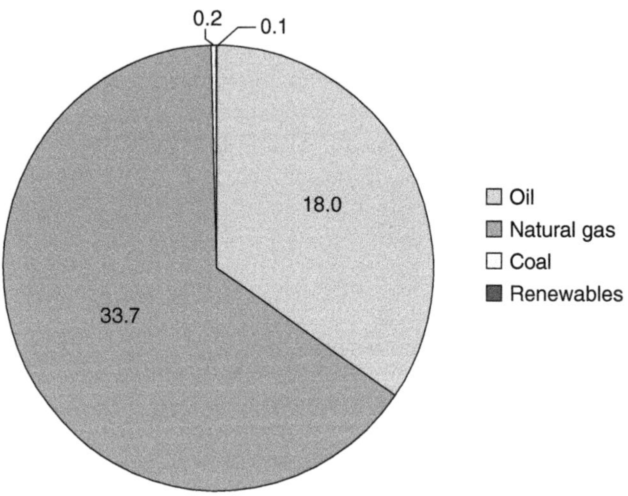

Figure 16.1 Algeria, primary energy consumption by fuel, 2014 (Mtoe).

Source: BP, 2015.

Given the predominance of hydrocarbons and Algeria's reliance on the revenue from these resources, rapidly increasing domestic oil and gas demand is a strain on the Algerian energy sector and reduces the surplus available for export. As shown in Figure 16.2, domestic consumption has more than doubled since the beginning of the twenty-first century while Algerian oil production has declined dramatically since it peaked in 2007, at 2 million barrels per day (mbd). As a result, the Algerian oil surplus has fallen from 1.7 mbd in 2007 to barely 1.1 mbd in 2014. The situation is even more problematic when it comes to natural gas, as seen in Figure 16.3. Algerian natural gas production peaked at 88 billion cubic meters (bcm) in 2005 before falling to around 80 bcm per year in 2009/2010. It has since grown to an estimated 85 bcm in 2015. While future gas production is expected to increase and reach 100 bcm by 2020 as the new South West gas projects come on stream, domestic consumption is also expected to increase.

Most Algerian gas exports are destined for Europe, mainly Spain, Italy and France (see Figure 16.4). Turkey is the main non-EU destination, followed by Morocco and Tunisia, which import Algerian gas as the transit fee for the pipelines crossing both countries toward Spain and Italy, respectively. More recently, Algeria has also exported small volumes to Egypt, along with marginal gas volumes to Brazil. Asian markets are also relatively important for Algeria, particularly Japan and South Korea.

Unless there is a fundamental policy change, domestic gas demand in Algeria is expected to continue to significantly increase. This threatens to reduce or – in the worst case – even stop gas exports in the mid- and long term.[6]

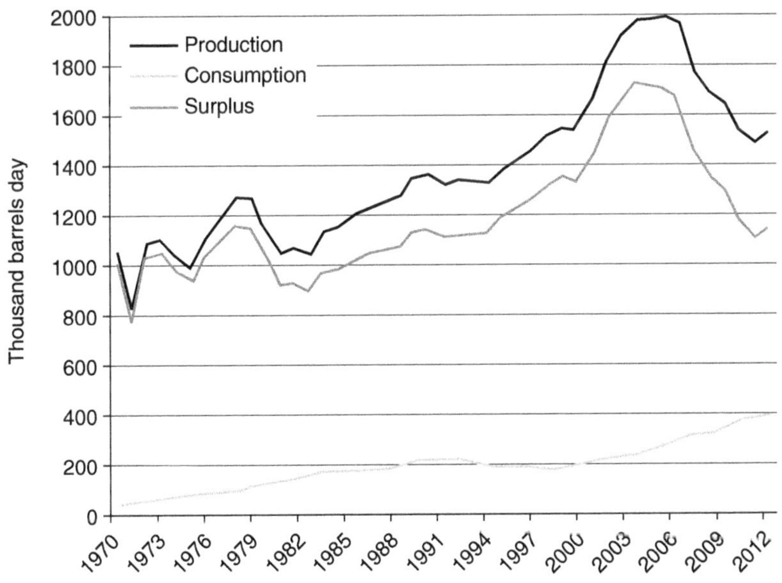

Figure 16.2 Algerian oil production, consumption, and surplus (1000 barrels/day).

Source: BP, 2015.

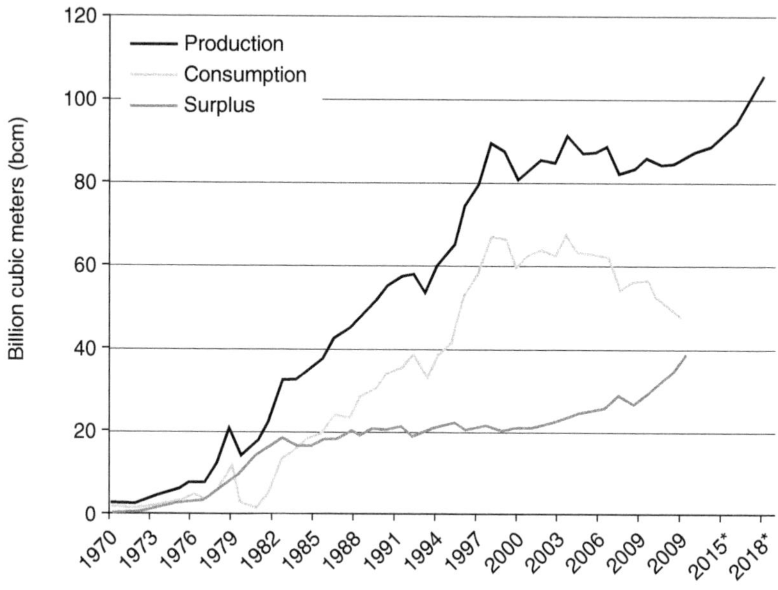

Figure 16.3 Algerian gas production, consumption, and surplus (bcm).

Sources: BP (2015) and (*) EIU (2016a) (2015, estimates; 2016 to 2020, forecasts).

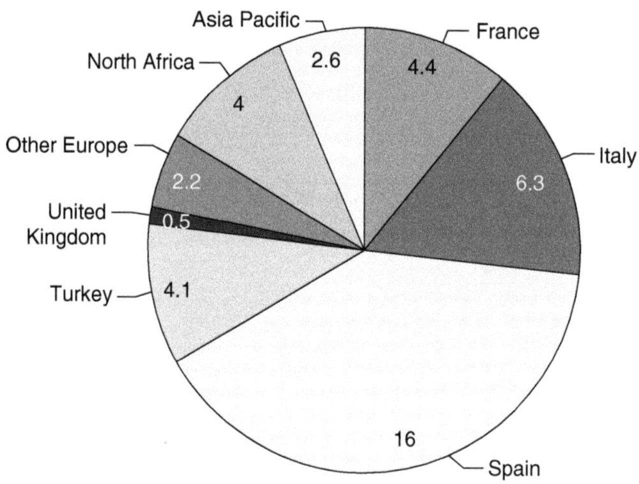

Figure 16.4 Algerian natural gas exports, 2014 (bcm).

Source: BP (2015).

Algeria also possesses vast untapped shale gas resources, the third-largest technically recoverable in the world.[7] In spite of favorable geology and a well-established gas industry, there are several obstacles to the development of unconventional gas. These obstacles include domestic opposition (including violent demonstrations in the south), water concerns, and long and bureaucratic procedures for the approval of projects.[8] Given these circumstances in addition to current low oil and gas prices, the short-term development of Algerian shale gas reserves seems unlikely. Aware of these constraints, the government is focusing on increasing exploration and production of conventional low-extraction cost resources, and looking at unconventional resources in the long run.

The influence of global and regional trends

Algeria's energy position is largely a function of the oil price collapse, the rise of US shale, booming domestic energy demand, and a deteriorating regional security context, along with the missed opportunity (to date) to project itself as a significant provider of energy security to the EU.

Oil price volatility has harsh implications for the Algerian economy. Due to the oil price counter-shock, exports have halved, from almost $73 billion in 2011 to $37.5 billion in 2015. As a result, the current account deficit reached a record 15.7 percent in 2015 according to IMF estimates. Between 2013 and 2015, foreign reserves plunged from $194 to $143 billion. The country's oil fund (*Fond de Régulation des Recettes* (FRR)) had fallen to 80 percent of its 2014 level by the end of 2016. The IMF recently stated that existing fiscal and external buffers provide a window of opportunity that "should be seized now, before a more rapid adjustment becomes unavoidable".[9]

Low oil and natural gas prices also deter investments in the Algerian energy sector by IOCs and public energy companies. While Sonatrach, the government-owned hydrocarbon company, can turn to international capital markets, this could prove difficult for Sonelgaz, as the state-owned electricity and natural gas distribution utility is cash-strapped due to low consumer prices.[10] Further postponing already delayed energy projects will worsen economic growth prospects and negatively impact the country's capacity to cope with lower oil prices in the medium term. Nevertheless, Algeria's geographical proximity to European markets, existing gas transport infrastructure, and the quality and relatively low cost of resources puts the country in a better position than other high-cost hydrocarbon producers, especially potential offshore Eastern Mediterranean and African gas producers.

The changing pattern of natural gas markets, both in geography and contractual terms, is the second global driver affecting Algeria's gas sector. From an international political economy perspective, these changes may be described as operating at two different levels: horizontal shifts rebalancing the geographies of energy, and vertical, normative shifts altering the contractual terms of energy flows.[11] Regarding the former, the US shale revolution has caused a horizontal shift in the geographies of energy power, altering global and regional natural gas flows. Algeria no longer exports oil or gas to the USA, and was facing an increasingly competitive LNG market even before the USA started exporting significant LNG volumes. African natural gas exporters could be the primary losers from US LNG exports to Europe, potentially suffering a 35 to 40 percent reduction in their export gas revenues, compared with a 27 to 38 peercent potential reduction for Russia.[12]

The emergence of a global LNG market has also caused a shift toward a more flexible and competitive market structure and new contractual patterns. This presents a challenge for Algeria which, while interested in participating in the global LNG market, has traditionally been reluctant to move away from oil-indexed, take-or-pay long-term contracts to spot prices set at (European) gas-trading hubs on the grounds that this would harm gas demand security and therefore upstream investment. As was the case with Russia, the changes in global gas markets may force Algerian policymakers to adopt a more flexible approach, namely partial indexing to European gas hubs, shorter term and more flexible contracts, and less stringent reselling clauses. There have been rumors that Sonatrach demonstrated readiness to improve both prices and quantities in 2015 negotiations with ENI. While contracts remain confidential, volumes are apparently set to increase, while the oil-linked gas price formula could be adjusted to the current price environment.[13]

Along with the rest of the MENA region, booming domestic energy demand is a challenge for Algeria's energy system. This problem will become especially acute if current investment projects are delayed and the existing investment conditions do not attract new projects, as demonstrated by the failures of the last Algerian oil and gas bidding rounds. High energy subsidies are also detrimental to the public utility Sonelgaz and deter investments in new generation and transmission capacity (including the deployment of renewables) and energy efficiency. Curbing domestic energy demand has become imperative not only in maintaining the sustainability of the Algerian energy sector, but also in keeping the fiscal deficit at manageable and financeable levels in the near term.

Like other MENA countries, Algeria also faces worsened regional security conditions in the Maghreb and the Sahel. While the internal security situation has greatly improved over the past years, with terrorist incidents peaking at 350 events in 1997 and numbering some 150 in 2006 before declining to under 20 incidents in 2014,[14] several "residual" terrorist groups are still active in the country. Algeria also has 5500 km of complex borders, including 1000 km shared with Tunisia, Libya, and Niger, and a 1400 km border with Mali. Despite significant efforts to increase border control, including a near doubling of its border police and increases in the security budget (the only budgetary allocation other than education to be increased in 2016), terrorist groups from neighboring countries continue to operate in Algerian territory.

The January 2013 jihadist attack on the In Amenas gas plant increased the risk perception of an energy supplier that had previously appeared immune to deteriorating regional security conditions. Following the attack, security risks, costs, and premiums increased accordingly, and in March 2016 al-Qaeda in the

Islamic Maghreb (AQIM) launched two missiles at the Kherichba gas facility. While the facility was not damaged in the attack, BP and Statoil evacuated personnel based on security concerns.[15] In a *communiqué*, AQIM threatened foreign energy companies and tried to link the attack to opposition to shale gas development and the presence of foreign companies.[16]

These developments have had a negative impact upon the Algerian economy, but at the same time have provided the impetus for reform. However, and perhaps more importantly, amid these developments Algeria has missed the opportunity to project itself as a significant provider of energy security to a EU attempting to diversify its gas supplies away from Russia. This positive and unexpected external geopolitical incentive should have further bolstered Algerian energy reforms. However, both parties share responsibility for failing to build a solid mechanism to manage their energy interdependency. To further explore the EU–Algeria energy relationship and examine this missed opportunity, the remainder of this section deals with the impact of EU energy policies upon Algeria.

Well before the 2014 annexation of Crimea, the *raison d'être* of European external energy policy was diversifying gas supplies in order to reduce reliance on Russia. However, when the EU looked around its neighborhood in search of new supplies, Algeria was apparently not in sight.[17] At the time, Algerian natural gas production was stagnating thanks to project delays resulting from bureaucratic lags and inefficiencies, difficulties in attracting foreign investment, infrastructure gaps, and technical problems. These difficulties should have come as no surprise, as several authors have provided warnings about this worrying trend and called for a comprehensive reform of the Algerian energy sector since the beginning of the decade.[18] These authors also called for an adaptation of EU policies toward Algeria based on the characteristics of the country, especially in designing an attractive and viable model to integrate Algerian gas into the European energy market.[19]

From the Algerian perspective, not only is it difficult to perceive what the contours of a future European energy model may look like (particularly when it comes to the role of gas, de-carbonization pathways, and insufficient intra-EU gas interconnections, especially between Mediterranean Europe and the rest of Europe). The existing Euro-Mediterranean framework fails to address Algerian preferences or to incentivize significant energy reform. Algeria is not interested in deepening its Free Trade Area with the EU, and in fact wants to renegotiate it. This is because, contrary to what may happen in Morocco, Egypt, or Tunisia, in Algeria's case the arrangement does not provide any preferential access for the country's exports, which are exclusively oil and gas.

Almost 90 percent of gas export capacities currently in operation in the Mediterranean region are in Algeria. Absent new investments in production and/or a tighter demand management policy, in the future much of this export capacity could sit idle, even as Algeria possesses the most significant available gas resources and established gas industry in the European neighborhood after Russia. European strategies moving forward can greatly influence Algerian policies, with the potential to reduce or increase the incentives for energy reform.

Shifting political economy balances

This section explores the economic consequences of the above-mentioned challenges, the Algerian government's policy response, and the political economy implications. In terms of consequences, as was the case in previous oil counter-shocks, the contraction of external revenue is having a severe impact upon Algerian economic growth. The Economist Intelligence Unit estimated that Algeria's GDP growth would be 3.9 percent in 2015, while its 2016 forecast predicts just 1.7 percent growth, based in part on a tighter than expected budget.[20] If this 2016 forecast holds true, it will be the lowest Algerian growth rate in over 20 years.

The 2016 budget is a reaction to the deterioration of the economy. The budget reduced public spending by 9 percent in an attempt to contain the public deficit at more manageable levels of around 7 percent of GDP. This is the equivalent of over 3 percent of GDP, a significant adjustment and comparable to the 1986 oil price collapse and ensuing recession, unemployment, and adjustment. While it must be acknowledged that current expenditures are being cut by more than 3 percent for the first time in years, the reductions appear less severe, as they do not substantially affect social benefits or key subsidies (food, housing, and energy). However, there are concerns about the impact of the fiscal adjustment upon employment and growth, as fiscal austerity requires reducing public investment by almost 20 percent, with investments in roads, railways, power stations, and other infrastructure taking a 50 percent cut. This could have a negative knock-on effect on economic growth and employment, both highly dependent on public investment.

The 2016 budget also includes some economic reforms that were fiercely opposed in the Parliament previously. In particular, in line with the newly announced investment regulations, the budget seeks to relax regulation 49/51, which limits the shareholdings of foreign companies to 49 percent (although not of course in the energy sector). This change would make it possible to channel foreign investments through the Algerian stock market without guaranteeing the right of first refusal to the Algerian State, which the opposition claims is a behind-the-door way to privatize public companies. This change also removes the obligation to reinvest tax breaks obtained by foreign companies. On the reformist side, there is widespread skepticism about the effective implementation of the reforms. Recent data show that the government has been unable to control the fiscal deficit, financing it at the expense of foreign reserves depletion. This will force the country to resort to debt financing, pushing public debt above 40 percent of GDP by 2020 from around 10 percent of GDP at the end of 2015.[21]

While the 2016 budget includes energy price increases for large consumers and industry and introduces a new tax on fuels, it is unlikely that such measures are enough to correct distortions in a country that ranks among the top energy subsidy providers in the world. In fact, the new budget includes an over 7 percent increase in the cost of direct subsidies, accounting for 23 percent of total public spending.[22] The government has repeatedly stressed the need for subsidy reform to make the system less socially regressive and fiscally burdensome, and more responsive to the basic needs of the most vulnerable groups in society. However, absent a drastic change in policy, the most likely path to reform is a gradual and incremental approach aimed at avoiding widespread social unrest. For instance, instead of reducing subsidies or implementing fuel tax increases, in March 2016 the government announced the issue of "compulsory" national public debt at a 5 percent interest rate.[23]

This underscores the usual depiction of Algerian political economy as a clear-cut struggle between reformists and conservatives, between the so-called "affairistes" (business elites) and the conservatives (members of the revolutionary family). The current divide mirrors the cleavages of the mid-1980s crisis in which conservatives thought the crisis would not last and thus minor reforms would be sufficient while waiting for oil prices to recover, while the reformists recognized the failure of the socialist economic model and the Algerian "rentier" state, and advocated for transitioning to a market economy.[24] The ensuing external debt crisis forced conservatives to accept economic stabilization and market-oriented reforms, but the deep micro-economic and institutional reforms remained incomplete. When oil prices started to rise again by the 2000s, the Algerian government had stabilized the economy, but had failed to accomplish a real modernization of its economic structure and institutions.[25]

Today, things are not that simple. Algeria currently has a business elite co-opted by the regime, favoring economic but not necessarily political reforms; a complex balance within the civilian and military branches of the "revolutionary family"; a slow and frustrating pace of generational change and almost no elite renewal; and overall uncertainty whether the Bouteflika wing has the capacity to continue to maintain a diversified network of alliances and balance among these actors given the President's poor health.[26] However, the fundamental cleavage regarding attitudes toward economic reform persists.[27] For instance, the *Forum des Chefs d'Entreprise* (FCE) has been pushing for unpopular reforms, like subsidy, fiscal, public administration, and foreign investment reforms, together with corporative demands and less liberal proposals such as creating a private national investment fund, industrial policy which picks national champions, and issuing national public debt.[28]

The oil price collapse may alter the balance of Algerian political economy in favor of economic reforms. In February 2016, President Bouteflika presided over a restricted council to adopt measures to promote oil and gas exploration and production, improve the efficiency of Sonatrach and Sonelgaz, and rationalize energy subsidies. Prime Minister Sellal has since gone even further, announcing a change of the Algerian economic model in spring 2016. While the details of this change remain to be seen, it is expected to include long-awaited reform of the Algerian energy sector.[29] However, few if any tangible results have emerged from such initiatives, while unclear paths toward economic or energy reform have spread a sense of governmental complacency and policy continuity driven by fears that reform can harm social stability.[30]

The absence of institutional reforms and the opacity of the Algerian regime lend credibility to suspicions that a corrupt business oligarchy controls the "system", and that economic reform is simply a disguise for the elites capturing new rents, either from privatization or liberalization (in particular the Bouteflika entourage). Given the country's governance failures, this discourse on rent seeking and capture is often considered a more plausible narrative by much of Algerian society than belief in the government's willingness to carry out much-needed and long-heralded reforms.

However, the country's difficult economic situation will make it increasingly difficult for the regime to continue pursuing this "reforms without change" strategy.[31] The recent policy measures (new budget, incremental reforms, and even calls for a more comprehensive economic reform), while incomplete and suboptimal, indicate that there is some propensity to reform. Whether such reforms will be implemented, at what pace, and to what extent, depends upon a combination of political economy factors represented in the different scenarios outlined in the concluding section of this chapter.

The Egyptian model, deteriorated continuity, and comprehensive reform

The combination of political disaffection and economic grievances creates a difficult scenario for a country also grappling with a deteriorating regional security environment. Some analysts have warned that this could eventually "degenerate into a pattern of urban violence last seen in 1988", outlining worrying scenarios similar to the ones that afflicted Algeria in the 1990s.[32] During that time, protests against the consequences of a deep economic recession, abrupt fiscal adjustment, and mass unemployment degenerated into outbreaks of violence and urban rebellion, forcing a political change, that was later overturned by the army following the victory of the FIS in the first round of the 1991 elections.

While the extreme scenario of internal instability cannot be ruled out, it is important not to overstate the comparison to the 1986 economic crisis or in extrapolating its consequences. Algeria's macroeconomic management has improved considerably since then, while the levels of foreign currency reserves and the oil fund provide a more comfortable cushion and foreign debt levels remain financeable. While the economic situation is admittedly difficult, the government appears to have reacted more quickly and assumed that low oil prices may persist. These factors should help prevent the kind of macroeconomic instability that prevailed between 1986 and 1989 and limit the toll on economic growth, which has slowed but remained positive compared with the severe three-year recession the country experienced at that time.

However, if Algeria's economic and social climate continues to deteriorate, the regime may respond in an authoritarian manner, resorting to repression and eventually degenerating into an Egyptian-like military-controlled political system.[33] Under such a scenario, it is difficult to predict the implications for energy sector reform, and indeed the Egyptian experience with energy reforms under Al Sisi does not offer much guidance for Algeria, as internal political conditions are quite different.

Should the government manage to prevent a severe economic crisis, it seems unlikely that major reforms like liberalizing the energy sector could be undertaken, at least not until uncertainty surrounding Bouteflika's succession can be dissipated. If the presidential wing remains confident that it can buy extra time through gradualism and partial reforms, the perennial debate between change and continuity in Algeria will probably play out in protracted and disputed economic reforms amid deteriorating political continuity.[34] Under such a scenario, tensions over political economy and social unrest would continue to arise, Algerian structural problems and macroeconomic unbalances would worsen, and political and economic adjustment costs would increase, culminating in a severe economic and political crisis.

Finally, there is a more optimistic scenario whereby substantial reforms may be implemented if sufficient incentives existed to override government hesitancy. Growing internal consensus on the need to modernize the Algerian economy and shifting political economy balances may create the conditions to enable genuine economic reform. Greater European engagement, from helping to diversify Algeria's economy, renegotiating the EU–Algeria Free Trade Area, enhancing renewable energy cooperation, or pursuing more political *rapprochement* pathways, could provide additional incentives.[35] In the event that the Algerian government's propensity for reform is increasing, the EU could offer an attractive model to integrate Algeria into the European energy market, addressing the country's expressed preferences regarding the security of European energy demand as an effective incentive for reform.[36]

It has been argued elsewhere that in light of shifting social, political, and economic balances in the Mediterranean, Europe should offer a more credible narrative for regional energy cooperation. To provide a more attractive framework for energy reform, the EU could consider offering Algeria better prospects of acceding to the EU's gas market in exchange for good energy governance.[37] A scenario in which the EU is unable to offer sufficient incentives to encourage a hesitant government, and/or Algeria proves incapable of reforming its energy sector, would be a serious failure for both sides. For Algeria, this could mean forfeiting the opportunity to capitalize on its vast energy resources, modernize its economy, and pursue an economically sustainable development path. For Europe, Algeria would go from being part of the solution to the EU's energy challenges to its next energy security problem, further destabilizing its southern neighborhood.

Regional turmoil and migration from the African continent to Europe are also linked to overall economic stability and the need for reform. The turmoil in Libya will continue to produce negative security spillovers for Algeria, the Sahel, and the Western Mediterranean, especially if ISIS is able to consolidate its strongholds and regional reach. Meanwhile, AQIM continues to target Algerian energy facilities and is attempting to link these attacks to the current energy debate and align with popular opposition against corrupt practices and shale gas development. In addition, the closure of the Eastern Mediterranean refugees' route has increased migratory pressure in the Western Mediterranean. Issues of migration and regional stability are linked to economic reform, and thus further make clear that it is time for Europe to develop a clear and attractive vision for its energy relations with Algeria. A comprehensive *rapprochement* that includes energy is the only kind of agreement that can deliver substantial incentives and resources that would enable the Algerian government to implement energy and economic reforms while maintaining political stability and internal and border security.

The May 2016 Algeria–EU business forum devoted to energy cooperation held in Algiers underscored the difficulties in advancing such a vision.[38] The European companies and the Commission emphasized the lack of quality offers, red tape, rigid contracts, and unfavorable fiscal terms.[39] However, there was some progress in establishing more constructive energy cooperation, including a €10 million technical assistance loan to support the Algerian renewables and energy efficiency programs.[40]

However, in Algeria the Forum was perceived as an instance of renewed European pressure to open up its energy sector and renegotiate long-term contracts that are set to expire through 2021. While the Algerian Energy Minister, Salah Khebri, was receptive to the companies' demands, he also proved reluctant to dismiss long-term contracts on the grounds that this would damage investments in the gas supply chain.[41] A former Algerian energy minister, Abdelmadjid Attar, declared that the Europeans did not propose anything new and focused exclusively on contractual and investment terms.[42] Thus, it remains to be seen whether the EU–Algeria Strategic Energy Partnership can offer a more attractive pattern of energy interdependency management beyond what transpired in its first business forum.

Notes

1 See Solana, 2016; Ghilès, 2016; Joffé, 2015; Lebovich, 2016, pp. 39–51; Tagliapietra/Zachmann, 2015.
2 Escribano, 2016.
3 EIA, 2016.
4 Brand, 2015.
5 OME, 2015, p. 26.
6 Ibid.; Darbouche/Hamilton, 2015; Aissaoui, 2016.
7 EIA, 2015.
8 Boersma et al., 2015.
9 IMF, 2016.
10 Maghreb Emergent, 2016.
11 Nye, 1990, pp. 153–171.
12 Bordoff/Hauser, 2014, fig. 15. The authors do not provide a breakdown by country, but given that Algeria is the main African gas exporter to the EU it is assumed that the country will bear most of such trade diversion.
13 Aissaoui, 2016, pp. 16–19; Verda, 2015.
14 Data on terrorist incidents from START, Global Terrorism Database.
15 El-Watan, 2016a.
16 Tout Sur l'Algérie, 2016.
17 See, for instance, Boersma et al., 2015; Chyong et al., 2015; Mokhefi, 2014.

18 Darbouche, 2011.
19 Darbouche, 2008; Darbouche/Dennison, 2011; Escribano, 2010.
20 EIU, 2016b.
21 Ibid.
22 EIU, 2015.
23 El-Watan, 2016b.
24 Martínez, 2010.
25 Escribano/Lorca, 2008, pp. 135–158.
26 For a more nuanced perspective on Algerian entrepreneurs see Boubekeur, 2013, pp. 469–481.
27 Escribano/Lorca, 2012.
28 Forum des Chefs d'Entreprise, 2015.
29 El-Watan, 2016e.
30 EIU, 2016c.
31 Aghrout/Zoubir, 2015, pp. 145–155.
32 Joffé, 2015, p. 12. Several authors have evoked the 1980s oil counter-shock consequences in fostering instability and ultimately the 1990s civil war; see, for instance, Fakir/Ghanem-Yazbeck, 2016.
33 Joffé, 2015.
34 Escribano, 2015, pp. 3–17.
35 See n. 1.
36 Escribano, 2016.
37 Escribano, 2015, pp. 3–17.
38 Escribano, 2015.
39 Reuters, 2016.
40 Forum d'affaires UE-Algérie sur l'Energie, 2016.
41 El-Watan, 2016c.
42 El-Watan, 2016d.

Bibliography

Aghrout, Ahmed/Yahia Zoubir (2015): *Algeria: Reform without Change?* London: Routledge.

Aissaoui, Ali (2016): *Algerian Gas: Troubling Trends, Troubled Policies*. OIES Paper, NG 108. Oxford: Oxford Institute for Energy Studies Available at: www.oxfordenergy.org/wpcms/wp-content/uploads/2016/05/Algerian-Gas-Troubling-Trends-Troubled-Policies-NG-108.pdf.

Boersma, Tim/Marie Vandendriessche/Andrew Leber (2015): *Shale Gas in Algeria. No Quick Fix*. Energy Security and Climate Initiative, Policy Brief 15–01. Washington, DC: Brookings. Available at: www.brookings.edu/wp-content/uploads/2016/07/no_quick_fix_final-2.pdf.

Bordoff, Jason/Trevor Hauser (2014): *American Gas to the Rescue?* New York: Center on Global Energy Policy, Columbia University. Available at: http://energypolicy.columbia.edu/sites/default/files/energy/CGEP_American%20Gas%20to%20the%20Rescue%3F.pdf.

Boubekeur, Amel (2013): Rolling Either Way? Algerian Entrepreneurs as Both Agents of Change and Means of Preservation of the System. *The Journal of North African Studies* 18(3), 469–481.

BP (2015): *Statistical Review of World Energy 2015*. London: BP.

Brand, Bernhard (2015): The Renewable Energy Targets of the MENA Countries: Objectives, Achievability, and Relevance for the Mediterranean Energy Collaboration. In

Rubino, Alessandro/Ilhan Ozturk/Veronica Lenzi/Maria Teresa Costa (Eds), *Regulation and Investments in Energy Markets. Solutions for the Mediterranean*. London: Academic Press, Elsevier.

Chyong, Chi-Kong et al. (2015): Europe's Alternatives to Russian Gas. *ECFR Commentary*.

Darbouche, Hakim (2008): Decoding Algeria's ENP Policy: Differentiation by Other Means? *Mediterranean Politics* 13(3), 371–389.

Darbouche, Hakim (2011): *Algeria's Shifting Gas Export Strategy – Between Policy and Market Constraints*. OIES Paper, NG 48. Oxford: Oxford Institute for Energy Studies. Available at: www.oxfordenergy.org/wpcms/wp-content/uploads/2011/03/NG48.pdf.

Darbouche, Hakim/Susi Dennison (2011): *A 'Reset' with Algeria: The Russia to the EU's South*. ECFR Policy Brief, 46. London: European Council on Foreign Relations. Available at: www.ecfr.eu/page/-/ECFR46_ALGERIA_BRIEF_AW.pdf.

Darbouche, Hakim/John Hamilton (2015): North Africa's Energy Challenges. In Zoubir, Yahia/Gregory White (Ed.): *North Africa Politics. Change and Continuity*. London: Routledge.

EIA (2015): *Shale Gas Resources: An Assessment of 137 Shale Formations in 41 Countries Outside the US*. Washington, DC: U.S. Energy Information Administration.

EIA (2016): *Country Analysis Brief: Algeria*. Washington, DC: U.S. Energy Information Adminstration.

EIU (2015): Government to Tighten Its Belt. October 13. Available at: http://country.eiu.com/article.aspx?articleid=243580008&Country=Algeria&topic=Economy_1.

EIU (2016a): Algeria Country Report. June 13. Available at: http://country.eiu.com/algeria.

EIU (2016b): Fiscal Policy Outlook: No Signs of Government Spending Restraint. June 7.

EIU (2016c): Policy Trends: New Economic Growth Model Launched. June 10.

El-Watan (2016a): In Salah: les dessous de l'attaque de la base de Kherchba. March 19.

El-Watan (2016b): L'Etat en quête d'argent. March 7.

El-Watan (2016c): Marché Européen du gaz: L'Algérie mise en difficulté. May 24.

El-Watan (2016d): Secteur Energétique: Les investisseurs restent frileux. May 25.

El-Watan (2016e): Sellal évoque un nouveau modèle économique. March 3.

Escribano, Gonzalo (2010): Convergence towards Differentiation: The Case of Mediterranean Energy Corridors. *Mediterranean Politics* 15(2), 211–229.

Escribano, Gonzalo (2015): The Political Economy of North African Political Transitions. In Zoubir, Yahia/Gregory White (Ed.): *North Africa Politics. Change and Continuity*. London: Routledge.

Escribano, Gonzalo (2016), *The Impact of Low Oil Prices on Algeria*. Columbia Center on Global Energy Policy Report.

Escribano, Gonzalo/Alejandro Lorca (2008): Economic Reform in the Maghreb. In Zoubir, Yahia/Haizam Amirah-Fernández (Eds): *North Africa: Politics, Region, and the Limits of Transformation*. London: Routledge.

Escribano, Gonzalo/Alejandro Lorca (2012): Modern Commercial and Social Entrepreneurship as a Factor of Change. In Merlini, Cesare/Olivier Roy (Eds): *Arab Society in Revolt: The West's Mediterranean Challenge*. Washington, DC: Brookings Institution Press.

Fakir, Intissar/Dalia Ghanem-Yazbeck (2016): Running Low: Algeria's Fiscal Challenges and Implications for Stability. *Carnegie Middle East Center*.

Forum d'affaires UE-Algérie sur l'Energie (2016): *Communiqué de presse conjoint*. Algiers: Alger.

Forum des Chefs d'Entreprise (2015): Pour l'Emergence de l'Economie Algerienne. FCE. Available at: www.fce.dz/wp-content/uploads/2015/09/plaidoyerfcefr.pdf.

Ghilès, Francis (2016): North African and European Strategic Interests Coincide. *Opinión CIDOB* April(403). Available at: www.cidob.org/es/publicaciones/serie_de_publicacion/opinion/mediterraneo_y_oriente_medio/north_african_and_european_strategic_interests_coincide.

IMF (2016): *IMF Staff Completes 2016 Article IV Mission to Algeria.* International Monetary Fund.

Joffé, George (2015): *The Outlook for Algeria.* IAI Working Papers 15/38. Istituto Affari Internazionali. Available at: www.iai.it/sites/default/files/iaiwp1538.pdf.

Lebovich, Andrew (2016): Algeria: The Stirrings of Change? In Dworkin, Anthony (ed.), *Five Years On: A New European Agenda For North Africa.* London: European Council on Foreign Relations.

Maghreb Emergent (2016): Algérie- Pour une nouvelle orientation de la politique énergétique et socio-économique. March 4. Available at: www.maghrebemergent.com/economie/algerie/56336-algerie-pour-une-nouvelle-orientation-de-la-politique-energetique-et-socio-economique-contribution.html.

Martínez, Luis (2010): *Violence de la Rente Pétrolière: Algérie, Irak, Libye.* Paris: Presses de Sciences Po.

Mokhefi, Mansouria (2014): Algeria – An Unsteady Partner for Europe. *ECFR Policy Memo.*

Nye, Joseph S. (1990): Soft Power. *Foreign Policy* (80), 153–171.

OME (2015): *Mediterranean Energy Perspectives 2015.* Paris: Observatoire Méditerranéen de l'Énergie.

Reuters (2016, 24): European Union and Energy Firms Court Algerian Gas Cooperation. May 24. Available at: http://af.reuters.com/article/algeriaNews/idAFL5N18L3AS.

Solana, Javier (2016): Peril and Promise in Algeria. World Affairs, Project Syndicate, February 25. Available at: www.project-syndicate.org/commentary/algeria-reform-challenges-opportunities-by-javier-solana-2016-02?barrier=true.

Tagliapietra, Simone/Georg Zachmann (2015): Reinvigorating EU–Algeria Energy Cooperation. Blog Post, Bruegel Blog, June 10. Available at: http://bruegel.org/2015/06/reinvigorating-the-eu-algeria-energy-cooperation/.

Tout Sur l'Algérie (2016): Aqmi dévoile des détails sur l'attaque du site gazier, menace les multinationales exploitant le gaz de schiste. March 19. Available at: www.tsa-algerie.com/20160319/aqmi-devoile-details-lattaque-site-gazier-menace-multi nationales-exploitant-gaz-de-schiste/.

Verda, Matteo (2015): *Italian Gas (Over)supply: How the Crisis Reshaped Imports.* ISPI Energy Watch, Italian Institute for International Political Studies, June 17. Available at: www.ispionline.it/en/energy-watch/italian-gas-oversupply-how-crisis-reshaped-imports-13515.

17 Energy security, sustainability, and development in Morocco

Georgeta Vidican-Auktor

Introduction

Energy dynamics at the international, regional, and national levels affect Morocco in various ways. This chapter seeks to examine these dynamics in more detail, with a particular focus on the implications of international and national developments for the country's energy mix and domestic consumption, as well as for politics and the economy.

Morocco is one of the most energy-poor countries in North Africa, satisfying more than 95 percent of its energy needs with imports of oil, coal, natural gas, and electricity.[1] This dependency increases its economic vulnerability to changes in conventional fuel prices on the global market, influencing its energy import patterns. Existing gas and electricity interconnections with neighboring countries (i.e., Algeria and Spain) are insufficient, while stronger regional cooperation in the energy sector (as well as in other sectors) has proved challenging.

In light of existing energy security concerns, expectations of increasing energy demand (estimated to double by 2020 and triple by 2030),[2] and difficult regional dynamics, Morocco has considered various possibilities to diversify its energy mix. The core focus has been on reducing its import dependency. Since Morocco possesses few natural resources, in 2009 the government focused on exploiting its abundant renewable energy (RE) resource potential (solar irradiation and wind speed). As such, Morocco's story is primarily one of transitioning toward increased utilization of renewables. Since 2010, large national and international investments have been made in this sector. Aside from improving energy security, supporting economic development through jobs and value creation (i.e., local manufacturing of parts and components and provision of associated services) is another key objective linked to RE investments. National-level action was also bolstered by changing global climate politics (i.e., increased international consensus on climate change), as Morocco has sought to raise its profile in such international forums. One result of these national and global dynamics has been increased availability of funds for RE projects.

Before delving into Morocco's energy system, this chapter first provides a short overview of the country's economic development and political climate, critical to understanding the national energy strategy. As energy is "part and parcel" of the social contract (see Chapter 1, this volume), as reflected in highly subsidized energy prices, this chapter then discusses the political economy of subsidy reform in Morocco. The difficult task of reducing or removing subsidies has been critical not only for increasing fiscal space in Morocco, but also for eliminating price disincentives for RE technologies, reducing energy consumption, and improving energy security. The chapter closes with an overview of the implications of broader energy dynamics for energy developments in Morocco.

Development context

Morocco began its post-colonial period in a challenging economic situation. Since that time, industrialization and close trade relations with the European continent have facilitated development in the country. Throughout its development, Morocco has succeeded in maintaining a stable political environment in a highly turbulent region. The significance of this approach became evident as the "Arabellion" swept across the region in 2010. The Moroccan Constitutional Monarchy showed tremendous resilience, thanks mostly to King Mohammed VI's reforms to modernize the country, and remained open to moderate levels of decentralization, improving their human rights record, and creating opportunities for a growing population.

In the past decade, Morocco has demonstrated positive economic growth, with a yearly average of around 4 percent.[3] Coupled with an increase in population, demand for energy has increased, putting mounting pressure on existing infrastructure and energy resources. At the same time, as a low- to middle-income country, Morocco faces the tremendous challenge of sustaining its economic growth record, improving private sector competitiveness, and reducing unemployment. According to recent estimates, 22 percent of educated youth in Morocco do not have a job,[4] a share that is slightly lower than in other MENA countries. But, if we consider the large informal sector, this share is certainly much higher.[5] To address this issue, energy investments need to take into account the goals of expanding employment opportunities and supporting private sector development.

Morocco's policymakers understand this challenge and have sought to closely integrate energy investments (especially those associated with renewables) with industrial policy. Such an approach is essential, not only given the tight synergies between energy and economic development, but also because of the vast opportunities that RE investments provide for localizing value creation and technology transfer.[6]

Energy sector: sources, policy, and strategy

Morocco's energy sector strategy is characterized by its high dependency on imports and vulnerability to price changes on the world market. Ensuring consistent supply of energy to power economic growth is crucial for Morocco's government. Climate concerns, while important, play a secondary role. Nevertheless, as most CO_2 emissions come from the power sector, Morocco took important steps toward aligning its actions in accordance with global climate initiatives.[7] To demonstrate its commitments to climate change mitigation, Morocco hosted the Conference of Parties (COP22) in November 2016, where follow-up actions to the Paris Agreement were discussed. Morocco's energy transition toward higher reliance on renewables may thus be viewed to result from an integration of these objectives (energy security, economy, climate).

Conventional and RE sources

Currently, Morocco's energy mix is dominated by oil (68 percent of total primary energy supply), followed by coal (16%), biofuels and waste (8%), and natural gas (6%).[8] Oil and oil products are imported from the world market, while natural gas is imported from Algeria. Electricity imports, which come from Spain, represent 2.2 percent and RE (mostly hydropower) accounts for about 1 percent of total primary energy supply (ibid.). The strong dependence on oil imports has placed a heavy burden on the government budget, particularly evident during the period of high oil prices in 2011 and 2012 when budget deficit increased to 7.3 percent.[9] Lower oil prices are expected to relieve some of the budgetary pressures, but the import dependence remains problematic from an energy security perspective. This explains why RE investment plans in Morocco have not been negatively affected by the drop in oil prices on the world market as has occurred in other countries.

Energy consumption is increasing rapidly due to economic and population growth (see Table 17.1). Over the ten-year period from 1993 to 2013, total energy consumption has more than doubled while oil and electricity consumption has more than tripled. The sectors that consumed most energy are industry, transport, and the residential sectors (see Table 17.2), while energy consumption increased the most in agriculture and transport sectors over the past decade.

Morocco is largely lacking in conventional energy resources. The country currently produces negligible amounts of oil and natural gas (6.5 kt and 0.06 bcm,

Table 17.1 Comparison of total final energy consumption, 1993 and 2013

	1993		*2013*		*% rate of change*
	Thousand toe	*%*	*Thousand toe*	*%*	
Coal	307	4.7	22	0.2	–92.8
Oil products	4,296	65.8	10,633	73.2	+147.5
Natural gas	18	0.3	46	0.4	+155.5
Biofuels and waste	1,082	16.6	1,387	9.5	+28.2
Electricity	826	12.7	2,441	16.8	+195.5
Total	**6,529**	**100**	**14,530**	**100**	**+122.5**

Source: IEA (n.d.).

Table 17.2 Comparison of total final energy consumption, 1993 and 2013 by sector

	1993		*2013*		*% rate of change*
	Thousand toe	*%*	*Thousand toe*	*%*	
Industry	1,864	28.6	3,143	21.6	+68.6
Transport	1,726	26.4	4,941	34.0	+183.3
Other, of which:	2,745	42.1	5,887	40.5	+114.5
• *Residential*	*1,379*	*50.2*	*2,912*	*49.5*	*+111.2*
• *Agriculture*	*690*	*25.1*	*1,821*	*30.9*	*+163.9*
Non-energy	193	3.0	558	3.8	+189.1
Total	**6,529**	**100**	**14,530**	**100**	**+122.5**

Source: IEA (n.d.).

respectively),[10] while proven oil shale reserves are estimated at 59 billion barrels[11] and shale gas reserves are estimated at 12 trillion cubic feet.[12]

In recent years, Morocco has modestly expanded its exploration of conventional energy sources. However, discussions of Morocco's conventional energy sources are overshadowed by controversies surrounding the Western Sahara territories. The region, thought to be the location of viable hydrocarbon reserves, is contested between the Moroccan government and the Polisario Front.[13] No solution to the territorial disputes is in sight, and thus these resources are considered to contribute to Morocco's energy security only in the mid-term.

Unlike oil, RE resources are widely available. The long coastline along the Mediterranean Sea and Atlantic Ocean provides Morocco with strong wind speeds, estimated at a potential 25 GW or 7936 TWh per year.[14] Positioned in the Sun Belt, Morocco also benefits from high solar radiation, with estimates of concentrated solar power (CSP) generation potential reaching 20,000 TWh per year.[15] Hydropower is another available resource, estimated at 5 TWh per year.[16] Thanks to a large agricultural sector along with animal and municipal waste, Morocco also has a solid bioenergy potential, estimated at 12.6 TWh per year, while biogas and biofuel are estimated at 13 TWh per year.[17]

The wide availability of RE sources could contribute to reducing Morocco's dependency on imports of electricity and conventional energy sources (i.e., oil, natural gas, and coal) and transitioning to a more sustainable growth pathway. However, increasing the share of RE beyond the current level of 1 percent is not free of challenges. Learning from these early projects needs to be intensified across organizations, as does awareness within the civil society. Removing energy subsidies and other barriers is also expected to increase the market for distributed generation. Finally, while there is always the risk that low oil prices could cause a slowdown in RE investment, Morocco's import reliance makes the urge to diversify and develop locally available energy sources fundamental to its future development.

Energy policy, strategy, and actors

Since the 1990s, Morocco's energy policy aims both to improve energy security and to ensure energy access to the growing population. It has pursued these objectives by securing imports from different sources, improving rural electrification rates, investing in RE, and reducing and more finely targeting fossil fuel subsidies. The integration of these different measures and implementation by various actors comprises Morocco's energy policy. The most recent national energy strategy, developed in 2009, reflects national and global changes in energy politics, and places a stronger emphasis on RE, energy efficiency, and sustainability.

Satisfying the increasing energy demand

To meet increasing energy demand, Morocco is investing in various conventional and RE generation projects. In terms of conventional energy generation, Morocco is planning for increases in coal power plants (2320 MW), combined cycle gas power plants (1600 MW), and fuel oil power plants (387 MW), along with nearly 5000 MW of planned RE power generation.[18]

Morocco is also seeking to maintain and expand its existing interconnections for electricity and natural gas imports. The country has two international electricity interconnections in operation, with Spain and Algeria,[19] and is part of the Maghreb–Europe Gas Pipeline that links the Hassi R'mel field in Algeria with Spain and Portugal. Morocco also cooperates with partners in the Maghreb Union and Europe to promote regional grid integration. The electricity interconnection with Spain (1400 MW) could also be used to export clean energy from Morocco to the Northern Mediterranean countries, an opportunity that was widely discussed under the Desertec framework a few years ago. However, while the potential for export exists amid Morocco's continued investment in RE electricity generation, political support for such a project in Europe has diminished due to the financial crisis and low political buy-in.

RE strategy and policy

The Moroccan Integrated Wind Program and the Moroccan Solar Plan have been expanded to support the progressive deployment of these technologies. While these deployment programs are ambitious (20 percent of electricity generation from solar and 20 percent from wind by 2030), the unique feature of Morocco's plan is the strategic link to industrial policy, aiming to increase local value creation from RE investments.[20] Currently, 180 MW of solar energy power has been installed, and several large- and medium-scale solar projects will be installed by 2020, totaling almost 2000 MW.[21] The largest of these projects is the CSP project in Ouarzazate.[22] The wind energy program aims to increase wind power capacity from 797 MW at present to nearly 5000 MW in 2030; by 2020, around 1200 MW of wind capacity is expected to be installed in different locations.[23] To ensure the implementation of these RE strategies and plans, a supportive institutional framework and new organizations have been developed and created.

Framework and design

The creation of a favorable legal framework was an important step in enabling the large-scale deployment of RE in Morocco. Law 13–09 allowed medium- and high-voltage projects to access the electricity network and opened up competition in this new market. More recently, a net metering scheme for solar and wind power plants connected to the high-/very high-voltage grid was introduced, allowing producers to sell surplus power to the grid, capped at 20 percent of their annual production. It is expected that the regulation will be extended to middle- and low-voltage projects in the future. The exclusion of low and middle voltage from the current regulation, and the limit of 20 percent on the sales to the grid, are important constraints for market development and local value creation.[24]

The development of a market for small independent (household) electricity producers could have wide implications for private sector development. Distributed generation of solar PV enables local small and medium enterprises (SMEs) to engage in the sector, not only in installation and maintenance, but also in manufacturing parts and components.[25] However, major hurdles to this development can arise in the institutional structure often prescribed to developing countries, specifically unbundling the energy system, as incumbents seek to protect existing market share. In Morocco, most electricity (in larger urban centers) is distributed by private entities, called *Regies*. These entities have so far blocked regulatory advancement that would support distributed electricity generation out of fear that such developments would result in their losing customers.[26]

Organizations and institutions

The creation of a new agency, initially called the Moroccan Agency for Solar Energy (MASEN), has been critical to the development of the solar energy sector and more recently of the wind sector as well. MASEN is specifically tasked with project development and the implementation of the *Plan Solaire*, and more recently its role was extended to the entire RE sector (not only solar) and its name changed to the Moroccan Agency for Sustainable Energy following the instruction of King Mohammed VI in December 2015.[27] MASEN seeks to harness co-benefits from power generation projects through its integrated approach to the development of RE projects, with a focus on electricity production, industrial integration, training, and R&D.

The *Societe d'Investisments Energetique* (SIE), created in 2010, is an organization endorsed by the state to support investments in RE projects, while the *Institut de Recherche en Energie Solaire et Energies Nouvelles* (IRESEN) was created in 2011 to bridge the gap between academia and the private sector in low-carbon energy research and to enhance innovation and entrepreneurship. IRESEN also created the innovation and education platform Green Energy Park in BenGuerir. Once fully operational, the Green Energy Park will be the first platform in Africa to create synergies between different research institutions in

Morocco and to contribute to building knowledge capabilities.[28] In addition, the *Agence Nationale pour le Developpement des Energies Renouvelables et de l'Efficacite Energetique* (ADEREE) was recently tasked with energy efficiency programs and developing a program to support large-scale deployment of solar water heaters.

Policy integration

Given the confluence of high RE investment requirements and the need to simultaneously address various development challenges, the Moroccan government aimed from the beginning to harness industrial development opportunities from large RE investments. Morocco's approach to achieving these objectives remains unique across the region, and while the results in terms of job creation and localization of value chains for RE parts and components remains limited at present, vast opportunities exist. Specifically, the government aims to enhance training and education, offer incentives for private sector development, and link RE strategy with other sectors.

The Ministry of Industry, Trade and New Technologies communicated a package of support measures promoting incentives for private sector development, While incentives have been recognized to be beneficial, further improvements are necessary, for example, with regard to enhancing standards, visibility, and processing time. The lack of a clear roadmap for industrial upgrading, which has been applied in the automotive and aeronautics sector, is being felt by companies operating in this emerging sector.[29]

With regard to training and education, extensive programs with a focus on vocational training are being implemented. At a more advanced level, a RE-focused curriculum has been introduced at most universities along with RE research platforms.

Morocco's RE strategy is also focused on linking solar energy applications to other sectors, such as housing (i.e., rooftop PV systems and SWH) and agriculture (i.e., solar water pumps). ADEREE has initiated collaborations with the Ministry of Agriculture and the Ministry of Housing and Urban Development to integrate RE technologies into new projects. Such initiatives are critical to introducing low-carbon technologies into Moroccan society more broadly. This was difficult as, until recently, high energy subsidies created cost disadvantages for RE, especially in electricity, hot water, and irrigation.

Energy subsidy reform

The reform of fossil fuel subsidies is a policy priority for Morocco, with the potential to affect the entire energy sector. Relative to other countries in the region, Morocco's energy prices have been quite high; however, fossil fuel subsidies have consumed a large part of the country's budget, caused inefficiencies in resource allocation, and lowered the incentives to invest in RE technologies. At its peak in 2012, Morocco's subsidy bill reached 6.6 percent of GDP. The amount spent on subsidies was equal to total investment spending and exceeded the amount spent on education and health combined.[30] Morocco has since made important steps toward reforming fossil fuel subsidies, reinforced by declining oil prices, and in 2013 subsidies amounted to less than 3.9 percent of GDP with the goal of dismantling the subsidy regime by 2017.[31]

Morocco's subsidy regime "began heading toward a crisis" in early 2011 (more than 5 percent of GDP) as the government began to sharply increase spending on subsidies to buy social peace[32] amid widespread uprisings in the region. Facing severe budgetary pressure, the Moroccan authorities started to reform in 2012, despite the opposition. By January 2014, gasoline and industrial fuel subsidies were eliminated, and prices are now reviewed twice a month by the Ministry of General Affairs and Governance.[33] In February 2014, the per-unit subsidy on diesel was reduced, with additional quarterly reductions announced for the remainder of 2014.[34]

The state utility, ONEE, benefited in 2013 from about 13 percent of the total subsidies (5.1 billion Moroccan Dirham) for the fuel needed to produce electricity.[35] The allocation of subsidies to the ONEE has been driven by increasing demand for electricity that placed pressure on the finances of ONEE. Due to regulated tariffs set below cost recovery levels, ONEE has reported losses every year since 2008.[36] To address this issue, a 5 percent price increase on retail tariffs was reported in January 2014 and an increase of up to 6.1 percent was announced in July 2014.[37]

The decision to link domestic fuel prices permanently to international prices makes Morocco a relatively unique case in the region.[38] The long-term benefits of reforming subsidies are clear, especially in eliminating large power market distortions, often a key factor influencing power sector investment. Resources formerly devoted to subsidies could be used to strengthen other relevant policy measures, such as infrastructure or R&D, to support on-grid (and off-grid) RE deployment, and could more generally contribute to policy de-risking.[39]

To avoid political backlash to subsidy reform, Morocco implemented a comprehensive and well-orchestrated communication strategy.[40] Campaigns in public media explained the economic reasons for price reforms, the different reform steps, the rationale for linking domestic to internationalprices, and the benefits that could result from these changes.[41] The government also assured the population that the increase in electricity prices would be gradual, and that LPG subsidies, mostly used by low-income population groups, would be continued.

Up until now, the effects of subsidy reform have been positive, both in terms of welfare and government savings. Reform saved the government about 5.5 billion Moroccan Dirhams (around 505 million euro) and did not result in any increases in poverty thanks to targeting energy products consumed mostly by higher income populations.[42]

Discussion

As a country almost entirely dependent on energy imports and in the midst of continuous economic growth, the changing dynamics of regional and global energy greatly influence Morocco's energy sector. Fluctuations in global oil prices have shown Morocco's leadership that investments in improving energy security (i.e., exploiting domestic energy sources) are essential. Furthermore, reducing energy subsidies is necessary to minimize vulnerabilities to changes in oil prices, increase fiscal space for other social and economic development objectives, reduce inefficiencies in energy consumption, and ultimately to avoid financial collapse. Moroccan decision-makers have sought to diversify the country's energy mix by exploiting both conventional (especially natural gas) and alternative energy sources (in particular solar and wind energy). Furthermore, in spite of the complex political economy context, fossil fuel subsidies have been systematically reduced since 2012. This decision is essential in an international environment defined by low oil prices, as reducing reliance on subsidies improves market efficiency and paves the way for more sustainable development pathways. In undertaking these measures, Morocco has aligned its national policies in keeping with the international climate change agenda.

As a result of limited conventional energy resource endowment, Morocco's energy strategy is based primarily on diversifying its energy mix through RE. Large investments have been made, along with the development of landmark projects and creation of new institutions and organizations. These efforts have been integrated with other strategies, including education and training, housing, and sustainable agriculture. Morocco's strong commitment to capitalizing on its vast RE resources, while linking these efforts to industrial development makes its strategy unique in the broader MENA region. Comprehensive subsidy reform aimed at balancing short-term (i.e., social instability) and long-term risks (i.e., fiscal instability) also differentiates Morocco from other countries in the region, such as Egypt. However, while much progress has been made, scaling up early RE projects beyond the 1 percent share in the energy mix will not be easy, as discussed previously. Many challenges remain, including promoting institutional coordination among actors, reducing market barriers to decentralized generation, enhancing expertise, and attracting private investment. Overcoming these challenges requires a long-term national vision that aligns different goals, coordinates interventions, and is based on systematic learning at different levels.[43]

Morocco's energy sector operates in a vast network of regional and international actors with different degrees of cooperation. Energy interconnection lines with Algeria (for natural gas imports) and Spain (for electricity imports) illustrate existing but limited cooperation in the sector. However, opportunities for electricity exports could foster enhanced cooperation across the Mediterranean. Meanwhile, development cooperation with international (multi- and bilateral) donors has intensified since 2010, especially in the energy sector.

Financial cooperation played an important role in enabling the rollout of the initial large-scale RE projects, while technical cooperation contributed significantly to enhancing knowledge capabilities and creating an institutional framework to support such developments.

Ultimately, Morocco demonstrates great potential in its transition toward a sustainable energy system, while simultaneously addressing fundamental political and economic challenges. Success will ultimately be defined by Morocco's ability to remain committed to political and economic reform and sustainable and inclusive growth, and energy will become increasingly important in sustaining the country's future development. Regional integration (within the North African region and across the Mediterranean) will depend on overcoming political differences and enhancing co-benefits from such cooperation. Finally, Morocco could capitalize on the emerging global commitment to climate change mitigation by further aligning its energy policy with sustainability goals and attracting further private investment.

Notes

1 MEMEE, 2013.
2 Ibid.
3 World Bank, 2016.
4 Haut Comissariat au Plan du Maroc, 2015.
5 Carnegie Middle East Center, 2013.
6 Vidican et al., 2013.
7 The government ratified the United Nations Framework Convention on Climate Change (UNFCCC) in 1995 and the Kyoto Protocol in 2002. Furthermore, in 1996 a National Committee on Climate Change was established, and in 2009 the National Plan to Combat Climate Change set the first targets for reducing emissions in the energy and industry sectors (IEA, 2014).
8 Ibid.
9 Amegroud, 2015.
10 Ibid.
11 IEA, 2014, p. 84.
12 Ibid., p. 103.
13 The Polisario Front, supported by Algeria since 1975, is a Sahrawi rebel national liberation movement seeking to end Moroccan presence in the Western Sahara.
14 Kingdom of Morocco, 2012.
15 DLR, 2005.
16 Kousksou et al., 2015.
17 Ibid.
18 ENPI, 2011.
19 ENPI, 2012.
20 Vidican-Auktor, 2016.
21 Schinke/Klawitter, 2016, p. 33.
22 When completed, the Ouarzazate project will be the largest CSP power plant worldwide. The first phase of the project has been developed by a Saudi–Spanish consortium led by ACWA Power. The Spanish companies involved are Acciona International and Sener.
23 ONEE, 2016.
24 Vidican-Auktor, 2016.

25 The importance of a large market for incentivizing private investments in manufacturing is illustrated by the wind energy sector in Morocco, where projects of more than 850 MW have been commissioned. As a result, Siemens Wind Power and Renewables is building a manufacturing plant for blades, committing an investment of 100 million euro expected to generate 1200 direct and indirect jobs (Innovant, 2016).
26 Vidican et al., 2013.
27 Schinke/Klawitter, 2016.
28 Among the international partners for the Green Energy Park are Fraunhofer CSP, the German Aerospace Center, PVcomB Helmholz Zentrum Berlin, and the Korea International Cooperation Agency.
29 Vidican et al., 2013.
30 El-Katiri/Fattouh, 2015.
31 Verme/El-Massnaoui, 2015.
32 Reuters, 2013.
33 El-Katiri/Fattouh, 2015.
34 Ibid.
35 Merrill et al., 2015, p. 43.
36 Ibid.
37 Ibid.
38 El-Katiri/Fattouh, 2015.
39 Carafa et al., 2016.
40 El-Katiri/Fattouh, 2015.
41 Ibid.
42 Verme/El-Massnaoui, 2015.
43 Vidican-Auktor, 2016.

Bibliography

Amegroud, Tayeb (2015): *Morocco's Power Sector Transition: Achievements and Potential.* IAI Working Papers 15, IAI–OCP Policy Center Partnership. Available at: www.iai.it/sites/default/files/iaiwp1505.pdf.

Carafa, Luigi/ Gianleo Frisari/Georgeta Vidican-Auktor (2016): Electricity Transition in the Middle East and North Africa: A De-risking Governance Approach. *Journal of Cleaner Production* 128, 34–47.

Carnegie Middle East Center (2013): The Bloated Informal Economies in Arab Countries. February 12. Available at: http://carnegie-mec.org/2013/02/12/bloated-informal-economies-in-arab-countries.

DLR (2005): *Concentrating Solar Power for the Mediterranean Region.* Stuttgart: German Aerospace Center.

El-Katiri, Laura/Bassam Fattouh (2015): *A Brief Political Economy of Energy.* OIES Paper, MEP 11. Oxford: The Oxford Institute for Energy Studies. Available at: www.oxfordenergy.org/wpcms/wp-content/uploads/2015/02/MEP-11.pdf.

ENPI (2011): *Paving the Way for the Mediterranean Solar Plan.* The European Neighbourhood and Partnership Instrument.

ENPI (2012): *Paving the Way for the Mediterranean Solar Plan. Power System 2020: Morocco.* The European Neighbourhood and Partnership Instrument.

Haut Comissariat au Plan du Maroc (2015): *Taux de chomage trimestriel selon le sexe.*

IEA (2014): *Morocco 2014: Energy Policies beyond IEA Countries.* Paris: International Energy Agency.

IEA (n.d.): *Energy Balance Dababase for Morocco 1993 and 2013.* Paris: International Energy Agency.

Innovant (2016): Siemens: Construction d'une usine de pales d'eoliennes au Maroc. June 8. Available at: http://magazine-innovant.com/?p=3598.

Kingdom of Morocco (2012): *Achievements and Perspectives from Rio to Rio +20.* Rabat: Ministry of Energy, Mines, Water and Environment.

Kousksou, T./A. Allouhi/M. Belattar/A. Jamil/T. El Rhafiki/A. Arid/Y. Zeraouli (2015). Renewable Energy Potential and National Policy Directions for Sustainable Development in Morocco. *Renewable and Sustainable Energy Reviews* 47, 46–57.

MEMEE (2013): *Secteur de l'energie: Chiffres cles pour l'annee 2012.*

Merrill, Laura/Andrea M. Bassi/Richard Bridle/Lasse T. Christensen (2015): *Tackling Fossil Fuel Subsidies and Climate Change: Levelling the Energy Playing Field.* Nordic Council of Ministers.

ONEE (2016): *Trends, Vision and Challenges for the Power Sector – Moroccan Electrical System.* Marrakesh: Office National de l'Electricité et de l'Eau Potable.

Reuters (2013): Morocco Prepares to Grasp Nettle of Subsidy Reform. January 16. Available at: www.reuters.com/article/morocco-subsidies-reform-idUSL6N0AJ81N20130116.

Schinke, Boris/Jens Klawitter (2016): *Country Fact Sheet Morocco: Energy and Development at a Glance 2016.* Bonn: German Watch.

Verme, Paolo/Khalid El-Massnaoui (2015): *An Evaluation of the 2014 Subsidy Reforms in Morocco and a Simulation of Future Reforms.* Policy Research Working Paper 7224. Washington, DC: World Bank Group. Available at: http://documents.worldbank.org/curated/en/978761467980552302/pdf/WPS7224.pdf.

Vidican-Auktor, Georgeta (2016): Renewable Energy as a Trigger for Industrial Development in Morocco. In Altenburg, Tilman S. (Ed.): *Green Industrial Policy in Emerging and Developing Countries.* Bonn: UNIDO.

Vidican, Georgeta/Matthias Böhning/Gina Burger/Elisa de Siqueira Regueira/Sandra Müller/Susanne Wendt (2013): *Achieving Inclusive Competitiveness in the Emerging Solar Energy Sector in Morocco.* Bonn: German Development Institute.

World Bank (2016): *Morocco – Country Overview: Context.* Washington, DC: World Bank.

18 The energy–security nexus in MENA region

Appraising the role of the USA, the EU, Russia, and China

Kirsten Westphal

Introduction

This chapter focuses on the energy relations between the MENA region and traditional major powers, such as the United States, Russia, and to a lesser extent Europe, that have historically been major players in the region, and also on the "newcomer": China. Energy is treated as a factor in international relations that drives securitization trends and geopolitics in both positive and negative directions.[1]

In several ways, the transformation of the energy system toward a more sustainable energy future and the reconfiguration of oil and gas markets change states' geopolitical positions, interests, and mind maps. Shifts in foreign interests and policies – real or anticipated – are thus factors as well. It is argued here that energy is a factor in geopolitics because "great power competition over access to strategic locations and natural resources"[2] has and continues to influence the course of international relations. Yet, energy is also a factor in international governance and cooperation.

The supply and demand balance is key for (power) relations between producers and consumers. The unconventional revolution impacts the supply side of oil and gas, while the sustainable energy transition will influence the demand side,[3] along with increasing domestic consumption in the MENA region.

The geography of oil demand has shifted over the past 15 years away from the Organization of Economic Cooperation and Development (OECD), whose consumption fell on average by nearly 250,000 barrels a day every year, while the year-on-year consumption increase in non-OECD countries exceeded 1.1 million barrels a day per year. China drove this increase, as its demand increased by more than 400,000 barrels a day per year. Middle Eastern consumption doubled over the same period.[4] Amid these shifts in demand, the rapid surge of US tight oil has shocked the market, rising from fewer than 0.5 million barrels a day in 2010 to 4.3 million barrels a day in 2015 and another 1.5 million barrels a day of natural gas liquids. This reversed a nearly 40-year decline in US production.[5] A similar pattern has emerged for natural gas, since the emergence of the USA and Australia as key LNG producers is reconfiguring gas markets.

Figure 18.1 shows the regional distribution of MENA exports of crude oil, illustrating the described trade shift to the Indo-Pacific.

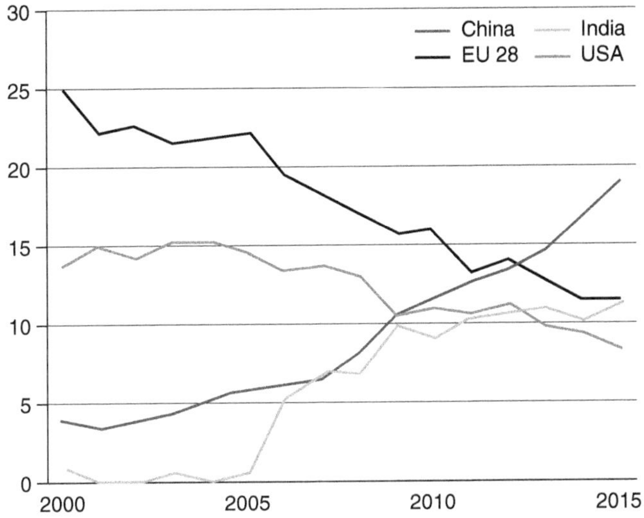

Figure 18.1 Regional distribution of MENA exports of crude oil (%).

Source: UNCTAD, UNCTADstat.

Figure 18.2 illustrates the MENA share of total crude oil imports in the respective destination markets, and Figure 18.3 shows the same pattern for natural gas imports. The Indo-Pacific oil and gas markets have become the major export destination for the GCC Monarchies. North African exports are more divided, as most Algerian oil and gas exports are destined for Europe[6] while more than two-thirds of Egyptian past LNG exports went to Asia.[7] Thus, while all hydrocarbon exporters are affected by price volatility, exporters face different situations in their major destination markets and must compete with other major suppliers over market share.

These trends that have unfolded over the past 15 years are likely to intensify in the future. The USA is set to become a net natural gas and crude oil exporter,[8] while import growth in the late 2020s will concentrate in China, the Middle East, and India.[9] Together, China and India will import nearly half of all internationally traded crude by 2040,[10] resulting in an additional three to five million barrels per day of traffic in the straits of Hormuz and Malacca.[11] The share of OPEC (and mostly MENA) oil will grow to almost 50 percent of global production in 2040 in a more carbon-constrained world.[12] These prospects will not only affect energy trade relations, but also have geopolitical and international security implications.

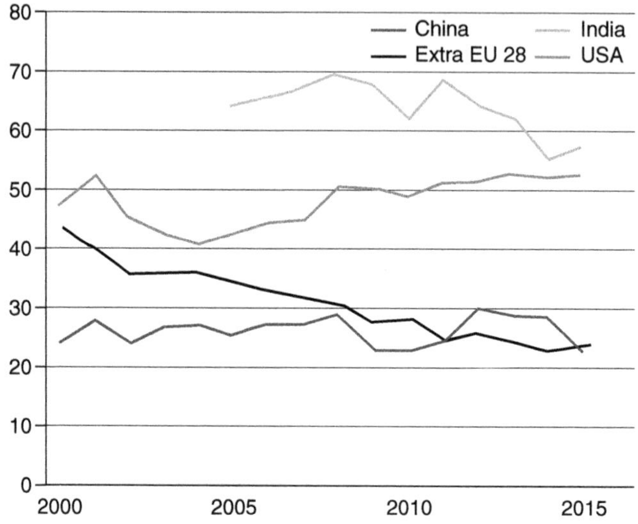

Figure 18.2 MENA states' shares of total imports of crude oil (%).
Source: UNCTAD, UNCTADstat. Figures for India available only after 2005.

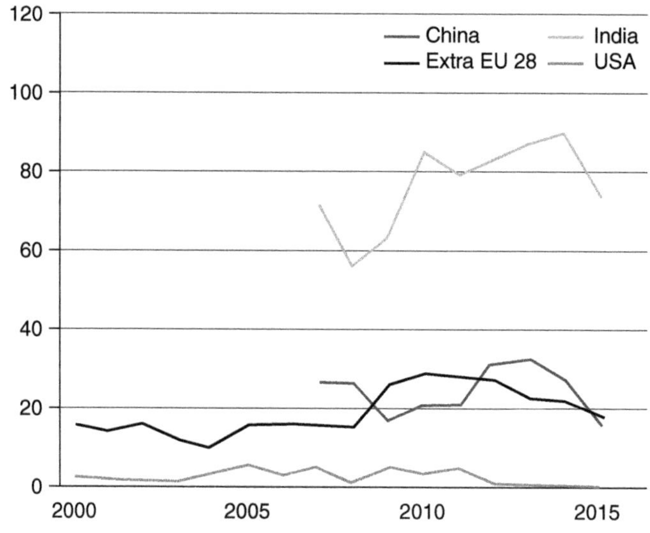

Figure 18.3 MENA states' shares of total imports of natural gas (%).
Source: UNCTADstat. Figures for India available only after 2005.

Conceptualizing the energy–security nexus

From the second half of 2014 until the time of writing in mid 2017, the world witnessed an unprecedented situation with low oil and gas prices despite simultaneous geopolitical turmoil in major producing regions. Oversupplied oil and gas markets and the sense of an "era of plenty" have (for the moment) eased energy security concerns.[13]

Traditionally, security drove energy relations with the MENA countries and shaped major powers' policy approaches toward the region. Securing access to and flows of energy from the region has been a major driver for US security engagement, both for itself and also for the sake of its European and Pacific allies. The nexus between energy and security is evident, as energy security, traditionally defined as secure, stable, affordable, and sustainable supplies, has implications for political, economic, societal, and environmental "arenas" and determines national economic well-being and growth potential. Energy is also a cross-cutting policy issue, as is the broader security agenda. Energy is "securitized" and treated accordingly because energy insecurity can quickly spill beyond the economy and have an "immediate and severe impact [...] on the functioning of a state".[14] The securitization of energy access and energy flow in sufficient quantity at appropriate prices at the time and place needed has national and international dimensions. In turn, energy insecurity emanates from interruptions of trade flows or high price volatility, (hybrid) warfare, terrorist attacks, and instability in producing regimes (among other causes).[15] Energy also exerts a transformative power and adds to the picture of the MENA region in search of new balances and stable future prospects for its states and societies, and in its external relations.

The (geo)politics of energy derives from the interactions of exporters and importers, the market position of producers and consumers, and the density of ties and interconnections. While energy relations are surrounded by politics, they are also tied to geography and geology, as energy resource deposits and locations as well as transport routes add to the "geo" in politics. At the same time, interactions in the energy system consist primarily of commercial transactions by companies – transactions that are driven, supported, or (rarely) obstructed by state policies. The geopolitics of energy predominantly serves self-interest, to secure either (from a consumer's point of view) energy supplies or markets, and (from a producer's point of view) customers for energy exports.

However, energy security can also be pursued through cooperative strategies driven by specific plurilateral interests intended to create and maintain a competitive, liberal global marketplace. Guaranteeing a level playing field based on shared rules and norms as well as free trade and transit provides a common good. The region in focus has been at the heart of both energy geopolitics *and* international governance initiatives such as OPEC[16] and the IEA, the International Energy Forum (IEF), the Gas Exporting Countries Forum (GECF), as well as IRENA.[17] Its key importance for a global energy transition is undergirded by its role as a major oil and gas supplier, high renewable potential, and its emergence as a demand-driven consumer center.

The United States: less engagement?

The US shale revolution is a central accelerating factor, transforming the international energy landscape and bilateral relations with other oil and gas exporters while also impacting international relations more broadly. The USA is not only one of the biggest energy consumers (alongside China), but is also a leading oil and gas producer. In fact, by mid-2013 the USA had become the world's largest energy producer, and the International Energy Agency outlined in its 2016 World Energy Outlook that the shale revolution will make North America self-sufficient in energy for the foreseeable future.

The impact of the tight oil boom upon bilateral trade between the USA and the GCC states has been limited thus far, as since the 1970s oil crises Washington has worked to reduce its dependence on Middle Eastern oil imports. Even before the shale revolution, the USA was no longer importing strategically relevant amounts from the Gulf; thus the direct impact upon Gulf exporters has been small to date (see Figure 18.4). This is also partly due to the configuration of refineries for specific grades of crude. American high-quality, low-sulfur tight oil has principally replaced West African crude of similar quality.

Gulf investors are also exploring business options in North America. Saudi Arabia, which supplies heavy oil with a high sulfur content, can to some extent secure the market for its own crude[18] as state-owned Saudi Aramco is active in the US refining sector. While the North American gas market detached from international LNG markets as imports decreased, it has reconnected through

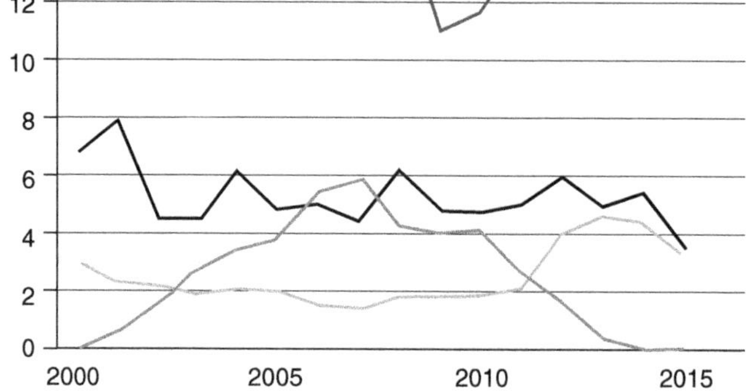

Figure 18.4 Share of US crude oil imports (%).

Source: UNCTAD, UNCTADstat.

developing its own exports. Qatar Petroleum has invested in LNG trains in the USA to diversify its overseas activities.[19]

The shale revolution has enabled access to stable, reliable, affordable, and – in the case of natural gas – relatively clean energy. As a result, US energy security has significantly improved thanks to domestic production that can respond relatively quickly to price movements, insulating the USA (to a degree) from turbulence on global oil and gas markets. The USA also proved its technological and innovative potential, putting it on a favorable energy development path.

As stated, increased oil independence from GCC countries has driven US energy policies since the oil crises of the 1970s. The USA also initiated the International Energy Agency in 1974, an importers' alliance created to counterbalance the OPEC producers' cartel. Against the backdrop of the unconventional revolution, the power of OPEC and its key regional producers has weakened. OPEC is losing its pricing power above the cost level of tight and shale oil production as US production is putting a cap on prices.[20] However, even though the organization no longer shapes the market, it still exerts a decisive influence in balancing the market, as evident in the "pump-at-will OPEC policy" from November 2014 until November 2016, during which time oil prices hovered at around US$50 per barrel.[21] OPEC's November 2016 agreement to limit production (jointly achieved with non-OPEC Russia) and the group's discipline (with Saudi Arabia cutting most) in curbing production by 1.1 million barrels a day initiated a price recovery. Yet, the price rise translates into increased US drilling activity, as the "frackers" immediately respond to price signals.[22] This dynamic interrelationship characterizes the new supply situation on global oil and gas markets.

While the market dynamics are visible, foreign and security policy consequences are still developing.[23] Since the 1970s, the USA has provided a de facto security guarantee to the GCC Monarchies, a central pillar of Gulf security without which Gulf Monarchies would have been incapable of defending themselves against powerful neighbors Iraq and Iran. In the course of three major wars (1980–1988, 1990–1991, 2003), Washington's alliance with the GCC states and interest in containing Iraq and Iran has drawn the USA ever deeper into the region's conflicts.[24] However, the divergence between the Gulf Monarchies' and Washington's foreign policy has grown since the 1990s, coming to a head over the 2003 Iraq War, as Riyadh in particular valued Saddam Hussein as a counterweight to Iran.

The relationship between the GCC countries and the Obama Administration represented a low point, driven by perceived indecisiveness in Syria, the nuclear deal with Iran, and public comments on the Gulf States'[25] "free-riding".[26] Asymmetrical interpretations of the security guarantee undergirded these disagreements. While Obama defined the guarantee in terms of the deterrence and containment of international conflict, the GCC assumed support for regime stability and internal security, which the Obama Administration's support for regime change in North Africa and Syria proved were not shared. The GCC States thus became suspicious that developments related to the shale revolution and the JCPOA with Iran would lay the groundwork for a US military withdrawal. Following the unconventional boom and amid growing political polarization and intervention fatigue, "economic statecraft" has indeed gained ground in the USA.[27] Military security and power projection have been noticeably subject to budget constraints,[28] even as the overall US presence in the MENA region, including the US Fifth Fleet in Bahrain and the Sixth Fleet in Italy and the Mediterranean, has increased during the Obama Administration.[29]

In sum, energy self-sufficiency has expanded Washington's policy options in the Gulf and North Africa. However, there was no evidence of a scaling down in diplomatic and military engagement in the MENA region during the Obama Administration. Significant non-energy-related interests, including the protection of Israel, non-proliferation of weapons of mass destruction, and maintaining a balance of power in the Gulf, dominate US policy. The fight against Islamic terrorism has also become a major factor.

Ultimately, there was a wide range of geopolitical reasons for a US presence in the region in the past that extended beyond energy exports to the USA and its IEA partners. Interest in free energy flows, open sea lanes, and liberal energy markets was a secondary argument for the US presence in the Gulf. This was part of US efforts to ensure global energy security as well as to support a liberal world (economy). The prospect of self-sufficiency allowed the Americans to demand that others – particularly the EU – increase military spending and engagement to ensure these global goods. However, as Figure 18.1 indicates, China and India are the major beneficiaries of free energy trade flows from the region.

This is an important caveat with respect to the new administration of President Trump and the "America First" motto. This may be the dawning of a new era with a paradigm change in international security and trade. Even if it is still too early in mid-2017 to draw conclusions, in the military security realm this manifests in strategic offshore balancing[30] and (again) a containment policy vis-à-vis Iran. From an economic perspective, the "America first" doctrine is a repudiation of liberalized global trade and division of labor. The fact that President Trump chose to travel first to Saudi Arabia for his initial visit abroad is telling. It plainly illustrates his preoccupation with striking deals for US industry and attracting investment in the USA. It also reflects that US relations with MENA have been transformed: oil supply security is no longer a determining factor. Indeed, the partnership is changing as the USA becomes a major oil and gas supplier in its own right. Exxon Mobil Group has teamed up with Saudi partners for its "Growing the Gulf" plan – meaning the US Gulf Coast.[31] The US seems to have discarded balancing regional powers in favor of a transactional relationship with Saudi Arabia and the United Arab Emirates. The US arms deals with Saudi Arabia are reminiscent of the traditionally close security partnership between the two countries, but are far more driven by profits and terrorism.

What these paradigm shifts mean for regional security and international energy trade is not yet clear. However, they may well add to the rift among the GCC countries and the isolation of Qatar as well as growing tensions with Iran in early summer 2017. While the USA has long played a key role in promoting global liberalized energy trade (including US natural gas and crude oil exports) and ensuring open sea lanes in the Greater Middle East, the role of the USA as a maintainer of the old order and upholder of the norm is seeming to fade, as power politics are increasingly favored over international governance and cooperation.

The EU: which role to play?

Figure 18.5 illustrates the share of the EU's oil imports from the MENA countries, while Figure 18.6 shows that Algeria is an important natural gas supplier for the EU. The share of EU imports from MENA countries is quite low, as Saudi Arabia provides the largest share of oil imports at 8 percent to the extra EU imports[32] while Qatar delivers 14 percent and Algeria 8 percent of natural gas imports from outside the EU.[33]

Qatar plays an important role as a LNG exporter and alternative supplier to Russia, which will increase in the future.[34] As a major net importer, the EU has significant market power that impacts the region, and proximity is an import element of the EU's energy policies toward its southern neighborhood. Moreover, the Eastern Mediterranean gas fields could potentially feed the important southern corridor for natural gas into the EU. Europe's wider neighborhood will remain decisive for its energy supply in the medium term, while the Gulf has long-term strategic (indirect) importance as a major crude oil supplier to world markets. "Geologics" and relatively low production costs drive the interest of

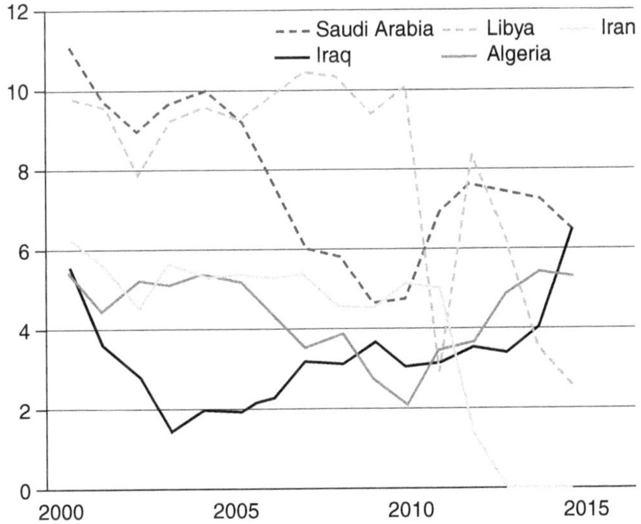

Figure 18.5 Share of extra EU 28 crude oil imports (%).

Source: UNCTAD, UNCTADstat.

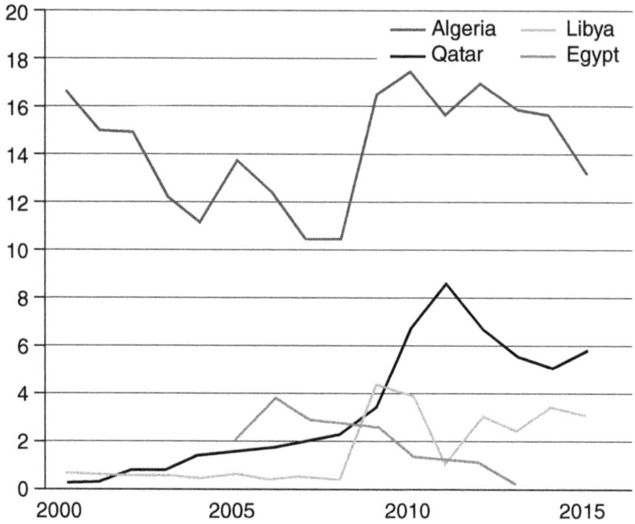

Figure 18.6 Share of extra EU 28 gas imports (%).

Source: Eurostat.

European international oil and gas companies in the MENA region as an attractive place to invest and diversify portfolio assets due to low below-ground geological risks.

The major European IOCs are driving conventional fossil fuel relations with energy-abundant MENA countries. The EU is a multifaceted actor with companies as the main providers of secure energy supplies to member states. The EU as an entity and the member states have traditionally backed international multilateral governance initiatives and relied on close cooperation with the USA in the past. On the institutional level, energy system transformation, market integration, and infrastructure development have become important reference points and fields of cooperation in EU external energy relations with certain MENA countries since the 2000s.[35] The EU and certain member states like Germany conduct energy partnerships to support the expansion of renewable energies and efficient and modern energy technology.[36] "Desert Power"[37] plans were supported by the Desertec Foundation and the Desertec Industrial Initiative comprising almost 20 shareholders, among others. These and other common projects and closer energy interconnections in renewable cooperation were also perceived as a vehicle for a EU–MENA energy space and market, and the Union for the Mediterranean incorporated this concept into its Solar Plan. However, despite the high expectations, these big plans have not produced concrete results in the short term. As a consequence, a silent scaling down of plans took place: the Union for the Mediterranean currently hosts energy platforms while the Desertec Industrial Initiative has had only three shareholders since 2014: German company RWE and, most tellingly, Saudi Acwa Power, and the State Grid of China.

Besides the (albeit limited) cooperation on sustainable energy,[38] the EU's integrated energy and climate policies have an indirect but decisive impact upon the MENA relationship. Despite the fact that the EU is a major net importer, its natural gas demand is stagnating and oil demand is decreasing. This limits the EU's attractiveness as a future market and raises uncertainty about demand prospects, particularly for natural gas, limiting to a degree its market and energy policy power projection. Algeria is a case in point[39] where the EU failed to combine energy and foreign policy interests for mutual benefits.

The close vicinity of North Africa and the Eastern Mediterranean and Turkey's crucial role as an energy transit corridor bring geography and geopolitics into play. The region is within the purview of an EU external energy governance approach that builds on the export of technical, legal, and regulatory norms and rules compatible or harmonized with the EU's energy *acquis communautaire*. Turkey is an energy community observer, and its grid is thus synchronized with continental Europe.[40] The EU has always considered the possibility of an energy community with its southern neighbors, but it has thus far failed to materialize in the same formal way as in the Balkans and Eastern Europe, as EU membership was never on the table and intra-regional cross-border trade and cooperation among North African and Eastern Mediterranean countries is marginal.[41] However, energy has been part and parcel of the EU's foreign policy approach toward the region.[42]

The EU's approach toward its southern neighbors began in the 1970s in response to war and conflict in the region, and the Euro–Arab dialogue started around the same time. Trade, aid, and labor migration were major dimensions in the relationship at that point.[43] The EU initialized the Barcelona process in 1995, which merged into the European Neighborhood Policy Instrument after 2003. The Union for the Mediterranean, launched in 2007, became a new framework for the EU's engagement with the wider Mediterranean basin. However, none of these governance mechanisms and institutions fulfilled the expectations for smooth cooperation, with blame found on both sides.

Since 2011, the Arab uprisings and their fallout have complicated already complex cooperation across the Mediterranean Sea. Like the USA, the EU has supported regime change in Tunisia and initially pinned hopes on regime change in Egypt, Libya, Yemen, and Syria.[44] While the volume of trade on both sides has more than doubled and in some cases tripled since 1995,[45] trade and aid are back on the agenda, but migration and terrorism[46] are predominant and sometimes calamitously intertwined issues.

The EU is confronted with its own limits and constraints against the backdrop of political turmoil, state fragility, migration across the Mediterranean, and the threat of transnational terrorism. This is true even as the EU's policy agenda for the MENA region builds on a comprehensive strategy for state and societal resilience and an integrated approach to conflict and crisis.[47] What sounds good on paper is in reality a Herculean task.

The EU and its member states have engaged in "capacity building" in the Mediterranean and North Africa to train local forces, primarily in response to migration and terrorism, aided by US information cooperation. In contrast, EU engagement in the Gulf is limited, even as the EU's 2014 Maritime Security Strategy[48] recognizes the importance of maritime security for energy supplies and identifies the protection of international shipping as a EU core interest. The EU is present in military and civilian missions in the Gaza Strip, in Libya, and around the Horn of Africa, countering piracy under the guise of its Common Security and Defense Policy.[49]

With regard to foreign and security policy, the EU's initial support for democratic transitions during the Arab Spring has relapsed to a security paradigm in response to migration (in some cases rhetorically intertwined with the fear of terrorist insurgency). The EU is heavily affected by the crisis of the "West" and the fact that the USA as the major partner is on a completely different energy trajectory. The EU has been relying on the USA as the major power responsible for projecting stability and security in the Greater Middle East in the past. The transatlantic partners have also shared efforts in fostering energy transition, supporting oil and gas supply security in the IEA, encouraging the association of more partners to the IEA, and phasing out fossil fuel subsidies among other G20 initiatives. Thus, the Trump Administration's disregard of this value-based transatlantic partnership hits the EU hard. The EU's own capacities are limited, as the EU is currently plagued by internal crises for the eighth consecutive year in a row, from the Eurozone and financial crises, to Brexit and migration, but the growing need for a concerted, independent, and self-directed approach is becoming evident.

Russia: filling the gap?

Russia is a top global energy supplier, on a par with Saudi Arabia and the USA. As a consequence, Russia's energy imports from the MENA are negligible to non-existent, as bilateral energy trade is generally temporary, consisting of swaps and short-term deals.

Moscow's geopolitical concerns coincide with its economic interests (through state-owned companies) in the region. Russia participated in the November 2016 OPEC deal and its subsequent reaffirmation in 2017. This started an unprecedented collaboration with Saudi Arabia. Beyond, that Russia has made significant inroads into the MENA countries' energy sector, as Russian oil companies Rosneft and Lukoil are present in Iran, Iraq, Egypt, Libya,[50] and Algeria. Russian gas giant Gazprom is present in Algeria and Iraq[51] and also plans to be active in Iran.[52] Energy cooperation is a key component of broader cooperation and stretches beyond oil and gas. Nuclear energy deals are an important element of Russia's strategy to maintain its energy superpower status and achieve global power status in the region. The state-owned nuclear company Rosatom conducts a range of activities, from nuclear power plant construction to fuel cycle services in the region.[53]

Through these interests, a web of reciprocal and dense ties is emerging. Middle Eastern wealth funds have reportedly invested in Russia,[54] particularly but not exclusively in response to Western sanctions related to the Ukraine crisis.[55] While current aggregate figures are lacking, there is ample evidence of single deals reported in the press, such as the Qatar Investment Authority's late 2016 purchase of stakes in Rosneft,[56] seen by some observers as part of a broader strategic partnership between Rosneft, ExxonMobil, and Qatar. These deals often go hand in hand with strengthening Russia's footprint in the respective country, as, for example, in Libya. Russia is also the primary partner for the nuclear fuel cycle. Package deals also undergird broader foreign and security policy, for example, in Iran, with whom Russia has signed a number of Memoranda of Understandings and hopes to engage in production, oil supplies, and swaps. This is a remarkable relationship given that the two countries compete for market share of gas and oil which is of a similar quality. In order to reduce dependency on one supplier, importing countries may strike deals with the other, as has Belarus.[57]

During the Cold War, the Soviet Union was a major player in the Middle East and North Africa, countering US influence in the wider region. This engagement was scaled down following the Soviet Union's dissolution in the 1990s and 2000s. However, during Putin's third term, Russian presence in the region became a centerpiece of Russian ambitions to regain global power status on a par with the USA. Geopolitical rivalries between the USA and Russia re-emerged in the European Neighborhood and heated up in Syria as the al-Assad regime, Russia's ally in the region, came under intense pressure. The Russian intervention in Syria has deepened the existing rifts with Europe and the USA, and exacerbated regional cleavages between a Saudi-led Sunni camp and the Russia–Iran–Syria–Hizbullah axis.[58]

Russia thus appears to be the global player in the MENA region whose diplomatic and security activities overlap and correspond with energy-related cooperation. Russia is the foreign actor that has expanded and consolidated its position in the political, energy, economic, and security realm with all major regional players. Moreover, Russia's Rosneft is not only engaging in joint production activities, but also emerging as a trader and aggregator of oil and LNG supplies from the region. While Russia's military power projection capabilities are limited, it appears to be a preferred partner, and has proven a reliable partner for existing regimes with respect to their domestic political stability. In short, Russia has moved from veto player to a major power shaping relations in the MENA region.

China: more than energy trade?

In 2013/2014, China became the world's largest oil importer. However, the geopolitical impact of this status is ambiguous. On the one hand, it makes China much more vulnerable to supply disruptions and changing terms of trade[59] due to price volatility than the USA, its competitor. On the other hand, market power is increasing with demand growth, and trade connections are intensifying in quantity and quality.

Given its heavy reliance on the Middle East (see Figure 18.7), Beijing has a strategy to hedge against supply disruptions and ensure reliable and adequate supplies, namely by backing its national oil companies in investing in upstream projects overseas and offering loans to producer countries that are repaid in oil or gas.[60] China has sought to diversify away from Gulf supplies since its demand surges in the early 2000s, but, aside from Russia and Angola, Saudi Arabia, Iraq, Oman, and Iran, provide two-thirds of China's imports.[61]

China is still heavily exposed to supply disruptions in the Gulf (and from Angola), which supplies 4 mb/d out of a total 7.7 mb/d Chinese imports.[62] Middle Eastern oil is in high demand in China due to its grade, which is highly compatible with domestic refining capacities.[63] Chinese companies are investing heavily in the Middle East because these grades will remain crucial feedstock. Iraq and Iran in particular have offered attractive deals in competition with other (Gulf) producers over market shares, and Chinese companies are active in these countries. Chinese companies now produce supplies for its domestic market in Iran, Iraq, Russia, and Angola.[64] China has also profited from the sanctions against Iran, capitalizing on the absence of Western companies.

China's hunger for energy has also driven security concerns, in particular over US maritime supremacy and its de facto dominance over major strategic ports and "choke points" like the Strait of Hormuz and the Strait of Malacca. Increasing import dependency will in turn mean increasing imports via sea lanes. Gulf producers remain strategically important not only for global energy supply but also for China, and several crucial trade routes pass through the Middle East. This includes the Strait of Hormuz, through which 20 percent of all internationally traded oil passes, as well as 20 percent of traded LNG, making the Strait the

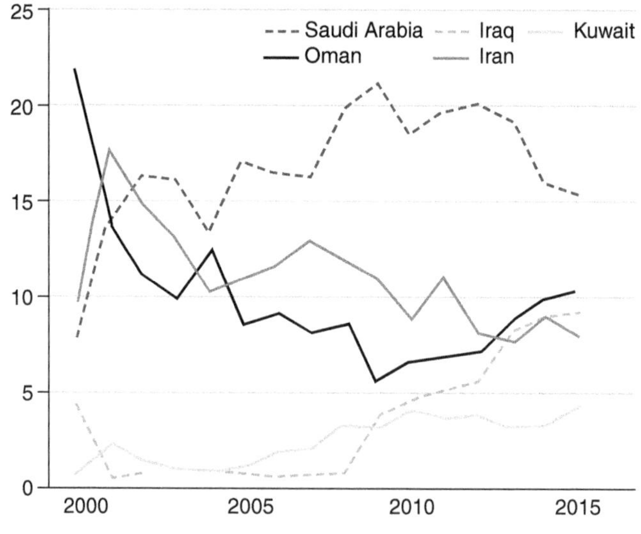

Figure 18.7 Share of China's crude oil imports (%).

Source: UNCTAD, UNCTADstat.

most important global energy supply choke point.[65] Securing this trade route is of particular strategic importance for Asia, as 85 percent of the oil shipped through Hormuz is destined for Asian markets (primarily Japan, India, South Korea, and China).[66] A grip on the sea lanes would also underpin China's dominance in Asia.

Therefore, the energy–security nexus and broader geopolitical rivalry with the USA drives Chinese ambitions and its security approach. China is enhancing its naval capacity, beginning with building a "string of pearls" comprising naval bases in Colombo (Sri Lanka), Gwadar (Pakistan), and Djibouti on the Horn of Africa, while Russia and China conducted a joint naval maneuver in the Mediterranean Sea in 2015. China's "Silk Road Initiative" also targets the Middle East and the Mediterranean as maritime routes and land-based belts cross the region toward Europe. The landmass between the Gulf and the Caspian Sea is also included in China's plan of "One Belt, one Road" which is part of China's geoeconomic power projection and need to export surplus capacities. Yet, the project is still in the early stages.

To conclude: after expanding energy ties China is slowly adapting its security and military capabilities alongside the major oil shipping lanes while pursuing its economic power projection. As part of this strategy, Chinese naval expansion could seriously clash with the interests of its Asian neighbors and/or the USA in the Greater Middle East, particularly if China were to back up its economic interests in the Gulf with security engagement. At the same time, China has reaffirmed its commitment to the Paris Agreement on Climate Change and has displayed a growing interest in a global energy architecture, for example, during its G20 presidency in 2016, but also in the International Energy Charter and the related process. China's growing investments in infrastructure abroad as well as in new technologies may be a reason for China's interest in these fora. Overall, Beijing has a record of mercantilist approaches toward natural resources and it remains to be seen how this will play out in the future when markets become tighter.

Conclusions and outlook

Changes in global energy trade and markets have knock-on effects for international relations. Changing dynamics between exporters and importers shape energy geopolitics, as do the different dependencies, asymmetric vulnerabilities, and relative exposure to changing terms of trade between the consumers who are the focus of this chapter. With the exception of the USA and Russia, all other major energy consumers are confronted with growing import dependency. After the 2014 to 2016 supply surplus, demand growth is once again on track to outstrip supply. Thus, the "geopolitics of energy" and "securitizing energy" will return, and perhaps be more acute given price volatility.[67] Russia has emerged at least tactically triumphant[68] and, as a major player in the region, boasts well-developed political, diplomatic, economic, and military ties. China is also preparing to take on the role of a newcomer in the region in the security and military realm, even as it remains to be seen how Beijing's "Silk Road Strategy" develops and materializes. The future of the "West" is also an open question. The obvious paradigm shift in US politics may well alter the delicate power balance in the region, and great power politics and economic rivalry may feed intra-regional tensions and conflict. Meanwhile, the development and adaptation of international energy governance to the challenges of the energy trilemma is well at stake. Common initiatives of the powers outside and inside the MENA region, as described in this chapter, are unlikely to be comprehensive, but rather ad hoc and issue based. Russia and the USA have made significant geopolitical moves. The EU's political and financial resources are tied up in internal crises and the security challenge in the Eastern neighborhood is acute.

The future of a liberal and globalized economy is in doubt. The animus against free trade, as reflected, for example, in President Trump's rhetoric, may breathe new life into mercantilist and self-serving approaches toward energy supply and trade. Whether this really erodes functioning energy markets may be questioned, but in any case, the USA, Russia, and China among others would be better positioned than the EU to play this new game, given their strategic approach toward energy trade.

Finally, as Steinberg and Werenfels emphasize,[69] we are observing a return of the security paradigm in the turmoil and fragility in the region but also in the magnitude of the new qualitative threat posed by terrorism in and beyond the region. The USA, the EU, Russia, and China are all more or less concerned with the fight against IS. Even in the West, which supported democratic regime change in the wake of the Arab uprisings, the return to traditional security is tangible, and has significant repercussions for the relationship with the MENA region. The desire for stability coincides with the consolidation of authoritarian states, breeding a precarious balance of superficial authoritarian stability and societal stagnation, leaving the pressing socioeconomic challenges that caused the uprisings in the first place still simmering beneath the surface.

For the energy and security nexus, the *duality* of the transformations – the changing energy landscape in parallel with turmoil, war, and state fragility in the MENA region[70] – creates a delicate (energy) security environment characterized by instability and uncertainty of future development paths. Energy trade has formed a two-way relationship between importing and exporting countries as the stability of the latter has depended on export revenues while the former has required stable, secure, and affordable supplies.

Finally, these mutual interdependencies, which create either tight or loose alliances and cooperation beyond the dense and intense web of energy ties, gives external powers a role to play. Currently, the prospects for international support for reforms are dubious, even as all states in the region are searching for a growth model to offer their societies an economic outlook that also (re-)positions the country in the global economy. Successfully implementing reforms in MENA countries will require support from partners, as will striking the delicate balance between transition and stability, as the former is contingent upon the latter. This is true not only in politics, but also in pursuing a successful and sustainable energy transformation.

Notes

1 Christou/Adamides, 2013, p. 519.
2 Overland, 2015, p. 3517.
3 Ibid.
4 IEA, 2016, p. 114.
5 Ibid., p. 132.
6 EIA, 2016.
7 EIA, 2015.
8 IEA, 2016, pp. 142, 182.
9 Ibid., p. 167.
10 Ibid., p. 143.
11 Ibid.
12 Ibid., p. 137.
13 In the past, the idea of "scarcity" underpinned the "rivalry" over the control of resources in the past (Overland, 2015, p. 3518).
14 Christou/Adamides, 2013, p. 514.
15 Ibid., p. 513.
16 See Luciani, Chapter 2, this volume.
17 See Roehrkasten and Qader, Chapter 4, this volume.
18 *New York Times*, 2013.
19 Golden Pass LNG Terminal, 2017.
20 Overland, 2015, p. 3526.
21 See: Bloomberg, 2016b.
22 Baker Hughes, 2017.
23 See Westphal et al., 2014.
24 Ibid., p. 29.
25 CNBC, 2016.
26 *New York Times*, 2016.
27 Westphal et al., 2014, p. 14.
28 Ibid., p. 27ff.
29 IISS, Military Balance, London, in ibid., p. 15.
30 Offshore balancing refers to a strategic approach in which the containment and deterrence of hostile countries is left to overseas partners while the USA remains safe and secure thanks to its "oceans and nukes".
31 *Wall Street Journal*, 2017.
32 EU Commission, 2014a, p. 32.
33 Ibid., p. 45.
34 Atradius, 2017, p. 3.
35 EU Commission, 2017.
36 Federal Ministry of Economic Affairs and Energy, 2017.
37 Dii, 2012, 2013.
38 Roehrkasten et al., 2016.
39 See Escribano, Chapter 16, this volume.
40 Ibid.
41 Werenfels/Westphal, 2010.
42 EU Commission, 2017.
43 Missiroli, 2016, pp. 124–125.
44 See Steinberg and Werenfels, Chapter 1, this volume.
45 Missiroli, 2016, p. 125.
46 In the past, the case of Libyan support to terrorism was an issue, leaving the country outside the Barcelona process.
47 EU Commission, 2016.
48 EU Commission, 2014b.

49 European Union External Action, 2016.
50 Lukoil Oil Company, 2017; Bloomberg, 2017.
51 Gazprom, 2017.
52 Bloomberg, 2016a.
53 Rosatom, 2017.
54 Economist Intelligence Unit, 2017.
55 Russia Beyond The Headlines, 2015.
56 *Financial Times*, 2016.
57 *Financial Tribune*, 2017.
58 See Steinberg and Werenfels, Chapter 1, this volume.
59 Terms of trade means the real exchange rate between exports and imports and influences the in-/outflow of capital.
60 Meidan, 2016, p. 1.
61 Ibid., p. 3.
62 Ibid., p. 16.
63 Ibid., p. 7.
64 Ibid., p. 3.
65 EIA, 2014.
66 Ibid.
67 CNBC, 2016.
68 Ibid.
69 See Steinberg und Werenfels, Chapter 1, this volume.
70 Ibid.

Bibliography

Atradius (2017): *Natural Gas Prices Have Reached a Turning Point*. Amsterdam: Atradius Economic Research. Available at: http://fcibglobal.com/pdf/atradius/Atradius_Economic_Research_Gas_Prices_Jan_2017_ERN01.pdf.

Baker Hughes (2017): *Rig Count Overview and Summary Count*.

Bloomberg (2016a): Gazprom Signs Oil Deal With Iran as Russians Return in Force. December 13. Available at: www.bloomberg.com/news/articles/2016-12-13/gazprom-neft-signs-oil-deal-as-russia-adds-to-presence-in-iran.

Bloomberg (2016b): Saudi Former Oil Minister Says OPEC Can't Cut Output by Itself. November 4. Available at: www.bloomberg.com/news/articles/2016-11-04/saudi-former-oil-minister-says-opec-can-t-cut-output-by-itself.

Bloomberg (2017): Rosneft Expands in Middle East With Libya and Iraq Oil Deals. February 21. Available at: www.bloomberg.com/news/articles/2017-02-21/rosneft-signs-libya-oil-deal-as-more-investors-return-to-country.

Christou, Odysseas/Constantinos Adamides (2013): Energy Securitization and Desecuritization in the New Middle East. *Security Dialogue* 44(5–6), 507–522.

CNBC (2016): The Next President Must Be Prepared to Act on the Middle East. July 14. Available at: www.cnbc.com/2016/07/14/trump-clinton-must-be-prepared-to-act-on-the-middle-east-commentary.html.

Dii (2012): *2050 Desert Power. Perspectives on a Sustainable Power System for EUMENA*. Munich: Dii. Available at: www.trec-uk.org.uk/reports/DII/DPP_2050_Study.pdf.

Dii (2013): *Desert Power: Getting Started, The Manual for Renewable Electricity in MENA*. Policy Report 2013. Munich: Dii. Available at: www.db.com/cr/en/docs/Desert-Power-Getting-Started-Full-Report-English-Screen(1).pdf.

Economist Intelligence Unit (2017): Country Report: Qatar. February 23. Available at: http://country.eiu.com/qatar.

EIA (2014): *World Oil Transit Chokepoints*. Washington, DC: U.S. Energy Information Administration. Available at: www.eia.gov/countries/regions-topics.cfm?fips=wotc&trk=p3.

EIA (2015): *Egypt – International Energy Data and Development*. Washington, DC: U.S. Energy Information Administration. Available at: www.eia.gov/beta/international/analysis_includes/countries_long/Egypt/egypt.pdf.

EIA (2016): *Country Analysis Brief: Algeria*. Washington, DC: U.S. Energy Information Adminstration.

EU Commission (2014a): *COMMISSION STAFF WORKING DOCUMENT. In-depth Study of European Energy Security. Accompanying the Document. Communication from the Commission to the Council and the European Parliament: European Energy Security Strategy*. Brussels: EU Commission. Available at: http://ec.europa.eu/energy/sites/ener/files/documents/20140528_energy_security_study.pdf.

EU Commission (2014b): *European Union Maritime Security Strategy. A Guide for Stakeholders*. Brussels: EU Commission. Available at: https://ec.europa.eu/maritimeaffairs/sites/maritimeaffairs/files/leaflet-european-union-maritime-security-strategy_en.pdf.

EU Commission (2016): *Shared Vision, Common Action: A Stronger Europe. A Global Strategy for the European Union's Foreign and Security Policy*. Brussels: Institute for Security Studies. Available at: www.iss.europa.eu/uploads/media/EUGS.pdf.

EU Commission (2017): *International Cooperation: Working With Our Energy Partners Abroad*. Brussels: EU Commission.

European Union External Action (2016): *Military and Civilian Missions and Operations*.

Federal Ministry of Economic Affairs and Energy (2017): *International Energy Policy*.

Financial Times (2016): Glencore and Qatar Take 19.5% Stake in Rosneft. December 10. Available at: www.ft.com/content/d3923b08-bf09-11e6-9bca-2b93a6856354.

Financial Tribune (2017): Belarus Buys Crude Oil from Iran. February 18. Available at: https://financialtribune.com/articles/energy/59762/belarus-buys-crude-oil-from-iran.

Gazprom (2017): *Fields*.

Golden Pass LNG Terminal (2017): *About Golden Pass*. Golden Pass LNG Terminal.

IEA (2016): *World Energy Outlook 2016*. Paris: International Energy Agency .

Lukoil Oil Company (2017): *Geographic Reach*.

Meidan, Michal (2016): *China's Loans for Oil: Asset or Liability?* OIES Paper, WPM 70. Oxford: Oxford Institute for Energy Studies. Available at: www.oxfordenergy.org/wpcms/wp-content/uploads/2016/12/Chinas-loans-for-oil-WPM-70.pdf.

Missiroli, Antonio (2016): *The EU and the World: Players and Policies Post-Lisbon. A Hand-book*. Paris: European Union Institute for Security Studies.

New York Times (2013): Texas Refinery is Saudi Foothold in US Market. April 4. Available at: www.nytimes.com/2013/04/05/business/texas-refinery-is-saudi-foothold-in-us-market.html?pagewanted=all&_r=1&.

New York Times (2016): Obama Criticizes the "Free Riders" among America's Allies. March 10. Available at: www.nytimes.com/2016/03/10/world/middleeast/obama-criticizes-the-free-riders-among-americas-allies.html?_r=0.

Overland, Indra (2015): Future Petroleum Geopolitics: Consequences of Climate Policy and Unconventional Oil and Gas. In Yan, Jinyue (Ed.). *Handbook of Clean Energy Systems*. New York: John Wiley & Sons. Available at: onlinelibrary.wiley.com/doi/10.1002/9781118991978.hces203/pdf.

Roehrkasten, Sybille/Rainer Quitzow/Georgeta Vidican-Auktor/Kirsten Westphal (2016): *Advancing an International Energy Transition Policy in North Africa and Beyond.*

IASS Policiy Brief No. 4. Potsdam: IASS. Available at: www.iass-potsdam.de/sites/default/files/files/policy_brief_4_2016_en_energy_transition_north_africa.pdf.

Rosatom (2017): *Global Presence*.

Russia Beyond The Headlines (2015): Why Arab Funds are Stepping Up Investments in Russia. November 25. Available at: http://rbth.com/business/2015/11/25/why-arab-funds-are-stepping-up-investments-in-rusia_543835.

Wall Street Journal (2017): U.S., Saudi Arabia Expect Deals, Investments Worth $300 Billion. May 22. Available at: www.wsj.com/articles/u-s-and-saudi-companies-sign-deals-worth-at-least-43-billion-1495287762.

Werenfels, Isabelle/Kirsten Westphal (2010): *Solar Power from North Africa. Frameworks and Prospects*. SWP Research Paper 2010/RP 03. Berlin: SWP. Available at: www.swp-berlin.org/fileadmin/contents/products/research_papers/2010_RP03_wrf_wep_ks.pdf.

Westphal, Kirsten et al. (2014): *The US Shale Revolution and the Arab Gulf States: The Economic and Political Impact of Changing Energy Markets*. SWP Research Paper. Berlin: SWP. Available at: www.swp-berlin.org/fileadmin/contents/products/research_papers/2014_RP11_wep_ovs_sbg.pdf.

Conclusions and outlook

David Ramin Jalilvand and Kirsten Westphal

This book has examined the political and economic challenges of energy for the MENA region, which remains in disarray more than six years after the Arab uprisings. The region has been afflicted by growing fragility, a result of the eroding efficacy and legitimacy of political regimes in many countries, which has amounted to failing states in some. This has led to what may be described as regional disorder, and is compounded by developments in the energy realm. The energy developments have a variety of impacts and also create their own regional, political, and economic dynamics.

Different energy dynamics

As in any country of the world, the availability of energy in the MENA region is central to economic competitiveness, prosperity, and socioeconomic development. In the region's energy-rich countries, energy is also an important production factor for national economies. Most economic diversification strategies, especially in the Gulf, rely on access to abundant and cheap energy for petrochemicals and energy-intensive industries as well as logistical hubs and airports. Energy is not only the backbone of oil-exporting economies in the region but also a foundational factor for polities in the Gulf region and at the heart of politics in any state. Moreover, it underpins the foreign policy of many countries.[1] Thus, the impact of a rapidly changing energy world on the MENA region cannot be overestimated.

One of the major observations of this volume is that while energy is an important driving factor for the future, dynamics differ substantially across countries. In some of the countries, such as Egypt, domestic factors are driving developments, as huge increases in domestic energy demand have altered export–import balances. In other countries, especially the smaller Gulf Monarchies, international price developments have been the most relevant drivers, namely the oil price slump since mid-2014. Unlike in the past, the region is no longer shaping outcomes, no longer in the driving seat, but rather a "taker" and affected by the developments and less able to influence outcomes proactively. Moreover, energy as a whole constitutes a broad category, and thus requires a more granular analysis of different energy sources.

Another observation from the book is that a diversification of energy developments is becoming evident. In the past, the MENA region's energy story was largely one of oil, both for importing and exporting countries. It was oil dynamics that drove many MENA countries to form and join OPEC and thus shape international energy developments (a function the cartel has proven unable to fulfill in the recent past). However, the MENA region's energy story has increasingly become a natural gas story as well, which has significant consequences for the region's energy landscape. While some countries (e.g., Iran) are endowed with large reserves of both oil and natural gas, oil-rich countries are not necessarily natural gas rich and vice versa.

This has led to a conundrum,[2] as many traditionally energy-rich (i.e., oil-rich) countries are facing natural gas deficits to meet their power generation needs even as they are located in a region endowed with natural gas reserves. This is leading to a "paradox of LNG imports".[3] For economic and environmental reasons, natural gas is the primary choice to meet domestic energy demand. However, regional cross-border gas trade has not (yet) lived up to expectations and potential, complicating the ability to meet rising demand with supplies from the region.

New energy discoveries and developments are also increasing the role of natural gas in the region's energy and geopolitical story. In the Eastern Mediterranean, the discovery of natural gas and early stages of exploitation could provide the basis or framework for a new energy region. However, the extent to which this will become a reality depends on the economic viability of developing the resources, which depends in turn on domestic demand in and export options for potential producing countries, along with resolving or coming to terms with long-standing political issues.

For energy-poor countries, renewable energies are becoming a dynamic factor driving the diversification of the energy mix. Some countries (e.g., Morocco) have made important progress in this regard.

The region's energy story is also becoming as much about demand as it has been about supply. Providing electricity to meet rising domestic demand – and to safeguard societal and political stability in many countries in the process – is both a challenge and a necessity across the region. To increase generation capacity, countries are not only expanding the share of natural gas and renewables, but also constructing and planning nuclear power plants. While the geopolitical motivation is strong in many countries (creating a nuclear weapons capability for the future), the security and safety challenges have remained under-discussed.

In sum, to understand the economic and political challenges of energy in the MENA region, the focus has to be broadened from oil to include the whole range of energy types. While it remains the case that the region is affected by the oil price decline, this is far from the only critical energy development. Rather, a broader structural transformation is also underway.

Readdressing the energy trilemma

Amid these developments, countries in the MENA region, much like other countries around the globe, must find solutions to address the "energy trilemma". This means simultaneously ensuring energy security, energy equity, and environmental sustainability, while progress or action in one area could jeopardize progress in others.[4] Balancing these three objectives is a particular challenge for any state, and each country approaches it from a different and unique development level and starting point.[5] Balancing the trilemma is even more complicated in the MENA region, as it occurs against the backdrop of political instability and changing political and economic circumstances. Given these unique dynamics, several observations specifically relevant to the challenge of meeting the energy trilemma in the MENA region are made below.

First, securing domestic and external energy sources to meet rising domestic demand is a key priority for most countries in the region. This has given energy security a new connotation in light of growing domestic consumption, as many countries are facing supply security risks. This is a shift from recent decades, when energy security concerns of the oil- (and gas-) exporting countries and fossil-fueled economies were related to demand security. Amid increases in electricity demand and the ongoing diversification in power generation, the reliability and stability of power grids is becoming more of an energy security concern than in the past, while the security of energy infrastructure is also closely intertwined with regional security developments and challenges posed by conflicts and terrorist attacks. Addressing these manifold dimensions of and challenges to energy security has qualitatively changed over the past decade.

Second, governments and leaders across the region are facing the challenge of ensuring accessibility and affordability of energy for their populations. The provision of energy has been a part of the political and social landscape in many MENA countries for decades. In energy-abundant countries, access to cheap energy is and has been part and parcel of the social contract, and energy subsidies have underpinned the political legitimacy of governments and the stability of regimes even in energy-poor countries. However, while the recent decline in oil prices may have lowered the cost of subsidization, this approach to energy provision is part of the past, and should not be extended. Energy subsidies not only undermine energy efficiency, they also burden national budgets thanks to growing domestic consumption needs. The current low oil price environment offers only temporary relief for oil-importing states, while falling revenue is putting additional pressure on oil-producing states to transform the system. While reducing subsidies and transforming energy systems is a challenge, the technological progress that produced lower energy prices provides opportunities for progress.

Third, climate and environmental stability have not yet become a major reference point for governments and policies in the region. That said, a reshuffling of energy policy objectives is gradually taking place, even if this is still in the very early stages. While climate change is not (yet) a major driver for policies, water scarcity concerns and the energy–water–food nexus are gaining political attention, along with economic and population growth and subsidies. Looking beyond 2020, the resilience of energy, water, and food supply is a real concern for the region, and could serve as an additional source of uncertainty or instability contributing to the precarious regional security situation. However, in the short term, preoccupation with the various security threats and the current low oil price environment could detract from the political will to properly address these longer term challenges.

Ultimately, when evaluating the energy trilemma, regional governments prioritize energy security and affordability, often at the expense of sustainability. This is because meeting domestic demand is key to political stability and government legitimacy, while climate and environmental concerns are (at present) of secondary importance.

Timing and time horizons matter

The observed global energy market dynamics and the dimensions of the energy trilemma challenge traditional political patterns and economic models, increasing the urgency to act upon these new developments. Moreover, meeting the obligations under the Paris Agreement and achieving energy transformation will require action now to achieve results over the medium and long term. In the December 2015 Paris Agreement, over 197 states and parties committed to limit greenhouse gas emissions and global warming to under 2C degrees above pre-industrial levels. While the agreement is legally binding in that the states must accept the 2C-degree target and adjust their policies accordingly, the commitments themselves are not. Meeting this climate target will require a transformation of the energy sector, responsible for more than two-thirds of greenhouse gas emissions. Looking ahead to 2030/2040, this transformation will require decisive political and economic adjustments. As the USA decided to withdraw from the deal, political pressure at the global level to proceed with implementing the Paris Agreement may have decreased. Nevertheless, in light of the dramatic consequences of climate change for the MENA region, countries in this part of the world are still challenged to develop and enforce policy solutions in this regard.

In this context, in the short term, most hydrocarbon-rich countries have to survive the low price era and (re-)position themselves in global oil and gas markets. This means competing with other suppliers over market shares, while retaining a certain international price level – a major challenge, as the nature of shale production changes market dynamics. Simultaneously, meeting growing energy demand is a challenge for all MENA countries. To meet rising demand and simultaneously avoid budget deficits and limit national debt, energy efficiency will have to be improved and domestic prices will have to be more cost-reflective. Achieving this will require painful adjustments to subsidy schemes and energy pricing, and measures to mitigate the effects on the poorer parts of the populations (including the establishment of capable government institutions).

Against the backdrop of climate change and the Paris Agreement, however, addressing the long-term challenge to move toward carbon-neutral energy systems globally and in the region is paramount. This is the case not only because of the general need to mitigate the potential impacts of climate, but also in light of the specific implications for the region, as the consequences, including extreme hot temperatures and rising sea levels, are anticipated to be harsher in the MENA region than in other parts of the world.

At any rate, despite the recognition of and commitment to climate goals, there is a high level of uncertainty about what the future energy path or pathways may look like given the gap between global climate ambitions and actual national energy plans. There is no clear practical and operational solution to achieve a sustainable and decarbonized energy system, and it is likely that there is no "one" solution. In addition to the lack of a clear path forward, fundamentally reforming energy systems could risk triggering or exacerbating political stability in many countries. Limiting energy subsidies, which enable growing energy consumption, is a particularly difficult task, as they often provide a minimum of social welfare, even if inefficiently administered. In the absence of capable state bureaucracies that can identify and provide for citizens in need in a more targeted manner, providing energy at subsidized prices is one of the few tools for governments to provide (or at least appear to provide) for their people (the Iranian example of 2010 demonstrates the dilemma[6]).

Providing a reliable energy supply that meets the needs of growing populations and building the pursuant infrastructure will require current and future investment. The mid-term challenges are particularly paramount, as development and growth models based on hydrocarbons can no longer be relied on. Even if oil and gas prices recover, it appears unlikely that they will return to the high and stable levels of the 2004 to 2009 and 2010 to 2014 periods in the foreseeable future due to structural changes in oil and gas markets.[7] The writing is on the wall for oil- and gas-exporting countries to read: oil prices will likely remain below the national fiscal break-even levels, which have risen substantially in the past. This leaves the governments in oil-exporting countries with two choices: to cut expenditure or generate alternative sources of income. At the same time, investments in nearly all branches of the energy sector are needed, as well as additional stimulus to diversify economies. Obviously, this system transformation will present challenges to political and societal stability.

Energy transformation will require political will and potentially involve some political cost. Since the level of climate ambition varies from country to country, the overall global commitment could erode if some countries feel they have to make greater efforts than others. Moreover, amid an uncertain time horizon and unclear transition paths, demand for both oil and natural gas around the globe will persist,[8] giving MENA energy producers some confidence in a long-term perspective for oil and natural gas exports. As a consequence, there is arguably no immediate pressure for these countries to reform their energy systems and diversify their economies – despite negative short-term effects from the oil price decline. Given this lack of incentive, it remains to be seen when and how MENA countries will engage in the implementation of the Paris Agreement.

A spatial reorganization of energy flows

Beyond the MENA region, changes in international energy are contributing to a reorganization of the global energy and financial landscape, including a reconfiguration of current patterns and scales of economic and social activity.[9] This is leading to a spatial reorganization of energy (and subsequently financial) flows, necessitating a closer look at the geographic distribution and movement of both, and how this is reshaping the landscape.

Geography is relevant to international energy in many ways. Energy is traded globally, while the capital used to purchase energy and finance energy projects also moves across borders. Through cross-border trade and the infrastructure that enables it, energy can have a direct impact upon regional dynamics and politics, and an indirect influence via financial flows. Both of these mechanisms of influence can underpin foreign policy objectives. As one of the major inputs in any domestic economy, energy also has a national dimension, and energy prices have a particularly strong impact upon national wealth and growth models.

A major factor that both illustrates and drives energy geography is the shifting center of demand-side gravity away from the OECD to the Asia-Pacific region, particularly China and India.[10] While energy demand in OECD countries is flattening or even declining, the Asia-Pacific region is driving up worldwide energy consumption. Inside the MENA region itself, energy consumption has increased dramatically. It seems logical, that – while starting from admittedly low levels – intra-regional trade within and across the MENA region, in particular of natural gas and electricity, has and will continue to grow. From this pragmatic and functional point of view, energy markets and trade are not only social constructions, they are also geographic ones, as energy locations and lines (e.g., power plants, processing units, sea lanes, pipelines, electric wires) craft "energy geographies". However, their functioning across borders requires political will, which has so far produced only limited progress with respect to international cooperation and governance. Electricity cooperation in the GCC countries is one example. The common and joint efforts across the Mediterranean to push for a renewable-based energy system (known as the Solar Plan) have been stalled among other factors by the non-cooperation between North African countries and the Israeli–Palestinian conflict. In sum, regional governance initiatives are in their fledging stages.

In light of this, (sub-) regional energy markets in MENA are developing. Thus, energy has a transformative impact in shaping the region from inside. Developments in the energy realm result in an intensification and densification of ties and relations (e.g., building a long-distance grid across the GCC countries), and can create shared interests or common energy spaces among countries. Another example of regional dynamics being shaped by energy are the natural gas discoveries in the Eastern Mediterranean region, which have spurred the idea of a regional identity and the imagination of a regional gas market,[11] while the prospect of these resources has and will likely continue to impact the conduct of international relations. Finally, the natural gas deficit in the Arab Gulf countries has made Iran consider regional export options. Should these gas trade relations materialize, it would signal that the countries are starting to apply energy logic over geopolitical considerations.

The spatial reorganization of energy flows underpins the view that economic development in MENA will be less oil (price) driven in the future than in the past, and will rather be influenced by regional dynamics and domestic activity. Moreover, structural shifts are looming on the horizon, as the diversification of the energy mix to include solar, wind, and nuclear energy also has implications for energy spaces and geography. For example, while wind and solar energy enable more local or domestic energy production and consumption, the proliferation of nuclear energy involves international cooperation.[12]

Thus, energy trade patterns are changing along with relations between exporting and importing countries. Previously, the MENA region's international energy trade was mostly with OECD or "Western" countries, which extended beyond energy to deepen the political and economic relations of MENA countries with Europe and North America. However, as MENA energy trade regionalizes and shifts toward the Asia-Pacific region, this will likely have consequences for political and economic relations with Europe and North America, and may arguably lead to a much more diversified matrix of international (energy) relations. This also impacts the IEA, as the major energy consumers' organization has associated Asian countries such as China and India among others, but also Morocco since 2015.

Toward a new center of marginal production?

The geography of energy is also changing on the supply side. Until recently, the MENA region was considered to be the global center of marginal energy production, as countries were able to respond flexibly to changes in global energy demand thanks in part to their extremely low production costs (especially in the Gulf region) and the fact that governments are in charge of industry. By increasing or decreasing production, MENA producers were able to balance markets, while agreements on production cuts in coordination with OPEC enabled MENA countries to raise oil prices. Saudi Arabia, OPEC and the MENA region's leading producer, was considered the "swing producer", effectively balancing markets through its oil policy.

However, change is underway as the "unconventional boom" in North America, starting in 2005 (for gas) and in 2008 (for oil), has expanded global supply. In response, Saudi Arabia and other OPEC members effectively abandoned ambitions to balance markets and instead increased output in what appeared to be a fight with the new North American competition for market share.[13] While this strategy was effective in causing oil prices to decline, North American unconventional oil and gas production proved more resilient than expected. After more than two years of competition and declining oil prices, many traditional producing countries experienced extreme pressures on their government budgets as revenue plummeted dramatically.[14] Even when OPEC members agreed on a production cut in late 2016, many unconventional rigs in the USA were still producing, while the price increase following the announcement of the OPEC cuts enabled US unconventional production to increase. This reflects the flexibility of unconventional producers to respond to changing market conditions, as the project size and timeline of unconventional production is smaller and shorter when compared to traditional production.

In light of these developments, some analysts have concluded that the center of the world's marginal oil and natural gas production is no longer in the MENA region. In this view, North America has taken over and will now act as swing producer – or, more precisely, swing producers, since there are no individual state-controlled energy companies as in the MENA region but rather a multitude of comparably smaller private companies – with the potential to balance markets.[15]

However, regardless of whether North America has actually taken over or is taking over the role of swing producer from the MENA region, the political and strategic implications of this development are already being assessed.[16] Inside the MENA region, especially in the GCC countries, policymakers fear a loss of relevance and the potential for this to lead to a reorientation of strategic relations with the USA to their disadvantage. While it is too early to draw any conclusions, the mere possibility that the MENA region's oil and natural gas reserves could lose importance is likely to have political and economic consequences. Economically, MENA countries would be less likely to be in a position to shape market conditions and more dependent on developments outside their control. Politically, Western governments may be less inclined to invest in the regime stability of MENA-producing countries, a trend that could be reinforced should the Trump Administration in the USA act on its stated preference for isolationist policies.

In light of these developments and against the backdrop of changing international energy flows and increasing intra-regional MENA trade, a reconfiguration of the MENA countries' position in global energy may be underway. After being the center of global energy supply, the MENA region's relative importance could decline, putting it on a more even footing with other world regions. While the countries still hold vast reserves, the region will need to increasingly address domestic consumption needs, while the development of alternative and unconventional supplies around the world could relegate the region to simply being one (albeit still crucial) center of supply among many. This possibility is more likely to be realized and reinforced if the transformation toward a sustainable energy system takes off.

Outlook

Oil and gas from the MENA region will comprise the bulk of global supplies for the foreseeable future. According to the IEA, the world's reliance on hydrocarbons from the region's OPEC member countries will increase in a carbon-constrained world.[17] From a technical perspective, the MENA region is uniquely positioned to attract investment due to its low-cost reserves. However, above the ground, geopolitical risks are high, and large question marks regarding the region's (future) stability remain.

The uncertainty of political and geopolitical developments is enhanced by the unpredictability of global, regional, and national energy trajectories. Energy trends are occurring simultaneously, making outcomes unpredictable and fluid, as it is not evident how these trends interact. This is particularly true for the boom in unconventional oil and gas (which stemmed from a technological evolution) and stricter climate policies. The former contributes to prolonging the fossil fuel era and drives demand, while the latter aims to rapidly curb greenhouse gas emissions from fossil fuels.[18] Given this ambiguity of trends and the visible paradox of developments, any conclusions are preliminary and can only provide a sense of potential developments.

Scarcity is no longer evident – rather, "an era of plenty" is apparent. At the same time, fossil fuel prices have slumped as a consequence of technological progress and strong investments in new reservoirs, leading to a decline in upstream investment. The new operating principle for oil and gas producers is "low for longer", and while boom-and-bust cycles have always been a part of the oil and gas history, it is easy to see how geopolitical turmoil could translate into supply disruptions. This new normal of relatively moderate and low prices is also reflected in the dramatic cost decline for renewables. The shorter time horizons of unconventional technologies, which enable more flexible and shorter contracts, means that volatile prices and markets will likely continue. In short, volatility is here to stay and will affect the terms of trade, as adapting to volatility is costly for consumers and producers alike.

This volume has addressed the changing energy landscape and its effects on the Middle East, North Africa, and the Eastern Mediterranean. While we have identified many trends and shifts in the landscape, we remain at the outset of a new energy era. While this era could be characterized by a more diversified energy supply, it is too early to draw final conclusions. While only time will tell how these energy dynamics will develop and play out, there are many questions we can ask in the meantime based on the observations and analyses in this volume. How long will the "era of plenty" last as advances in technology lead to more discoveries and production? Will MENA countries be able to adapt their energy systems to the changing circumstances? Are the oil- and natural gas-exporting countries of the MENA region willing and able to capitalize on the current situation as an opportunity to diversify their economies and overcome fossil fuels revenue-based social contracts? Will there be shifts in power from larger national energy companies to smaller private companies as part of the "unconventional revolution"? Last but not least, will the trend of increasing geopolitical instability and crises in the region continue and how will they affect energy?

Regardless of how these questions will be answered, its vast reserves guarantee that the MENA region will remain important to global energy. At the same time, energy will continue to be of central importance to politics and economies within the MENA region. While it remains unclear how developments will unfold, it is certain that the countries of the MENA region face tremendous political and economic challenges of energy to confront in the future. For the countries between the Atlantic Ocean and Central Asia, these challenges are likely to shape the course of future development.

Notes

1 Orttung/Overland, 2011.
2 Jaffe et al., 2013.
3 Corbeau, Chapter 3, this volume.
4 World Energy Council, 2016, pp. 33–36.
5 Bradshaw, 2010, pp. 275–290.
6 In 2010, Iran's government reduced many subsidies and intended to provide lower income households with cash in exchange. The vast majority of Iranian citizens applied for cash handouts and government authorities were unable to effectively assess claims. Eventually, cash handouts exceeded the savings from the subsidy cuts.
7 See Luciani, Chapter 2, and Corbeau, Chapter 3, this volume.
8 IEA, 2016.
9 Bridge et al., 2013, p. 331.
10 See Westphal, Chapter 18, this volume.
11 Goldthau et al., 2017.
12 See Westphal, Chapter 18, this volume.
13 *The Economist*, 2014.
14 See Sons, Chapter 9, and El-Katiri, Chapter 6, this volume.
15 Stevens, 2016.
16 See Westphal, Chapter 18, this volume.
17 IEA, 2016, p. 137.
18 Overland, 2015.

Bibliography

Bradshaw, Michael J. (2010): Global Energy Dilemmas: A Geographical Perspective. *The Geographical Journal* 176(4), 279–290.

Bridge, Gavin/Stefan Bouzarovski/ Michael Bradshaw/Nick. Eyre (2013): Geographies of Energy Transition: Space, Place and the Low-carbon Economy. *Energy Policy* 53, 331–340.

Economist, The (2014): The New Economics of Oil: Sheikhs v Shale. December 6. Available at: www.economist.com/news/leaders/21635472-economics-oil-have-changed-some-businesses-will-go-bust-market-will-be.

Goldthau, Andreas/Stephan Stetter/Jörn Richert (2017): *Leviathan Awakens: The World Energy System and the Birth of the Eastern Mediterranean as a Geo-Political Region.* Paper presented at the ISA Annual Convention.

IEA (2016): *World Energy Outlook 2016*. Paris: International Energy Agency.

Jaffe, Amy Myers/Jareer Elass/Keily Miller (2013): *The Gulf Cooperation Council Natural Gas Conundrum: Geopolitics Drive Shortages amid Plenty*. Geopolitics of Energy Case Chapter. Harvard/Baker Institute Study. Available at: www.belfercenter.org/sites/default/files/legacy/files/MO-CES-pub-GeoGasGCC-102513.pdf.

Orttung, Robert W/Indra Overland (2011): A Limited Toolbox: Explaining the Constraints on Russia's Foreign Energy Policy. *Journal of Eurasian Studies* 2(1), 74–85.

Overland, Indra (2015): Future Petroleum Geopolitics: Consequences of Climate Policy and Unconventional Oil and Gas. In Yan, Jinyue (Ed.): *Handbook of Clean Energy Systems*, 1–29.

Stevens, Paul (2016): *International Oil Companies: The Death of the Old Business Model*. London: Chatham House, Royal Institute of International Affairs. Available at: www.chathamhouse.org/sites/files/chathamhouse/publications/research/2016-05-05-international-oil-companies-stevens.pdf.

World Energy Council (2016): *Energy Trilemma Index*. World Energy Council. Available at: https://trilemma.worldenergy.org/reports/main/2016/2016%20Energy%20Trilemma%20Index.pdf.

Index

For Product Safety Concerns and Information please contact our EU representative GPSR@taylorandfrancis.com
Taylor & Francis Verlag GmbH, Kaufingerstraße 24, 80331 München, Germany

www.ingramcontent.com/pod-product-compliance
Ingram Content Group UK Ltd.
Pitfield, Milton Keynes, MK11 3LW, UK
UKHW022014180926
475701UK00003B/353
9781032096070